salon FUNDAMENTALS®

Art & Science Salon

A Resource for Your Cosmetology Career

STUDY GUIDE

by
Clif St. Germain, Ph.D.

Learning is a treasure that will follow its owner everywhere.
— Chinese Proverb

A Resource for Your Cosmetology Career
STUDY GUIDE

© 2000, 2010, 2014 Pivot Point International
and Clif St. Germain Ph.D.

ISBN 978-1-937964-82-5

3rd Edition
4th Printing, August 2016
Printed in Hong Kong

This publication is protected under U.S. and worldwide copyright laws and may not be copied, reproduced, stored in a retrieval system, transmitted, broadcast or quoted in whole or in part in any form, or by any means: electronically or mechanically, printed, photocopied, recorded, scanned or otherwise, nor may derivative works be created from it without written permission from Pivot Point International, Inc. More detailed information on copyright can be found at: http://www.pivot-point.com/copyright.html.

Trademarks: Pivot Point, the Pivot Point Logo, the P Design, and *Salon Fundamentals* are trademarks or registered trademarks of Pivot Point International, Inc., in the United States and other countries, and may not be used without written permission.

Pivot Point International, Inc.
World Headquarters
8725 W. Higgins Road, Suite 700
Chicago, IL 60631 USA

847-866-0500
pivot-point.com

CONTENTS

UNIT 1 THEORY ESSENTIALS
1. **PROFESSIONAL DEVELOPMENT** 11
    - Brain Conditioner 23
2. **SALON ECOLOGY** 26
    - Brain Conditioner 39
3. **ANATOMY AND PHYSIOLOGY** 45
    - Brain Conditioner 86
4. **ELECTRICITY** 96
    - Brain Conditioner 109
5. **CHEMISTRY** 115
    - Brain Conditioner 136
6. **SALON BUSINESS** 142
    - Brain Conditioner 161

UNIT 2 HAIR SERVICES
7. **TRICHOLOGY** 165
    - Wet Hair Service Draping, Shampooing and Conditioning Rubric 175
    - Basic Scalp Massage Rubric 176
    - Brain Conditioner 177
8. **DESIGN DECISIONS** 184
    - Brain Conditioner 192
9. **HAIRCUTTING** 195
    - Solid Form Haircut Rubric 204
    - Increase-Layered Form Haircut Rubric 205
    - Graduated Form Haircut Rubric 206
    - Uniformly Layered Form Haircut Rubric 207
    - Combination Form Haircut Rubric 208
    - Square Form/Uniform Haircut Rubric 209
    - Fade Haircut Rubric 210
    - Brain Conditioner 212
10. **HAIRSTYLING** 215
    - Air Forming Solid Form Rubric 222
    - Scrunching Layered Form Rubric 223
    - Air Forming Graduated Form: 9-Row Brush Rubric 224
    - Air Forming Layered Form: Round Brush Rubric 225
    - Air Forming Combination Form: 9-Row Brush Rubric 226
    - Air Forming Combination Form: Round Brush/Curling Iron Rubric 227
    - Pressing and Curling Rubric 228
    - Fingerwaves and Flat Pincurls Rubric 232
    - Straight Volume Rollers and Pincurls Rubric 233
    - Curvature Volume Rollers and Pincurls Rubric 234
    - Three-Strand Overbraid Rubric 236
    - Three-Strand Underbraid Rubric 237
    - French Twist Rubric 238
    - Brain Conditioner 243
11. **WIGS AND HAIR ADDITIONS** 247
    - Brain Conditioner 256
12. **CHEMICAL TEXTURIZING** 260
    - Rectangle Perm Wrap Rubric 267
    - Bricklay Perm Wrap Rubric 268
    - Spiral Bricklay Perm Wrap Rubric 269
    - Bricklay With Directional Fringe Perm Wrap Rubric 270
    - Virgin Thio Relaxer Rubric 274
    - Sodium Hydroxide Relaxer Retouch Rubric 275
    - Curl Reforming Service: Contour Wrap Rubric 277
    - Brain Conditioner 282
13. **HAIR COLORING** 289
    - Semi-Permanent Color Rubric 302
    - Oxidative Color: Darker Result Rubric 303
    - Freehand Painting Rubric 304
    - Partial Highlights: Slicing Rubric 305
    - Full Highlights: Weaving Rubric 306
    - Double-Process Blond Rubric 307
    - Brain Conditioner 308

UNIT 3 NAIL AND SKIN SERVICES
14. **THE STUDY OF NAILS** 314
    - Basic Manicure Rubric 320
    - Basic Pedicure Rubric 321
    - Nail Tips Rubric 323
    - Tips with Acrylic Overlay Rubric 324
    - Pink and White Sculptured Nails Rubric 325
    - Brain Conditioner 331
15. **THE STUDY OF SKIN** 336
    - Basic Facial Rubric 344
    - Basic Waxing Rubric 346
    - Basic Makeup Application Rubric 351
    - Brain Conditioner 355

GLOSSARY 388

STUDY GUIDE OVERVIEW

OVERVIEW

Welcome to the world of cosmetology.

Maybe you wonder why there are two books instead of one. Well, that's easy enough. Your text was written by experts—women and men who have proven their skills in the world you want to enter. Your study guide will be written by YOU. It is the place where learning will become your own. **Everything you need to know to be successful in *Salon Fundamentals* is included in your study guide.** It is designed to boost your learning potential and take the fear and confusion out of your professional preparation.

Because everyone learns in different ways, it is reasonable to expect parts of this study guide to be easy for you and others difficult. Most of your life you have practiced certain ways of learning and avoided others. Take a moment now to think of some ways of learning that you avoid whenever you can. Over the next few days, talk with a few other people and find out what ways of learning they avoid.

Most of those preferred and avoided ways of learning will be included in this study guide in order to make your learning more complete. You can gain confidence by thinking of your study guide as a jigsaw puzzle. Each piece involves a special way of learning, of using your brainpower. Put the easiest pieces together first. (Remember that the easiest pieces for you may be the hardest for someone else.) That way you will have more experience when you attempt the more difficult pieces. The more you practice the difficult parts, the easier they become and **the smarter your brain becomes**. Successful students are not born, after all. They evolve by developing a diverse set of learning tools that helps them connect new information to what they already know. This study guide aims to help you build as diverse a set of learning tools as you possibly can.

Many of these tools can be grouped in a category called **MINDFRAMES**. Each MINDFRAME is a specific way of using your brainpower to make you smarter. Your study guide is organized into 7 different MINDFRAMES: PREVIEWING, NAMING, CONNECTING, SELF-CHECKING, APPLYING, SELF-TESTING and JOURNALING. These MINDFRAMES overlap in rich and rewarding ways just the way your mind itself does. One MINDFRAME flows into another.

To help you identify the specific MINDFRAME each activity requires, there is an icon on every study guide page. You can identify what kind of brainpower you will be using most on that page. The MINDFRAME you need on each page is highlighted in cyan. On some pages, two MINDFRAMES are suggested. Here is how the MINDFRAMES help you become a more successful learner.

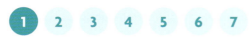

MINDFRAME ICON

MINDFRAME 1: PREVIEWING

Previewing sets the stage for purposeful learning. It enables you to get the big picture, the overall design of what you will study before you turn your attention to the details.

Research tells us that 80% of what you need to learn is contained in 20% of the material you study. Known as the 80-20 rule, this finding supports the importance of knowing what to study before you begin. Your study guide aims to take the mystery out of what's important by showcasing the most important material on the first page or two of each chapter. It gives you a sneak preview of the whole chapter.

Let's see how it works. Here is a sample of what you will see on the first page or two of each study guide chapter. The **VALUE STATEMENT** tells you why this material is important to you personally. The **MAIN IDEA** states the fundamental message of the chapter. The **PLAN** gives a graphic preview of the general content of the chapter. Together these pieces represent the "warm-up" stages of learning. "Warming up" by surveying the chapter and generating a few insights and questions *before* beginning greatly improves your concentration, memory and learning.

If you've already looked at a chapter in your *Salon Fundamentals* textbook, this first-page lineup in your study guide will look familiar. You have a VALUE STATEMENT, a MAIN IDEA and a PLAN there as well. Focus on these three important areas of your study:

- **Its importance to you personally (VALUE STATEMENT)**
- **Its major message (MAIN IDEA)**
- **The way the ideas in the chapter will be developed (PLAN)**

As you proceed, you will notice that the Plan in the textbook has words, as do the Plans in the theory chapters of your study guide. The Plans in the more hands-on, practical chapters of the guide have pictures. Throughout your study, try to link words and pictures in order to make your thinking visible to yourself and others. As you move from chapter to chapter, make sure to discuss with someone else how the words and pictures in the two Plans fit together. When you see a study guide Plan with no words, look at the corresponding Plan in your textbook. Write the words from the textbook Plan on or near their corresponding pictures in the study guide Plan. That way you are creating a linkage of verbal and visual knowing.

MINDFRAME 2: NAMING

Once you've seen the big picture, your MINDFRAME shifts. You begin NAMING what you are coming to know, putting it into your own words, arranging the material in a form that makes sense to you. Some years ago, Dr. Walter Pauk, from Cornell University, developed an excellent system of note-taking. This second MINDFRAME is modeled on his system and is called **SmartNotes**. Look at a sample page of **SmartNotes**. What do you see? Take a moment to identify how these pages are built and how many ways they offer clues for your learning.

STUDY GUIDE OVERVIEW

At the top of each **SmartNotes** page are the main topics you are studying and the corresponding page numbers in the textbook to consult for additional information. Familiarize yourself right away by referring to those pages in the text whenever you have questions or want clarification. That simple practice will deepen your learning and save you time. Instead of searching aimlessly for answers, you will know right where to go.

The rest of the page is divided into two columns. Key terms and ideas are listed in the smaller left column. This column is commonly referred to as the "cue" column. The cue column has lots of white space so you can search the words and easily locate important ideas. All of the words in the cue column are important. These words are arranged in ways that help you connect segments of the chapter that should be studied together. They are presented in an order that eventually will help you tell a story about what you are learning. When you put ideas into a story, you are building important links that your brain can use to remember what you are learning.

Here are some recommendations for using these pages:
- **Pay particular attention to these key terms and ideas.**
- **Note your thoughts in the right-hand column while reading your** textbook.
- **Refer to the glossary at the end of your study guide for terms that you may need as a quick review.**
- **Add what you hear during a class discussion to your notes in the right column.**
- **Try to use your growing set of notes to tell a story.**

How exactly do you fill in the right-hand column of your **SmartNotes** using the prompts in the left column? Experts say that when taking notes it is best to use short phrases, written in your own words, to describe what is most important to know about the word in the cue column. Include only the most essential information. Your brain will notice that the most important ideas are given more space in the notes column. If you see more space in the notes column this should alert you to the relative importance of the concept you are studying.

Many future hair designers have wonderful spatial intelligence. The design of your study guide encourages you to put that spatial intelligence to work learning the content you are studying. These notes do not need to make sense to anyone but yourself. **If they help you learn and remember this material, they are indeed SmartNotes because they're helping to make you smarter!** By translating the ideas of the chapter into your own words and images, you are actively processing the material. You are making sense of what you are learning. You are actually rewriting your textbook in ways that make sense to you. Copying answers word for word from your textbook is not recommended. Copying answers in someone else's words usually makes them more difficult to remember.

SmartNotes contain a running total of all you are learning about a particular idea. Simply completing this section guarantees that you are on the right track to learning the most important ideas. **SmartNotes** also provide a ready-made personal outline for connecting important ideas and building the references you will need to deepen your understanding of the material to be learned.

STUDY GUIDE OVERVIEW

MINDFRAME 3: CONNECTING

Successfully NAMING what you are learning lays the foundation for making connections of all kinds. Your CONNECTING skill rapidly increases your ability to learn and retain what you learn. Sometimes in your study guide, CONNECTING activities are inserted within the **SmartNotes**. Other times they are placed after your **SmartNotes**. The most creative learners are energized by novelty. They use creative expressions to "jump start" their thinking. For that reason, you will see many different kinds of exercises included as connectors.

An excellent way for your brain to make connections is by building **Thinking Maps**. **Thinking Maps** create pictures of what you know using shapes, patterns, words, doodles and connections of all kinds. Once again your spatial intelligence has a chance to shine. **Thinking Maps make your thoughts visible so that you can think about them in different ways.** They promote discussion and help you explore specific topics in creative and organized ways. You can use them as "roadmaps" to deeper understanding. Because they tap into your ability to create relationships among the concepts you are learning, **Thinking Maps** are powerful memory joggers. Once you can picture how words and ideas fit together, you will remember them more easily.

Thinking Maps appeal to the creative side of your intellect as well as to your spatial intelligence. For this reason, they are usually enjoyable for students who are studying to be designers and cosmetologists. These maps of colors, pictures and symbols, when coupled with words, create powerful associations in your brain that will ensure better understanding and recall.

You're probably wondering: **How do I make a Thinking Map?**

First… Start with a topic and circle it in the center of your paper.

Then… Add branches to hold key subtopics. Gather subtopics from your memory, your **SmartNotes**, the PLAN or from the **Jump Start Box** of terms and ideas on each **Thinking Map** page. Branches can also be categories such as who, what, where, when, how or why.

Next… Use the words in the **Jump Start Box** to explore all the possible links you can create. If you have questions about any words, you may also refer to the glossary at the end of your study guide.

Finally… Share and compare. Let others see your map and gain ideas and connections from you. Add to your map realizations you have while looking at someone else's map. Shared knowledge makes each person better.

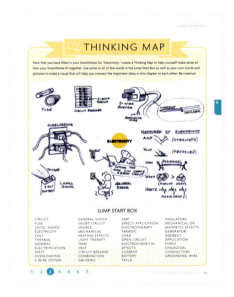

As you follow and intermingle these steps, make sure that you personalize your map with your style. Use more than two colors. Doodle. Vary size and shape for effect. Be creative. Your map can continue to grow in extent and interrelationships. You can always add more insights as you discover them. There is no single, correct way to build a **Thinking Map**. In fact, each **Thinking Map** you make for this study guide will probably be different from the others. You are not making carbon copies. You are creating original images of your growing understanding of a topic.

STUDY GUIDE OVERVIEW

MINDFRAME 4: SELF-CHECKING

The connections you are making need to stand up to scrutiny, your own first of all. They need to be challenged for accuracy and depth. In the past, you may have regarded that as the job of someone like a teacher or outsider. No longer. That's what your own brain does for you during SELF-CHECKING. Your brain actually doubles back on itself and asks the question: How well am I relating to this new material? Do I know it well enough to advance to the next step in my education and professional development? The more skilled you become at SELF-CHECKING, the more prepared you will be to learn the rest of the information in the chapter. It offers a diagnostic check midway through a chapter to validate and reinforce *to yourself* that you really are learning, that much of what you need to know is already in place. SELF-CHECKING allows you to tell yourself you're doing fine, to give yourself a pat on the back.

It is also a quick reminder to go back and pick up anything you missed along the way. The better a student you become, the more you will self-check automatically. You will know that before you move forward you need to pause and check your location. You pause to pay attention to certain areas of the text you might ordinarily skip. Remember what I said earlier about ways of learning you avoid? Your natural learning style tends to skip what it considers unpleasant. SELF-CHECKING cues your brain about possible gaps that may exist and gives you time to fill those gaps with new learning.

In this study guide, your SELF-CHECKING opportunity takes the form of **The Challenge**. You are encouraged to review your study guide before completing **The Challenge**. The questions represent the most basic ideas in the chapter. You should expect to get at least 80% of these answers correct before you continue on with your work in the rest of the study guide. If you find **The Challenge** questions too difficult, take time to return to your textbook and your **SmartNotes** and re-learn the material. You may also wish to review with someone else or approach your teacher for extra help and suggestions.

How do you know exactly which answers you have correct? Following every **Challenge** is a **Memory Box**, a self-monitoring activity designed to provide you with immediate feedback about your progress. Here are its parts: First you use the page references to look up the answers in your textbook. Then check "got it" for all correct answers and "not yet" for all incorrect ones. Next, using the *Know Chart*, record the correct answers in the *I Know* column. Correct the incorrect answers and record the corrected response in the *I Need to Study* column. In this way, you can monitor your progress and clearly determine what you need to study to become more successful.

STUDY GUIDE OVERVIEW

MINDFRAME 5: APPLYING

Here is your long-awaited chance to put your knowledge into action. Many students feel at their best when they are actually doing something. After all, you dream of being a cosmetologist because you sense a personal talent for doing creative work with hair, skin and nails. There are several different learning exercises in the APPLYING sections of your study guide. Learning exercises in this MINDFRAME are **Talking Points**, **Show You Know** and the **Rubrics**. **SmartNotes** and **Thinking Maps** give you lots to talk about with others. Experts tell us that we really don't "personalize" what we learn until we express it. Part of your reputation as a stylist will rest on your ability to talk clearly and confidently with your clients. That's why **Talking Points** are part of your guide – to encourage you to talk about what you know and how you know it. Talking out your ideas is a great way to discover your comfort level with the information. It is another concrete way to monitor your progress and build your skills.

In order to refine your communication skills, you need practice in a non-threatening environment. In your study guide, each **Talking Point** is placed next to a miniature "card," representing an index card. On it you can jot down your key points. You may choose to transfer some **Talking Points** to real cards and use the cards to role play actual conversations. These practice conversations can be shared with a friend, a parent, classmate or anyone who will listen. The goal of the activity is to learn to explain and communicate your ideas with poise and confidence.

Many chapters have a **Show You Know** project designed to give you the opportunity to be creative and expressive. These activities will reinforce to you that you really do understand and can apply what you are learning. If you devote some time and energy to them, you will begin to realize how smart you really are.

Each **Show You Know** is matched to specific professional standards in the cosmetology industry. By completing each one you will gain valuable exposure to professional standards and have fun demonstrating that you can apply what you are learning.

In all the practical chapters, your central way of APPLYING what you learn will be through practicing the procedures for that skill. Each procedure has its own evaluation form called a RUBRIC. The word RUBRIC translates as "something written in red" from the Latin word for red or red chalk. It means simply a set of standardized directions.

In your study guide, a RUBRIC is a self-assessment tool that will help you gauge your level of performance. It is designed to compare your skill and technique to industry standards. On the following page is a sample RUBRIC. Look at the page and see what you can learn immediately about how the RUBRICS are set up. You see under the directions the name of the procedure you will be practicing followed by the industry standard to which it relates.

Then you see a bulleted list of steps under "Preparation," "Procedure" and "Completion." Each bulleted item is followed by three boxes, Levels 1, 2 and 3. For each RUBRIC form you complete, you will be asked to check for each item your level of accomplishment at that time.

STUDY GUIDE OVERVIEW

RUBRIC

This rubric is a self-assessment tool designed to compare your skill to industry standards. Indicate your present level of performance by checking the appropriate box. See overview for instructions.

Pink and White Sculptured Nails

Industry Standard – to meet entry-level proficiency, industry standards require that you:
- Provide and conduct basic manicure and pedicure services in a safe environment, free from disease.

	Level 1	Level 2	Level 3	To Improve, I Need To:	Teacher Assessment
Preparation					
Clean nail table; place fresh soaking lotion and disinfected nail implements on nail table; review and arrange products in order of use	☐	☐	☐		☐
Procedure					
Wash and sanitize hands; perform visual analysis; remove nail polish	☐	☐	☐		☐
Perform thorough hand and nail examination and consultation	☐	☐	☐		☐
File free edge; buff surface of nail lightly; remove filing residue	☐	☐	☐		☐
Apply dehydrant; apply nail form; apply primer if directed	☐	☐	☐		☐
Measure out required amount of pink and white acrylic powder; form bead of white acrylic on side of brush	☐	☐	☐		☐
Apply acrylic bead to form to create free edge (zone 1); rotate brush; pat and press toward edges of nail form	☐	☐	☐		☐
Define shape and length of free edge	☐	☐	☐		☐
Create second acrylic pink bead; place second bead in middle section (zone 2); pat, press and stroke acrylic into place	☐	☐	☐		☐
Place smallest pink acrylic bead just below cuticle (zone 3); pat, press and stroke acrylic down to base of nail	☐	☐	☐		☐
Apply fourth bead across stress area (optional); repeat on remaining nails	☐	☐	☐		☐
Remove form; file and buff; remove nail dust; buff	☐	☐	☐		☐
Completion					
Offer a prebook visit; recommend retail products; discard non-reusable materials, replace used towels with fresh towels, arrange all products and implements in proper order; disinfect acrylic overlay service implements and equipment; wash your hands with liquid soap.	☐	☐	☐		☐

Total = addition of all Teacher Assessment boxes

TOTAL POINTS = ☐
39

Percentage = student score / highest possible score

_____ %

SALON FUNDAMENTALS COSMETOLOGY

Level 1 means you're still "In Progress."
    You complete the task with assistance and/or prompting.
    You complete the task with inconsistent quality.
    You perform the task with several errors evident in technique.
    You describe the technique with vague understanding.

Level 2 means you're "Getting Better."
    You complete the task alone.
    You complete the task approaching the industry standard.
    You perform the task with occasional errors evident in technique.
    You describe the technique with prompting.

Level 3 means you've reached "Entry-Level Proficiency" for the beginning stylist.
    You complete the task alone.
    You complete the task and meet the industry standard described in the text.
    You perform the task with very few errors evident in technique.
    You communicate and reflect upon the technique to others.
    You complete the entire procedure in accordance with required timing.

Next to the boxes is a line where you can jot down some areas in which you wish to improve. Finally, when you are ready, you can ask your teacher to complete a RUBRIC form for you. The teacher will assess your level of competence and place a 1, 2 or 3 in each "Teacher Assessment" box, total your score and determine your percentage for that procedure.

As you use the RUBRIC, remember that some tasks will be easier for you than others. On these tasks you will achieve "Entry Level Proficiency" sooner. For more difficult tasks, your RUBRIC—no matter in what color you write it—will remind you of where you need to practice your technique.

MINDFRAME 6: SELF-TESTING

Your study guide is designed to take the mystery and fear out of tests. Experts remind us that SELF-TESTING, actually practicing in a test-like format, builds confidence and reduces test anxiety. If you practice enough by testing yourself, your licensure exam will not seem as threatening.

The activity designed for SELF-TESTING is called a **Brain Conditioner**. The **Brain Conditioner** is a test-event designed to simulate your certification test.

STUDY GUIDE OVERVIEW

Practice really does make perfect. If you practice the actual test event, you will learn many valuable things like:
- **How to relax enough to deal with test anxiety**
- **How to skip hard questions until later**
- **How to space your energy and brainpower over the entire test so that you have as much energy at the end of the test as you had at the beginning**
- **How to avoid discouragement if you don't know every answer**
- **How to read each question calmly and understand what it is asking**
- **How to stay in a flow state (a positive place) as long as you can**

Although the **Brain Conditioner** is an actual test event, it is also a learning activity. For that reason, you should use your **Memory Box** just as you did after **The Challenge** to gather information you still need to review a bit more.

MINDFRAME 7: JOURNALING

True learning is a deeply personal experience. It engages the person you are and begins your transformation into the person you wish to become. As this growth is happening in you, you need some kind of record of what is going on with your feelings as well as in your thinking. **SmartNotes** and other activities here in the guide give you records of your thinking. JOURNALING offers the opportunity to honor what you are feeling, realizing and questioning at levels even deeper than thought.

At the end of each chapter, it is important to jot down your feelings about what you have just studied. Especially important to note are things that surprised you, learning tasks that you found difficult and how you dealt with those difficulties. Also helpful to record are suggestions you received from friends or others that might help you enjoy learning more. You will be surprised how your comments change as you go through the chapters of your *Salon Fundamentals* textbook, giving your energy to each MINDFRAME in its turn.

Now you have an overview of this entire book—your book—the place where the knowledge of the experts takes on personal meaning. Everyone's textbook is identical. Everyone's study guide, if done correctly, will be unique. Your mind will frame the material to suit your specific learning preferences and needs.

You can make your study guide a real part of your professional journey by adding to it and improving it every day. If you do, new possibilities for creativity and opportunity will appear in your work. As you improve your study guide, you improve yourself. The study guide is designed to be a developing learning guide, a portfolio, of what you can do and your commitment to your future. As you learn to grow what you know, grow it with passion, integrity and commitment.

CHAPTER 1
PROFESSIONAL DEVELOPMENT

VALUE
Professional development will enable you to improve your health, professional status and positive relationships with clients and co-workers.

MAIN IDEA
A Healthy Body and Mind + Effective Communication + Positive Human Relations = **SUCCESS**

PLAN

1.1 **HEALTHY BODY AND MIND**
Rest and Relaxation
Exercise
Nutrition
Hygiene
Image
Ergonomics

1.2 **EFFECTIVE COMMUNICATION**
Nonverbal Communication
Verbal Communication

1.3 **HUMAN RELATIONS**
Personality
Teamwork
Ethics

CHAPTER 1

smartNOTES

1.1 HEALTHY BODY AND MIND   pages 25-27

Rest and Relaxation

Exercise

Nutrition

Hygiene

Record Your Week

	MONDAY	TUESDAY	WEDNESDAY	THURSDAY	FRIDAY	SATURDAY	SUNDAY
Hours of sleep per night							
How much exercise							
Calories burned							

(Refer to Salon Fundamentals Cosmetology coursebook page 26)

PUBLIC HYGIENE

PERSONAL HYGIENE

12 UNIT 1 THEORY ESSENTIALS   1 **2** 3 4 5 6 7

PROFESSIONAL DEVELOPMENT

smartNOTES

1.1 HEALTHY BODY AND MIND pages 27-30

PRIMARY HEALTH HAZARDS
- Impure air ventilation
- Inadequate _____
- Improper disinfection practices
- Improper _____ or use of food

Oral Hygiene

Bad breath = _____
Maintaining healthy teeth and keeping breath fresh

Reducing Body Odor

Bathe regularly using soap and use deodorant

Image

Hair care: Clean, healthy hair = beautiful _____
Good nutrition, exercise and rest = healthy, glowing skin

Tips

Foundation should always match skin _____
Contouring with lights – _____
Contouring with darks – _____

Dress for Success

Clothing must be clean, shoes _____
Dress well

Posture Tips

Good _____ enhances your physical well-being and reduces physical fatigue
- Use height adjustments on _____
- Keep head up, chin level, shoulders _____
- When sitting, keep knees together, feet on floor, sit well back in chair

1 2 3 4 5 6 7

SALON FUNDAMENTALS COSMETOLOGY 13

CHAPTER 1

smartNOTES

1.1 HEALTHY BODY AND MIND
pages 31-33

Ergonomics

Ergonomics is the science that looks at how you do your work, what body movements, positions, tools, etc., you use and the effect it has on your body.

Prevent Neck and Back Problems

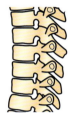

- Work with _____ straight
- Use freestanding sink
- Adjust _____ of chair
- Tilt client's head
- Use tilted _____ or wedge
- Bend _____ slightly

- Place one foot up
- Avoid high _____
- Stand on foot stool
- Work with client standing (if long hair)

Prevent Foot and Leg Problems

- Don't _____ for a long time
- Raise feet on stool during break
- Wear comfortable, rubber-soled shoes
- Use shock-absorbing _____
- Use _____ hose/socks
- Hydraulic chairs should adjust at least _____ inches

- Use _____ floor mat
- Avoid shoes with high _____ or pointed toes

Prevent Hand and Wrist Problems

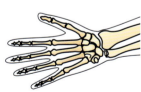

- Swivel chair
- Tilt client's head
- Use _____ shears, well-oiled
- Twirl handles
- Manicure stations – use _____ rests

- Adjust _____ of chair
- Use procedural techniques to keep _____ straight

Prevent Shoulder Problems

- Adjust _____ of chair
- Swivel chair
- Tilt client's _____
- Hold _____ so you don't have to raise arms
- When doing nails have client extend arm
- Use arm rest

PROFESSIONAL DEVELOPMENT

smartNOTES

1.2 EFFECTIVE COMMUNICATION   pages 34-37

Communication

Nonverbal Communication

BODY LANGUAGE	MEANING
SMILING	•
NODDING	•
HANDSHAKE	•
LEANING FORWARD	•
ARMS CROSSED ON CHEST	•

Verbal Communication

Grammar

Keys to Effective Two-Way Communication
-
-
-
-

1 2 3 4 5 6 7

SALON FUNDAMENTALS COSMETOLOGY   15

CHAPTER 1

smartNOTES

1.2 EFFECTIVE COMMUNICATION page 37

Keys to Effective Two-Way Communication (Cont'd)

-
-
-
-
-

1.3 HUMAN RELATIONS pages 38-42

Personality

-
-

POSITIVE PERSONALITY TRAITS

-
-
-
-

-
-
-
-

PROFESSIONAL DEVELOPMENT

smartNOTES

1.3 HUMAN RELATIONS pages 42-43

Teamwork

The existence of a harmonious environment depends heavily on _____
- Keeping your workstation _____, with all your tools in place, is usually set forth by a regulating agency
- The key words for _____ are consideration and cooperation

Ethics

As your personality develops, you establish your own personal system of moral principles and values, which become known as your personal _____

GIVE EXAMPLES OF THE FOLLOWING:

Respect →

Courtesy →

Eagerness To Learn →

Honesty →

Loyalty →

Trustworthiness →

Cleanliness And Safety →

Pride In Your Profession →

1 **2** 3 4 5 6 7

SALON FUNDAMENTALS COSMETOLOGY 17

CHAPTER 1

THINKING MAP

Now that you have filled in your SmartNotes for "Professional Development," create a Thinking Map to help make sense of how your SmartNotes fit together. Use some or all of the words in the Jump Start Box as well as your own words and pictures to make a visual that will help you connect the important ideas in this chapter to each other. Be creative!

PROFESSIONAL DEVELOPMENT

JUMP START BOX

REST	EXERCISE	CONTOURING	NONVERBAL
CALORIES	RDA	PERSONALITY	PUBLIC HYGIENE
PERSONAL HYGIENE	GROOMING	VERBAL	PROFESSIONAL PRIDE
DARK	POSTURE	ENERGY	LIGHTING
LANGUAGE	POSITIVE ATTITUDE	RESPECT	
ETHICS	NUTRITION	LIGHT	
VENTILATION	HYGIENE	COMMUNICATION	

PROFESSIONAL DEVELOPMENT

TALKING POINTS

Your next challenge is to be ready to talk about some of the important ideas in this chapter. Follow the directions listed next to each box. Then practice talking about your ideas with others.

-
-
-

Using your own words, describe 3 things you can do to ensure a healthy body and mind.

-
-
-

List 3 nonverbal behaviors you observe in clients that indicate satisfaction or approval.

Design a bumper sticker or banner that expresses your personal code of ethics. Compare your code with others.

THE CHALLENGE

Now it's time to see how well you know your new material. First answer these questions. Then use the Memory Box that follows to check yourself. Look up each answer on the corresponding page in the *Salon Fundamentals* textbook. Check "got it" for all correct answers and "not yet" for all incorrect responses. Using the "Know Chart," record all of your correct responses in the "I Know" column. After correcting incorrect answers, record all of your corrected responses in the "I Need to Study" column. That way you know exactly what to review before continuing in this study guide.

1. Establishing routines to maintain a healthy body and mind is the first step toward _____ _____.

2. Dedication to proper nutrition, image and hygiene are important steps that will ensure a healthy body and mind. Name two other areas that will aid in developing a healthy body and mind. _____ _____

3. TRUE   FALSE   Most people need six to eight hours of sleep or they become fatigued and cannot function properly.

4. The practice of public hygiene is important because it helps to preserve the health of the _____.

5. How you do your work, what body movements, positions, tools and equipment you should use and the effect all these things have on you and your client's health and comfort is the science called _____.

6. The exchange of thoughts and information through conversation or writing is defined as _____

7. Appearance, posture and facial expression would be examples of _____ communication.

8. TRUE   FALSE   Religion and politics are acceptable topics of discussion between a cosmetologist and a client.

9. The psychology of getting along with others is referred to as _____.

10. The outward reflection of your inner feelings, thoughts, attitudes and values is referred to as your _____.

CHAPTER 1

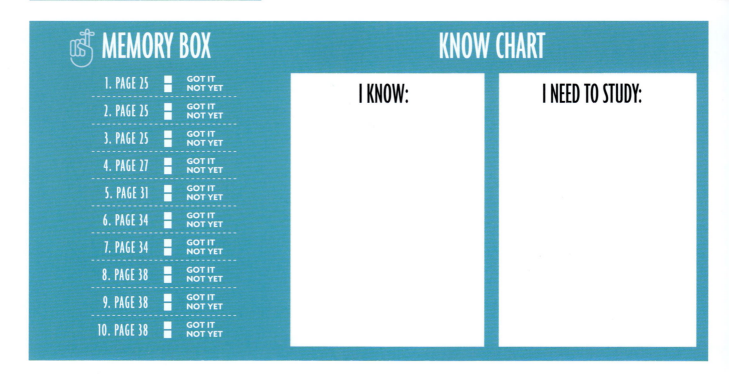

SHOW YOU KNOW...

Select a person you know that models or represents lifelong learning and health and well-being. In other words, this person is a true role model. Indicators of such performance might include:

- Participating in industry-related shows and educational seminars
- Subscribing to cosmetology journals and professional organizations
- Taking appropriate measures to protect personal health

The work styles of this person might be described using some of the following words or phrases:

Achiever	Social orientation	Persistent
Adaptable/Flexible	Shows initiative	Attentive to detail
Exhibits leadership	Independent	Cooperative
Innovative	Shows concern	

KNOWLEDGE GRID

Start at the top of the Knowledge Grid and work your way down, answering each question to check your understanding of *Chapter 1, Professional Development*. The questions found here will help you deepen your understanding, build self-confidence and increase your awareness of different ways of thinking about a subject.

KNOW	LIST THE RECOMMENDED NUMBER OF HOURS TO SLEEP AT NIGHT.	
COMPREHEND	COMPARE PERSONAL HYGIENE TO PUBLIC HYGIENE.	
APPLY	DESCRIBE A TIP FOR ENHANCING A NARROW FOREHEAD.	
ANALYZE	ANALYZE THE FOLLOWING NONVERBAL MESSAGES AND IDENTIFY WHAT EACH MESSAGE COMMUNICATES:	Smile Person standing straight with squared shoulders, head held high Bowed shoulders and sloping body posture
SYNTHESIZE	FORMULATE THE TOPICS OF DISCUSSION THAT SHOULD BE AVOIDED WITH CLIENTS.	
EVALUATE	DEFEND WHAT A "CODE OF PROFESSIONAL ETHICS" STATES ABOUT YOU.	

CHAPTER 1

BRAIN **BUILDER**

Questions help us think. Write a challenging question about four of the important words or phrases below and be prepared to answer it. (The following stems generate the most thought-provoking questions: Why does? Why are? What if? How would? Try them!) Then try your questions out on your friends. How well can they answer them?

- Cosmetology
- Professional Development
- Hygiene
- Ergonomics
- Nonverbal Communication
- Personality
- Code Of Ethics

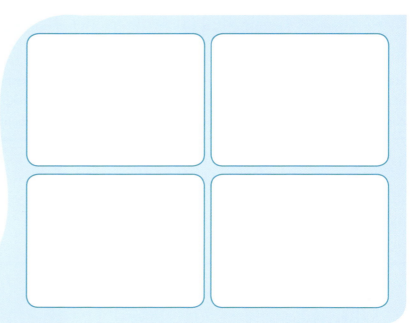

PUTTING YOUR HEADS TOGETHER

FIRST... THE GOAL OF THIS ACTIVITY IS TO CLARIFY YOUR IDEAS BY WORKING TOGETHER IN SMALL GROUPS. COMPLETE THE FOLLOWING SHORT-ANSWER QUESTIONS WITH A PARTNER OR IN A SMALL GROUP...

THEN... DISCUSS YOUR ANSWERS...

FINALLY... LOOK UP EACH ANSWER IN YOUR TEXTBOOK, USING THE PAGE REFERENCE TO THE LEFT, TO SEE IF YOU ARE CORRECT. MAKE CORRECTIONS OR ADDITIONS AS NECESSARY.

PAGE 24 1. The art and science of beauty care is known as _____ .

PAGE 25 2. The two emotions that can be injurious to your health are _____ and _____ .

PAGE 27 3. Hygiene is the science that deals with _____ _____ .

PAGE 30 4. Good posture will (a) _____ , (b) _____ , (c) _____ .

PAGE 35 5. List 3 examples of nonverbal communication: (1) _____ , (2) _____ , (3) _____ .

PAGES 36-37 6. Describe behaviors of a good communicator: _____ _____ .

PAGE 38 7. Personality is defined as the _____ _____ .

PAGE 42 8. Ethical conduct is _____ .

22 UNIT 1 THEORY ESSENTIALS

1 2 3 4 **5** 6 7

PROFESSIONAL DEVELOPMENT

BRAIN CONDITIONER
MULTIPLE CHOICE. CIRCLE THE CORRECT ANSWER.

1. The art and science of beauty care is defined as:
   a. charisma
   b. personal hygiene
   c. cosmetology
   d. ethical conduct

2. How many hours of sleep do most people need to function properly?
   a. 1 to 2 hours
   b. 3 to 4 hours
   c. 6 to 8 hours
   d. 9 to 12 hours

3. Which of the following activities is NOT a recommended way to relax and get away from it all?
   a. reading a book
   b. listening to music
   c. going for a walk
   d. sleeping 1 to 2 hours a day

4. What will make you feel, look and work better?
   a. skipping lunch
   b. sleeping 1 to 2 hours a day
   c. drinking coffee
   d. a regular exercise program

5. Which of the following activities helps stimulate blood circulation in your body?
   a. watching TV
   b. reading a good book
   c. listening to music
   d. exercise

6. Worry is an emotion that could have which of the following effects?
   a. vitalize mental health
   b. injurious to mental health
   c. tones muscles
   d. stimulates exercise

7. Which of the following items is one of the three energy nutrients almost all foods contain?
   a. fats
   b. salt
   c. sugar
   d. calories

8. The energy contained in food is measured in:
   a. degrees
   b. protein content
   c. calories
   d. fat content

9. The energy in food can be stored in the body as:
   a. fat
   b. protein
   c. carbohydrates
   d. vitamins

10. The science that deals with healthful living is called:
    a. hygiene
    b. nutrition
    c. ergonomics
    d. mental health

11. The practice of public hygiene covers all of the following health issues EXCEPT:
    a. impure air
    b. bad breath
    c. poor ventilation
    d. improper use of food

12. Bathing regularly with soap, using deodorant and washing clothes are examples of:
    a. oral hygiene
    b. public sanitation
    c. personal hygiene
    d. excessive grooming

13. Halitosis is the technical term for:
    a. poor posture
    b. bad breath
    c. poor nutrition
    d. poor public hygiene

14. Healthy skin is dependent on all of the following health techniques EXCEPT:
    a. rest
    b. exercise
    c. good nutrition
    d. lack of sleep

15. Which of the following statements is true about contouring?
    a. light colors broaden
    b. light colors narrow
    c. dark colors broaden
    d. light colors can narrow or broaden

CHAPTER 1

16. **An overly wide jaw can be visually narrowed by applying:**
    a. lighter contour creme on the inner areas of the jaw
    b. lighter contour creme on the outer areas of the jawline
    c. darker contour creme on the outer areas of the jawline
    d. lighter contour creme around the lips

17. **What type of shoes should be worn to reduce the fatigue from standing all day?**
    a. old   b. tennis   c. high-heeled   d. low, broad-heeled

18. **A foot doctor is called a:**
    a. psychologist   b. gynecologist   c. pediatrician   d. podiatrist

19. **Maintaining good posture and moving properly will:**
    a. present an attractive image
    b. cause fatigue
    c. cause injury
    d. hurt your feet

20. **All of the following can help prevent neck and back strain EXCEPT:**
    a. working with the back straight
    b. reaching overhead for supplies
    c. using freestanding shampoo bowls
    d. adjusting the height of the client's chair

21. **All of the following movements cause carpal tunnel EXCEPT:**
    a. bending your wrist a lot
    b. gripping with force
    c. repeating a motion over and over
    d. using sharp shears

22. **Facial expressions, posture and poise are examples of:**
    a. hygiene
    b. verbal communication
    c. public hygiene
    d. nonverbal communication

23. **The exchange of thoughts, ideas or feelings with someone is called:**
    a. public relations   b. personality   c. communication   d. language

24. **To be a good communicator, you also have to be:**
    a. loud   b. a good listener   c. a good story teller   d. able to stretch the truth

25. **An outward reflection of your feelings, thoughts, attitudes and nature defines your:**
    a. hygiene   b. posture   c. personality   d. sense of humor

26. **When having a two-way conversation with a client, it is best to focus your conversation on:**
    a. controversial topics
    b. the weather
    c. your client's lifestyle and salon-related needs
    d. famous personalities

27. **The psychology of getting along with others is called:**
    a. communication   b. human relations   c. philosophy   d. attitude

28. **Personal ethics include the following attributes EXCEPT:**
    a. values   b. personality   c. moral principles   d. negative attitude

29. **Following a regulating agency's requirement to keep your workspace uncluttered is:**
    a. almost impossible to do
    b. disrespectful toward other co-workers
    c. also visually appealing to the overall atmosphere of the workstation
    d. something you should do only because it's a rule

30. **Proper conduct in relationships with your employer, co-workers and clients is known as:**
    a. personal hygiene   b. professional ethics   c. professional connecting   d. economics

PROFESSIONAL DEVELOPMENT

FINAL REVIEW

Check your answers as you did before. Place a check mark next to the page number for any incorrect answer. On the lines below, jot down topics that you still need to review.

☐ 1.	page 24	☐ 9.	page 26	☐ 17.	page 29	☐ 25.	page 38
☐ 2.	page 25	☐ 10.	page 27	☐ 18.	page 29	☐ 26.	page 38
☐ 3.	page 25	☐ 11.	page 27	☐ 19.	page 30	☐ 27.	page 38
☐ 4.	page 25	☐ 12.	page 27	☐ 20.	page 31	☐ 28.	page 42
☐ 5.	page 25	☐ 13.	page 27	☐ 21.	page 32	☐ 29.	page 42
☐ 6.	page 25	☐ 14.	page 28	☐ 22.	page 34	☐ 30.	page 43
☐ 7.	page 26	☐ 15.	page 29	☐ 23.	page 34		
☐ 8.	page 26	☐ 16.	page 29	☐ 24.	page 37		

NOTES TO MYSELF

Experts tell us that it is important to summarize your feelings and reactions about what you are learning. Note especially things that surprised you, things you found difficult to learn, suggestions and ideas you received from friends that helped make learning this chapter easier and more enjoyable.

My reflections about Professional Development:

LESSONS LEARNED

- *Establishing routines to maintain a healthy body and mind puts you on the right track toward attaining your professional goals.*
- *Effective communication reflects your professionalism and includes both verbal and nonverbal messages.*
- *Positive human relations are influenced by personality, teamwork and ethical conduct.*

SALON FUNDAMENTALS COSMETOLOGY

CHAPTER 2

CHAPTER 2
SALON ECOLOGY

VALUE
Your understanding of Salon Ecology will help you protect your clients and yourself from the unnecessary spread of infectious diseases.

MAIN IDEA
Microbiology + Infection Control + First-Aid Procedures =
A Healthy and Safe Environment

PLAN

2.1 **MICROBIOLOGY**
Bacteria
Growth of Bacteria
Viruses
External Parasites
Infection
Immunity

2.2 **INFECTION CONTROL**
Sanitation
Disinfection
Sterilization
Infection Control Guidelines

2.3 **FIRST AID**
Bleeding and Wounds
Burns
Choking
Fainting
Eye Injury

SALON ECOLOGY

smartNOTES

2.1 MICROBIOLOGY   pages 47-48

Bacteria

DIFFERENCES

NONPATHOGENIC
-
-
-
-

PATHOGENIC
-
-
-
-

Pathogenic Bacteria

Cocci →

Staphylococci →

Streptococci →

Diplococci →

Bacilli →

Spirilla →

ACTIVITY

What if the terms in pathogenic bacteria were given really creative, fun names? Would you be able to recognize them? Listed below is a list of "alias" names and their descriptions. See if you can determine the term that matches their identity or "alias," and draw a picture of it.

My name is Curly.
I am very "coiled" and curvy!

My real name is _____ .

My name is Phyl.
I hang out with a "bunch" of guys and sometimes we "boil" up lots of trouble.

My real name is _____ .

My name is Pearl.
I come from a long "chain" of hot oysters, so hot we bring a "fever"!

My real name is _____ .

Our names are Arnold and Danny.
We are a "pair" and when we are around everyone starts coughing!

Our real name is _____ .

My name is Rodney.
I'm a tough guy with lots of muscle. I have the power to lock your jaw!

My real name is _____ .

SALON ECOLOGY

smartNOTES

2.1 MICROBIOLOGY   pages 49-50

Growth of Bacteria

DIFFERENCES

ACTIVE	INACTIVE
•	•
•	•
•	•
•	

Movement of Bacteria

Viruses

External Parasites

PARASITIC FUNGI	PARASITIC MITES

SALON FUNDAMENTALS COSMETOLOGY   29

CHAPTER 2

smartNOTES

2.1 MICROBIOLOGY pages 50-52

Infection

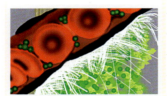

Local

General

Asymptomatic Carrier

Universal Precautions

Immunity

ACTIVE	PASSIVE
•	•
•	•
•	•

2.2 INFECTION CONTROL pages 52-59

Infection Control

1:64 (2 ozs. of this product per gallon of water or 16 ml per liter).

Beauty and Barber Shop, Instruments and Tools: Thoroughly pre-clean. Completely immerse brushes, combs, scissors, clipper blades, razors, tweezers, manicure and other shop tools for 10 minutes (or as required by local authorities). Wipe dry before use. Fresh solution should be prepared daily or more often when the solution becomes diluted or soiled.

*Virucidal: For Complete Instructions For Hepatitis B Virus (HBV) and Human Immunodeficiency Virus (HIV-1) DISINFECTION Refer To Enclosed Hang Tag.

Statement of Practical Treatment: In case of contact immediately flush eyes or skin with plenty of water for at least 15 minutes. For eye contacts, call a physician. If swallowed, drink egg whites, gelatin solution or if these are not available, drink large quantities of water. Avoid alcohol. Call a physician immediately.

Note to Physician: Probable mucosal damage may contra-indicate the use of gastric lavage.

SALON ECOLOGY

INFECTION CONTROL PYRAMID

HIGH LEVEL
STERILIZATION
KILLS: _____

BLOODBORNE PATHOGEN DISINFECTION
KILLS: _____

MEDIUM LEVEL
DISINFECTION
KILLS: _____

ANTISEPTIC
PREVENTS: _____

LOW LEVEL
SANITATION
REMOVES: _____

KEY TERMS

Antiseptic:

Bloodborne Pathogen Disinfection:

Broad Spectrum:

Efficacy Label:

MATCHING

Draw a line from the initials to the correct match.

OSHA	Key info on product ingredients
MSDS	Department of Labor regulatory agency
EPA	Approves efficacy of products

BASICS OF HANDWASHING

1. Use _____ water and _____ soap
2. Work up a good lather for at least _____ seconds
3. Position hands and fingertips _____ while rinsing
4. Dry hands to remove remaining _____

SALON FUNDAMENTALS COSMETOLOGY

CHAPTER 2

smartNOTES

2.3 FIRST AID
pages 60-61

Bleeding and Wounds

Write the correct first-aid procedures in sequential order

Step 1

Step 2

Step 3

Step 4

Never use a tourniquet unless you cannot control the bleeding.

Have emergency personnel check victim for shock if necessary.

Burns

FIRST-AID PROCEDURES

CHEMICAL	HEAT OR ELECTRICAL
1.	1.
2.	2.
3.	3.

32 UNIT 1 THEORY ESSENTIALS

SALON ECOLOGY

smartNOTES

2.3 FIRST AID   pages 61-62

Choking

Step 4 Perform upward thrust by grasping _____ with other hand and pulling it quickly toward you; repeat if necessary

Step 3 Make a thumbless fist with one hand and place that fist just above _____ and well below the ribs with thumb and forefinger side toward the victim

Step 2 Stand behind _____; wrap arms around his or her stomach

Step 1 Determine if victim can _____ or cough. If no, have someone call 911 while you do abdominal thrusts

Fainting

Step 1 Lay victim down on _____ ; allow plenty of fresh air

Step 2 Reassure victim and _____ cold compress to face

Step 3 If victim vomits, roll onto _____ , keep windpipe clear

Call 911 if victim does not regain consciousness

Eye Injury

FIRST-AID PROCEDURES

CHEMICAL

- Hold _____ apart - flush eyeball with lukewarm water for 15-30 minutes; don't let runoff flow into the other eye
- Place gauze pad or cloth over both _____ and secure with bandage
- Get to an eye specialist or emergency room immediately

CUT, SCRATCH OR EMBEDDED OBJECT

- Place gauze pad or cloth over both eyes and secure with a bandage
- Do not try to remove an embedded _____
- Get to an eye specialist or emergency room immediately

1 2 3 4 5 6 7

SALON FUNDAMENTALS COSMETOLOGY   33

CHAPTER 2

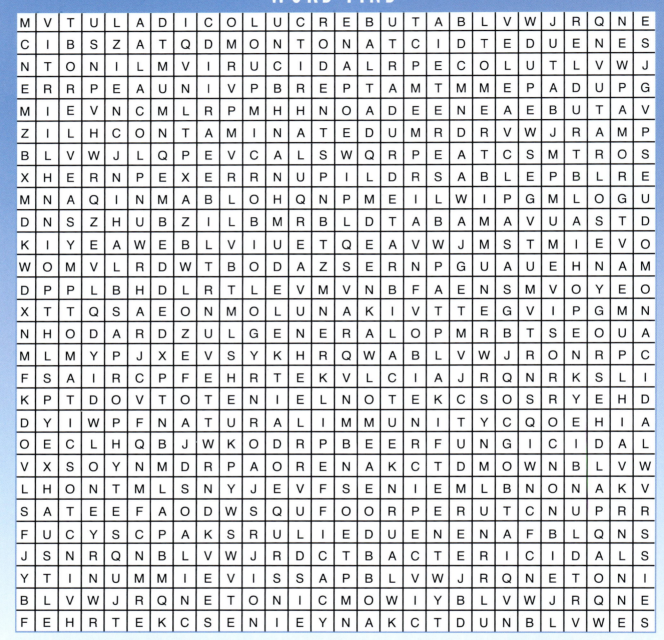

In the word find, circle the words listed below. Words are listed forward, backward and diagonally. Listings that have punctuation or two words are found without punctuation or spacing in the puzzle. How many of these words can you define?

CONTAMINATED	MICROBIOLOGY	SAPROPHYTES	PARASITES
BACTERICIDAL	IMMUNE	ASYMPTOMATIC	PSEUDOMONACIDAL
LOCAL	TUBERCULOCIDAL	GENERAL	NATURAL IMMUNITY
VIRUCIDAL	POLLUTANT	EXHAUST	RODENTS
PASSIVE IMMUNITY	MSDS	FUNGICIDAL	NON-CORROSIVE
EFFICACY	HAZARDOUS	PUNCTURE PROOF	CALIBRATED
TOURNIQUET	COMPRESS	EMBEDDED	EPA

TALKING POINTS

Your next challenge is to be ready to talk about some of the important ideas in this chapter. Follow the directions listed next to each box. Then practice talking about your ideas with others.

Describe in your own way the most common means of spreading infection.

Make and explain a creative sign depicting how to prevent the spread of infection.

Design and share a poster displaying safety precautions for the salon.

CHAPTER 2

THE CHALLENGE

Now it's time to see how well you know your new material. First answer these questions. Then use the Memory Box that follows to check yourself. Look up each answer on the corresponding page in the *Salon Fundamentals* textbook. Check "got it" for all correct answers and "not yet" for all incorrect responses. Using the "Know Chart," record all of your correct responses in the "I Know" column. After correcting incorrect answers, record all of your corrected responses in the "I Need to Study" column. That way you know exactly what to review before continuing in this study guide.

1. Keeping the special environment of the salon in balance to guarantee everyone's well-being involves _____ _____.

2. The study of small organisms is called _____.

3. The type of bacteria that causes infection and disease and can be found everywhere in our environment is called _____.

4. The common cold, hepatitis and measles are examples of _____ diseases.

5. TRUE   FALSE Bacilli are the most common form of bacterial cells and can produce a variety of diseases including tetanus, bacterial influenza and tuberculosis.

6. The term used to describe efforts to prevent the spread of disease and kill certain or all microbes is called _____.

7. What a product will destroy or be effective against is stated on the _____ _____.

8. TRUE   FALSE The 2001 OSHA Bloodborne Pathogens Standard requires the use of an EPA-registered disinfectant with an efficacy against HIV and HBV or tuberculocidal to be used on implements that have accidentally come into contact with blood or body fluids.

9. Laws that most states have enacted to encourage people to help others in emergency situations by providing legal protection are _____ _____ _____.

10. TRUE   FALSE The first step in treating a chemical burn is to rinse away all traces of chemical while moving away any contaminated clothing from the burn area.

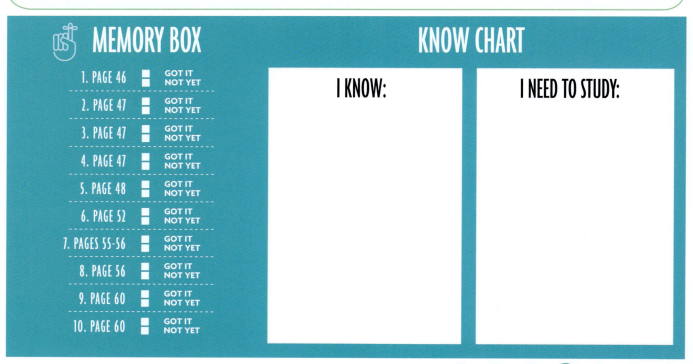

36   UNIT 1 THEORY ESSENTIALS

SALON ECOLOGY

SHOW YOU KNOW...

Relate the information you have reviewed in this chapter to other professional occupations by listing infection control or safety steps that you have observed or are aware of within these professions.

Medical Doctor:

Dentist:

Chef:

Find three efficacy labels from products found in your home. List your findings here and discuss these findings with your friends.

Label 1:

Label 2:

Label 3:

KNOWLEDGE GRID

Start at the top of the Knowledge Grid and work your way down, answering each question to check your understanding of *Chapter 2, Salon Ecology*. The questions found here will help you deepen your understanding, build self-confidence and increase your awareness of different ways of thinking about a subject.

KNOW	DEFINE MITOSIS.	
COMPREHEND	DESCRIBE THE DIFFERENCE BETWEEN ACTIVE AND PASSIVE IMMUNITY.	

1 2 3 4 **5** 6 7

SALON FUNDAMENTALS COSMETOLOGY   37

CHAPTER 2

APPLY	DIFFERENTIATE BETWEEN SANITATION, DISINFECTION AND STERILIZATION STANDARDS.	
ANALYZE	• EXAMINE THE FOLLOWING BRUSH OR COMB DISINFECTION PROCEDURES NOTING THAT THERE ARE ONLY 5 OF THE 6 LISTED AND THEY ARE OUT OF ORDER. ARRANGE THEM IN THE CORRECT SEQUENCE AND FILL IN THE MISSING PROCEDURE. • IMPLEMENTS MUST BE NONPOROUS TO BE DISINFECTED. USING THIS GUIDING PRINCIPLE, CONSTRUCT A LIST OF 3 ITEMS THAT ARE POROUS AND NEED TO BE DISCARDED.	1. Remove the brush or comb with forceps, tongs or gloved hands. 2. Wash the brush or comb thoroughly with soap and water to remove any dirt, grease or oil 3. Remove all hair from the brush or comb 4. Store in a disinfected, dry, covered container or cabinet until needed 5. Rinse the brush or comb thoroughly and pat dry to avoid dilution when immersed in disinfectant Missing step: _____ _____
SYNTHESIZE	DEFEND THE IMPORTANCE OF DOUBLE-BAGGING ALL BLOOD-SOILED ARTICLES.	

BRAIN **BUILDER**

Questions help us think. Write a challenging question about four of the important words or phrases below and be prepared to answer it. (The following stems generate the most thought-provoking questions: Why does? Why are? What if? How would? Try them!) Then try your questions out on your friends. How well can they answer them?

- Bacteriology
- Nonpathogenic Bacteria
- Bloodborne Pathogen Disinfection
- Broad Spectrum Disinfection
- Efficacy Label
- Material Safety Data Sheet

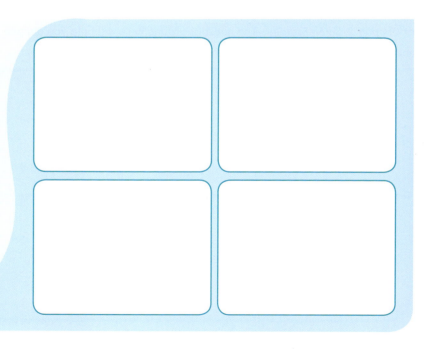

SALON ECOLOGY

PUTTING YOUR HEADS TOGETHER

With a partner or in a small group, quiz each other using the words below. Make notes for future study.

CONTAMINATED	PARASITES	HAZARDOUS	EXHAUST
BACTERICIDAL	RODENTS	COMPRESS	MSDS
LOCAL	EPA	PSEUDOMONACIDAL	FUNGICIDAL
VIRUCIDAL	MICROBIOLOGY	NON-CORROSIVE	PUNCTURE PROOF
PASSIVE IMMUNITY	IMMUNE	SAPROPHYTES	EMBEDDED
EFFICACY	TUBERCULOCIDAL	ASYMPTOMATIC	ACTIVE IMMUNITY
TOURNIQUET	POLLUTANT	GENERAL	CALIBRATED

BRAIN CONDITIONER
MULTIPLE CHOICE. CIRCLE THE CORRECT ANSWER.

1. Bacteriology is the study of:
   a. bacteria   b. personal hygiene   c. toxins   d. disease

2. Bacteria are:
   a. always infectious   b. multi-celled microorganisms
   c. one-celled microorganisms   d. harmless

3. Bacterial cells that are harmless to humans and can even be beneficial are called:
   a. nonpathogenic bacteria   b. pathogenic bacteria
   c. viruses   d. microbes

4. Which of the following do not produce disease?
   a. saprophytes   b. staphylococci   c. streptococci   d. diplococci

5. A communicable disease refers to a disease that is easily:
   a. vaccinated   b. immunized
   c. not spread from one person to another   d. spread from one person to another

6. The common cold, hepatitis, and measles are examples of:
   a. beneficial diseases   b. harmless diseases   c. communicable diseases   d. nonpathogenic diseases

7. Another term that means the same as germ or bacteria is:
   a. parasite   b. microbe   c. mite   d. lice

SALON FUNDAMENTALS COSMETOLOGY 39

CHAPTER 2

8. Pathogenic bacteria are responsible for all of the following EXCEPT:
    a. causing disease
    b. producing toxins
    c. causing infection
    d. causing refuse to decay

9. The most common form of bacterial cells are:
    a. bacilli
    b. spirilla
    c. cocci
    d. streptococci

10. This type of bacterial cell is a coiled, corkscrew-shaped organism that can cause highly contagious diseases:
    a. spirilla
    b. bacilli
    c. streptococci
    d. staphylococci

11. Pus-forming bacterial cells that form grape-like clusters and are present in abscesses are called:
    a. staphylococci
    b. streptococci
    c. diplococci
    d. spirilla

12. Which of the following sources does NOT allow bacteria or viruses to enter the body?
    a. nose
    b. mouth
    c. healthy skin
    d. broken skin

13. Which of the following phrases describes bacteria?
    a. used to control infections
    b. always external parasites
    c. with three basic shapes
    d. beneficial to your health

14. Which of the following conditions is NOT a disease caused by a virus?
    a. mumps
    b. tuberculosis
    c. common cold
    d. respiratory infection

15. Personal service workers such as nurses, doctors, teachers and cosmetologists may be inoculated against which highly infectious disease?
    a. Hepatitis B
    b. strep throat
    c. ringworm
    d. the common cold

16. Human Immunodeficiency Virus (HIV) can be transferred by all of the following sources EXCEPT:
    a. blood
    b. semen
    c. body fluids
    d. holding hands

17. Organisms that live on or obtain nutrients from another organism are known as:
    a. external parasites
    b. internal parasites
    c. viruses
    d. bacteria

18. All of the following are examples of contagions EXCEPT:
    a. fungi
    b. bacteria
    c. flagella
    d. mites

19. Which of the following conditions would be considered a local infection?
    a. septicemia
    b. rheumatic fever
    c. pus-filled boil
    d. AIDS

20. Universal precautions require you to perform infection control procedures with which clients?
    a. all
    b. sick
    c. children
    d. elderly

21. A person who carries a disease-producing bacteria with no recognizable symptoms of the disease is a(n):
    a. asymptomatic carrier
    b. nonpathogenic carrier
    c. pathogenic carrier
    d. parasitic carrier

22. What is provided when a person is given antibodies to a disease rather than producing them through his or her own immune system?
    a. natural immunity
    b. active immunity
    c. passive immunity
    d. parasitic immunity

23. All of the following results are true about active immunity, EXCEPT:
    a. the result of the production of antibodies
    b. lasts only for a few weeks or months
    c. long-lasting and sometimes lifelong
    d. disease organism triggers the immune system

24. Where can the information about what the product is "effective in fighting against" be found?
    a. efficacy label
    b. name
    c. directions
    d. OSHA comments

25. All of the following categories describe infection control EXCEPT:
    a. immunity   b. disinfection   c. sterilization   d. sanitation

26. What products are used to reduce the growth of microbes on the skin?
    a. antiseptics   b. disinfectants   c. fungicidals   d. bactericidals

27. What term describes when all microbes are killed or destroyed?
    a. sterilization   b. sanitation   c. disinfection   d. ventilation

28. The term used to describe efforts to prevent the spread of disease and kill certain or all microbes is known as:
    a. first aid   b. ventilation   c. contamination   d. infection control

29. Sanitation is a term that means:
    a. to remove dirt to aid in reducing the growth of microbes
    b. to destroy or kill a broad spectrum of microbes
    c. to kill fungus
    d. the study of microorganisms

30. What type of soap should cosmetologists avoid using because it can harbor and transmit microbes?
    a. liquid soap from a pump dispenser
    b. bar soap
    c. antiseptic
    d. disinfectant

31. Key information on a specific product regarding ingredients, associated hazards, combustion levels and storage requirements can be found on:
    a. MSDS   b. product cap   c. efficacy label   d. registration

32. The regulating agency under the Department of Labor that enforces safety and health standards in the workplace is:
    a. MSDS   b. DNR   c. USDA   d. OSHA

33. What agency approves the efficacy of products used for infection control?
    a. EPA   b. DNR   c. OSHA   d. MSDS

34. Disinfectants that kill bacteria, viruses, fungi and pseudomonas are:
    a. bacterial disinfectants
    b. viral disinfectants
    c. broad spectrum disinfectants
    d. narrow spectrum disinfectants

35. All implements must be thoroughly cleaned before:
    a. purchasing   b. disposal   c. lending   d. immersion

36. Implements that come into contact with the client must be:
    a. sanitized at the beginning of each day
    b. sanitized at the end of each day
    c. disinfected on a weekly basis
    d. disinfected or discarded

37. It is important to follow all of these steps when disinfecting a brush or comb EXCEPT:
    a. remove hair from the implement
    b. wash the implement with soap and water
    c. completely immerse the implement in the disinfectant
    d. partially immerse the implement in the disinfectant

38. Disinfection can only be practiced on:
    a. porous surfaces   b. nonporous surfaces   c. plastic   d. uneven surfaces

39. All of the following terms describe the type of container disinfected implements are stored in EXCEPT:
    a. open   b. clean   c. covered   d. disinfected

40. All of the following descriptions are precautions to take when using chemical disinfectants EXCEPT:
    a. wear safety glasses
    b. tightly cover and label all containers
    c. purchase chemicals in small quantities
    d. store implements in a warm, moist area.

CHAPTER 2

41. Which of the following statements is NOT a step associated with a blood spill procedure?
    a. wash hands
    b. apply lotion
    c. cover hands with protective gloves
    d. double-bag blood-soiled articles

42. Disinfecting solutions should be stored in a cool, dry area, because:
    a. air, light and heat can weaken their effectiveness
    b. they can be easily found there
    c. it is required by the IRS
    d. they can melt

43. What is recommended for a person who has an electrical or a heat burn but the skin is not broken?
    a. apply an ointment or cream to the burned area
    b. immerse the burned area in cool water
    c. break any blisters that may form
    d. pour hot water on the burned area

44. Which of the following steps is recommended for flushing the eyes if chemicals should get into them?
    a. 15 to 30 minutes with cold water
    b. 15 to 30 minutes with lukewarm water
    c. 15 to 30 minutes with hot water
    d. 15 to 30 minutes with a mild antiseptic

45. In the event of an embedded object in the eye, a person should:
    a. remove the embedded object with the corner of a damp cloth
    b. place a gauze pad over the eye only if object has been successfully removed
    c. get to an eye specialist or emergency room immediately
    d. wait for a few days before seeking medical attention

FINAL REVIEW

Check your answers as you did before. Place a check mark next to the page number for any incorrect answer. On the lines on the next page, jot down topics that you still need to review.

☐ 1. page 47	☐ 13. page 48	☐ 25. page 52	☐ 37. page 57
☐ 2. page 47	☐ 14. page 49	☐ 26. page 52	☐ 38. page 57
☐ 3. page 47	☐ 15. page 49	☐ 27. page 52	☐ 39. page 57
☐ 4. page 47	☐ 16. page 50	☐ 28. page 52	☐ 40. page 58
☐ 5. page 47	☐ 17. page 50	☐ 29. page 53	☐ 41. page 58
☐ 6. page 47	☐ 18. page 50	☐ 30. page 53	☐ 42. page 58
☐ 7. page 47	☐ 19. page 51	☐ 31. page 55	☐ 43. page 61
☐ 8. page 47	☐ 20. page 51	☐ 32. page 55	☐ 44. page 62
☐ 9. page 48	☐ 21. page 51	☐ 33. page 55	☐ 45. page 62
☐ 10. page 48	☐ 22. page 51	☐ 34. page 55	
☐ 11. page 48	☐ 23. page 51	☐ 35. page 56	
☐ 12. page 48	☐ 24. page 52	☐ 36. page 57	

SALON ECOLOGY

Experts tell us that it is important to summarize your feelings and reactions about what you are learning. Note especially things that surprised you, things you found difficult to learn, suggestions and ideas you received from friends that helped make learning this chapter easier and more enjoyable.

My reflections about Salon Ecology:

LESSONS LEARNED

- *A basic knowledge of microbiology provides the foundation for preventing the spread of disease through proper disinfection in the salon.*

- *Infection control involves the steps you take to prevent the spread of disease and kill certain or all microbes.*

- *First-aid safety precautions allow a salon professional to help people in emergency situations.*

CHAPTER 2

smartNOTES

CHAPTER 3
ANATOMY AND PHYSIOLOGY

VALUE
Because cosmetologists touch and care for the human body, you have the responsibility as a professional to know and understand how the body functions.

MAIN IDEA
Proper hair, nail and skin care depends on your knowledge of the body's anatomy.

PLAN

3.1 **BUILDING BLOCKS OF THE HUMAN BODY**
    Cells
    Tissues
    Organs
    Body Systems

3.2 **BASIC BODY SYSTEMS**
    The Skeletal System
    The Muscular System
    The Circulatory System
    The Nervous System
    The Digestive System
    The Excretory System
    The Respiratory System
    The Endocrine System
    The Reproductive System
    The Integumentary System

CHAPTER 3

smartNOTES

3.1 BUILDING BLOCKS OF THE HUMAN BODY pages 65-66

Anatomy

DIFFERENCES

GROSS

MICROSCOPIC

Physiology

Cells

Protoplasm

ANATOMY AND PHYSIOLOGY

smartNOTES

3.1 BUILDING BLOCKS OF THE HUMAN BODY   page 66

Nucleus

Cytoplasm

Cell Membrane

Label the Cell

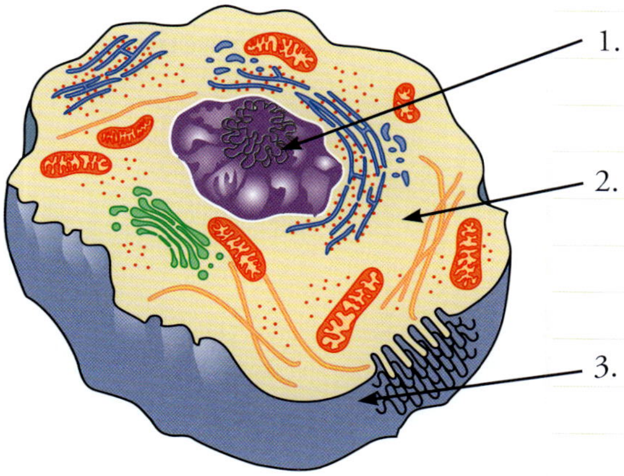

1.

2.

3.

Metabolism

ANABOLISM	CATABOLISM

1 2 3 4 5 6 7

SALON FUNDAMENTALS COSMETOLOGY   47

CHAPTER 3

smartNOTES

3.1 BUILDING BLOCKS OF THE HUMAN BODY — page 67

Tissues

Five Types by Function

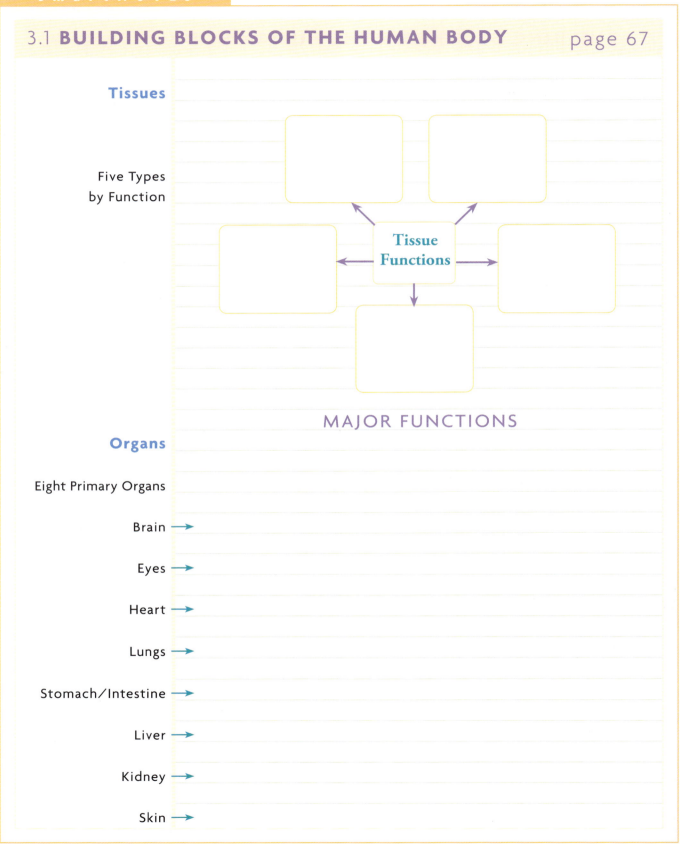

MAJOR FUNCTIONS

Organs

Eight Primary Organs

Brain →

Eyes →

Heart →

Lungs →

Stomach/Intestine →

Liver →

Kidney →

Skin →

ANATOMY AND PHYSIOLOGY

smartNOTES

3.1 BUILDING BLOCKS OF THE HUMAN BODY — page 68

Body Systems

VITAL FUNCTIONS

Skeletal →

Muscular →

Circulatory →

Nervous →

Digestive →

Excretory →

Respiratory →

Endocrine →

Reproductive →

Integumentary →

Mini-Review

- SYSTEMS:
- ORGANS:
- TISSUES:
- CELLS:

CHAPTER 3

smartNOTES

3.2 BASIC BODY SYSTEMS   page 69

The Skeletal System

206

Osteology

Types of Bones   Long bones are found in _____

Flat bones are found in _____

Irregular bones are found in _____

Bone

Composition

Four Major Functions of   1.
the Skeletal System
2.

3.

4.

smartNOTES

3.2 BASIC BODY SYSTEMS   pages 69-70

The Skull

Major Parts of the Cranium

DESCRIBE IN YOUR OWN WORDS

Frontal

Parietal

Occipital

Temporal

Sphenoid

Ethmoid

Label the Cranium

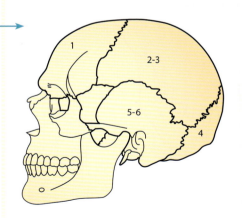

1.

2-3.

4.

5-6.

CHAPTER 3

smartNOTES

3.2 BASIC BODY SYSTEMS   page 70

Facial Skeleton

Parts of the Facial Skeleton

Mandible

Maxillae

Nasal

Zygomatic (Malar)

Lacrimal

DESCRIBE IN YOUR OWN WORDS

Label the Facial Skeleton

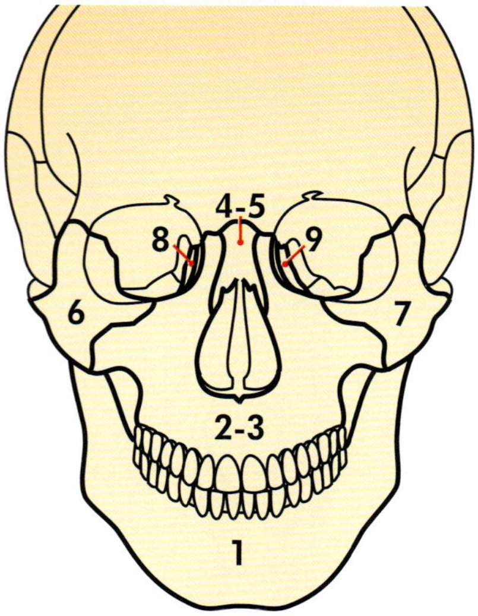

1.

2-3.

4-5.

6-7.

8-9.

52 UNIT 1 THEORY ESSENTIALS

ANATOMY AND PHYSIOLOGY

smartNOTES

3.2 BASIC BODY SYSTEMS   pages 70-71

Neck Bones

Cervical Vertebrae

Hyoid

Label the Neck Bones

1-7.

8.

Back, Chest and Shoulder Bones

Thorax

Clavicle

Scapula

Label the Back, Chest and Shoulder Bones

1.

2.

3-14.

15.

16.

SALON FUNDAMENTALS COSMETOLOGY 53

CHAPTER 3

smartNOTES

3.2 BASIC BODY SYSTEMS   page 71

Arm, Wrist and Hand Bones

    Humerus
    Radius
    Ulna
    Carpals
    Metacarpals
    Phalanges

Label the Arm, Wrist and Hand Bones →

1.
2.
3.
4.
5.
6.

Leg, Ankle and Foot Bones

Femur   1. Thigh bone or _____ bone in the body

Patella   2. Kneecap, sits over the _____ of the knee joint

Tibia   3. Inner and _____ of the two lower leg bones

Fibula   4. Extends from the _____ to the ankle

Talus   5. Talus, tibia and fibula _____ the ankle joint

Tarsal   6. Seven bones that makeup the _____ foot and _____ foot

Metatarsals   7. Five bones that connect the _____ to the tarsals

Phalanges   8. Fourteen bones that form the _____

54   UNIT 1 THEORY ESSENTIALS

ANATOMY AND PHYSIOLOGY

WORD SORT GAME
DEM BONES

THIS GAME WILL HELP YOU REMEMBER DIFFICULT WORDS.

Directions:
1. Select a team
2. Review the words in the Jump Start Box
3. Place each word in the correct Mystery Box
4. Check your answers in the *Salon Fundamentals* coursebook

CRANIUM

NECK BONES

FACIAL SKELETON

ARM, WRIST & HAND BONES

LEG, ANKLE & FOOT BONES

BACK, CHEST & SHOULDER BONES

JUMP START BOX

FRONTAL	PATELLA	OCCIPITAL	TALUS
HYOID	METACARPALS	TIBIA	NASAL
CLAVICLE	PHALANGES	LACRIMAL	SCAPULA
THORAX	CERVICAL VERTEBRAE	ULNA	HUMERUS
FEMUR	PHALANGES	MANDIBLE	RADIUS
ZYGOMATIC	CARPALS	FIBULA	PARIETAL
METATARSALS	TEMPORAL	MAXILLAE	TARSAL

1 2 3 4 **5** 6 7

SALON FUNDAMENTALS COSMETOLOGY

CHAPTER 3

smartNOTES

3.2 BASIC BODY SYSTEMS   page 72

Muscular System

Myology

500

Four Major Functions of the Muscular System
1.
2.
3.
4.

Two Types of Muscle Tissue

STRIATED

NON-STRIATED

ANATOMY AND PHYSIOLOGY

smartNOTES

3.2 BASIC BODY SYSTEMS pages 72-73

Special Terminology

Anterior →

Posterior →

Superioris →

Inferioris →

Levator →

Depressor →

Dilator →

Cosmetologist's Primary Concern

Cardiac Muscle

Three Parts of the Muscle
1. Origin:

2. Belly:

3. Insertion:

How the Muscle Produces Movement

SALON FUNDAMENTALS COSMETOLOGY   57

CHAPTER 3

smartNOTES

3.2 BASIC BODY SYSTEMS   page 73

Seven Ways to Stimulate Muscles

Muscular Stimulation

Scalp and Face Muscles

Epicranium

Epicranius

Frontalis Muscle

Occipitalis Muscle

Label the Scalp Muscles

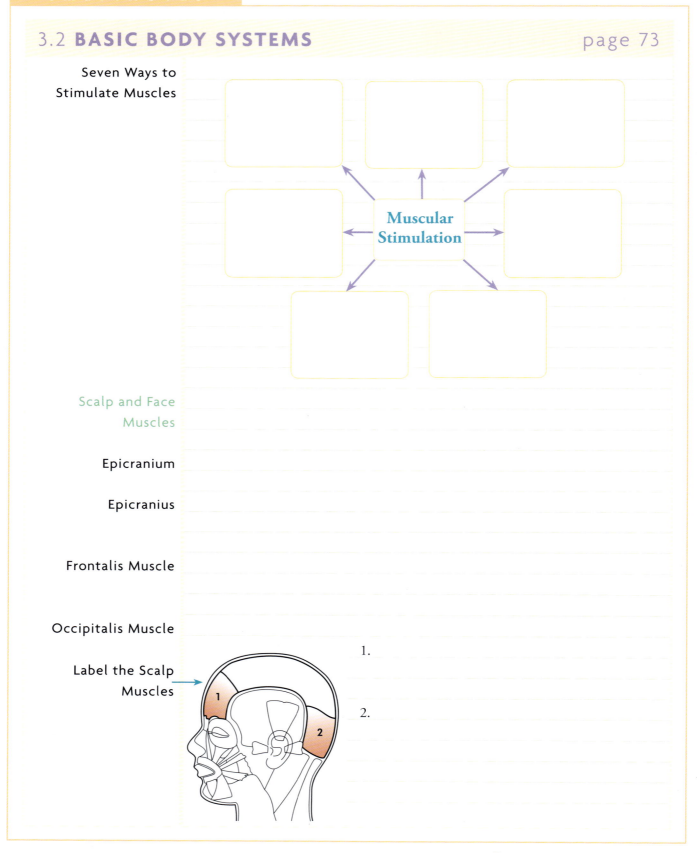

1.

2.

58 UNIT 1 THEORY ESSENTIALS

smartNOTES

3.2 BASIC BODY SYSTEMS   page 74

Ear Muscles

Auricularis Anterior

Auricularis Superior

Auricularis Posterior

Label the Ear Muscles

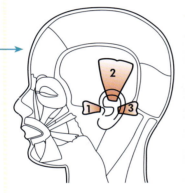

1.

2.

3.

Eye and Nose Muscles

Corrugator

Levator Palpebrae Superioris

Orbicularis Oculi

Procerus

CHAPTER 3

smartNOTES

3.2 BASIC BODY SYSTEMS   pages 74-75

Label the Eye and Nose Muscles

1.
2.
3.
4.

Mouth Muscles

Orbicularis Oris

Quadratus Labii Superioris
(Levatator Labii Superioris)

Quadratus Labii Inferioris
(Depressor Labii Inferioris)

Mentalis

Risorius

Caninus
(Levator Anguli Oris)

Triangularis
(Depressor Anguli)

Zygomaticus

Buccinator

Label the Mouth Muscles

1.
2.
3.
4.   7.
5.   8.
6.   9.

smartNOTES

3.2 BASIC BODY SYSTEMS   page 75

Mastication Muscles

Temporalis

Masseter

Label the Mastication Muscles

1.
2.

Neck and Back Muscles

Platysma

Sternocleido Mastoideus

Trapezius

Latissimus Dorsi

Label the Neck and Back Muscles

3.
4.
5.
6.

CHAPTER 3

smartNOTES

3.2 BASIC BODY SYSTEMS   page 76

Shoulder, Chest and Arm Muscles

Pectoralis

Serratus Anterior

Deltoid

Bicep

Tricep

Supinator

Pronator

Flexor

Extensor

Label the Shoulder, Chest and Arm Muscles

Anterior View   Posterior View

1a.   6.
1b.   7.
2.   8.
3.   9.
4.
5.

ANATOMY AND PHYSIOLOGY

smartNOTES

3.2 BASIC BODY SYSTEMS   page 76-77

Hand Muscles

Abductor

Adductor

Opponens

Label the Hand Muscles

Palm Down   Palm Up

1.

2.

3.

Leg and Foot Muscles

Tibialis Anterior — 1. Bends the foot upward and _____

Gastrocnemius — 2. Pulls the foot _____

Peroneus Longus — 3. Causes the foot to invert and turn _____

Peroneus Brevis — 4. Bends the foot down and _____

Soleus — 5. Bends the foot _____

Extensor Digitorum Longus — 6. Bends foot up and _____ the toes

Extensor Hallucis Longus — 7. Extends the _____ toe and flexes the foot

Flexor Digiti Minimi Brevis — 8. Flexes the joint of the _____ toe

Flexor Digitorum Brevis — 9. Flexes toe digits _____ through _____

Abductor Hallucis — 10. Moves the _____ toe away from the other toes

Abductor Digiti Minimi — 11. Moves the _____ toe away from the other toes

1 2 3 4 5 6 7

SALON FUNDAMENTALS COSMETOLOGY   63

CHAPTER 3

MATCHING

Match the term with the best description by placing the number of the description in the space to the left of the term.

DESCRIPTION

1. Close Eyelids
2. Opens and Closes Jaw
3. Separates Fingers
4. Bends the foot upward and inward
5. Raise Nostrils (distaste)
6. Draws Fingers Together
7. Raise Eyebrows
8. Draws Mouth Up (grin)
9. Causes the foot to invert and turn outward
10. Thumb Movement
11. Wrinkles Chin (doubt)
12. Chewing
13. Controls Swinging of Arms
14. Bends the foot down
15. Assists in Breathing
16. Raise Eyelids
17. Kissing
18. Flexes toe digits 2 through 4
19. Draws Corners of Mouth Up (laugh)
20. Wrinkles Nose
21. Pulls Lip Down (sarcasm)
22. Moves the big toe away from the other toes
23. Controls Eyebrows

TERM

_____ Frontalis
_____ Corrugator
_____ Levator Palpebrae Superioris
_____ Soleus
_____ Orbicularis Oculi
_____ Procerus
_____ Orbicularis Oris
_____ Quadratus Labii Superioris
_____ Quadratus Labii Inferioris
_____ Flexor Digitorum Brevis
_____ Mentalis
_____ Risorius
_____ Zygomaticus
_____ Temporalis
_____ Peroneus Longus
_____ Masseter
_____ Latissimus Dorsi
_____ Serratus Anterior
_____ Abductor
_____ Abductor Hallucis
_____ Adductor
_____ Opponens
_____ Tibialis Anterior

WORD SORT GAME
DEM MUSCLES

THIS GAME WILL HELP YOU REMEMBER DIFFICULT WORDS.

Directions:
1. Select a team
2. Review the words in the Jump Start Box
3. Place each word in the correct Mystery Box
4. Check your answers in the *Salon Fundamentals Textbook*

| EAR | SCALP & FACE | HAND | MASTICATION |

| NECK & BACK | SHOULDER, CHEST & ARM | EYE & NOSE |

| MOUTH | LEG AND FOOT MUSCLES |

JUMP START BOX

ABDUCTOR	FLEXOR	PERONEUS LONGUS
ABDUCTOR DIGITI MINIMI	FLEXOR DIGITI MINIMI BREVIS	PLATYSMA
ABDUCTOR HALLUCIS	FLEXOR DIGITORUM BREVIS	PROCERUS
ADDUCTOR	FRONTALIS	QUADRATUS LABII INFERIORIS
AURICULARIS ANTERIOR	GASTROCNEMIUS	QUADRATUS LABII SUPERIORIS
AURICULARIS POSTERIOR	LATISSIMUS DORSI	SERRATUS ANTERIOR
AURICULARIS SUPERIOR	LEVATOR PALPEBRAE SUPERIORIS	SOLEUS
BICEP	MASSETER	STERNOCLEIDO MASTOIDEUS
BUCCINATOR	MENTALIS RISORIUS	SUPINATOR
CANINUS	OCCIPITALIS	TEMPORALIS
CORRUGATOR	OPPONENS	TIBIALIS ANTERIOR
DELTOID	ORBICULARIS OCULI	TRAPEZIUS
EXTENSOR	ORBICULARIS ORIS	TRIANGULARIS
EXTENSOR DIGITORUM LONGUS	PECTORALIS	TRICEP
EXTENSOR HALLUCIS LONGUS	PERONEUS BREVIS	ZYGOMATICUS

CHAPTER 3

smartNOTES

3.2 BASIC BODY SYSTEMS   page 77

The Circulatory System

MAJOR FUNCTIONS

Cardiovascular System

Lymph-Vascular System

Lymph

Glands

Nodes

> **Note:**
> Lymph, which also transports disease-fighting white blood cells (lymphocytes), circulates only as a result of muscle movement; there is no heart-like pump.

smartNOTES

3.2 BASIC BODY SYSTEMS page 77-78

The Circulatory System (continued)

The Heart

Pericardium

Four Compartments

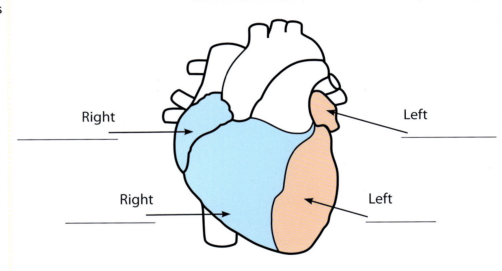

Right

Left

Right

Left

Heart Rate

CHAPTER 3

smartNOTES

3.2 BASIC BODY SYSTEMS
pages 77-78

Label the Heart

1.

2.

3.

4.

5.

The Blood

8 to 10 Pints

Erythrocytes (RBC)

Leukocytes (WBC)

Thrombocytes (Clot)

Interesting fact: One square inch (6.5 sq. cm) of skin contains up to 15 feet (4.5 m) of blood vessels.

smartNOTES

3.2 BASIC BODY SYSTEMS   pages 78-79

Blood Vessels

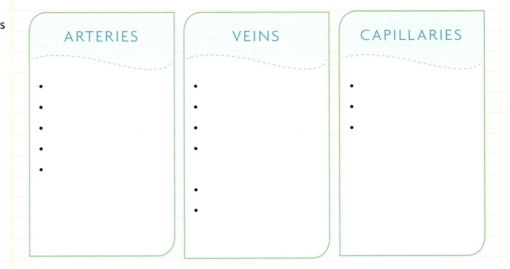

ARTERIES
-
-
-
-
-

VEINS
-
-
-
-
-
-

CAPILLARIES
-
-
-

1. Systemic Circulation

TO THE HEART

Blood enters the right _____ of the heart through the _____ _____ _____ . Then it is pumped through the _____ _____ into the _____ _____ .

2. Pulmonary Circulation

TO THE LUNGS

From the _____ _____ , blood is pumped into the _____ _____ , then through the _____ _____ to the lungs.

3. Systemic Circulation

BACK TO THE HEART

Blood returns to the heart from the lungs via the _____ _____ and enters the left _____ . From the left atrium it goes to the _____ _____ by way of the _____ valve. From the left ventricle it goes to the _____ .

TO THE BODY

Blood then flows throughout the body and returns to the heart via the _____ _____ _____ .

CHAPTER 3

smartNOTES

3.2 BASIC BODY SYSTEMS   page 80

Arteries of the Face, Head and Neck

Common Carotid (CCA)

Blood supplied to: The _____ _____ _____ supplies blood to the brain, eyes and forehead. _____ _____ branches into smaller arteries, supplying blood to the skin and muscles of the head.

Returns blood from: All blood from the head, face and neck returns through two veins, the _____ _____ _____ and the _____ _____ _____.

External Carotid Artery

Occipital

Posterior Auricular

Superficial Temporal

External Maxillary

ANATOMY AND PHYSIOLOGY

smartNOTES

3.2 BASIC BODY SYSTEMS   page 80

Label the Veins and Arteries of the Face, Head and Neck →

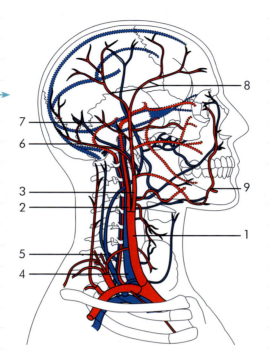

1.
2.
3.
4.
5.
6.
7.
8.
9.

ARTERIES OF THE HAND AND ARM →

Ulnar — 1. Supplies blood to the _____ finger side of forearm

Radial — 2. Supplies blood to the _____ side of the arm

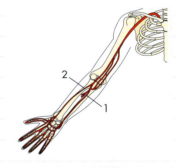

ARTERIES OF THE LOWER LEG AND FOOT →

Popliteal — 1. Supplies blood to _____ joint and muscles in thigh and calf

Anterior tibial — 2. Supplies blood just _____ the knee

Posterior tibial — 3. Supplies blood _____ the calf muscle

Dorsalis pedis — 4. Carries blood to the upper surface of the _____

Saphenous vein — 5. Transports blood _____ veins in the foot

Femoral vein — 6. Transports blood to the heart and lungs for _____

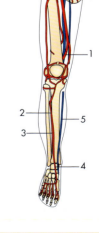

SALON FUNDAMENTALS COSMETOLOGY   71

CHAPTER 3

smartNOTES

3.2 BASIC BODY SYSTEMS   pages 81-82

The Nervous System

Central Nervous System

Brain

Four Parts of the Brain

CEREBRUM	CEREBELLUM	PONS	MEDULLA OBLONGATA
• •	• •	• •	•

> Spinal cord originates in base of brain and extends to the base of the spine; holds 31 pairs of cranial nerves

Peripheral Nervous System

Nerve Cells

Types of Nerves

MOTOR	SENSORY	MIXED
• •	• • •	•

> **Interesting fact:**
> At birth the brain weighs about one pound. By one year it has doubled in size and reaches 90% of adult size (approximately 3-4 pounds) by age 4.
>
> Millions of dendrites (nerve impulses) travel across the brain. Research tells us that reading is the best form of aerobics for the brain, causing the dendrites to travel back and forth, from left brain to right brain to transfer the image of the printed word to a comprehensive thought or idea.

ANATOMY AND PHYSIOLOGY

smartNOTES

3.2 BASIC BODY SYSTEMS   pages 83-84

Face, Head and Neck Nerves

Trifacial and Facial Nerves

Label the Nerves of the Face, Head and Neck

Trifacial is also called trigeminal or the 5th cranial nerve. Facial is also called the 7th cranial nerve. Numbers 14-17 represent the 11th cranial nerve or sometimes referred to as the accessory nerve. The textbook refers to this group as other cervical nerves.

1.
2.
2a.
3.
4.
5.
6.
7.
8.
9.
10.
11.
12.
13.
14.
15.
16.
17.

SALON FUNDAMENTALS COSMETOLOGY   73

CHAPTER 3

smartNOTES

3.2 BASIC BODY SYSTEMS   page 85

Label the Nerves of the Arm and Hand

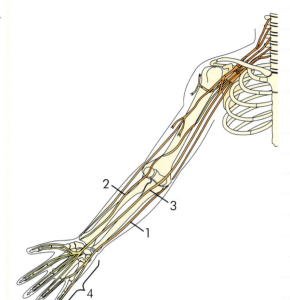

1.

2.

3.

4.

Label The Nerves of the Lower Leg and Foot

1.   5.

2.   6.

3.   7.

4.   8.

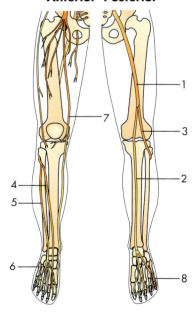

Anterior   Posterior

The Autonomic Nervous System

74   UNIT 1 THEORY ESSENTIALS

smartNOTES

3.2 BASIC BODY SYSTEMS   pages 86-88

The Digestive System

The digestive system breaks down _____ into simpler _____ compounds that can be easily _____ by cells or, if not absorbed, eliminated from the body in _____ products

The Excretory System

The excretory system _____ solid, liquid and gaseous waste products from the body

Skin

Liver

Kidneys

The Respiratory System

Primary Functions

The Endocrine System

The Reproductive System

The Integumentary System

Two Primary Glands

CHAPTER 3

THINKING MAP

Now that you have filled in your SmartNotes for "Anatomy and Physiology," create a Thinking Map to help make sense of how your SmartNotes fit together. Use some or all of the words in the Jump Start Box as well as your own words and pictures to make a visual that will help you connect the important ideas in this chapter to each other. Be creative!

ANATOMY AND PHYSIOLOGY

JUMP START BOX

BODY SYSTEMS	ENDOCRINE	STOMACH/INTESTINE	MUSCULAR
SKELETAL	REPRODUCTIVE	LIVER	CELLS
MUSCULAR	INTEGUMENTARY	KIDNEYS	NUCLEUS
CIRCULATORY	ORGANS	SKIN	CYTOPLASM
NERVOUS	BRAIN	TISSUES	CELL MEMBRANE
DIGESTIVE	EYES	EPITHELIAL	PROTOPLASM
EXCRETORY	HEART	CONNECTIVE	METABOLISM
RESPIRATORY	LUNGS	NERVE	

ANATOMY AND PHYSIOLOGY

MEMORY JOGGER

AN "OLOGY" IS THE STUDY OF SOMETHING.
Define the following ology's.

PHYSIOLOGY

OSTEOLOGY

MYOLOGY

COSMETOLOGY

NEUROLOGY

FORM FOLLOWS FUNCTION

In this chapter several important terms describe major functions of the human body. Can you describe the "action" these terms describe?

FORM	FUNCTION
Cells	
Tissues	
Organs	
Systems	
Cranium	
Thorax	
Muscles	
Heart	
Blood	
Erythrocytes	

SALON FUNDAMENTALS COSMETOLOGY 77

CHAPTER 3

FORM FOLLOWS FUNCTION

FORM	FUNCTION
Leukocytes	
Thrombocytes	
Arteries	
Veins	
Capillaries	
Carotid Arteries	
Lymph System	
Central Nervous System	
Peripheral Nervous System	
Trifacial Nerve	
Autonomic Nervous System	
Digestive System	
Enzymes	
Excretory System	
Skin	
Liver	
Kidneys	
Respiratory System	
Lungs	
Diaphragm	
Endocrine System	

MEMORY JOGGER

BY THE NUMBERS

The chapter on Anatomy and Physiology has several important numbers and measurements. Can you recall...? If not, look them up.

NUMBER/MEASUREMENT	WHY IMPORTANT
_____	The number of primary tissues
_____	The number of primary organs
_____	The number of vital body systems
_____	The number of bones in the body
_____	Average resting heart rate
_____	Time it takes the body to complete digestion
_____	The number of bones in the cranium
_____	The number of facial bones
_____	The number of muscles (large & small) in the body
_____	Approximate weight of the human brain
_____	The number of spinal nerves (pairs) in the spinal cord
_____	The number of lymph nodes
_____	The number of square feet of body surface covered by the skin

CHAPTER 3

MATCHING
ALSO KNOWN AS

In this chapter many terms have a scientific name and a common name. Can you match the following? Place the number of the common name in the space next to the scientific name found on the right.

COMMON NAME

1. Spine
2. Collar Bone
3. Heart
4. Front
5. Larger
6. Back
7. Open
8. Scalp
9. Kissing Muscle
10. White Blood Cells
11. Lymph-Vascular System
12. Red Blood Cells
13. Nerve Cells
14. Blood Platelets
15. Sensory Nerves
16. Trifacial Nerve
17. Motor Nerve
18. Autonomic Nervous System
19. Vascular

SCIENTIFIC NAME

_____ Thoracic Vertebrae
_____ Cardiac Muscle
_____ Anterior
_____ Dilator
_____ Clavicle
_____ Posterior
_____ Superioris
_____ Epicranium
_____ Thrombocytes
_____ Erythrocytes
_____ Oribicularis Oris
_____ Lymphatic System
_____ Leukocytes
_____ Neuron
_____ Afferent Nerves
_____ Sympathetic Nervous System
_____ Efferent Nerves
_____ Trigeminal Nerve
_____ Circulatory

ANATOMY AND PHYSIOLOGY

TALKING POINTS

Your next challenge is to be ready to talk about some of the important ideas in this chapter. Follow the directions listed next to each box. Then practice talking about your ideas with others.

Describe in your own way the relationship between cells, tissues, organs and systems. Use examples.

Draw a chart you can use to tell others about the blood flow through the heart to the body and back.

Select one of the visuals you reviewed in this chapter. Draw it here and label its parts with an explanation of why it is important for a cosmetologist to understand this information.

CHAPTER 3

THE CHALLENGE

Now it's time to see how well you know your new material. First answer these questions. Then use the Memory Box that follows to check yourself. Look up each answer on the corresponding page in the *Salon Fundamentals* textbook. Check "got it" for all correct answers and "not yet" for all incorrect responses. Using the "Know Chart," record all of your correct responses in the "I Know" column. After correcting incorrect answers, record all of your corrected responses in the "I Need to Study" column. That way you know exactly what to review before continuing in this study guide.

1. The basic units of living matter are _____.

2. Groups of cells of the same kind make up _____.

3. Separate body structures that perform specific functions are called _____.

4. Name the five primary types of tissues in the human body. _____
   _____ _____
   _____ _____

5. A group of body structures and/or organs that together perform one or more vital functions is a _____.

6. Four functions of the _____ system include supporting the body by giving it shape and strength, surrounding and protecting internal organs, providing a framework to which muscles can attach and allowing body movement.

7. TRUE   FALSE   Bone is the hardest structure of the body with a composition of ⅔ mineral matter and ⅓ organic matter.

8. Flat bones are plate-shaped. Where are they located? _____

9. The study of the structure, function and diseases of the muscles is known as _____.

10. What are the two types of muscle tissue? _____

11. The three parts of a muscle are its origin, its belly and its _____.

12. The vascular or circulatory system controls the circulation of blood and _____ through the body.

13. The system responsible for the circulation of blood which includes the heart, arteries, veins and capillaries is the _____ system.

14. TRUE   FALSE   Arteries have thinner walls than veins because they carry oxygen-rich blood that is transferred to the cells throughout the body.

15. TRUE   FALSE   The lymph-vascular system is responsible for reaching parts of the body not reached by blood.

16. The study of the nervous system is known as _____.

17. The primary components of the nervous system are _____, _____ and _____.

18. The nervous system can be divided into three subsystems. They are _____, _____ and _____.

19. TRUE   FALSE   The nervous system coordinates and controls the overall operation of the human body.

20. Nerve cells, like any other cells in the body, have a nucleus, cytoplasm and cell membrane. They differ from other cells in the body in that they have threadlike fibers called _____.

21. The system that breaks food down into simpler compounds that can be easily absorbed by cells is the _____ system.

82   UNIT 1 THEORY ESSENTIALS

22. TRUE   FALSE Pepsin is an enzyme responsible for the breakdown of protein into polypeptide molecules and free amino acids, which are of particular importance to the production of hair, nails and skin.

23. The skin, liver and kidneys are all part of the _____ system.

24. TRUE   FALSE The largest organ of the body is the liver.

25. The system responsible for the intake of oxygen to be absorbed by the blood and the exhalation of carbon dioxide is the _____ system.

26. The two main organs of the respiratory system are the _____ and the _____.

27. A carefully balanced mechanism that directly affects hair growth, skin conditions and energy levels is the _____ system.

28. The two primary glands of the integumentary system are _____ and _____.

29. TRUE   FALSE Ductless glands manufacture hormones that are secreted directly into the bloodstream.

MEMORY BOX

1. PAGE 66 — GOT IT / NOT YET
2. PAGE 67 — GOT IT / NOT YET
3. PAGE 67 — GOT IT / NOT YET
4. PAGE 67 — GOT IT / NOT YET
5. PAGE 68 — GOT IT / NOT YET
6. PAGE 69 — GOT IT / NOT YET
7. PAGE 69 — GOT IT / NOT YET
8. PAGE 69 — GOT IT / NOT YET
9. PAGE 72 — GOT IT / NOT YET
10. PAGE 72 — GOT IT / NOT YET
11. PAGE 73 — GOT IT / NOT YET
12. PAGE 77 — GOT IT / NOT YET
13. PAGE 77 — GOT IT / NOT YET
14. PAGE 78 — GOT IT / NOT YET
15. PAGE 77 — GOT IT / NOT YET

KNOW CHART

I KNOW:

I NEED TO STUDY:

CHAPTER 3

MEMORY BOX

16. PAGE 81	☐	GOT IT / NOT YET
17. PAGE 81	☐	GOT IT / NOT YET
18. PAGE 81	☐	GOT IT / NOT YET
19. PAGE 81	☐	GOT IT / NOT YET
20. PAGE 82	☐	GOT IT / NOT YET
21. PAGE 86	☐	GOT IT / NOT YET
22. PAGE 86	☐	GOT IT / NOT YET
23. PAGE 87	☐	GOT IT / NOT YET
24. PAGE 87	☐	GOT IT / NOT YET
25. PAGE 87	☐	GOT IT / NOT YET
26. PAGE 87	☐	GOT IT / NOT YET
27. PAGE 88	☐	GOT IT / NOT YET
28. PAGE 88	☐	GOT IT / NOT YET
29. PAGE 88	☐	GOT IT / NOT YET

KNOW CHART

I KNOW:	I NEED TO STUDY:

SHOW YOU KNOW...

Using 20 of the terms found in this chapter and a minimum of 10 sentences, write a short story that includes your newly understood terms. Be creative and at the same time make sure everyone will understand the area of the body to which you might be referring. An example sentence is shown here to help spark your creativity. When you have completed your story, share it with a partner and see if he or she can interpret it back to you with a full understanding. Sample: As I combed my hair over my temporalis, I realized that the incident of hitting the door jamb of the car had left a large bump on my frontal that extended to my parietal.

ANATOMY AND PHYSIOLOGY

KNOWLEDGE GRID

Start at the top of the Knowledge Grid and work your way down, answering each question to check your understanding of *Chapter 3, Anatomy and Physiology*. The questions found here will help you deepen your understanding, build self-confidence and increase your awareness of different ways of thinking about a subject.

KNOW	LIST THE 3 BASIC PARTS OF A CELL.
COMPREHEND	EXPLAIN THE RELATIONSHIP BETWEEN CELLS, TISSUES, ORGANS AND SYSTEMS.
APPLY	DISTINGUISH 9 OF THE 14 FACIAL SKELETON BONES AFFECTED BY MASSAGE.
ANALYZE	OUTLINE THE FUNCTIONS OF THE MUSCULAR SYSTEM.
SYNTHESIZE	COMPARE THE RESPONSIBILITY OF THE LYMPH-VASCULAR SYSTEM TO THE CARDIOVASCULAR SYSTEM.
EVALUATE	IMAGINE YOU HAVE TIGHT OR FATIGUED MUSCLES. WHAT EFFECT COULD MASSAGE MANIPULATIONS HAVE ON THOSE MUSCLES AND WHY?

1 2 3 4 **5** 6 7

CHAPTER 3

BRAIN BUILDER

Questions help us think. Write a challenging question about four of the important words or phrases below and be prepared to answer it. (The following stems generate the most throught-provoking questions: Why does? Why are? What if? How would? Try them!) Then try your questions out on your friends. How well can they answer them?

- Gross Anatomy
- Physiology
- Cytoplasm
- Organ
- Myology
- Trifacial Nerve
- Sudoriferous

BRAIN CONDITIONER
MULTIPLE CHOICE. CIRCLE THE CORRECT ANSWER.

1. **What is physiology?**
   a. the study of the functions of organs and systems of the body
   b. the study of organs and systems of the body
   c. the study of structures that can be seen with the naked eye
   d. the study of structures too small to be seen

2. **What is another name for histology?**
   a. gross anatomy   b. microscopic anatomy   c. osteology   d. physiology

3. **Anatomy is the study of:**
   a. small organisms
   b. the chemical properties of the hair
   c. the organs and systems of the body
   d. human relations

4. **Which of the following terms is NOT a building block of the human body?**
   a. cells   b. tissues   c. organs   d. muscles

5. **Which of the following is NOT one of the three basic parts of the cell?**
   a. nucleus   b. cytoplasm   c. nerve   d. cell membrane

6. **Cells are composed of a gel-like substance called:**
   a. an atom   b. a molecule   c. protoplasm   d. cytoplasm

7. **Which of the following descriptions is NOT an example of metabolism?**
   a. building up of larger molecules from smaller ones
   b. controlling the basic functions and activities of the cell
   c. releasing energy to perform specific body functions
   d. breaking down of larger molecules or substances into small ones

8. Most of the activities or production of the cell take place in the:
   a. nucleus   b. cytoplasm   c. stomach   d. cell membrane
9. The basic units of living matter are:
   a. nerves   b. muscles   c. cells   d. organs
10. The control center of cell activities, including reproduction, is called the:
    a. cytoplasm   b. cell membrane   c. protoplasm   d. nucleus
11. What is the process of breaking down larger molecules into smaller ones called?
    a. anabolism   b. catabolism   c. cell division   d. erosion
12. The process of building up larger molecules from smaller ones is called:
    a. anabolism   b. catabolism   c. cell division   d. mutation
13. The chemical process in which cells receive nutrients for all growth and reproduction is called:
    a. metabolism   b. cell growth   c. cell division   d. protoplasm
14. All of the following statements are true about the nucleus EXCEPT:
    a. located in the cytoplasm   b. coordinates body functions
    c. surrounded by cell membrane   d. is the control center of cell activities
15. A separate body structure composed of two or more different tissues is a(n):
    a. system   b. tissue   c. organ   d. muscle
16. Which type of tissue supports, protects and holds the body together?
    a. epithelial   b. connective   c. nerve   d. muscular
17. Groups of cells of the same kind make up:
    a. organs   b. tissues   c. systems   d. muscles
18. Which tissue contracts when stimulated to produce motion?
    a. epithelial   b. connective   c. nerve   d. muscular
19. What is the role of epithelial tissue?
    a. contracts to produce motion   b. carries messages to and from the brain
    c. supports, protects and holds the body together   d. covers and protects body surfaces and internal organs
20. All of the following are organs of primary importance EXCEPT the:
    a. eyes   b. skeleton   c. heart   d. brain
21. All of the following examples are bones of the cranium EXCEPT:
    a. frontal   b. occipital   c. temporal   d. metacarpal
22. Which of the following items is NOT a function of the skeletal system?
    a. allowing body movement   b. sending and receiving body messages
    c. providing a frame to which muscles can attach   d. surrounding and protecting internal organs
23. An example of a long bone would be the:
    a. humerus   b. wrist bones   c. cervical vertebrae   d. mandible
24. The skeleton of the head that encloses and protects the brain and primary sensory organs is the:
    a. skull   b. mandible   c. thorax   d. vertebrae
25. Which bone forms the back of the skull?
    a. occipital   b. parietal   c. temporal   d. sphenoid
26. Which of the body's systems has the function to give the body shape and strength?
    a. skeletal   b. circulatory   c. nervous   d. endocrine

CHAPTER 3

27. How many bones of the cranium are affected by a scalp massage?
    a. 4	b. 6	c. 8	d. 14

28. What are the two bones that form the crown and upper sides of the head?
    a. frontal	b. parietal	c. temporal	d. ethmoid

29. Osteology is the study of:
    a. muscles	b. nerves	c. bones	d. organs

30. The bone that is located behind the eyes and nose and connects all the bones to the cranium is the:
    a. temporal	b. ethmoid	c. occipital	d. sphenoid

31. The spongy bone between the eyes which forms the nasal cavity is the:
    a. sphenoid	b. temporal	c. ethmoid	d. occipital

32. How many bones are involved in a facial massage?
    a. 8	b. 9	c. 12	d. 14

33. What is the largest bone of the facial skeleton?
    a. mandible	b. maxillary	c. malar	d. palatine

34. Which of the following are two bones that join to form the bridge of the nose?
    a. nasal	b. mandible	c. zygomatic	d. lacrimal

35. What are the two bones of the upper jaw?
    a. maxillae	b. turbinals	c. palatines	d. vomers

36. The smallest bones of the facial skeleton that form the front part of the inner, bottom wall of the eye socket are the:
    a. zygomatic	b. nasal	c. malar	d. lacrimal

37. The thumb has how many phalanges?
    a. 2	b. 3	c. 4	d. 5

38. What is also known as the collar bone?
    a. thorax	b. hyoid	c. clavicle	d. patella

39. Which of the following bones protects the heart, lungs and other internal organs?
    a. thorax	b. hyoid	c. spine	d. cranium

40. Eight carpals held together with ligaments form the carpus or the:
    a. knee	b. elbow	c. wrist	d. hand

41. The humerus is an example of what type of bone?
    a. flat	b. long	c. irregular	d. short

42. Which of the following is the outer and narrower of the two leg bones?
    a. fibula	b. femur	c. talus	d. patella

43. How many bones are included in the cervical vertebrae?
    a. 3	b. 6	c. 7	d. 9

44. Which muscle is the only one of its kind in the human body?
    a. striated	b. non-striated	c. involuntary	d. heart

45. Striated muscles can be described by which of the following statements?
    a. controlled by the autonomic nervous system	b. respond to commands regulated by will
    c. involuntary muscles	d. only found in the heart

46. What term means "located above" or "is larger"?
    a. depressor b. dilator c. superioris d. inferioris
47. What term means "behind" or "in back of"?
    a. inferior b. posterior c. depressor d. anterior
48. Muscle makes up approximately what percentage of the body's weight?
    a. 10 b. 20 c. 40 d. 70
49. Myology is the study of the structure, function and diseases of the:
    a. cells b. organs c. muscles d. skeleton
50. The muscles that respond automatically to control various body functions are referrred to as:
    a. cardiac b. voluntary c. non-striated d. striated
51. What term means "in front of"?
    a. posterior b. superior c. anterior d. inferior
52. The muscle that raises eyebrows is the:
    a. auricularis anterior b. epicranius c. frontalis d. occipitalis
53. The portion of muscle joined to movable attachments, such as bones is the:
    a. origin b. belly c. insertion d. ligament
54. Muscles affected by massage are generally manipulated from the:
    a. origin to insertion b. insertion to origin c. belly to insertion d. insertion to belly
55. The non-moving portion of the muscle attached to bone or other fixed muscle is the:
    a. origin b. belly c. insertion d. synapse
56. The epicranium is covered by a large muscle called the:
    a. frontalis b. occipitalis c. auricularis d. epicranius
57. The midsection of a muscle is called its:
    a. belly b. contraction point c. origin d. insertion
58. Which of the following is NOT a part of the muscle?
    a. pons b. belly c. origin d. insertion
59. When you raise your eyelid, which muscles are being used?
    a. orbicularis oculi b. auricularis posterior c. levator palpebrae superioris d. auricularis superior
60. Which muscle is being used when you wrinkle your chin?
    a. mentalis b. caninus c. triangularis d. risorius
61. Which muscle circles the eye socket and closes the eyelid?
    a. corrugator b. orbicularis oculi c. auricularis d. buccinator
62. Which muscle circles the mouth and is responsible for puckering and wrinkling the lips?
    a. risorius b. quadratus labii superioris c. orbicularis oculi d. triangularis
63. Which muscle is responsible for compressing the cheek to release air outwardly, as in blowing?
    a. caninus b. buccinator c. triangularis d. risorius
64. When you laugh, you draw your mouth up and back by using which of these muscles?
    a. caninus b. zygomaticus c. buccinator d. risorius

CHAPTER 3

65. What are the deltoid muscles?
 a. muscles that extend across the chest
 b. muscles that cover the shoulders
 c. muscles located between the shoulder and the elbow
 d. muscles responsible for thumb movement

66. Which muscle moves the smallest toe away from the other toes.
 a. abductor hallucis
 b. abductor digiti minimi
 c. flexor digitorum brevis
 d. flexor digiti minimi brevis

67. What nourishes the parts of the body not reached by blood?
 a. hemoglobin
 b. platelets
 c. lymph
 d. carbon dioxide

68. Which muscles are used to separate the fingers?
 a. adductor
 b. abductor
 c. extensor
 d. flexor

69. Which of the following is the average resting heart rate?
 a. 40 to 50
 b. 50 to 60
 c. 60 to 100
 d. 100 to 120

70. Which of the following phrases describes the function of white corpuscles?
 a. increase in number when there is an infection
 b. carry oxygen
 c. clot the blood
 d. carry carbon dioxide

71. Which of the following terms is another name for white blood cells?
 a. leukocytes
 b. thrombocytes
 c. erythrocytes
 d. red corpuscles

72. An adult human has how much blood circulating throughout the body?
 a. 4 to 6 pints
 b. 4 to 6 quarts
 c. 8 to 10 pints
 d. 8 to 10 quarts

73. What are thrombocytes?
 a. blood platelets
 b. oxygen carriers
 c. hemoglobin carriers
 d. carbon dioxide removers

74. What does hemoglobin do?
 a. reacts with oxygen to create red blood cells
 b. repels oxygen
 c. attracts oxygen
 d. changes oxygen into carbon dioxide

75. Thick-walled vessels that carry blood away from the heart are:
 a. arteries
 b. veins
 c. lymph vessels
 d. capillaries

76. Which of the following is true of arteries?
 a. Arteries contain cup-like valves to prevent backflow
 b. Arteries have thicker walls than veins
 c. Arteries carry oxygen-poor blood
 d. Arteries are thin, small vessels

77. The fluid part of the blood is called:
 a. hemoglobin
 b. red blood cells
 c. white blood cells
 d. plasma

78. Cells that fight bacteria and other foreign substances are called leukocytes or:
 a. red blood cells
 b. plasma
 c. white blood cells
 d. hemoglobin

79. The entire process of blood traveling from the heart, throughout the body and back to the heart is called:
 a. systemic or general circulation
 b. massive circulation
 c. local circulation
 d. arterial circulation

80. Which of the following vessels take waste products from the cells to the veins?
 a. capillaries
 b. arteries
 c. veins
 d. varicose veins

81. Blood travels from the heart to the lungs by way of the:
 a. super vena cava
 b. aorta
 c. pulmonary vein
 d. pulmonary artery

82. What refers to the phase of circulation in which the blood is oxygenated in the lungs?
 a. respiration
 b. pulmonary circulation
 c. interior circulation
 d. general circulation

ANATOMY AND PHYSIOLOGY

83. Oxygen-poor blood enters which part of the heart?
    a. right atrium   b. left atrium   c. pulmonary vein   d. left ventricle
84. Which artery supplies the lower portion of the face, including the mouth and nose?
    a. superficial temporal   b. posterior auricular   c. occipital   d. external maxillary
85. Which artery supplies blood to the face, head and neck?
    a. internal jugular   b. external jugular   c. posterior auricular   d. common carotid artery
86. What controls all three subsystems of the nervous system?
    a. brain   b. eyes   c. lungs   d. heart
87. What is the study of the nervous system called?
    a. neurology   b. philosophy   c. anatomy   d. physiology
88. The brain, nerves and spinal cord are primary components of what system?
    a. circulatory   b. muscular   c. skeletal   d. nervous
89. The average human brain weighs between:
    a. 20 and 24 ounces   b. 44 and 48 ounces   c. 60 and 68 ounces   d. 100 and 120 ounces
90. The brain, spinal cord and spinal and cranial nerves make up the:
    a. central nervous system   b. peripheral nervous system   c. autonomic nervous system   d. sympathetic nervous system
91. Which system is responsible for all voluntary body actions?
    a. autonomic nervous system   b. dendrites
    c. axons   d. central nervous system
92. What is the substance that travels through glands or nodes to help filter out toxic substances?
    a. lymph   b. hemoglobin   c. keratin   d. oxygen
93. The spinal cord holds how many pairs of spinal nerves that branch out to muscles, internal organs and the skin?
    a. 12   b. 14   c. 31   d. 206
94. Which system is composed of sensory and motor nerves that extend from the spinal cord and brain to other parts of the body?
    a. peripheral nervous system   b. autonomic nervous system
    c. zygomatic nervous system   d. cerebrum
95. What connects the other parts of the brain to the spinal column?
    a. cerebrum   b. cerebellum   c. pons   d. clavicle
96. What is the part of the brain responsible for mental activity and is located in the upper front portion of the cranium?
    a. cerebrum   b. cerebellum   c. pons   d. medulla oblongata
97. Another name for a nerve cell is:
    a. neuron   b. dendrite   c. axon   d. cerebrum
98. Nerves that perform both sensory and motor functions are called:
    a. afferent nerves   b. efferent nerves   c. mixed nerves   d. central nerves
99. How many pairs of cranial nerves are there?
    a. 12   b. 18   c. 24   d. 36
100. Another name for a sensory nerve is:
    a. dendrite nerve   b. axon   c. afferent nerve   d. efferent nerve
101. Which nerves determine the sense of smell, touch, sight, hearing and taste?
    a. dendrite   b. motor   c. sensory   d. axon

CHAPTER 3

102. The cranial nerve responsible for transmitting facial sensations to the brain is the:
    a. trifacial b. facial c. radial d. ulnar

103. Which of the following nerves is the primary motor nerve of the face?
    a. fifth b. seventh c. ulnar d. radial

104. Which of the following terms is NOT associated with the functions found within the nervous system?
    a. motor b. mixed c. deltoid d. sensory

105. The posterior auricular, temporal and zygomatic are all branches of which nerve?
    a. buccal b. cervical c. mandibular d. facial

106. The digestive, respiratory and circulatory systems are controlled by the:
    a. ophthalmic branch b. autonomic nervous system c. voluntary nervous system d. skeletal system

107. Which of the following examples is NOT a primary nerve found in the arm and hand?
    a. ulnar b. radial c. buccal d. digital

108. Peristalsis refers to:
    a. a blister from a severe burn
    b. the motion of the esophagus when swallowing
    c. the breakdown of food by enzymes
    d. the elimination of waste products from the body

109. Finger-like projections of the intestine walls are called:
    a. villi b. peristalsis c. cilia d. enzymes

110. The digestive system includes all of the following components EXCEPT:
    a. pharynx b. stomach c. diaphragm d. esophagus

111. Which body system breaks food down into simpler chemical compounds that can easily be absorbed by cells?
    a. digestive b. lymph c. excretory d. respiratory

112. The system that eliminates solid, liquid and gaseous waste products from the body is the:
    a. digestive b. excretory c. endocrine d. respiratory

113. Nephrons would be associated with which of the following organs?
    a. lungs b. liver c. heart d. kidney

114. The system responsible for taking in oxygen and exhaling carbon dioxide is the:
    a. circulatory system b. excretory system c. endocrine system d. respiratory system

115. The largest organ of the body is the:
    a. skin b. liver c. brain d. stomach

116. The endocrine system is responsible for:
    a. eliminating waste products from the body
    b. producing hormones required by the body
    c. carrying lymph to parts of the body not reached by the circulatory system
    d. building larger molecules from smaller ones

117. What converts and neutralizes ammonia from the circulatory system to urea?
    a. liver b. skin c. heart d. lungs

ANATOMY AND PHYSIOLOGY

118. All of the following are organs of the excretory system EXCEPT:
    a. skin	b. lungs	c. liver	d. kidneys

119. The skin and all of its layers make up which of the following sytems?
    a. integumentary	b. excretory	c. endocrine	d. respiratory

120. A sebaceous gland is part of which body system?
    a. respiratory	b. digestive	c. nervous	d. integumentary

FINAL REVIEW

Check your answers as you did before. Place a check mark next to the page number for any incorrect answer. On the lines on the next page, jot down topics that you still need to review.

☐	1. page 65	☐	16. page 67	☐	31. page 70	☐	46. page 72
☐	2. page 65	☐	17. page 67	☐	32. page 70	☐	47. page 72
☐	3. page 65	☐	18. page 67	☐	33. page 70	☐	48. page 72
☐	4. page 65	☐	19. page 67	☐	34. page 70	☐	49. page 72
☐	5. page 66	☐	20. page 67	☐	35. page 70	☐	50. page 72
☐	6. page 66	☐	21. page 69	☐	36. page 70	☐	51. page 72
☐	7. page 66	☐	22. page 69	☐	37. page 71	☐	52. page 73
☐	8. page 66	☐	23. page 69	☐	38. page 71	☐	53. page 73
☐	9. page 66	☐	24. page 69	☐	39. page 71	☐	54. page 73
☐	10. page 66	☐	25. page 69	☐	40. page 71	☐	55. page 73
☐	11. page 66	☐	26. page 69	☐	41. page 71	☐	56. page 73
☐	12. page 66	☐	27. page 69	☐	42. page 71	☐	57. page 73
☐	13. page 66	☐	28. page 69	☐	43. page 71	☐	58. page 73
☐	14. page 66	☐	29. page 69	☐	44. page 72	☐	59. page 74
☐	15. page 67	☐	30. page 70	☐	45. page 72	☐	60. page 74

CHAPTER 3

FINAL REVIEW *continued*

☐ 61.	page 74	☐ 76.	page 78	☐ 91.	page 81	☐ 106.	page 85
☐ 62.	page 74	☐ 77.	page 78	☐ 92.	page 81	☐ 107.	page 85
☐ 63.	page 75	☐ 78.	page 78	☐ 93.	page 82	☐ 108.	page 86
☐ 64.	page 75	☐ 79.	page 79	☐ 94.	page 82	☐ 109.	page 86
☐ 65.	page 76	☐ 80.	page 79	☐ 95.	page 82	☐ 110.	page 86
☐ 66.	page 77	☐ 81.	page 79	☐ 96.	page 82	☐ 111.	page 86
☐ 67.	page 77	☐ 82.	page 79	☐ 97.	page 82	☐ 112.	page 87
☐ 68.	page 76	☐ 83.	page 79	☐ 98.	page 83	☐ 113.	page 87
☐ 69.	page 78	☐ 84.	page 80	☐ 99.	page 83	☐ 114.	page 87
☐ 70.	page 78	☐ 85.	page 80	☐ 100.	page 83	☐ 115.	page 88
☐ 71.	page 78	☐ 86.	page 81	☐ 101.	page 83	☐ 116.	page 88
☐ 72.	page 78	☐ 87.	page 81	☐ 102.	page 83	☐ 117.	page 87
☐ 73.	page 78	☐ 88.	page 81	☐ 103.	page 83	☐ 118.	page 87
☐ 74.	page 78	☐ 89.	page 81	☐ 104.	page 83	☐ 119.	page 88
☐ 75.	page 78	☐ 90.	page 81	☐ 105.	page 84	☐ 120.	page 88

UNIT 1 THEORY ESSENTIALS

ANATOMY AND PHYSIOLOGY

 **NOTES TO MYSELF**

Experts tell us that it is important to summarize your feelings and reactions about what you are learning. Note especially things that surprised you, things you found difficult to learn, suggestions and ideas you received from friends that helped make learning this chapter easier and more enjoyable.

My reflections about Anatomy and Physiology:

LESSONS LEARNED

- The building blocks of the human body include cells that make up tissues, tissues that make up organs and organs that make up systems.

- The skeletal system supports the body, surrounds and protects internal organs, provides a frame to which muscles can attach and allows body movement.

- The muscular system supports the skeleton, produces body movements, contours the body and aids in the functions of other body systems.

- The circulatory system controls the circulation of blood and lymph through the body.

- The nervous system coordinates and controls the overall operation of the human body by receiving and interpreting stimuli and sending messages away from the nerve cells to the appropriate tissues, muscles and organs.

THINGS TO DO

☐   ☐
☐   ☐
☐   ☐
☐   ☐
☐   ☐
☐   ☐
☐   ☐
☐   ☐

1 2 3 4 5 6 **7**

SALON FUNDAMENTALS COSMETOLOGY 95

CHAPTER 4

CHAPTER 4
ELECTRICITY

VALUE
Understanding the basics of electricity enables you to serve your clients efficiently and safely, especially when working with electrotherapy and specialized electrical appliances.

MAIN IDEA
Electricity is a fundamental tool for safe and efficient treatments and services for clients.

PLAN

4.1 PRINCIPLES OF ELECTRICITY
Vocabulary of Electricity
Electric Current
Safety Measures

4.2 ELECTRICITY IN COSMETOLOGY
Effects of Electric Current
Electrotherapy
Light Therapy

smartNOTES

4.1 PRINCIPLES OF ELECTRICITY pages 91-93

Vocabulary of Electricity

Electricity

Electrons

Current

Load

Conductors
-
-

Insulators
-

Cord Safety

Measures of Electricity

AMP	VOLT	OHM	WATT	HERTZ

CHAPTER 4

smartNOTES

4.1 PRINCIPLES OF ELECTRICITY   pages 93-95

Electric Current

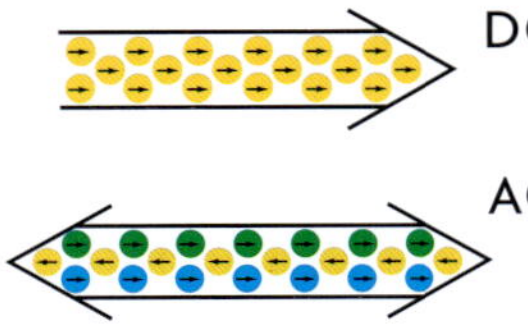

DC

AC

Sources of Electricity

DIFFERENCES

GENERATOR	BATTERY
•	•
•	•
•	•

Frequency

How Electric Current is Produced

Circuit

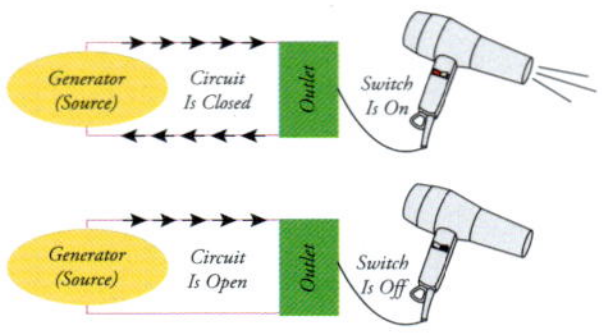

CLOSED	OPEN

ELECTRICITY

smartNOTES

4.1 PRINCIPLES OF ELECTRICITY   pages 95-97

Parallel Wiring

Series Wiring

Overload

Short Circuit

Safety Devices

ALERT
! Electric shock can be fatal.

Safety Measures

FUSE	CIRCUIT BREAKER	GROUNDING WIRE (3-wire system)
•	•	•
•	•	•
•	•	•
•		

1 **2** 3 4 5 6 7

CHAPTER 4

smartNOTES

4.1 PRINCIPLES OF ELECTRICITY   page 98

First Aid for Shock

Step 1:

Step 2:

Step 3:

Local Shock Procedure
-
-

General Shock Procedure

First:

Then:

Electrical Fires Emergency Procedures

Remember: NO WATER

-
-

ELECTRICITY

ELECTRICITY BY USE IN THE SALON

Thermal/Heat
Examples:

-

Combination
Examples:

-

Mechanical
Examples:

-

TALKING POINTS

Your next challenge is to be ready to talk about some of the important ideas in this chapter. Follow the directions listed next to each box. Then practice talking about your ideas with others.

Describe in your own way three common electrical accidents that could happen in the salon.

Using words and symbols, make a sign for emergency procedures for electrical fires. Explain your sign to a friend or family member.

SALON FUNDAMENTALS COSMETOLOGY   101

CHAPTER 4

smartNOTES

4.2 ELECTRICITY IN COSMETOLOGY   pages 99-101

Effects of Electric Current

| HEATING | MECHANICAL OR MAGNETIC | ELECTROCHEMICAL |

Electrotherapy

Electrode

Galvanic Current
-
-
-
-

Phoresis (Bleaching)

ALERT

A person with any potentially restrictive medical condition should always consult a physician before receiving electrotherapy treatment.

smartNOTES

4.2 ELECTRICITY IN COSMETOLOGY   pages 101-103

Anaphoresis

Cataphoresis

ANAPHORESIS	CATAPHORESIS
negative (-) pole	positive (+) pole

Galvanic Current Electrotherapy

Iontophoreses

Faradic Current

Sinusoidal Current

Tesla Current

ALERT
! Do not use the Galvanic Current over an area that has many broken capillaries.

CHAPTER 4

smartNOTES

4.2 ELECTRICITY IN COSMETOLOGY — pages 105-108

WEB

- Galvanic Current Precautions
- Tesla Current Precautions
- Faradic Current Precautions
- Sinusoidal Current Precautions

Topic: Electrotherapy

General Precautions
Always read manufacturer's directions
_____ should never touch each other

Heat Energy
Conduction, _____ , radiation
Mild - _____ muscles, causes blood circulation to _____
Intense - _____ cells and tissues

Topic: Light Therapy
- Benefits of Light Therapy
- Visible Light
- Ultraviolet Light
- Invisible Light
- Infrared Light
- Types of Medical Devices

ELECTRICITY

THINKING MAP

Now that you have filled in your SmartNotes for "Electricity," create a Thinking Map to help yourself make sense of how your SmartNotes fit together. Use some or all of the words in the Jump Start Box as well as your own words and pictures to make a visual that will help you connect the important ideas in this chapter to each other. Be creative!

ELECTRICITY

JUMP START BOX

CIRCUIT	GENERAL SHOCK	AMP	INSULATORS
FUSE	SHORT CIRCUIT	DIRECT APPLICATION	MECHANICAL OR MAGNETIC EFFECTS
LOCAL SHOCK	SOURCE	ELECTROTHERAPY	GENERATOR
ELECTRICITY	MECHANICAL	FARADIC	INDIRECT APPLICATION
VOLT	HEATING EFFECTS	LOAD	
THERMAL	LIGHT THERAPY	OPEN CIRCUIT	FORCE
GENERAL ELECTRIFICATION	OHM	ELECTROCHEMICAL EFFECTS	SINUSOIDAL
WATT	HEAT	CURRENT	CONDUCTORS
OVERLOADING	CIRCUIT BREAKER	BATTERY	GROUNDING WIRE
3-WIRE SYSTEM	COMBINATION	TESLA	
	GALVANIC		

SALON FUNDAMENTALS COSMETOLOGY

CHAPTER 4

THE CHALLENGE

Now it's time to see how well you know your new material. First answer these questions. Then use the Memory Box that follows to check yourself. Look up each answer on the corresponding page in the *Salon Fundamentals* textbook. Check "got it" for all correct answers and "not yet" for all incorrect responses. Using the "Know Chart," record all of your correct responses in the "I Know" column. After correcting incorrect answers, record all of your corrected responses in the "I Need to Study" column. That way you know exactly what to review before continuing in this study guide.

1. Electricity is a form of energy that produces _____, _____, _____ and _____ changes.

2. What are the two forms of electricity, both of which are used in a salon? _____ _____.

3. Two common sources of electricity are _____ and _____.

4. The three kinds of effects that can be created by electric current during cosmetology services are _____, _____ and _____.

5. TRUE   FALSE   Galvanic Current is the only form of electrotherapy that uses direct current and has an electrochemical effect.

6. The process of forcing acid or alkali solutions into the skin by applying current to the solution is known as _____.

7. What percentage of sunlight is composed of invisible rays beyond red, called infrared? _____

8. Benefits derived from using _____ light include increased circulation, increased skin gland secretions, and relaxation of muscles.

9. Small doses of ultraviolet light can tan the skin and may help the body produce _____.

10. TRUE   FALSE   Ultraviolet rays are the least penetrating light rays in the spectrum; therefore, there is no danger of overexposure.

MEMORY BOX

1. PAGE 91 — GOT IT / NOT YET
2. PAGE 93 — GOT IT / NOT YET
3. PAGE 94 — GOT IT / NOT YET
4. PAGE 99 — GOT IT / NOT YET
5. PAGE 100 — GOT IT / NOT YET
6. PAGE 101 — GOT IT / NOT YET
7. PAGE 107 — GOT IT / NOT YET
8. PAGE 107 — GOT IT / NOT YET
9. PAGE 107 — GOT IT / NOT YET
10. PAGES 107, 108 — GOT IT / NOT YET

KNOW CHART

I KNOW:

I NEED TO STUDY:

ELECTRICITY

SHOW YOU KNOW...

You are teaching a group of young adults safety measures. Your next topics are local and general shock. Create a poem, a song or a catchy poster that will help your class remember the steps for local or general shock safety precautions.

KNOWLEDGE GRID

Start at the top of the Knowledge Grid and work your way down, answering each question to check your understanding of *Chapter 4, Electricity*. The questions found here will help you deepen your understanding, build self-confidence and increase your awareness of different ways of thinking about a subject.

KNOW	WHAT IS THE DEFINITION OF ELECTRICITY?	
COMPREHEND	WHAT IS THE DIFFERENCE BETWEEN ALTERNATING AND DIRECT CURRENT?	
APPLY	IF A FIRE RESULTS FROM AN OVERLOAD OF AN ELECTRIC CIRCUIT AND AN APPLIANCE MELTS AND BURNS, HOW WOULD YOU RESPOND?	

SALON FUNDAMENTALS COSMETOLOGY

CHAPTER 4

KNOWLEDGE GRID *continued*

ANALYZE	DISTINGUISH BETWEEN HEAT, MECHANICAL AND ELECTROCHEMICAL EFFECTS.	
SYNTHESIZE	IN YOUR OWN WORDS, GENERATE A RESPONSE TO IDENTIFY THE BENEFITS OF USING INFRARED LIGHT.	
EVALUATE	JUSTIFY THE NEED FOR SALONS TO HAVE BOTH INCANDESCENT AND FLUORESCENT LIGHTING.	

BRAIN **BUILDER**

Questions help us think. Write a challenging question about four of the important words or phrases below and be prepared to answer it. (The following stems generate the most thought-provoking questions: Why does? Why are? What if? How would? Try them!) Then try your questions out on your friends. How well can they answer them?

- Current
- Conductor
- Insulator
- Circuit Breaker
- Electrotherapy
- Tesla
- Light Therapy

108   UNIT 1 THEORY ESSENTIALS

BRAIN CONDITIONER
MULTIPLE CHOICE. CIRCLE THE CORRECT ANSWER.

1. Light, heat, chemical and magnetic changes are all produced by:
   a. electricity   b. short circuit   c. force   d. conductors

2. The movement of electricity along a conductor is called:
   a. voltage   b. wattage   c. electric current   d. magnetic conductance

3. What is the technical name for any electrically powered appliance?
   a. force   b. closed circuit   c. load   d. short circuit

4. Since silver and copper transport electricity easily, they are called:
   a. insulators   b. conductors   c. electrons   d. closed circuits

5. Materials such as glass, rubber or paper that do not allow electricity to flow through them are called:
   a. insulators   b. conductors   c. open circuits   d. closed circuits

6. An ampere is a unit of electric:
   a. pressure   b. strength   c. resistance   d. frequency

7. A volt is a unit of electric:
   a. pressure   b. strength   c. resistance   d. frequency

8. Which of the following materials does NOT allow a current to pass through it?
   a. metal   b. water   c. carbon   d. alcohol

9. A unit of electrical resistance is called a(n):
   a. ohm   b. watt   c. insulator   d. volt

10. The measure of how difficult it is to push electrons through a conductor is called:
    a. resistance   b. amperage   c. voltage   d. wattage

11. The measure of how much electrical energy is being used is called a(n):
    a. volt   b. watt   c. ohm   d. ampere

12. A constant electrical current flowing in one direction is called a(n):
    a. Sinusoidal Current   b. alternating current   c. Faradic Current   d. direct current

13. What changes direct current into alternating current?
    a. rectifier   b. converter   c. meter   d. circuit breaker

14. Electric current that flows first in one direction and then the other is called:
    a. direct current   b. alternating current   c. Galvanic Current   d. incandescent current

15. What changes alternating current into direct current?
    a. converter   b. rectifier   c. circuit breaker   d. short circuit

16. The power source used most often in a salon is a:
    a. battery   b. wall outlet   c. generator   d. switch

17. The very minimum ampere rating of a circuit operating a single 1,000-watt blow dryer would be:
    a. 1 ampere   b. 10 amperes   c. 60 amperes   d. 120 amperes

CHAPTER 4

18. If appliances are causing more current to flow than what the circuit is designed to carry, what could occur?
    a. overloading   b. downsizing   c. converting   d. rectifying

19. A closed path through which electrons travel is referred to as a:
    a. circuit   b. short circuit   c. source   d. resistance

20. Which of the following actions would be an example of closing a circuit?
    a. turning on a light switch   b. turning off a circuit breaker
    c. blowing a fuse   d. unplugging a lamp

21. Dropping an electrical appliance into water is an example of:
    a. overloading   b. open circuit   c. closed circuit   d. short circuit

22. What is the name of a device with a fine metal wire running through it which will melt and open the circuit if too much current is flowing through it?
    a. circuit breaker   b. resistor   c. fuse   d. grounding wire

23. What is a device used to protect a circuit from being overloaded?
    a. ground wire   b. on-off switch   c. rectifier   d. circuit breaker

24. A special wire used on some appliances for conducting high and sudden flows of electric current out of the appliance is called a:
    a. positive wire   b. negative wire   c. grounding wire   d. fuse

25. What type of shock passes through the nervous system?
    a. local   b. general   c. direct   d. indirect

26. Which of the following methods is NOT recommended for extinguishing an electrical fire?
    a. use a fire extinguisher   b. pour water on it   c. smother it with a towel   d. pour corn starch on it

27. Curling irons and heat lamps are examples of which type of electrically powered equipment?
    a. thermal   b. mechanical   c. combination   d. electrochemical

28. What does a local shock do?
    a. causes the heart to stop   b. causes breathing to halt
    c. passes through a small part of the body   d. always requires medical attention

29. Using electric clippers in cosmetology work would be an example of which kind of electrical effect?
    a. heating   b. mechanical   c. electrochemical   d. electrochemical and heating

30. Which of the following steps should NOT be followed to break the circuit when a person comes into contact with an electric current?
    a. unplug the appliance   b. turn off all the circuit breakers
    c. touch the person to ground the circuit   d. knock the person out of the circuit using an insulator

31. The application of special electric currents that have certain effects on the skin is known as:
    a. cosmetology   b. chemotherapy   c. shock therapy   d. electrotherapy

32. Which of the following currents is an example of low-voltage direct current and high amps?
    a. Faradic   b. Sinusoidal   c. Tesla   d. Galvanic

33. In order to apply special currents to the skin, what device is used to reduce the current from a typical 120-volt power source to a level safely handled by the human body?
    a. rectifier   b. converter   c. wall plate   d. electrode

34. When performing an electrotherapy procedure, what apparatus or current conductor is used to bring the current from the appliance to the client's skin?
    a. resistor   b. watt   c. wall plate   d. electrode

35. The oldest form of electrotherapy used in the salon is:
    a. Galvanic Current   b. Tesla Current   c. Sinusoidal Current   d. Faradic Current

36. What is the type of current that has an electrochemical effect?
    a. Tesla   b. Faradic   c. Galvanic   d. Sinusoidal

37. Which of the following statements is NOT true about the anode?
    a. shows a large "P"   b. is usually colored red   c. is usually colored black   d. shows a positive sign

38. Which process uses a negative pole or electrode to force negatively charged (alkaline) solutions into the skin without breaking the skin?
    a. anaphoresis   b. cataphoresis   c. Faradic therapy   d. Sinusoidal therapy

39. Which process uses the positive electrode to force acidic solutions into the skin without breaking the skin?
    a. anaphoresis   b. cataphoresis   c. Faradic therapy   d. Tesla therapy

40. Which of the following statements is NOT true about cataphoresis?
    a. slows the blood flow
    b. soothes nerves
    c. softens tissues and opens pores
    d. decreases redness of simple blemishes

41. What process can use either the negative or positive pole to introduce water-soluble treatment products to the skin?
    a. anaphoresis   b. cataphoresis   c. iontophoresis   d. Faradic therapy

42. Which of the following descriptions is NOT a temporary effect of the positive pole of Galvanic Current?
    a. softens tissues
    b. soothes nerves
    c. produces an acidic reaction
    d. slows blood flow by contracting the vessels

43. Which of the following statements is NOT true about a positive pole of Galvanic Current?
    a. soothes nerves
    b. produces an acidic reaction
    c. opens pores after facial treatment
    d. slows the blood flow by contracting the vessels

44. What type of electrotherapy current is considered superior to Faradic Current therapy because it penetrates more deeply?
    a. Tesla   b. direct current   c. Galvanic   d. Sinusoidal

45. Which of the following items would be used during a Faradic Current treatment?
    a. amperages of more than 1 milliampere
    b. 120 volts
    c. direct method
    d. indirect method

46. High Frequency and alternating current are characteristics of which type of electrotherapy?
    a. Tesla   b. direct current   c. Galvanic   d. Sinusoidal

47. A benefit of Tesla Current therapy may include:
    a. improved muscle tone
    b. stimulation of hair growth
    c. soothed nerves
    d. improved blood circulation

48. Which of the following benefits is NOT believed to be derived through application of the High Frequency current?
    a. improved blood circulation
    b. increased rate of metabolism
    c. decreased rate of metabolism
    d. increased sebaceous glandular activity

CHAPTER 4

49. The maximum amount of current used in a Galvanic treatment should not exceed:
    a. 1 milliampere   b. 1 ampere   c. 2 amperes   d. 10 amperes

50. Tesla treatments should be limited to no more than how many minutes in duration?
    a. 1   b. 5   c. 10   d. 30

51. The chemical breakdown of the skin caused by intense heat is called:
    a. psoriasis   b. pyrolysis   c. melting   d. vaporizing

52. The portion of the electromagnetic spectrum that humans can see is called:
    a. visible light   b. infrared light   c. ultraviolet light   d. X-rays

53. White light can be broken down into its individual wavelengths by the use of a:
    a. rectifier   b. converter   c. prism   d. fluorescent light

54. Which type of light can create blue or cool tones?
    a. fluorescent   b. incandescent   c. sunlight   d. invisible

55. Which of the following types of light carries the most energy?
    a. ultraviolet   b. violet   c. infrared   d. red

56. Which of the following types of light has the shortest wavelength?
    a. ultraviolet   b. violet   c. infrared   d. red

57. What light creates the closest substitute for natural sunlight?
    a. fluorescent   b. red   c. violet   d. incandescent

58. Bacteria that cause skin infections can be killed by which kind of light?
    a. incandescent   b. fluorescent   c. infrared   d. ultraviolet

59. Small doses of ultraviolet light may help the body produce:
    a. Vitamin A   b. Vitamin B   c. Vitamin C   d. Vitamin D

60. Which of the following effects is NOT a benefit of using infrared light during a facial?
    a. increased circulation   b. relaxation of muscles
    c. increased skin gland secretions   d. decreased skin gland secretion

FINAL REVIEW

Check your answers as you did before. Place a check mark next to the page number for any incorrect answer. On the lines on the next page, jot down topics that you still need to review.

☐ 1.	page 91	☐ 7.	page 92	☐ 13.	page 93	☐ 19.	page 95
☐ 2.	page 91	☐ 8.	page 92	☐ 14.	page 93	☐ 20.	page 95
☐ 3.	page 91	☐ 9.	page 93	☐ 15.	page 93	☐ 21.	page 96
☐ 4.	page 92	☐ 10.	page 93	☐ 16.	page 94	☐ 22.	page 96
☐ 5.	page 92	☐ 11.	page 93	☐ 17.	page 95	☐ 23.	page 97
☐ 6.	page 92	☐ 12.	page 93	☐ 18.	page 95	☐ 24.	page 97

FINAL REVIEW *continued*

- [ ] 25. page 98
- [ ] 26. page 98
- [ ] 27. page 98
- [ ] 28. page 98
- [ ] 29. page 98
- [ ] 30. page 98
- [ ] 31. page 99
- [ ] 32. page 100
- [ ] 33. page 100
- [ ] 34. page 100
- [ ] 35. page 100
- [ ] 36. page 100
- [ ] 37. page 100
- [ ] 38. page 101
- [ ] 39. page 101
- [ ] 40. page 101
- [ ] 41. page 101
- [ ] 42. page 101
- [ ] 43. page 101
- [ ] 44. page 102
- [ ] 45. page 102
- [ ] 46. page 103
- [ ] 47. page 103
- [ ] 48. page 103
- [ ] 49. page 105
- [ ] 50. page 105
- [ ] 51. page 105
- [ ] 52. page 106
- [ ] 53. page 106
- [ ] 54. page 106
- [ ] 55. page 106
- [ ] 56. page 107
- [ ] 57. page 107
- [ ] 58. page 107
- [ ] 59. page 107
- [ ] 60. page 107

CHAPTER 4

NOTES TO MYSELF

Experts tell us that it is important to summarize your feelings and reactions about what you are learning. Note especially things that surprised you, things you found difficult to learn, suggestions and ideas you received from friends that helped make learning this chapter easier and more enjoyable.

My reflections about Electricity:

LESSONS LEARNED

- *Using electricity safely ensures the well-being of the salon professional and the client.*
- *Electric current may result in heat, mechanical or magnetic and electrochemical effects.*
- *Electric currents used during electrotherapy and light therapy treatments include Galvanic Current to produce chemical effects, Faradic and Sinusoidal Currents to produce mechanical, non-chemical reactions and Tesla Current to produce heat.*

CHAPTER 5
CHEMISTRY

VALUE
Chemistry helps you use a variety of products to improve the personal well-being of your client.

MAIN IDEA
Marketing products, making sound decisions about services and guarding your client's safety all require some knowledge of chemistry.

PLAN

5.1 **MATTER**
   Elements
   Chemical Bonds

5.2 **THE pH SCALE**

CHAPTER 5

smartNOTES

5.1 MATTER   pages 111-112

Matter

Three Forms

ORGANIC

INORGANIC

Changes in Matter

PHYSICAL

CHEMICAL

Properties
1.
2.
3.
4.

CHEMISTRY

smartNOTES

5.1 MATTER
pages 112-114

Elements

Number	Element	Symbol	Form
1			GAS
6			SOLID
7			GAS
8			GAS
16			SOLID

Atoms

3 Parts of Atom

proton

neutron

electron

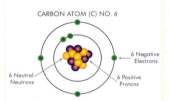

Molecule

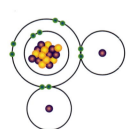

1 2 3 4 5 6 7

CHAPTER 5

TALKING POINTS

Your next challenge is to be ready to talk about some of the important ideas in this chapter. Follow the directions listed next to each box. Then practice talking about your ideas with others.

Describe the three forms of matter...

and the elements that make up hair.

Draw an atom. Compare your drawing with a friend's.

MATCHING

1. Change in a substance's characteristics without making a new substance

2. Negative electrical charge

3. Change in a substance that creates a new substance, new characteristics

4. Anything that occupies space

5. Smallest complete unit of an element

_____ atom

_____ matter

_____ physical change

_____ electron

_____ chemical change

118 UNIT 1 THEORY ESSENTIALS

smartNOTES

5.1 MATTER
pages 114-117

Chemical Bonds	_____ combine chemically to create compounds that eventually create protein of hair

Amino Acids	Compounds of C, O, H, N - 22 common amino acids; join together in chains to make _____

Protein	Hair is made up of protein called _____
Hair is 97% keratin and 3% trace materials
Hair contains 19 of 22 common amino acids

Hydrogen Bond	The hydrogen atom in one molecule is attracted to an atom of another molecule that has many negative _____; hair has many hydrogen bonds, which are individually very weak and can easily be _____ by heat or water

Salt Bond	This bond is a result of the _____ of unlike charges; the negative charge in one amino acid grouping attracts the positive charge in another amino acid grouping

Disulfide Bond	A chemical bond that forms between protein structures; sulfur-type side chains join with other sulfur-type side chains; they form the disulfide bond

van der Waals Forces	Atomic groups prefer an environment with other groups that have structures _____ to theirs

CHAPTER 5

smartNOTES

5.1 MATTER
pages 115-117

End Bonds
(Peptide Bonds)

Side Bonds

END BOND	SIDE BOND

Label the bonds

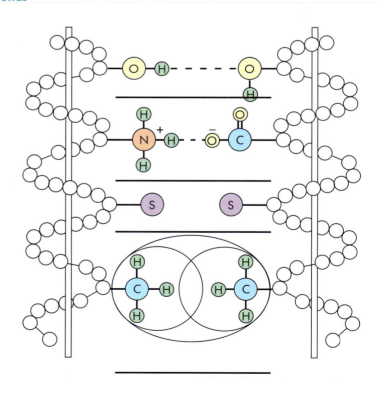

120 UNIT 1 THEORY ESSENTIALS

CHEMISTRY

TALKING POINTS

Your next challenge is to be ready to talk about some of the important ideas in this chapter. Follow the directions listed next to each box. Then practice talking about your ideas with others.

Describe each of these in your own way:

The importance of an end bond.

How side bonds are affected by chemical treatment.

ATOM → AMINO ACID → PROTEIN → HAIR

The importance of this graphic.

CHAPTER 5

THINKING MAP

Now that you have filled in your SmartNotes for "Chemistry," create a Thinking Map to help yourself make sense of how your SmartNotes fit together. Use some or all of the words in the Jump Start Box as well as your own words and pictures to make a visual that will help you connect the important ideas in this chapter to each other. Be creative!

CHEMISTRY

JUMP START BOX

NITROGEN	PHYSICAL CHANGE	GAS	7
HYDROGEN	MOLECULES	6	DISULFIDE
CARBON	AMINO ACID	PEPTIDE BOND	HYDROGEN BONDS
CHEMICAL CHANGE	PROTEIN	POLYPEPTIDE BOND	SALT BONDS
1	KERATIN	SIDE BOND	MATTER
PROTON	HAIR	BONDS	OXYGEN
NEUTRON	SOLID	ATOMS	16
ELECTRON	LIQUID	SULFUR	VAN DER WAALS FORCES
8			

smartNOTES

5.2 THE pH SCALE
pages 118-119

Potential Hydrogen

Water-Based Solutions

Acid

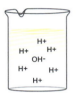

Neutral

Alkaline

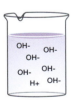

ACID	ALKALINE

CHAPTER 5

smartNOTES

5.2 THE pH SCALE   pages 118-119

pH scale — Unit of measurement - determines if substance is _____, neutral or _____; ranges from 0 to 14; ___ is neutral

0-6.99 — Acid range (orange); more _____ hydrogen ions
Neutral (water); _____ hydrogen and hydroxide ions

7.01-14 — Alkaline range (ammonia); more negative hydroxide ions

Logarithm — Each number increases by multiples of ___

```
  7      8      9      10      11      12      13           14
___x ___x ____x _____x _____x _____x 1,000,000x _____x
```

14 is 10,000,000 times more alkaline than 7

Testing pH
1. pH (Nitrazine) paper
2. pH pencil
3. pH meter

Acid balanced — Within the same range as hair, skin and scalp, ____ to ____

CHEMISTRY

TALKING POINTS

Your next challenge is to be ready to talk about some of the important ideas in this chapter. Follow the directions listed next to each box. Then practice talking about your ideas with others.

Draw and label the pH scale. Explain the pH scale to someone.

Explain the term acid balanced.

Give examples of acidic, alkaline and neutral pH items.

MATCHING

Match the term with the best description by placing the number of the description in the space to the left of the term.

1. Substance with a pH value of 4.5-5.5
2. Alkaline pH range
3. Acidic pH range
4. Water
5. Each number increases by multiples of 10

_____ 0-6.99
_____ Neutral
_____ 7.01-14
_____ Logarithm
_____ Acid balanced

SALON FUNDAMENTALS COSMETOLOGY 125

CHAPTER 5

smartNOTES

5.3 CHEMISTRY OF COSMETICS   pages 120-125

Cosmetic Classifications	Based on how well substance _____ and physical characteristics
Solutions	Mixture of 2 or more kinds of _____; do not _____; can be solid, liquid or gas
Suspensions	Mixture of 2 or more kinds of molecules; _____; need to be shaken, such as vinegar and oil
Emulsions	2 or more non-mixable substances united by a _____ (gum), e.g., oil in water (perms), water in oil (cold cream)
Ointments	Mixture of organic substance and a _____ agent (semi-solid form); no water, e.g., lipstick
Soaps	Mixtures of fat and oil converted to fatty _____ by heat and then purified
Powders	Equal mixtures of inorganic and organic substances that do NOT _____ in water; sifted and mixed until free of coarse grit
Shampoos	Clean _____ and hair; remove all foreign debris without adversely affecting scalp or hair
How Shampoo Works	A "push-pull" action caused by a surface active _____ causes the oil to "roll up" into droplets that are lifted and rinsed away.
Surfactant	Surface active agent; has a water-loving and _____-loving part
The Role of Water	Universal _____; neutral; hard water = minerals; soft water preferred (allows lather); hard water is hard to lather

126 UNIT 1 THEORY ESSENTIALS

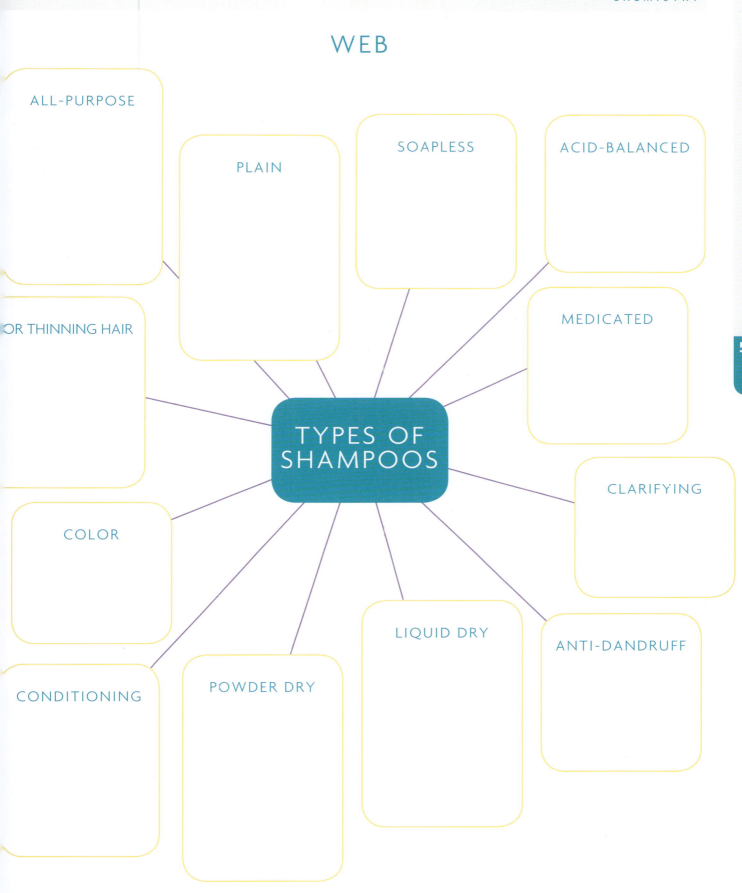

CHAPTER 5

smartNOTES

5.3 CHEMISTRY OF COSMETICS   pages 125-128

Rinses and Conditioners

Appearance

Porosity

Manageability

Elasticity

Types of Rinses

1.

2.

3.

Conditioners

1.

2.

3.

4.

5.

smartNOTES

5.3 CHEMISTRY OF COSMETICS
pages 128-130

Perms — Hair is wrapped around tool; processing lotion is applied to break disulfide _____; hair softens to shape of perm tool; rinsing removes lotion; _____ reforms disulfide bonds to new shape

Alkaline — Processes without _____; pH 8.0 - 9.5; thioglycolic acid and ammonium hydroxide are main ingredients

Acid wave — Main ingredient = glycerylmonothioglycolate; speed is sacrificed for a more controlled curl; heat may be used

Neutralizers — Main ingredients: hydrogen _____, sodium perborate or sodium bromate

Relaxers — Reduce curl in excessively curly or wavy hair by changing molecular _____

Sodium Hydroxide — Formulated with 2% to 3% sodium hydroxide in heavy cream base with ____ of 11.5 to 14

ALERT! — Sodium Hydroxide and _____ are NOT compatible. Do NOT use one on top of the other. The straightened hair must grow out before additional chemical services can be performed.

Thioglycolate — Formulated with 4% to 6% thioglycolic acid with 1% ammonium hydroxide; pH 8.5 to 9.5; cream base usually added

Lanthionization — When chemically relaxing hair with _____ _____, the disulfide bonds are broken at point "X" between the first sulphur atom and the adjacent carbon atom, resulting in one sulphur atom being lost.

Curl Reformation — Loosens _____ of curly-to-tightly curled hair; hair is smoothed with thioglycolic-based cream, rinsed, curl booster applied; hair is then _____ around perm tool, processed to desired shape, rinsed and neutralized

CHAPTER 5

smartNOTES

5.3 CHEMISTRY OF COSMETICS pages 131-132

Hair Color

REDUCTION (Redox)

Nonoxidative

1.

2.

Oxidative

3.

4.

ALERT! Perform patch test 24 hours prior to application of aniline derivative color

Allergies – Perform Patch Test

Oxidants

smartNOTES

5.3 CHEMISTRY OF COSMETICS
pages 132-134

Hair Lighteners

ON-THE-SCALP

OFF-THE-SCALP

Developers

Hydrometer

Vegetable, Metallic and Compound Dyes

CHAPTER 5

TALKING POINTS

Your next challenge is to be ready to talk about some of the important ideas in this chapter. Follow the directions listed next to each box. Then practice talking about your ideas with others.

Describe each of these in your own way:

Two types of perms.

The lasting effects caused by sodium hydroxide and why it must be handled with professional care.

The use of oxidants.

THE CHALLENGE

Now it's time to see how well you know your new material. First answer these questions. Then use the Memory Box that follows to check yourself. Look up each answer on the corresponding page in the *Salon Fundamentals* textbook. Check "got it" for all correct answers and "not yet" for all incorrect responses. Using the "Know Chart," record all of your correct responses in the "I Know" column. After correcting incorrect answers, record all of your corrected responses in the "I Need to Study" column. That way you know exactly what to review before continuing in this study guide.

1. Anything that occupies space is called _____.

2. List the five elements that form the structure of hair. _____ _____ _____ _____ _____

3. Hair is a form of protein called _____.

4. Hair is a _____ because it has definite weight, volume and shape.

5. TRUE   FALSE   As a cosmetologist, many of the chemical services you perform, primarily perming and relaxing, directly affect the disulfide bond by either breaking the bond or reforming it into a new shape.

6. List the three major chemical services a cosmetologist performs on hair. _____ _____ _____.

7. TRUE   FALSE   Permanent waves using thioglycolic acid have a higher pH value than those using glycerylmonothioglycolate.

8. TRUE   FALSE   It is safe to use a sodium hydroxide relaxer on hair that has already been relaxed with a thioglycolate relaxer.

9. List the five general categories of hair coloring products. _____ _____ _____ _____ _____.

10. Hair colors using an oxidation system that starts out with colorless molecules are referred to as _____.

132   UNIT 1 THEORY ESSENTIALS

CHEMISTRY

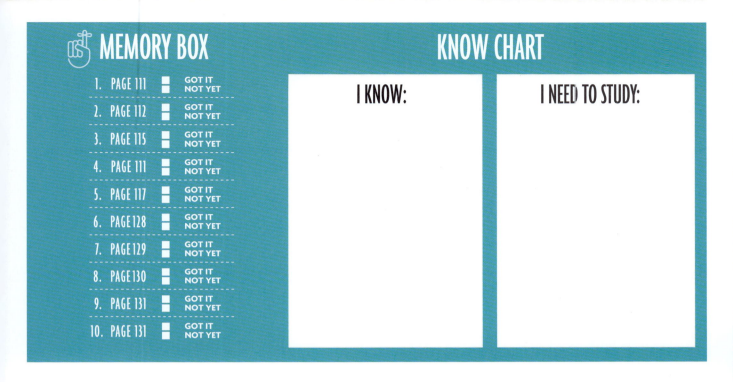

MEMORY BOX

1. PAGE 111 — GOT IT / NOT YET
2. PAGE 112 — GOT IT / NOT YET
3. PAGE 115 — GOT IT / NOT YET
4. PAGE 111 — GOT IT / NOT YET
5. PAGE 117 — GOT IT / NOT YET
6. PAGE 128 — GOT IT / NOT YET
7. PAGE 129 — GOT IT / NOT YET
8. PAGE 130 — GOT IT / NOT YET
9. PAGE 131 — GOT IT / NOT YET
10. PAGE 131 — GOT IT / NOT YET

KNOW CHART

I KNOW:

I NEED TO STUDY:

SHOW YOU KNOW...

You have just developed a new conditioner to be used for all hair types. The major marketing point this product has is that it will add body to the hair. List below a name for your product, a sample list of ingredients that might be found in your product, directions for use of your product and an advertising phrase that might be used to help "sell" your product. Be sure to include any safety precautions for the user. Be creative!

Product Name:

List of Ingredients:

Directions:

Advertising Phrase:

SALON FUNDAMENTALS COSMETOLOGY   133

CHAPTER 5

KNOWLEDGE GRID

Start at the top of the Knowledge Grid and work your way down, answering each question to check your understanding of *Chapter 5, Chemistry*. The questions found here will help you deepen your understanding, build self-confidence and increase your awareness of different ways of thinking about a subject.

KNOW	IDENTIFY THE FIVE ELEMENTS FOUND IN HAIR.
COMPREHEND	WHY IS THE pH SCALE IMPORTANT TO A COSMETOLOGIST
APPLY	COMPARE THE FUNCTION OF A HYDROPHILIC MOLECULE TO A LIPOPHILIC MOLECULE.
ANALYZE	CLARIFY THE RESPONSIBILITY OF AMMONIUM HYDROXIDE WITHIN AN ALKALINE WAVE.
SYNTHESIZE	DIFFERENTIATE BETWEEN THE PROCESS INVOLVED WHEN CHEMICALLY RELAXING THE HAIR WITH EITHER A SODIUM HYDROXIDE RELAXER OR A THIOGLYCOLATE RELAXER.
EVALUATE	DEFEND HOW OXIDATIVE COLORS ARE ABLE TO CAUSE A CHEMICAL CHANGE IN THE HAIR.

BRAIN BUILDER

Questions help us think. Write a challenging question about four of the important words or phrases below and be prepared to answer it. (The following stems generate the most throught-provoking questions: Why does? Why are? What if? How would? Try them!) Then try your questions out on your friends. How well can they answer them?

- Matter
- Chemical Change
- Amino Acids
- Chemical Bonds
- pH Scale
- Solutions
- Porosity

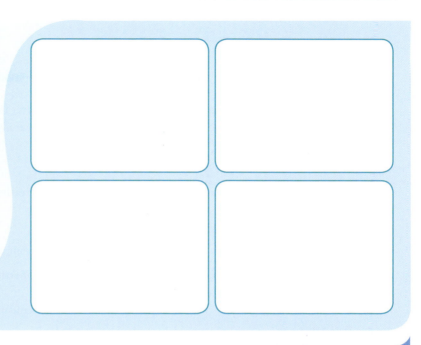

PUTTING YOUR HEADS TOGETHER

With a partner or in a small group, quiz each other using the words below. Make notes for future study.

CHEMISTRY	ELEMENTS	OXYGEN
PROTEIN	MATTER	ATOMS
SULFUR	KERATIN	LIQUID
MOLECULES	NUCLEUS	HAIR
SOLID	HYDROGEN	PROTON
PEPTIDE BOND	GAS	CARBON
ELECTRON	POLYPEPTIDE	PHYSICAL CHANGE
NITROGEN	AMINO ACID	CHEMICAL CHANGE
SIDE BOND	BONDS	POSITIVE ION
SHELL ORBIT	UNSTABLE ATOM	ATOMIC NUMBER
MIXTURE	NEGATIVE ION	BASE pH
NITRAZINE PAPER	ACID	ALKALINE

1 2 3 4 5 6 7

CHAPTER 5

BRAIN CONDITIONER
MULTIPLE CHOICE. CIRCLE THE CORRECT ANSWER.

1. The scientific study of matter and the physical changes in matter is called:
   a. chemistry   b. physics   c. anatomy   d. physiology

2. How many different forms of matter are there?
   a. 2   b. 3   c. 4   d. 7

3. Matter with definite weight, volume and shape, such as your leather shoes, is which form of matter?
   a. solid   b. liquid   c. gas   d. inorganic

4. Melting an ice cube would be an example of a(n):
   a. chemical change   b. physical change   c. chemical reaction   d. organic change

5. A change in a substance that creates a new substance with properties or characteristics different from the original substance is a(n):
   a. chemical change   b. physical change   c. elemental change   d. anatomical change

6. What form of matter is hair?
   a. solid   b. liquid   c. inorganic   d. gas

7. Which of the following activities is NOT an example of a physical change?
   a. rusting of a nail   b. performing a haircut   c. shattering a piece of glass   d. performing a thermal style

8. All matter that is living or once was living contains carbon and deals with:
   a. organic chemistry   b. physics   c. anatomy   d. inorganic chemistry

9. Everything that is alive or was once alive contains:
   a. oxygen   b. hydrogen   c. nitrogen   d. carbon

10. The study of minerals would involve:
    a. organic chemistry   b. inorganic chemistry   c. living matter   d. chemical bonds

11. The smallest complete unit of an element is a(n):
    a. atom   b. proton   c. electron   d. neutron

12. Within an atom, protons and neutrons are found in the:
    a. orbit   b. shell   c. nucleus   d. protoplasm

13. The atomic number of an atom indicates the number of what in the nucleus:
    a. electrons   b. protons plus neutrons   c. neutrons plus electrons   d. protons

14. The shell of an atom consists of:
    a. neutrons   b. protons   c. electrons   d. protons and neutrons

15. The molecule formed when different elements are joined together chemically is called a:
    a. mixture   b. compound   c. solid   d. liquid

16. Carbon, nitrogen, oxygen and hydrogen are the basis of:
    a. amino acids   b. solutions   c. mixtures   d. end bonds

17. Amino acids join together in chains to become:
    a. compounds   b. solutions   c. chemicals   d. proteins

18. Hair is an example of a(n):
    a. element   b. form of protein   c. mixture   d. solution

136 UNIT 1 THEORY ESSENTIALS

CHEMISTRY

19. **Hair is primarily composed of:**
    a. keratin   b. trace minerals   c. protons   d. electrons

20. **The backbone of all protein molecules is the:**
    a. side bond   b. hydrogen bond   c. peptide bond   d. amino acid

21. **What types of bonds are individually very weak?**
    a. hydrogen bonds   b. side bonds   c. disulfide bonds   d. peptide bonds

22. **The most important side bond a cosmetologist is concerned with is the:**
    a. hydrogen bond   b. van der Waals forces   c. salt bond   d. disulfide bond

23. **An example of a chemical change is:**
    a. shampooing hair   b. styling the hair on rollers   c. perming   d. using a blow dryer

24. **The pH measurement scale indicates whether a substance is:**
    a. a liquid, solid or gas   b. organic or inorganic
    c. hard or soft   d. acidic, neutral or alkaline

25. **Substances of acidic or alkaline nature dissolve in water and/or contain:**
    a. water   b. hydrogen   c. carbon   d. salt

26. **A substance with a pH of 6 would be:**
    a. neutral   b. acidic   c. alkaline   d. salty

27. **A pH of 5 is how many more times acidic than a pH of 6:**
    a. 1.5   b. 10   c. 100   d. 1,000

28. **The pH of skin, hair and scalp is in which of the following ranges?**
    a. 4.5 to 5.5   b. 6.5 to 7.5   c. 8.5 to 10.5   d. 11.0 to 12.0

29. **All of the following statements regarding pH are true EXCEPT:**
    a. pH measurement scale ranges from 0 to 14
    b. a solution is acidic if it has more negative hydroxide ions
    c. solutions with equal hydrogen and hydroxide ions are neutral
    d. pH is a unit of measurement that indicates whether a substance is acidic, neutral or alkaline

30. **Distilled water with a pH of 7 is:**
    a. salt   b. alkali   c. acid   d. neutral

31. **Most shampoos and conditioners are acid-balanced to what range on the pH scale?**
    a. 2.5 to 3.5   b. 4.5 to 5.5   c. 6.5 to 7.5   d. 7

32. **What defines cosmetics as articles intended to be rubbed, poured, sprinkled, or otherwise applied to the human body or any part thereof for cleansing, beautifying, promoting attractiveness or altering the appearance?**
    a. The Federal Food, Drug and Cosmetic Act of 1938   b. OSHA
    c. The EPA   d. The USDA

33. **How many general classifications are assigned to categorize cosmetics used in the cosmetology industry?**
    a. 3   b. 4   c. 5   d. 6

34. **A mixture of two or more kinds of molecules, evenly dispersed would be a(n):**
    a. solution   b. suspension   c. emulsion   d. ointment

35. **Water is considered to be a universal solvent because it is:**
    a. not capable of dissolving more substances than any other solvent
    b. capable of dissolving more substances than any other solvent
    c. a dilute solution
    d. a concentrated solution

CHAPTER 5

36. What substance is formed when two or more nonmixable substances are united with the help of a binder?
    a. solutions b. powders c. ointments d. emulsions

37. Mixtures of organic substances and a medicinal agent are:
    a. solutions b. emulsions c. ointments d. suspensions

38. Which type of hair usually needs to be shampooed more often?
    a. oily b. dry c. normal d. blond

39. A surfactant is used to:
    a. change hair color b. condition hair c. add oil to hair d. remove oil from hair

40. Another name for the oil-loving part of a surfactant is:
    a. lipophilic b. hydrophilic c. peroxide d. hydroxide

41. Which of the following statements about surfactants is NOT true?
    a. contains a lipophilic part b. contains a hydrophilic part
    c. used to remove oil from the hair d. prevents shampoo from lathering

42. Which type of shampoo contains low alkaline content and a low concentration of surface acting agents and generally does not correct any special condition?
    a. plain b. all-purpose c. clarifying d. medicated

43. Which of the following shampoos would NOT be used for chemically treated or damaged hair?
    a. plain b. non-stripping c. all-purpose d. acid-balanced

44. Shampoos that often have a higher alkalinity in order to be able to remove residue, such as product build-up or dirt, are:
    a. clarifying b. powder dry c. thinning hair d. conditioning

45. A shampoo that contains orris root powder to absorb soil and oil is classified as a(n):
    a. color shampoo b. powder dry shampoo c. anti-dandruff shampoo d. liquid dry shampoo

46. The ability of hair to stretch and then return to its natural shape without breaking is referred to as:
    a. porosity b. elasticity c. manageability d. luster

47. Acid rinses help:
    a. open the cuticle b. close the cuticle c. add softness d. control dandruff

48. What types of conditioners contain hydrolyzed animal proteins and are recommended for dry, brittle hair that has been mechanically or chemically damaged?
    a. moisturizing b. normalizing c. customized d. body-building

49. What type of conditioners coat the hair shaft and restore moisture and oils, but do not penetrate into the cortex or replace keratin in the shaft?
    a. instant b. moisturizing c. body-building d. normalizing

50. Using a conditioner would help achieve all of the following results EXCEPT:
    a. fortify damaged areas b. increase new hair growth
    c. alter the way the hair behaves d. protect against further damage

51. The purpose of a waving lotion is to:
    a. break disulfide bonds b. break salt bonds
    c. restore salt bonds d. restore disulfide bonds

52. The purpose of a neutralizer is to:
    a. break disulfide bonds b. break salt bonds c. restore salt bonds d. restore disulfide bonds

53. Which of the following is an appropriate description of alkaline waves?
    a. processed with heat
    b. processed without heat
    c. pH of 6.9 to 7.2
    d. contains glyceryl monothioglycolate

54. The main ingredient found in most neutralizers is either:
    a. hydrogen peroxide, sodium perborate or sodium bromate
    b. hydrogen sulfide, thioglycolic acid or ammonium hydroxide
    c. quats, disulfides or sodium hydroxide
    d. mineral water, wheat germ or dimethicones

55. Sodium hydroxide and thioglycolate relaxers:
    a. should be used together
    b. are not compatible
    c. have the same pH
    d. are physical processes

56. What is another name for temporary colors?
    a. developers
    b. certified
    c. peroxide
    d. an oxidative system

57. What type of color is most frequently used in permanent hair color?
    a. aniline derivative
    b. certified
    c. vegetable dye
    d. progressive

58. What product is usually used for lightening procedures such as highlighting and weaving?
    a. oil lighteners
    b. cream lighteners
    c. on-the-scalp lighteners
    d. powder bleaches

59. The most common oxidizing agent used in hair coloring and in hair lightening is:
    a. water
    b. hydrogen peroxide
    c. henna
    d. all of the above

60. Which item is incompatible with other chemical procedures such as perms and oxidative hair coloring?
    a. metallic dyes
    b. temporary colors
    c. semi-permanent colors
    d. cream lighteners

FINAL REVIEW

Check your answers as you did before. Place a check mark next to the page number for any incorrect answer. On the lines on the next page, jot down topics that you still need to review.

☐ 1.	page 111	☐ 8.	page 112	☐ 15.	page 114	☐ 22.	page 117		
☐ 2.	page 111	☐ 9.	page 112	☐ 16.	page 115	☐ 23.	page 117		
☐ 3.	page 111	☐ 10.	page 112	☐ 17.	page 115	☐ 24.	page 118		
☐ 4.	page 111	☐ 11.	page 113	☐ 18.	page 115	☐ 25.	page 118		
☐ 5.	page 111	☐ 12.	page 113	☐ 19.	page 115	☐ 26.	page 118		
☐ 6.	page 111	☐ 13.	page 113	☐ 20.	page 115	☐ 27.	page 118		
☐ 7.	page 111	☐ 14.	page 113	☐ 21.	page 116	☐ 28.	page 118		

CHAPTER 5

FINAL REVIEW *continued*

☐ 29.	page 118	☐ 37.	page 121	☐ 45.	page 124	☐ 53.	page 129
☐ 30.	page 119	☐ 38.	page 122	☐ 46.	page 125	☐ 54.	page 129
☐ 31.	page 119	☐ 39.	page 122	☐ 47.	page 126	☐ 55.	page 130
☐ 32.	page 120	☐ 40.	page 122	☐ 48.	page 127	☐ 56.	page 131
☐ 33.	page 120	☐ 41.	page 122	☐ 49.	page 127	☐ 57.	page 132
☐ 34.	page 120	☐ 42.	page 123	☐ 50.	page 127	☐ 58.	page 133
☐ 35.	page 120	☐ 43.	page 123	☐ 51.	page 128	☐ 59.	page 133
☐ 36.	page 121	☐ 44.	page 124	☐ 52.	page 129	☐ 60.	page 134

NOTES TO MYSELF

Experts tell us that it is important to summarize your feelings and reactions about what you are learning. Note especially things that surprised you, things you found difficult to learn, suggestions and ideas you received from friends that helped make learning this chapter easier and more enjoyable.

My reflections about Chemistry:

LESSONS LEARNED

- The bonding of protein chains to other protein chains makes human hair.
- The pH scale indicates whether a substance is acidic, neutral or alkaline to assist professionals in keeping the hair, skin and scalp in the best condition possible.
- Knowledge of the six classifications of cosmetics helps professionals understand product labels and usage directions.

CHEMISTRY

THINGS TO DO

THINGS TO DO

THINGS TO DO

CHAPTER 6

CHAPTER 6
SALON BUSINESS

VALUE

The ability to select the right salon will ensure financial rewards and personal and professional opportunity.

MAIN IDEA

The areas in which you choose to develop your expertise will shape your career future. Choice + Hard Work = **Success**

PLAN

6.1 **THE BEAUTY INDUSTRY**
What You Need to Know
Your Professional Goals

6.2 **JOB SEARCH**
Resumés
Job Interviews
Evaluating the Salon

6.3 **PROFESSIONAL RELATIONSHIPS**
Networking
Building a Clientele
The Stylist-Client Relationship
The Stylist-Staff Relationship
Performance Review

6.4 **SALON OWNERSHIP**
Self-Appraisal
Types of Salon Ownership
Requirements of a Salon
Getting the Right Advice
Space Requirements and Floor Plans
Borrowing Money
Rental Agreements
Types of Insurance
Taxes
Expenses and Income
Salon Philosophy, Policies and Procedures
Salon Operation

6.5 **SALON RETAILING**
Selling
Professional Products
Closing the Sale
Buyer Types
Follow Up
Effective Displays

SALON BUSINESS

smartNOTES

6.1 THE BEAUTY INDUSTRY — pages 141-142

Personal Profile

I enjoy learning about (personal interests):

I like (working conditions):

Greek Proverb "Know Thyself"

I hope to become (career goals):

I plan to achieve my goals (career path):

First:

Then:

Finally:

CHAPTER 6

smartNOTES

6.2 JOB SEARCH   pages 142-144

Strategies You Would Use

1.

2.

3.

4.

Resumés

Components

Resumé

Cover Letter

Dear _____,

I am writing this letter to introduce myself and describe my personal and professional aspirations. It is my intention to interview for a position at

Salon Name _____.

Present Work Status My name is _____ and I am presently _____
_____.

smartNOTES

6.2 JOB SEARCH
pages 143-144

Formal School Experience
For the past _____ (months) I have studied cosmetology at _____.

Graduation Date
I plan to complete my schooling and licensure by
_____.

Specialty Skills
In addition to my salon preparation I have also
_____
_____
_____.

Position Applied For
At this point in my career I am especially interested in working on a
_____.

Opportunity
I have selected your salon because _____
_____
_____.

Contact Info
My application and resumé are attached. Please know that I am available for a personal interview at your convenience. Should you require additional information or references please contact me at _____.

I look forward to talking with you soon.

Respectfully,
_____

CHAPTER 6

smartNOTES

6.2 JOB SEARCH   pages 143-146

Application Quick Reference Guide

Complete this guide and use it for application completion

PERSONAL INFORMATION
Name:
Address:
Telephone:

SCHOOL INFORMATION
School Attended:
Graduation Date:
State Board Date Completed:

OTHER SKILLS/SPECIALTIES
Special Training:
Work Experience:
Awards:

CAREER OBJECTIVES

REFERENCES

QUESTIONS YOU CAN ASK
Product Line:
Salon Fee Structure:
Staff Size:
Specialty Services:
Dress Code:
Work Schedule:
Pay:

Illegal Interview Questions

SALON BUSINESS

smartNOTES

6.2 JOB SEARCH   pages 146-150

Evaluating the Salon Consider not only your salary or commission on services or retail, but also the benefits provided.

Benefits Inquiry List
Paid Holidays:
Sick Days:
Insurance Benefits:
Educational Opportunities:
Retirement:

Notes to Yourself

PROS   CONS

6.3 Professional Relationships   pages 148-150

Networking Professional relationships based on open, honest, well-developed communication

Building a Clientele

CHAPTER 6

smartNOTES

6.3 PROFESSIONAL RELATIONSHIPS pages 150-151

The Stylist-Client Relationship

Success Checklist
- [ ] Determine client's needs
- [ ] Describe finished looks
- [ ] Keep changes conservative at first
- [ ] Discuss style maintenance
- [ ] Provide product information
- [ ] Remember to prebook
- [ ] Notify clients of schedule changes well in advance

With a partner, role play your success procedures using the success checklist above.

Self-Assessment

INCLUDED	NEGLECTED

6.4 SALON OWNERSHIP page 153

Ownership Skills Profile

Review the nine ownership skills listed on page 153. Decide on the 4 most important and list them in the order of importance.

Most Important _____

Very Important _____

Somewhat Important _____

Also Important _____

smartNOTES

6.4 SALON OWNERSHIP pages 154-156

Assets

Cash Value Items

Liabilities

Net Worth

Personal Loan Rate

Types of Salon Ownership

- SOLE PROPRIETORSHIP
- PARTNERSHIP
- CORPORATION
- FRANCHISE

Requirements of a Salon

Location

Market Need

Improvement Costs

CHAPTER 6

smartNOTES

6.4 SALON OWNERSHIP   pages 156-158

Getting the Right Advice

SERVICES INCLUDE:

Accountants

Insurance Agents

Lawyer

Distributor Sales Consultant

IRS — Internal Revenue Service
OSHA — Occupational Safety and Health Administration
ADA — Americans with Disabilities Act

Space Requirements and Floor Plans

Floor Plans

L x W = Square Foot

Service Area 120-150

Workstation Area:
Reception:
Receiving:
Dispensary:
Restroom:
Shampoo:
Display:

SALON BUSINESS

smartNOTES

6.4 SALON OWNERSHIP   pages 159-162

Rental Agreements

Lease for 5 or more years to help control costs

FIXED RENT	VARIABLE RENT

Types of Insurance

Required by Law

Malpractice:

Premise:

Product Liability:

Workers' Compensation:

Taxes

Social Security Tax:

Sales Tax:

Income Tax:

Expenses and Income

Profit
Loss
Independent
Contractors

CHAPTER 6

smartNOTES

6.4 SALON OWNERSHIP   pages 163-166

Federal Employer Identification Number

Payment Plan

> Using each one of the payment plans, create a sample pay period, income amount, hours worked, tax deductions and final paycheck example.

Commission

Salary

Salary plus Commission

Pricing

Advertising

Inventory and Product Control

Receptionist Duties

Making Change

SALON BUSINESS

smartNOTES

6.4 SALON OWNERSHIP   pages 166-168

Telephone Techniques

1.
2.
3.
4.
5.
6.

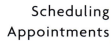

Scheduling Appointments

6.5 SALON RETAILING   pages 173-175

Buyer Types

Ready Buyer

Logical

Emotional

Bargain

Stubborn

Role play each of these buyer types and see if others can guess the type. Explain key attributes.

Buyer Motivation

CHAPTER 6

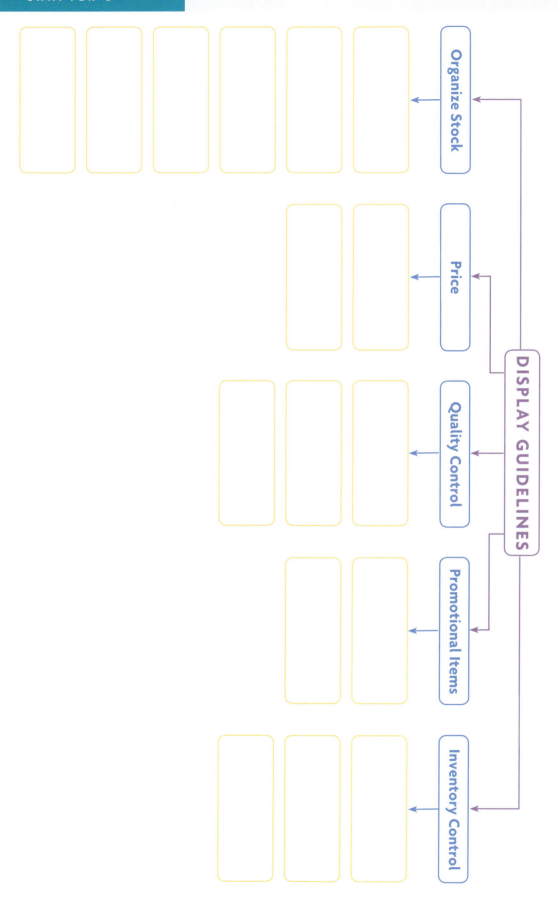

154 UNIT 1 THEORY ESSENTIALS

TALKING POINTS

Your next challenge is to be ready to talk about some of the important ideas in this chapter. Follow the directions listed next to each box. Then practice talking about your ideas with others.

Create a chart of your best personal attributes. BE CREATIVE! Ask someone you trust to discuss your chart with you.

Make a note card you can use to explain Assets, Liabilities, Net Worth.

Describe in your own way, the 4 types of salon ownership.

THE CHALLENGE

Now it's time to see how well you know your new material. First answer these questions. Then use the Memory Box that follows to check yourself. Look up each answer on the corresponding page in the *Salon Fundamentals* textbook. Check "got it" for all correct answers and "not yet" for all incorrect responses. Using the "Know Chart," record all of your correct responses in the "I Know" column. After correcting incorrect answers, record all of your corrected responses in the "I Need to Study" column. That way you know exactly what to review before continuing in this study guide.

1. A goal identifying what you would like to achieve in the next year is called a _____-_____ _____.

2. TRUE FALSE A good first impression can be obtained at an interview if you are neat and fashionably dressed.

3. TRUE FALSE Since you will be spending much of your time at a salon developing your career, the most important aspect in applying for a job is the size of the salon.

4. The best form of advertising is _____ _____ _____.

5. List the four types of salon ownership.
   _____   _____
   _____   _____

6. TRUE FALSE Owning a salon requires expertise in all areas of a salon.

7. Who is responsible for the salon's compliance with all local, state and federal rules, regulations and laws?
   _____ _____

8. Successful selling could be best defined as the art of _____ _____.

9. Statistics show that 45% to 65% of all purchases involve some form of _____ buying.

10. TRUE FALSE All clients share similar motivations for buying which include need, desire to look good, profit or gain, and impulse.

1 2 3 4 5 6 7

CHAPTER 6

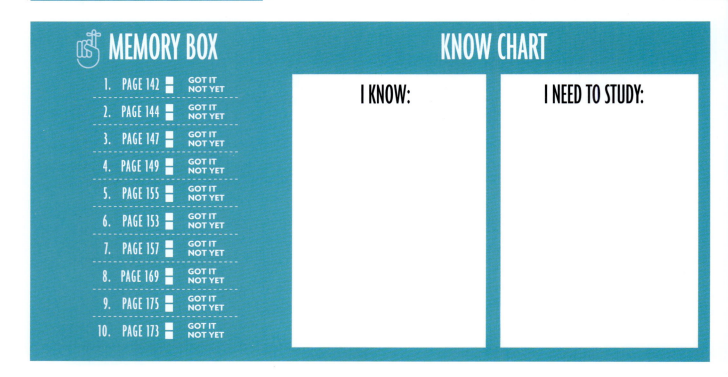

SHOW YOU KNOW...

With the thought in mind of the salon you would like to work for, design a promotional contest that could be offered in the salon that would encourage retail sales. Be creative and innovative. Think of an idea that will gain the attention of the clients and still be exciting for the stylists. Your theme (idea) might include a seasonal or community event or focus on wellness or personal development. Include incentives, goals, time frames, motivators (spirit builders or "rah rah" rallies) or decorating ideas you have that will support this promotional contest.

Contest Theme (Name):

Promotion:

Goals:

Time Frames:

Motivators:

Decorating:

KNOWLEDGE GRID

Start at the top of the Knowledge Grid and work your way down, answering each question to check your understanding of *Chapter 6, Salon Business*. The questions found here will help you deepen your understanding, build self-confidence and increase your awareness of different ways of thinking about a subject.

KNOW	LIST AT LEAST SIX AREAS LOCATED ON A RESUMÉ.
COMPREHEND	IDENTIFY WHAT IS CONSIDERED TO BE THE MOST EFFECTIVE ADVERTISING FOR BUILDING A CLIENTELE.
APPLY	PLEASE OFFER A BRIEF DESCRIPTION OF EACH OF THE FOUR TYPES OF SALON OWNERSHIP.
ANALYZE	JUSTIFY THE IMPORTANCE OF MALPRACTICE INSURANCE FOR A SALON OWNER.
SYNTHESIZE	SUSAN IS PAID A 15% COMMISSION ON RETAIL PRODUCTS SHE SELLS TO HER CLIENTS. THIS WEEK SUSAN SOLD $120 IN RETAIL TO HER CLIENTS. WHAT WOULD SUSAN'S COMMISSION BE THIS WEEK, PRIOR TO ANY DEDUCTIONS?
EVALUATE	OFFER YOUR OPINION ON WHAT THE BENEFITS TO A CLIENT MIGHT BE FOR A PRODUCT THAT FEATURES A SMALL CONTAINER, PROTEIN AS A PRIMARY INGREDIENT AND A CONCENTRATED FORMULA THAT REQUIRES ONLY A SMALL AMOUNT FOR PRODUCT USAGE.

CHAPTER 6

PUTTING YOUR HEADS TOGETHER

FIRST... With a partner review this chapter and jot down notes for an essay titled "Why the Cosmetology Industry Will Be Better Because I am a Part of It."

THEN... Create a short outline or thinking map of your ideas.

FINALLY... Write your essay in the space provided on the following pages.

NOTES:

THINKING MAP

Now that you have filled in your SmartNotes for "Professional Development," create a Thinking Map to help yourself make sense of how your SmartNotes fit together. Use some or all of the words in the Jump Start Box as well as your own words and pictures to make a visual that will help you connect the important ideas in this chapter to each other. Be creative!

SALON BUSINESS

158 UNIT 1 THEORY ESSENTIALS

SALON BUSINESS

ESSAY WIZARD

Writing doesn't have to be a chore.
Here's how to make it easy!

PURPOSE

FIRST

Choose a purpose...
to describe, explain,
entertain, refute

INTRODUCTION

THEN

Write what you
are going to
write about...

TEXT

NEXT

WRITE IT!

Continue on next page

CONNECTION
but
altogether
nevertheless
despite
however
except

EMPHASIS
moreover
in addition
also
furthermore

EXPLANATION
because
since
hence
for

CONCLUSION
therefore
thus
so
as a result

1 2 3 4 **5** 6 7

SALON FUNDAMENTALS COSMETOLOGY   159

CHAPTER 6

TEXT

SUMMARY

LAST

Summarize and give your conclusions.

BRAIN CONDITIONER
MULTIPLE CHOICE. CIRCLE THE CORRECT ANSWER.

1. Which of these descriptions is NOT a guideline to be used when creating a resumé?
   a. list awards and special recognition
   b. show prior employment information
   c. provide at least eight pages of information
   d. write the resumé in a brief and concise manner

2. During a job interview it is very important to:
   a. stay calm and be yourself
   b. tell a lot of stories
   c. stretch the truth if necessary
   d. tell the interviewer whatever you think he or she wants to hear

3. Which of the following abilities is NOT necessary for a salon owner?
   a. ability to recognize fashion trends
   b. ability to exert self-control
   c. ability to communicate with the public
   d. ability in all practical skills

4. A list of all the property you own is called your:
   a. assets
   b. net profit
   c. net worth
   d. liabilities

5. A list of all the money owed to others is called:
   a. net worth
   b. total liabilities
   c. assets
   d. net assets

6. Total assets minus total liabilities is called:
   a. borrowing capacity
   b. net worth
   c. gross assets
   d. gross worth

7. On a financial statement, the $3,000 balance owed on a car would be listed as:
   a. an asset
   b. a net worth
   c. a liability
   d. a bad business risk

8. On a financial statement, the $6,000 a car is actually worth is listed as:
   a. a liability
   b. a net worth
   c. an asset
   d. a bad investment

9. A bank will generally lend money based on:
   a. total liabilities
   b. personal appearance
   c. total assets
   d. net worth

10. A business owned by one person who is in complete control of the business is a:
    a. partnership
    b. sole proprietorship
    c. corporation
    d. franchise

11. A business in which two or more persons share management responsibilities is a:
    a. partnership
    b. sole proprietorship
    c. corporation
    d. franchise

12. A form of operation in which a fee is paid to a parent corporation is a:
    a. partnership
    b. corporation
    c. franchise
    d. entity

13. Which of the following businesses is owned by the shareholders and is formed under legal guidelines?
    a. corporation
    b. franchise
    c. partnership
    d. proprietorship

14. Location is the most important factor in:
    a. choosing a distributor
    b. choosing a lawyer
    c. choosing an accountant
    d. opening a salon

15. All of the following items should be important requirements in the process of salon planning EXCEPT:
    a. location
    b. market need
    c. cost of necessary improvements
    d. the distance from the Social Security office

16. Which of the following professionals can offer advice on the operating capital needed to open a salon and pay the expenses of your business?
    a. accountant
    b. lawyer
    c. distributor sales consultant
    d. banker

CHAPTER 6

17. **An efficient working space for each stylist is:**
    a. 50 to 75 square feet b. 120 to 150 square feet c. 200 to 300 square feet d. over 300 square feet

18. **A lawyer can help ensure that a salon owner is in compliance with all of the following areas EXCEPT:**
    a. tax responsibilities
    c. local, state and federal codes
    b. signing rental agreements
    d. inventory needs

19. **Which of the following professionals is most likely able to assist a salon owner with an inventory-saving idea?**
    a. lawyer
    c. distributor sales consultant
    b. insurance agent
    d. accountant

20. **It would be unwise to install a salon without a rental agreement of less than:**
    a. 2 years b. 5 years c. 10 years d. 15 years

21. **What type of rental contract has a set dollar amount plus a percentage of the monthly income paid?**
    a. variable b. fixed c. monthly d. yearly

22. **In order to protect the employee, states require that salons:**
    a. carry worker's compensation insurance
    c. retain an accountant
    b. have a lawyer
    d. have a sales consultant

23. **What type of tax dictates that for every dollar an employee pays, the salon owner needs to also pay the same amount to the government?**
    a. federal income
    c. local income
    b. state income
    d. Social Security or (Canadian Pension Tax)

24. **Before collecting sales taxes on products or services sold, a salon owner must:**
    a. make money
    c. pay state income taxes
    b. apply for a state sales tax permit
    d. apply for a federal sales tax permit

25. **On the average, the largest expense in operating a salon would be:**
    a. salaries or commissions b. rent c. supplies d. utilities

26. **Which of the following items is/are required by law?**
    a. parking facilities b. recordkeeping c. variable rent d. retailing salon products

27. **It is wise to keep all records of daily sales and service for how long?**
    a. 2 to 4 years b. 5 to 7 years c. 10 to 12 years d. 14 to 16 years

28. **What percentage of salon expenses represents compensation for the employer and employees?**
    a. 10 b. 25 c. 50 d. 75

29. **What form of employee compensation guarantees a certain amount of money on a regular basis and allows additional payment based on the number of clients the cosmetologist brings into the salon?**
    a. salary b. salary plus commission c. commission d. bonus

30. **One of the best forms of advertising for the stylist is:**
    a. word-of-mouth b. billboards c. pamphlets d. television

31. **For each dollar a stylist brings into the salon for services, it is an industry-recommended goal for the stylist to bring in what additional amount in sales of home care products?**
    a. $1.00 b. $2.00 c. $3.00 d. $4.00

32. **What amount of commission will a salon owner usually pay an employee for the retail sales of home care products?**
    a. 2% to 5% b. 8% to 15% c. 20% to 25% d. 50%

33. In many cases, the first person to greet a client is the:
    a. stylist   b. manager   c. receptionist   d. owner

34. When counting back change to a client it is recommended to:
    a. not count out loud   b. use as many bills as possible
    c. count back from smaller denomination to larger   d. count back from larger denomination to smaller

35. The art of professional recommendation could best be described as:
    a. successful selling   b. making appointments   c. proper phone procedures   d. stylist-staff relations

36. To become an asset to any salon staff, the stylist should peform all of the following actions EXCEPT:
    a. listen to clients   b. offer sound advice
    c. make negative comments   d. communicate professionally

37. Which buyer type is open-minded and will take a chance on a new product without hesitation?
    a. ready   b. logical   c. emotional   d. bargain

38. Which buyer type is more interested in price than quality?
    a. logical   b. bargain   c. stubborn   d. emotional

39. Which buyer type makes purchases more on personal reasons than on facts?
    a. logical   b. bargain   c. emotional   d. stubborn

40. Impulse buying accounts for about what percent of all purchases?
    a. 10% to 20%   b. 45% to 65%   c. 70% to 80%   d. 85% to 95%

FINAL REVIEW

Check your answers as you did before. Place a check mark next to the page number for any incorrect answer. On the lines on the next page, jot down topics that you still need to review.

☐ 1. page 143	☐ 9. page 154	☐ 17. page 157	☐ 25. page 161
☐ 2. page 144	☐ 10. page 155	☐ 18. page 157	☐ 26. page 161
☐ 3. page 153	☐ 11. page 155	☐ 19. page 157	☐ 27. page 161
☐ 4. page 154	☐ 12. page 155	☐ 20. page 159	☐ 28. page 161
☐ 5. page 154	☐ 13. page 155	☐ 21. page 159	☐ 29. page 155
☐ 6. page 154	☐ 14. page 156	☐ 22. page 160	☐ 30. page 154
☐ 7. page 154	☐ 15. page 156	☐ 23. page 160	☐ 31. page 165
☐ 8. page 154	☐ 16. page 156	☐ 24. page 160	☐ 32. page 165

CHAPTER 6

FINAL REVIEW *continued*

- [ ] 33. page 165
- [ ] 34. page 166
- [ ] 35. page 169
- [ ] 36. page 170
- [ ] 37. page 173
- [ ] 38. page 173
- [ ] 39. page 173
- [ ] 40. page 175

NOTES TO MYSELF

Experts tell us that it is important to summarize your feelings and reactions about what you are learning. Note especially things that surprised you, things you found difficult to learn, suggestions and ideas you received from friends that helped make learning this chapter easier and more enjoyable.

My reflections about Salon Business:

LESSONS LEARNED

- *Establishing short and long-range goals and following a plan to achieve those goals support the professional in reaching clear-cut levels of achievement.*
- *Evaluating the advantages and disadvantages of working at a particular salon is a prerequisite to accepting a job offer.*
- *The ability to develop meaningful relationships with the general public and professionals at all levels of the industry is a necessity for career success.*
- *Knowing the principles of salon ownership operations allows a professional to work productively with employers or to eventually own a salon.*
- *Recommending products to clients and teaching them how to use those products to achieve their desired image will help grow a loyal, appreciative client base.*

CHAPTER 7
TRICHOLOGY

VALUE

Your shampoo and massage ability increases as you learn more about hair theory and care.

MAIN IDEA

Knowledge of the study of hair + care and skill during shampoo and massage = **quality salon services**

PLAN

7.1 HAIR THEORY
Hair Bulb Formation
Hair Growth
Hair Structure and Behavior
Natural Hair Color

7.2 HAIR CARE
Hair Evaluation
Common Hair Conditions
Common Scalp Conditions
Hair Loss

7.3 DRAPING, SHAMPOOING AND SCALP MASSAGE
Draping Theory
Shampooing and Conditioning Theory
Scalp Massage Theory
Draping, Shampooing and Scalp Massage Essentials
Infection Control and Safety
Basic Draping, Shampooing and Conditioning
Basic Scalp Massage

CHAPTER 7

smartNOTES

7.1 HAIR THEORY   pages 181-183

Trichology

Hair Bulb Formation

Two primary parts of the hair

HAIR ROOT	HAIR FIBER

Three Shapes of Follicles
-
-
-

Hair Growth

Papilla

Three Major Layers

Medulla —
Cortex —
Cuticle —

Keratinization

Three Stages of Growth

STAGE	COMMON NAME	CHARACTERISTIC

First
Then
Finally

166 UNIT 2 HAIR SERVICES   1 2 3 4 5 6 7

TRICHOLOGY

smartNOTES

7.1 HAIR THEORY   pages 184-186

Hair Structure and Behavior

Three Factors That Affect Behavior
-
-
-

Cuticle/Cortex Ratio

Natural Hair Color

1.
2.
3.

Eumelanin
Brown/Black

Pheomelanin
Red/Yellow

Albinism

7.2 HAIR CARE   pages 187-188

Hair Evaluation

	TYPES	CHARACTERISTICS	NOTES
Texture	1. Fine	feel of _____	Degree of _____
	2. Medium	feel of _____	or _____ of hair fiber
	3. Coarse	feel of _____	
Density	1. Thick (heavy)	_____ active follicles	Judged by number of active _____ per square inch
	2. Thin (light)	_____ active follicles	
	3. Medium	_____ active follicles	
Porosity	1. Resistant	Absorbs _____ moisture	Amount of _____, liquids or chemicals able to be absorbed
	2. Average	Normal ability to _____ moisture	
	3. Extreme	Damaged	
	4. Uneven	_____ of two or more porosities	
Elasticity	1. Normal	Lively, springs back; stretches about _____ of its length	Ability of hair to _____ and _____ to original shape without _____
	2. Wet	Stretches 40% to ____% of its length	

Test for Structural Strength
1. Remove strand of hair and hold between thumb and forefinger; ribbon
2. Pull hair taut for ____ seconds; release
3. Good condition = returns to curl pattern
4. Weak condition = returns to ____% or less of curl pattern

SALON FUNDAMENTALS COSMETOLOGY   167

CHAPTER 7

COMMON HAIR CONDITIONS

Fill in the missing elements for the following charts.

CONDITIONS	ALSO KNOWN AS	CAUSE/TREATMENT
Broken Hair		
Split Ends		
Matting		
Nodules		
Canities		
Ringed Hair		
Hypertrichosis		
Monilethrix		

COMMON SCALP CONDITIONS

DISORDER OR DISEASE	MEDICAL TERM	DESCRIPTION	TREATMENT
Psoriasis			
Dandruff			
Dry Dandruff			
Grease or Waxy Dandruff			

The leading cause of dandruff is a naturally occurring microscopic fungus called Malassezia. The _____ feeds on the scalp's natural oils and creates by-products that cause irritation on the scalp. The body reacts to the irritation by accelerating the amount and rate of _____ of dead skin cells.

EXTERNAL PARASITES

Be advised that the conditions listed on the chart below are contagious. Refer clients with these conditions to a physician before performing any salon services.

Ringworm

Ringworm of the scalp

Honeycomb Ringworm

Itch Mite

Head Lice

smartNOTES

7.2 HAIR CARE   pages 191-196

Hair Loss

Normal Hair Loss

Androgenetic Hair Loss

Androgenetic Alopecia

Males

Females

Other Types of Hair Loss

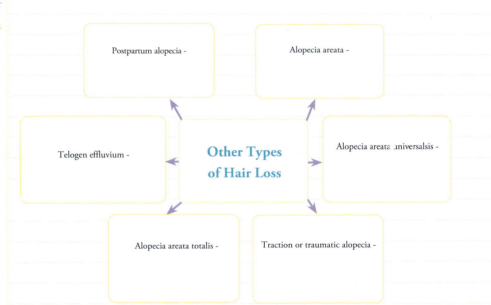

- Postpartum alopecia -
- Alopecia areata -
- Telogen effluvium -
- Other Types of Hair Loss
- Alopecia areata universalsis -
- Alopecia areata totalis -
- Traction or traumatic alopecia -

Hair Loss Treatments
1.
2.
3.
4.
5.

CHAPTER 7

smartNOTES

7.3 DRAPING, SHAMPOOING AND SCALP MASSAGE
pages 197-201

Purpose of Shampooing

To cleanse the scalp and hair by removing dirt, oils and _____ build-up

If hair is not cleansed properly an accumulation of oil and dirt can lead to scalp disorders

Draping Theory

Prior to hair care services; to _____ client's skin and clothing

Regulating agencies require shampoo capes used to drape clients be laundered in solution to disinfect

Make sure neck of cape does not come in direct contact with client's skin; use neck strip

Shampooing and Conditioning Theory

Performed before most _____ except before certain color and chemical services

Water

Understanding the pH level of shampoos and conditioners will help make the right selection

Soft

Rain water or chemically treated water generally preferred for shampooing

Hard

Contains minerals, does not allow shampoo to lather freely

Temperature

Monitor water temperature before applying to scalp

Brushing and Combing

- Removes _____
- Stimulates _____ circulation
- Removes dust, dirt and build-up

Scalp Massage Theory

Involves manipulations performed to relax muscles and stimulate scalp

Important Steps
- Establish a soothing or stimulating _____
- Maintain _____ with the client throughout the manipulations
- Carry out manipulations with firm, controlled movements
- Keep fingernails at a moderate _____

smartNOTES

7.3 DRAPING, SHAMPOOING AND SCALP MASSAGE
pages 201; 214-215

Five Basic Manipulations of Massage

MOVEMENT	EFFECT
Effleurage	
Petrissage	
Tapotement	
Friction	
Vibration	

AROMATHERAPY

Directions: Using the words in the Jump Start Box, fill in the blanks for the conditions in the left-hand column.

Normal Hair
Oily Hair and Scalp
Dry Hair and Scalp
Oily Dandruff

Alopecia (Hair Loss)

JUMP START BOX

Rosemary	Thyme	Patchouli
Clary Sage	Cedarwood	Chamomile
Lavender	Lemon	Bay
Sandalwood	Ylang Ylang	

CHAPTER 7

TALKING POINTS

Your next challenge is to be ready to talk about some of the important ideas in this chapter. Follow the directions listed next to each box. Then practice talking about your ideas with others.

[   ] Describe the process of hair follicle formation and the stages of hair growth.

[   ] Explain the three layers of hair and their importance to cosmetologists.

[   ] Discuss the eight common hair disorders and their causes.

THE CHALLENGE

Now it's time to see how well you know your new material. First answer these questions. Then use the Memory Box that follows to check yourself. Look up each answer on the corresponding page in the *Salon Fundamentals* textbook. Check "got it" for all correct answers and "not yet" for all incorrect responses. Using the "Know Chart," record all of your correct responses in the "I Know" column. After correcting incorrect answers, record all of your corrected responses in the "I Need to Study" column. That way you know exactly what to review before continuing in this study guide.

1. What are the three major layers of the hair? _____ _____ _____
2. Hair is primarily made of _____.
3. What three factors dictate why everyone's hair is so different, even though all hair is primarily made of the same thing? _____ _____ _____
4. TRUE FALSE The cuticle is the protective layer of the hair shaft and is made up of a harder protein than the cortex.
5. The amount, size, type and distribution of _____ will determine the natural color of hair.
6. Two types of melanin that create the large variety of hair colors are _____ and _____ .
7. During your professional analysis of a client's hair fiber, a number of observations will alert you to possible problems you might encounter as you service the hair. List seven of these observations. _____
   _____ _____ _____
   _____ _____ _____
8. TRUE FALSE A dryer or a curling iron could cause the hair to become brittle and the cortex of the hair could melt.
9. The most common form of hair loss is androgenetic alopecia. What are some of the other types of hair loss?
   _____ _____ _____ _____
10. TRUE FALSE The FDA has ruled that products claiming hair regrowth or hair loss prevention cannot be marketed without prior FDA review and approval.

172 UNIT 2 HAIR SERVICES   1 2 3   6 7

TRICHOLOGY

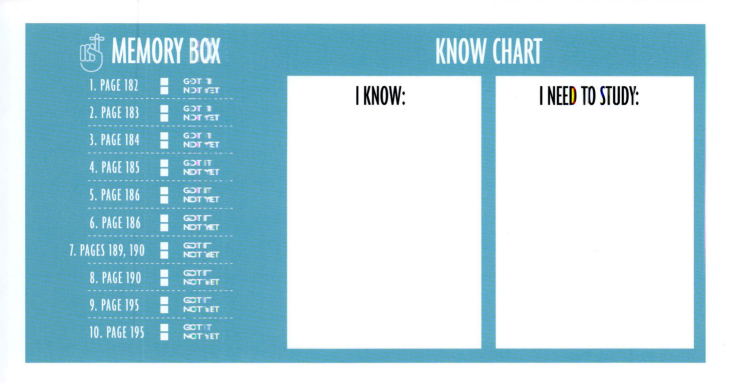

SHOW YOU KNOW...

Pair up with a partner and show you know how to shampoo by performing a shampoo service on each other for evaluation. Shown below is a score sheet to use for each other. Score 1 point for each area successfully completed by your partner. Show you know by earning all 10 points!

1st Partner

____ You were welcomed with a warm greeting and handshake.
____ You were properly draped for the shampoo service.
____ Communication was professional, friendly and pertained to the service.
____ Examination of your scalp and hair was performed prior to the service.
____ Your hair was brushed, and tangles were removed comfortably.
____ Water temperature and pressure were comfortable.
____ The massage manipulations were performed in a comfortable, confident manner.
____ Concern was exhibited to not allow your face or clothing to become wet.
____ Thorough lathering and rinsing procedures were followed.
____ Your hair was adequately towel-dried and detangled following the service.
____ TOTAL POINTS

2nd Partner

____ You were welcomed with a warm greeting and handshake.
____ You were properly draped for the shampoo service.
____ Communication was professional, friendly and pertained to the service.
____ Examination of your scalp and hair was performed prior to the service.
____ Your hair was brushed, and tangles were removed comfortably.
____ Water temperature and pressure were comfortable.
____ The massage manipulations were performed in a comfortable, confident manner.
____ Concern was exhibited to not allow your face or clothing to become wet.
____ Thorough lathering and rinsing procedures were followed.
____ Your hair was adequately towel-dried and detangled following the service.
____ TOTAL POINTS

SALON FUNDAMENTALS COSMETOLOGY

CHAPTER 7

KNOWLEDGE GRID

Start at the top of the Knowledge Grid and work your way down, answering each question to check your understanding of *Chapter 7, Trichology*. The questions found here will help you deepen your understanding, build self-confidence and increase your awareness of different ways of thinking about a subject.

KNOW	LIST THE THREE MAJOR LAYERS OF THE HAIR.	
COMPREHEND	COMPARE THE ANAGEN, CATAGEN AND TELOGEN STAGES OF HAIR GROWTH.	
APPLY	OFFER AN EXAMPLE OF HOW THE HAIR CUTICLE CAN BE DAMAGED.	
ANALYZE	ANALYZE THE IMPORTANCE OF EVALUATING YOUR CLIENT'S HAIR PRIOR TO A SERVICE.	
SYNTHESIZE	SUGGEST A TREATMENT OPTION FOR ANDROGENETIC ALOPECIA.	
EVALUATE	STATE YOUR OPINION ON THE USE OF AROMATHERAPY ON THE SCALP.	

TRICHOLOGY

RUBRIC

This rubric is a self-assessment tool designed to compare your skill to industry standards. Indicate your present level of performance by checking the appropriate box. See overview for instructions.

Wet Hair Service Draping, Shampooing and Conditioning

Industry Standard – to meet entry-level proficiency, industry standards require that you:
- Provide hair-related services in accordance with a client's needs or expectations in a safe environment.

	Level 1	Level 2	Level 3	To Improve, I Need To:	Teacher Assessment
Preparation					
Assemble the essential products, implements/supplies and equipment for the procedure	☐	☐	☐		☐
Procedure					
Wash and sanitize hands	☐	☐	☐		☐
Ask client to remove jewelry and glasses and secure in a safe place	☐	☐	☐		☐
Clip client's hair out of the way (if applicable)	☐	☐	☐		☐
Turn client's collar inward (if applicable)	☐	☐	☐		☐
Place towel lengthwise over client's shoulders, cross ends in front	☐	☐	☐		☐
Position plastic cape over towel, secure and fold towel outward over neckband of cape	☐	☐	☐		☐
Examine the client's hair and scalp	☐	☐	☐		☐
Position cape over chair	☐	☐	☐		☐
Brush the hair	☐	☐	☐		☐
Test the temperature and pressure of the water; wet the hair; apply shampoo	☐	☐	☐		☐
Perform scalp massage manipulations	☐	☐	☐		☐
Rinse thoroughly; repeat shampoo and rinse procedures if necessary	☐	☐	☐		☐
Apply rinse or conditioner, rinse thoroughly	☐	☐	☐		☐
Towel dry client's hair; detangle the hair	☐	☐	☐		☐
Completion					
Clean shampoo service area before continuing with client; ensure there is no water left standing in the shampoo service area	☐	☐	☐		☐
Discuss the products you used on the client and proceed to the next service.	☐	☐	☐		☐

TOTAL = ADDITION OF ALL TEACHER ASSESSMENT BOXES

TOTAL POINTS = ☐

51

PERCENTAGE = STUDENT SCORE / HIGHEST POSSIBLE SCORE _____ %

SALON FUNDAMENTALS COSMETOLOGY 175

CHAPTER 7

RUBRIC

This rubric is a self-assessment tool designed to compare your skill to industry standards. Indicate your present level of performance by checking the appropriate box. See overview for instructions.

Basic Scalp Massage

Industry Standard – to meet entry-level proficiency, industry standards require that you:
- Provide hair-related services in accordance with a client's needs or expectations in a safe environment.

	Level 1	Level 2	Level 3	To Improve, I Need To:	Teacher Assessment
Preparation					
• Assemble the essential products, implements/supplies and equipment for the procedure	☐	☐	☐		☐
Procedure					
• Wash and sanitize hands	☐	☐	☐		☐
• Drape client for a wet hair service	☐	☐	☐		☐
• Detangle hair	☐	☐	☐		☐
• Apply scalp product	☐	☐	☐		☐
• Perform effleurage scalp manipulations	☐	☐	☐		☐
• Perform petrissage scalp manipulations	☐	☐	☐		☐
• Perform effleurage scalp manipulations	☐	☐	☐		☐
• Perform tapotement	☐	☐	☐		☐
• Rotate the scalp	☐	☐	☐		☐
• Conclude scalp massage	☐	☐	☐		☐
• Shampoo and rinse client's hair	☐	☐	☐		☐
• Dry hair or move to next service	☐	☐	☐		☐
Completion					
• Discuss and offer to prebook your client's next visit	☐	☐	☐		☐
• Recommend appropriate retail products to your client	☐	☐	☐		☐
• Clean your work area	☐	☐	☐		☐

TOTAL = ADDITION OF ALL TEACHER ASSESSMENT BOXES   TOTAL POINTS = ☐
                                                              48

PERCENTAGE = STUDENT SCORE / HIGHEST POSSIBLE SCORE   ____ %

BRAIN CONDITIONER
MULTIPLE CHOICE. CIRCLE THE CORRECT ANSWER.

1. The technical name for the study of hair is:
   a. trichology
   b. hairology
   c. biology
   d. cosmetology

2. Which of the following items is alive?
   a. hair fiber
   b. hair bulb
   c. hair strand
   d. keratin

3. The cluster of cells in the epidermis from which the hair follicle forms is called the:
   a. hair fiber
   b. hair strand
   c. primitive hair germ
   d. root sheath

4. The root sheath of hair is typically oval or round in:
   a. tightly curled hair
   b. curly hair
   c. wavy or straight hair
   d. coarse hair

5. What item needs nourishment to grow into a fully developed hair follicle?
   a. primitive hair germ
   b. cortex
   c. root sheath
   d. cuticle

6. Which of the following functions is NOT one of the main purposes of hair?
   a. support
   b. adornment
   c. protection from cold
   d. protection from injury

7. Which item produces oil and sends it up through the hair follicles to the surface of the skin?
   a. papilla
   b. root sheath
   c. sebaceous gland
   d. arrector pili

8. Which section of the hair structure is the area where mitosis takes place?
   a. germinal matrix
   b. root sheath
   c. hair follicle
   d. cuticle

9. The outer covering of the hair fiber is called the:
   a. sebum
   b. medulla
   c. cuticle
   d. cortex

10. What does sebum mix with to form the acid mantle?
    a. perspiration
    b. oil
    c. amino acid
    d. protein

11. What layer of the hair fiber gives hair its pigment and elasticity?
    a. cuticle
    b. cortex
    c. medulla
    d. sebum

12. Which layer of hair may be absent in fine or very fine hair?
    a. cuticle
    b. outer
    c. medulla
    d. cortex

13. The helix or coil shape of what part of the hair follicle gives hair the ability to stretch?
    a. medulla
    b. cortex
    c. cuticle
    d. root sheath

14. Hair falls out during which stage of growth?
    a. active
    b. anagen
    c. catagen
    d. telogen

15. On the average, what stage of hair growth lasts from two to six years?
    a. resting
    b. anagen
    c. catagen
    d. telogen

16. Which of these factors does NOT affect hair growth?
    a. frequent exercise
    b. disease
    c. lack of vitamins
    d. medication

17. Which of these factors does NOT influence the behavior of hair?
    a. heredity
    b. exercise routine
    c. environment
    d. products or appliances used

CHAPTER 7

18. The structural organization of the hair can be affected by all of the following factors EXCEPT:
    a. hair dryers   b. perms   c. shears   d. shampoo

19. How is the protein in the cuticle different than the protein in the cortex?
    a. harder   b. more elastic   c. softer   d. more abundant

20. Which of the following statements describes fine hair?
    a. may be up to 40% cuticle   b. may be more receptive to permanent waves
    c. may not have any cuticle at all   d. may be less than 10% cuticle

21. Which term describes bundles of a pigment protein complex called melanosomes?
    a. amino acids   b. proteins   c. melanocytes   d. keratin

22. Melanin in brown/black hair is called:
    a. pheomelanin   b. eumelanin   c. albinism   d. melanosome

23. The amount and type of melanin produced is determined by:
    a. papilla   b. genes   c. melanosomes   d. the dermal papilla

24. People with lighter-colored hair have melanin in the:
    a. cuticle only   b. cortex only   c. cuticle and cortex   d. medulla only

25. A high concentration of pheomelanin will result in:
    a. red hair   b. black hair   c. brown hair   d. dense hair

26. The degree of coarseness or fineness of the hair fiber is referred to as:
    a. density   b. porosity   c. viscosity   d. texture

27. What condition is determined by the number of active hair follicles per square inch of scalp?
    a. texture   b. density   c. porosity   d. viscosity

28. The ability of the hair to absorb moisture, liquids or chemicals is known as:
    a. texture   b. density   c. capacity   d. porosity

29. The ability of hair to stretch and return to its original shape without breaking is called:
    a. elasticity   b. texture   c. porosity   d. breaking point

30. Which type of porosity describes hair that is able to absorb the least amount of moisture, usually due to the closeness of the cuticle layers?
    a. resistant   b. average   c. extreme   d. uneven

31. Hair damaged due to chemical services or environment is said to have:
    a. extreme porosity   b. resistant porosity   c. uneven porosity   d. average porosity

32. Normal dry hair is capable of being stretched to what fraction of its length?
    a. one-tenth   b. one-fifth   c. one-half   d. three-fourths

33. Wet hair is able to be stretched to what percent of its length?
    a. 10% to 20%   b. 40% to 50%   c. 70% to 80%   d. 100%

34. Split hair ends start as cracks in the:
    a. medulla   b. cuticle   c. cortex   d. DNA

35. Fragilitis crinium is the technical name for:
    a. alopecia   b. split ends   c. ringed hair   d. matting

36. An abraded cuticle can result from all of the following actions EXCEPT:
    a. brushing   b. shampooing
    c. clipping hair back tightly   d. manipulating the hair when wet

37. A term applied to matting of the hair is:
    a. alopecia   b. pilica polonica   c. ringed hair   d. monilethrix
38. This hair condition may be caused by an inherited defect in the hair's keratin protein structure:
    a. pilica polonica   b. alopecia   c. trichorrhexis nodosa   d. trichonodosis
39. Grayness or whiteness of hair is called:
    a. hypertrichosis   b. canities   c. monilethrix   d. androgenetic alopecia
40. An abnormal coverage of hair on areas of the body where normally only lanugo or baby fine hair appears is a condition known as:
    a. hypertrichosis   b. monilethrix   c. trichorrhexis nodosa   d. pilica polonica
41. A condition in which beads or nodes form on the hair shaft is called:
    a. hypertrichosis   b. monilethrix   c. canities   d. nodules
42. A condition in which alternating bands of gray and dark hair exist is called:
    a. ringed hair   b. canities   c. monilethrix   d. hypertrichosis
43. Removal methods used for hypertrichosis range from tweezing to electrolysis, depending on all of the following factors EXCEPT:
    a. client preference   b. location of the hair
    c. cosmetologist's preference   d. amount of hair to be removed
44. The average head contains how many strands of hair per square inch of surface?
    a. 1,000   b. 2,000   c. 3,000   d. over 5,000
45. People with what color of hair, on the average, have the fewest hair strands?
    a. black   b. red   c. blond   d. brown
46. People with what color of hair, on the average, have the most hair strands?
    a. red   b. brown   c. brunette   d. blond
47. The medical term for head lice is:
    a. scabies   b. tinea favosa   c. pediculosis capitis   d. pityriasis steatoides
48. The medical term for a chronic scalp condition with excess flaking, which accumulates on the scalp or falls to the shoulders is a disorder known as:
    a. tinea capitis   b. tinea favosa   c. scabies   d. pityriasis
49. The medical term for greasy or waxy dandruff is:
    a. tinea capitis   b. pityriasis capitis c. pityriasis steatoides   d. tinea favosa
50. What is the term applied to the baby fine hair that is shed shortly after birth?
    a. lanugo   b. vellus   c. alopecia   d. follicle
51. The term used for excessive hair loss is known as:
    a. alopecia   b. abraded hair   c. fragilitis crinium d. trichonodosis
52. The average daily hair loss is:
    a. fewer than 20 strands   b. 40 to 100 strands   c. 250 to 500 strands   d. over 1,000 strands
53. Long, thick, pigmented hair like scalp and eyebrow hair is referred to as:
    a. vellus   b. lanugo   c. body   d. terminal
54. The most common form of hair loss in both men and women is:
    a. androgenetic alopecia   b. exposure to sunlight   c. telogen effluvium   d. exposure to chlorine

CHAPTER 7

55. In androgenetic alopecia, a combination of heredity, hormones and age causes:
    a. the shrinking of scalp follicles
    b. the lengthening of the hair's growing cycle
    c. the anagen phase to become longer
    d. the telogen phase to become shorter

56. Alopecia, or excessive hair loss, may be caused by any one of the following EXCEPT:
    a. fungal infection
    b. bacterial infection
    c. parasitic organism
    d. inflammatory disease of the scalp

57. Hair loss identification systems identify the:
    a. pattern and density of the client's hair
    b. texture of the client's hair
    c. hair color variations of the client's hair
    d. treatment options

58. Hair loss caused by excessive stretching is called:
    a. telogen effluvium
    b. fragilitis crinium
    c. pilica polonica
    d. traction alopecia

59. Products claiming hair regrowth or hair loss prevention cannot be marketed without what agency's review and approval?
    a. OSHA
    b. EPA
    c. USDA
    d. FDA

60. Sudden hair loss in round or irregular patches without the display of an inflamed scalp is referred to as:
    a. postpartum alopecia
    b. alopecia areata
    c. telogen effluvium
    d. traumatic alopecia

61. Which term is a temporary hair loss that occurs only in women?
    a. postpartum alopecia
    b. alopecia areata
    c. telogen effluvium
    d. androgenetic alopecia

62. The premature shedding of hair in the resting phase is:
    a. telogen effluvium
    b. alopecia areata
    c. traumatic alopecia
    d. postpartum alopecia

63. Cleansing the scalp and hair by removing dirt, oils and product build-up is the purpose of:
    a. scalp massage
    b. shampooing
    c. draping
    d. perming

64. What should be done if a client has an infectious disease or disorder of the scalp?
    a. proceed with the service, with caution
    b. refuse the service and refer the client to a physician
    c. use a disinfecting shampoo before proceeding with the service
    d. proceed with the service

65. Which term describes the scientific method of manipulating the body by rubbing, pinching, tapping, kneading or stroking with the hands, fingers or an instrument?
    a. cosmetology
    b. trichology
    c. anatomy
    d. massage

66. When dealing with a client, a professional cosmetologist is responsible for all of the following items EXCEPT:
    a. safety
    b. comfort
    c. transportation
    d. protection

67. Which of the following statements is NOT true about draping?
    a. performed prior to hair care service
    b. protects client's skin and clothing
    c. performed after client removes jewelry
    d. performed after shampooing is complete

68. What type of cape is generally used for shampooing, wet haircutting, wet styling or chemical services?
    a. plastic or waterproof cape
    b. cloth cape
    c. double-layered cloth cape
    d. lightweight cape

69. Many regulating agencies require all of the following steps EXCEPT:
    a. use of a neck strip
    b. preventing direct contact with the client's skin and cape
    c. use of a laundered cape
    d. shampoo prior to draping

70. What kind of shampoos will make hair dry and brittle?
    a. shampoos with a high pH
    b. shampoos that are acid-balanced
    c. shampoos with a pH of 4.5 to 5.5
    d. shampoos with a low pH

71. Which type of water contains minerals and does not allow shampoo to lather freely?
    a. warm
    b. cold
    c. soft
    d. hard

72. Brushing the hair prior to a shampoo service accomplishes all of the following EXCEPT:
    a. removing tangles
    b. removing dust and dirt
    c. stimulating blood circulation
    d. decreasing blood circulation

73. Which of the following statements is true of removing tangles from the hair?
    a. start at lowest point of tangled area
    b. start at the scalp and progress toward the ends of hair
    c. use long, firm strokes
    d. start at the highest point of the tangled area

74. Scalp massage involves manipulations performed on the scalp to relax the muscles and stimulate:
    a. blood circulation
    b. relaxation
    c. the hair shaft
    d. the cortex

75. What kind of massage uses light, gliding strokes or circular motions made with the palms of the hands or pads of the fingertips?
    a. petrissage
    b. tapotement
    c. friction
    d. effleurage

76. What kind of massage uses heavy kneading and rolling of the muscles?
    a. petrissage
    b. tapotement
    c. friction
    d. vibration

77. Light tapping or slapping massage movements are known as:
    a. petrissage
    b. tapotement
    c. friction
    d. effleurage

78. The most important scalp massage manipulation that stimulates the sebaceous glands is known as:
    a. effleurage
    b. petrissage
    c. tapotement
    d. friction

79. What type of shampoos cleanse the hair without correcting any special conditions?
    a. all-purpose
    b. medicated
    c. clarifying
    d. anti-dandruff

80. What type of shampoos are used to remove residue such as product build-up?
    a. liquid dry
    b. powder dry
    c. clarifying
    d. plain

81. What type of shampoos are especially good for cleansing lightened, color-treated or dry, brittle hair?
    a. acid-balanced
    b. all-purpose
    c. soapless
    d. liquid dry

82. What type of rinse is used after a color service to prevent the color from fading?
    a. cream
    b. color
    c. medicated
    d. acid-balanced

83. What type of conditioner helps close the cuticle after an alkaline chemical service?
    a. normalizing
    b. moisturizing
    c. customized
    d. instant

84. Avoid giving a scalp massage prior to all of the following services EXCEPT:
    a. relaxing healthy hair
    b. coloring healthy hair
    c. perming healthy hair
    d. shampooing healthy hair

85. What term is used to describe the combination of the sense of smell and the use of plant extracts and their healing abilities?
    a. electrology
    b. massage therapy
    c. aromatherapy
    d. trichology

CHAPTER 7

FINAL REVIEW

Check your answers as you did before. Place a check mark next to the page number for any incorrect answer. On the lines following the answers, jot down topics that you still need to review.

☐	1.	page 181	☐	23.	page 186	☐	45.	page 191
☐	2.	page 181	☐	24.	page 186	☐	46.	page 191
☐	3.	page 181	☐	25.	page 186	☐	47.	page 191
☐	4.	page 181	☐	26.	page 187	☐	48.	page 191
☐	5.	page 181	☐	27.	page 187	☐	49.	page 191
☐	6.	page 181	☐	28.	page 188	☐	50.	page 192
☐	7.	page 182	☐	29.	page 188	☐	51.	page 192
☐	8.	page 182	☐	30.	page 188	☐	52.	page 192
☐	9.	page 182	☐	31.	page 188	☐	53.	page 192
☐	10.	page 182	☐	32.	page 188	☐	54.	page 192
☐	11.	page 182	☐	33.	page 188	☐	55.	page 192
☐	12.	page 182	☐	34.	page 189	☐	56.	page 192
☐	13.	page 183	☐	35.	page 189	☐	57.	page 194
☐	14.	page 183	☐	36.	page 189	☐	58.	page 195
☐	15.	page 183	☐	37.	page 190	☐	59.	page 195
☐	16.	page 183	☐	38.	page 190	☐	60.	page 195
☐	17.	page 184	☐	39.	page 190	☐	61.	page 195
☐	18.	page 182	☐	40.	page 190	☐	62.	page 195
☐	19.	page 185	☐	41.	page 190	☐	63.	page 197
☐	20.	page 185	☐	42.	page 190	☐	64.	page 197
☐	21.	page 186	☐	43.	page 190	☐	65.	page 197
☐	22.	page 186	☐	44.	page 191	☐	66.	page 197

FINAL REVIEW *continued*

- 67. page 197
- 68. page 198
- 69. page 198
- 70. page 199
- 71. page 199
- 72. page 199
- 73. page 200
- 74. page 200
- 75. page 201
- 76. page 201
- 77. page 201
- 78. page 201
- 79. page 202
- 80. page 202
- 81. page 202
- 82. page 203
- 83. page 203
- 84. page 205
- 85. page 214

NOTES TO MYSELF

Experts tell us that it is important to summarize your feelings and reactions about what you are learning. Note especially things that surprised you, things you found difficult to learn, suggestions and ideas you received from friends that helped make learning this chapter easier and more enjoyable.

My reflections about Trichology:

LESSONS LEARNED

- The hair strand consists of three layers: the medulla, the cortex and the cuticle.
- Two types of the pigment melanin give hair its variety of hair colors.
- Evaluating the texture, density, porosity and elasticity of clients' hair and determining if there are any noteworthy hair or scalp conditions is done before beginning the client service.
- Proper draping is important to protect clients' skin and clothing.
- The shampooing and conditioning procedure is designed to ensure client comfort as well as to cleanse and prepare the hair for additional services.
- Scalp massage can both relax muscles to soothe the client and stimulate blood circulation to improve the condition of the hair and scalp.

CHAPTER 8

CHAPTER 8
DESIGN DECISIONS

VALUE
Clients will depend on you as their image-maker.

MAIN IDEA
Design composition + client consultation + client proportions
= **design decisions to consider**

PLAN

8.1 **DESIGN DECISION CONSIDERATIONS**
   Proportion
   Hair
   Personality
   Clothing
   Lifestyle

8.2 **CLIENT CONSULTATION**
   Communication

8.3 **DESIGN COMPOSITION**
   Design Elements
   Design Principles

DESIGN DECISIONS

smartNOTES

8.1 DESIGN DECISION CONSIDERATIONS pages 219-225

Proportion

3 Main Body Shapes

- TALL & LANKY
- AVERAGE
- SHORT & STURDY

Standard Design Considerations

DOMINANT FEATURE	ADD OR AVOID FOR BALANCE
Short Neck	
Long Neck	
Wide Shoulders	
Narrow Shoulders	
Large Figure	
Small Figure	

Neck

Shoulders

Entire Body Shape

Face Shape

DO	DON'T

Oval

Round

Square

CHAPTER 8

smartNOTES

8.1 DESIGN DECISION CONSIDERATIONS   pages 225-236

	DO	DON'T
Face Shape (cont'd)

Oblong

Pear

Diamond

Heart

3 Profile Types   Most noticeable features:

Straight Profile

Convex Profile

Concave Profile

Special Considerations
-
-
-

Hair
Hair Color

Hair Texture

Activated

Unactivated

smartNOTES

8.1 DESIGN DECISION CONSIDERATIONS   pages 237-242

Personality

OUTGOING	RESERVED

Clothing

General Clothing Styles
1.
2.
3.
4.
5.
6.

Lifestyle

8.2 CLIENT CONSULTATION   pages 243-244

Communication

5 Steps to Consultation

	HOW	WHY	MATERIAL
Greeting		Break the ice	
Ask, Analyze and Assess		Discover needs	
Agree		Gain feedback	
Deliver		Satisfy needs	
Complete		Build relationships	

SALON FUNDAMENTALS COSMETOLOGY   187

CHAPTER 8

smartNOTES

8.3 DESIGN COMPOSITION   pages 245-251

Design Elements

Form

Line

Horizontal
-
-

Vertical
-
-

Diagonal
-
-

Curved
-
-

Texture

Texture Speed

Color

Effects

| WARM COLORS | COOL COLORS |
| LIGHT COLORS | DARK COLORS |

Design Principles
-
-
-
-

Balance

Symmetrical

Asymmetrical

DESIGN DECISIONS

TALKING POINTS

Your next challenge is to be ready to talk about some of the important ideas in this chapter. Follow the directions listed next to each box. Then practice talking about your ideas with others.

	Discuss how you would identify the proper design proportions using the client's dominant features.
	Role play the 5 steps to consultation.
	Tell how clothing styles influence design decisions.

THE CHALLENGE

Now it's time to see how well you know your new material. First answer these questions. Then use the Memory Box that follows to check yourself. Look up each answer on the corresponding page in the *Salon Fundamentals* textbook. Check "got it" for all correct answers and "not yet" for all incorrect responses. Using the "Know Chart," record all of your correct responses in the "I Know" column. After correcting incorrect answers, record all of your corrected responses in the "I Need to Study" column. That way you know exactly what to review before continuing in this study guide.

1. Sound design decisions begin with an understanding of proportion. According to the standard proportions used by most artists, the head of a woman should be ___ of her overall height, and the head of a man should be ___ of his overall height.

2. What are the three main body shapes that need to be considered when making a design decision?
   _____ _____ _____

3. Which of the following statements is/are true regarding design decisions concerning the neck and shoulder?
   a) Long necks need mass and fullness around them.   b) Wide shoulders need a narrowing design line in back.
   c) A tall and lanky person will often have narrow shoulders.   d) All of the above.

4. TRUE FALSE Concerning the overall body shape, a person with a large body will easily become overpowered by a large hairstyle.

5. The facial shape needs to be considered when making design decisions. Name the seven most common facial shapes.
   _____ _____ _____
   _____ _____ _____
   _____

6. Since clients are viewed from various angles, it is important that their hairstyle complement their profile as well. The three different types of profiles are _____, _____ and _____.

7. TRUE FALSE A basic guideline for selecting glasses is to select large glasses for a large face and select small glasses for a small face.

8. A cosmetologist should never make a design decision without analyzing his or her primary working material—the hair. List six hair factors that should be considered before deciding on a particular style.
   _____ _____ _____
   _____ _____ _____

9. Describe the difference between activated and unactivated texture.
   activated _____ unactivated _____

10. TRUE FALSE A client's personality, clothing style and lifestyle should all be considered when making a design decision.

1 2 3 4 5 6 7

SALON FUNDAMENTALS COSMETOLOGY 189

CHAPTER 8

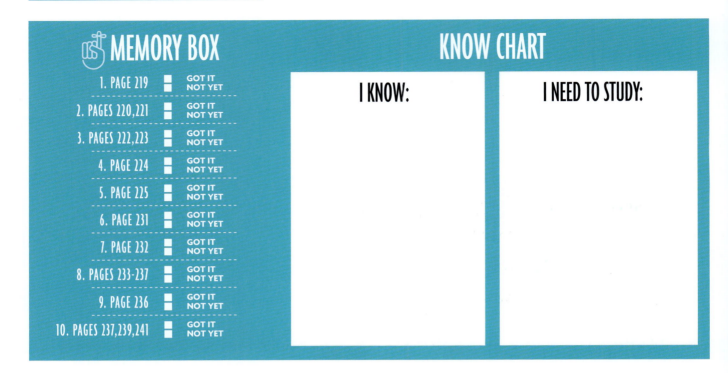

MEMORY BOX

1. PAGE 219 ☐ GOT IT / NOT YET
2. PAGES 220, 221 ☐ GOT IT / NOT YET
3. PAGES 222, 223 ☐ GOT IT / NOT YET
4. PAGE 224 ☐ GOT IT / NOT YET
5. PAGE 225 ☐ GOT IT / NOT YET
6. PAGE 231 ☐ GOT IT / NOT YET
7. PAGE 232 ☐ GOT IT / NOT YET
8. PAGES 233-237 ☐ GOT IT / NOT YET
9. PAGE 236 ☐ GOT IT / NOT YET
10. PAGES 237, 239, 241 ☐ GOT IT / NOT YET

KNOW CHART

I KNOW:

I NEED TO STUDY:

SHOW YOU KNOW...

Show You Know the facial shapes by placing photos from magazines or photo albums in the frames provided below:

KNOWLEDGE GRID

Start at the top of the Knowledge Grid and work your way down, answering each question to check your understanding of *Chapter 8, Design Decisions*. The questions found here will help you deepen your understanding, build self-confidence and increase your awareness of different ways of thinking about a subject.

KNOW	WHAT IS THE STANDARD MOST ARTISTS USE TO DETERMINE THE PROPORTION OF A WOMAN'S HEAD TO HER OVERALL BODY HEIGHT?	
COMPREHEND	STATE WHAT IS MEANT BY THREE-SECTIONING IN RELATION TO BODY PROPORTIONS?	
APPLY	DRAW AN APPROPRIATE HAIR DESIGN FOR A CLIENT WITH A ROUND FACIAL SHAPE.	
ANALYZE	PLEASE COMPARE A HAIR DESIGN FOR A TALL AND LANKY BODY SHAPE AND SHORT AND STURDY BODY SHAPE.	
SYNTHESIZE	CREATE A RHYME USING ONE OF THE SEVEN FACIAL SHAPES AS A FOCUS POINT.	
EVALUATE	IN YOUR OPINION, WHICH OF THE SIX MAIN STYLE CATEGORIES WILL DESCRIBE MOST OF THE CLIENTS YOU WILL SEE IN THE SALON?	

CHAPTER 8

BRAIN CONDITIONER
MULTIPLE CHOICE. CIRCLE THE CORRECT ANSWER.

1. Design decision considerations involve all of the following techniques EXCEPT:
   a. ability to communicate
   b. knowledge of the body and its proportions
   c. understanding of design composition
   d. viewing the client's baby photos

2. According to the standard most artists use, the head of a woman should be how much of her overall body height?
   a. 1/5th   b. 1/6th   c. 1/7th   d. 1/8th

3. According to the standard most artists use, the head of a man should be how much of his overall body height?
   a. 1/5th   b. 1/6th   c. 1/7th   d. 1/8th

4. A man would be considered to have what type of body shape if he is between 5'7" (1.7 m) and 6'1" (1.8 m) tall?
   a. tall and lanky   b. average   c. short and sturdy   d. very tall

5. Narrow shoulders are enhanced by all of the following design lines EXCEPT:
   a. horizontal lines
   b. lines that create an "A"-shape
   c. flat, wide and oval lines
   d. lines that create a "V"-shape

6. When determining facial shape, which of the following areas is NOT a consideration?
   a. analysis of the hairline
   b. analysis of bone structure
   c. analysis of the widest area
   d. analysis of the least dominant area

7. Three-sectioning is an effective way to measure the proportions of the:
   a. shoulders   b. neck   c. entire body shape   d. face

8. Which of the following guidelines is NOT true if a client has a diamond facial shape?
   a. add width at the cheekbones
   b. use a side part and diagonal fringe
   c. add width at the forehead
   d. add width at the jawline

9. Which of the following guidelines is true if a client has a round facial shape?
   a. add height to the crown
   b. add a full fringe
   c. add width to the sides
   d. add equal fullness around the entire face

10. Which of the following guidelines is true if a client has a heart facial shape?
    a. add width at the forehead
    b. add width at the cheekbones
    c. leave fullness at nape that can be seen from the front
    d. leave hair close at nape

11. Which of the following guidelines is true if a client has an oblong facial shape?
    a. add width at the jawline
    b. add width at the forehead
    c. add width at the sides
    d. use a middle part and horizontal fringe

12. A client with what type of profile has a very strong outward curvature from the front hairline to the tip of the nose and from the tip of the nose to the chin?
    a. concave   b. convex   c. straight   d. angled

13. Which of the following statements is true regarding design decisions about clients who wear glasses?
    a. a square-shaped pair of glasses can give a square face more interest
    b. select small glasses for a large face
    c. select large glasses for a large face
    d. a narrow frame can add width to a narrow face

14. Warm colors contain yellow, orange and/or:
    a. red   b. blue   c. green   d. violet

15. Clients with which type of hair density generally do not have enough fullness for longer designs that go past the shoulders?
    a. light b. medium c. heavy d. thick
16. Which of the following terms does NOT describe hair texture?
    a. fine b. blond c. coarse d. medium
17. Clients who usually wear their hair short and have an eye for interesting detail choose what kind of clothing style?
    a. dramatic b. classic c. natural d. gamine
18. The three major design elements are texture, color and:
    a. porosity b. aroma c. form d. composition
19. The surface appearance of hair such as curly or straight, smooth or layered is called:
    a. form b. texture c. composition d. color
20. The size of the actual texture pattern is called:
    a. texture speed b. composition c. form d. appearance

FINAL REVIEW

Check your answers as you did before. Place a check mark next to the page number for any incorrect answer. Review that material.

- 1. page 218
- 2. page 219
- 3. page 219
- 4. page 221
- 5. page 223
- 6. page 224
- 7. page 225
- 8. page 230
- 9. page 230
- 10. page 230
- 11. page 230
- 12. page 231
- 13. page 232
- 14. page 233
- 15. page 236
- 16. page 236
- 17. page 240
- 18. page 245
- 19. page 247
- 20. page 247

NOTES TO MYSELF

Experts tell us that it is important to summarize your feelings and reactions about what you are learning. Note especially things that surprised you, things you found difficult to learn, suggestions and ideas you received from friends that helped make learning this chapter easier and more enjoyable.

My reflections about Design Decisions:

CHAPTER 8

LESSONS LEARNED

- *Proportion plays a major part in how people perceive beauty and compose designs.*
- *Hair designs should be adapted to each client's body and facial shape, features, hair, clothing and lifestyle.*
- *Greeting, Ask, Agree, Deliver and Complete are the five steps that lead to a successful consultation.*
- *Personality, schedule, environment and professional appearance are key factors that contribute to effective client-stylist communication.*
- *The three design elements of form, texture and color are also the major components of an art form.*
- *The four design principles of repetition, alternation, progression and contrast are the patterns used to arrange design elements within a composition.*

THINGS TO DO

THINGS TO DO

CHAPTER 9
HAIRCUTTING

VALUE
Haircutting is a valuable skill that will allow you to dramatically change a client's total look or offer subtle nuances.

MAIN IDEA
Theory of hair + ability to perform haircutting = **a satisfied clientele and a successful foundation for further services**

PLAN

9.1 HAIRCUTTING THEORY
Form
Haircutting Essentials
Haircutting Fundamentals
Infection Control and Safety
Client Consultation

9.2 HAIRCUTTING PROCEDURES
Haircutting Procedures Overview
Solid Form Haircut
Solid Form Variation: Increase-Layered Front Hairline
Increase-Layered Form Haircut
Graduated Form Haircut
Uniformly Layered Form Haircut
Combination Form Haircut
Square Form/Uniform Haircut
Overcomb Techniques
Fade Haircut

CHAPTER 9

smartNOTES

9.1 HAIRCUTTING THEORY — pages 255-258

Haircutting f

Form

FORM	SHAPE
three-dimensional representation of a shape. it has length, width and depth	Two-dimensional representation of form because it consists of length and width only.

Points, Lines and Angles

POINT

·

HORIZONTAL   VERTICAL   DIAGONAL

LINES: there are three basic straight lines, which are horizontal, vertical and diagonal

Concave lines curves inward, like the inside of a sphere.

Convex lines curve outward, like the outside of a sphere

Most Common Angles
- angles are 45 and 90
- are used to created the shape and form of the haircut

Structure of a haircut consists of the arrangement of lengths across the various curves of the head

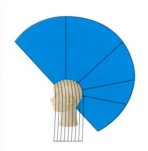

NATURAL FALL	NORMAL PROJECTION
Natural Fall describes the hair as the lengths lay or fall naturally over the curve of the head when identifying a haircut according to its Natural	another way to analize the structure or length arrangement of a haircut is in Normal projected at a 90°

1 **2** 3 4 5 6 7

HAIRCUTTING

smartNOTES

9.1 HAIRCUTTING THEORY   pages 258-260

Texture

UNACTIVATED	ACTIVATED
Texture can be described as unactivated (smooth)	activated (rough) in haircutting texture is Activated

Basic Haircuts
4 Basic Forms

SOLID
- Structure: shorter exterior progressing to longer
- Shape: Rectangle
- Texture: unactivated

GRADUATED
- Structure: shorter exterior gradually progressing to
- Shape: triangle
- Texture: unactivated/activated

INCREASE-LAYERED
- Structure: shorter interior progressing to longer
- Shape: oval
- Texture: activated

UNIFORMLY LAYERED
- Structure: Same length throughout
- Shape: Circular
- Texture: Activated

COMBINATION
- Structure: two or more forms in any combination
- Shape: Reflects forms chosen
- Texture: Activated unactivated

CHAPTER 9

smartNOTES

9.1 HAIRCUTTING THEORY — pages 260-268

GRADATION

Structure: Very short exterior gradually progressing to longer interior

Shape: rectangle or oval   Texture: Activated

SQUARE COMBINATION

Structure: Uniform at center top to increase layered at front and crown

Shape: square/rectangle   Texture: Activated

Haircutting Essentials

Shears
- Characteristics:
- Primary Use:
- Familiarity with cutting positions: Level 1   Level 2   Level 3
- Date: ☐   ☐   ☐

Taper Shears
- Characteristics:
- Primary Use:
- Familiarity with cutting positions: Level 1   Level 2   Level 3
- Date: ☐   ☐   ☐

Razor
- Characteristics:
- Primary Use:
- Familiarity with cutting positions: Level 1   Level 2   Level 3
- Date: ☐   ☐   ☐

Clippers
- Characteristics:
- Primary Use:
- Familiarity with cutting positions: Level 1   Level 2   Level 3
- Date: ☐   ☐   ☐

smartNOTES

9.1 HAIRCUTTING THEORY   pages 269-271

Haircutting Fundamentals

Areas of the Head

Sectioning

Label the sectioning positions using the words in the Jump Start Box →

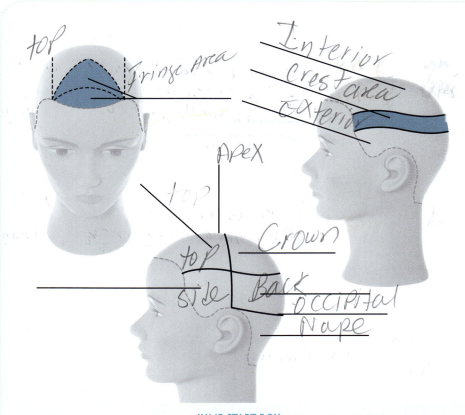

JUMP START BOX

Crest area	Back	Side	Apex	Nape
Crown	Top	Interior	Exterior	Fringe area
Occipital				

Head Position

The most common head positions are upright, forward or tilted to either side.

Parting

Are lines that subdivide sections of hair in order to separate, distribute and control the hair while cutting. Generally, the parting pattern will be parallel to the design line, which is the guideline used while cutting.

CHAPTER 9

smartNOTES

9.1 HAIRCUTTING THEORY — pages 271-273

Distribution

NATURAL	PERPENDICULAR
distribution is the direction the Hair assumes as it Falls naturally from the head due to gravity	the Hair is combed at 90° angle from its parting
SHIFTED	**DIRECTIONAL**
It is generally used for exaggerated length increases and blending between different forms	distribution results in length increases due to the curve of the head

Projection (Elevation) — between 0° and 30° are considered to be low projection, between 30° and 60° medium projection and between 60°-90° high projection

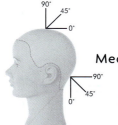

Low

Medium

High

Finger and Shear Position
-
-

Design Line

Stationary

Mobile

Crosschecking

200 UNIT 2 HAIR SERVICES

HAIRCUTTING

smartNOTES

9.1 HAIRCUTTING THEORY   pages 273-277

Texturizing

BASE	MIDSTRAND	END

Razor Etching

Slithering

Razor Rotation

Texturizing Considerations

FINE
MEDIUM
COARSE

Outlining
-
-

Special Grooming

Other Fundamental Considerations

Fringe and Nape Variations

Growth Patterns
- • •
- •

1 2 3 4 5 6 7

SALON FUNDAMENTALS COSMETOLOGY   201

CHAPTER 9

TALKING POINTS

Your next challenge is to be ready to talk about some of the important ideas in this chapter. Follow the directions listed next to each box. Then practice talking about your ideas with others.

	Compare solid, graduated, increase-layered and uniformly layered forms to clothing.
	List 3 examples of where you would find horizontal, vertical and diagonal lines used in architecture.
	Create a slogan used to promote a haircut combined with another service in the salon.

THE CHALLENGE

Now it's time to see how well you know your new material. First answer these questions. Then use the Memory Box that follows to check yourself. Look up each answer on the corresponding page in the *Salon Fundamentals* textbook. Check "got it" for all correct answers and "not yet" for all incorrect responses. Using the "Know Chart," record all of your correct responses in the "I Know" column. After correcting incorrect answers, record all of your corrected responses in the "I Need to Study" column. That way you know exactly what to review before continuing in this study guide.

1. Almost everything that exists in nature is composed of form, texture and color. Which one of these three characteristics is the foundation of every haircut? _____

2. Texture can refer to the surface appearance of hair. Describe the difference between activated and unactivated texture.
   Activated_____
   Unactivated_____

3. What are the seven basic forms used in haircutting? _____ _____
   _____ _____ _____ _____ _____

4. What are the five hand-held implements used in a haircutting procedure?
   _____ _____ _____ _____ _____

5. TRUE   FALSE   The hand-held implements you use during a haircutting procedure must be disinfected after each use.

6. Every successful haircut begins with sectioning. The most common sectioning pattern divides the head into four sections. On a separate sheet of paper describe the dividing lines of these four sections.

7. Distribution refers to the direction hair is combed in relation to the parting. What are the four types of distribution?
   _____ _____ _____ _____

8. _____, also known as elevation, is the angle at which the hair is held in relation to the curve of the head prior to cutting.
   a) Projection   b) Crosschecking   c) Slithering   d) Texturizing

9. TRUE   FALSE   Never thin the very ends of hair or anywhere around the hairline.

202   UNIT 2 HAIR SERVICES

HAIRCUTTING

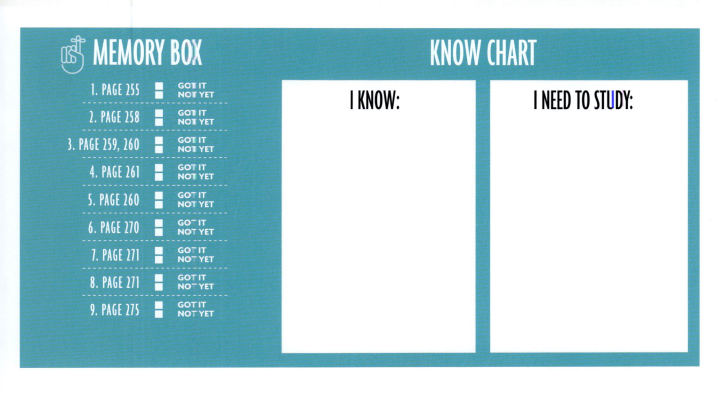

SHOW YOU KNOW...

Show You Know the basic forms of haircutting by identifying a current celebrity's haircut that exhibits the following forms and write a short statement of why you think the haircut they wear is perfect for them.

Solid Form
The solid form haircut is perfect for _____ because _____

Increase-Layered Form
The increase-layered form haircut is perfect for _____ because _____

Graduated Form
The graduated form haircut is perfect for _____ because _____

Uniformly Layered Form
The uniformly layered form haircut is perfect for _____ because _____

Combination Form
The combination form haircut is perfect for _____ because _____

CHAPTER 9

RUBRIC

This rubric is a self-assessment tool designed to compare your skill to industry standards. Indicate your present level of performance by checking the appropriate box. See overview for instructions.

Solid Form Haircut

Industry Standard — to meet entry-level proficiency, industry standards require that you:
- Consult with and provide a haircut in accordance with a client's needs or expectations.

Preparation

	Level 1	Level 2	Level 3	To Improve, I Need To:	Teacher Assessment
• Disinfect workstation; assemble implements/supplies; wash hands; analyze hair/scalp; ask client to remove jewelry; drape/shampoo/condition client; replace towel with neck strip	☐	☐	☐		☐

Procedure

	Level 1	Level 2	Level 3		Teacher Assessment
• Subdivide hair into four sections	☐	☐	☐		☐
• Position head upright	☐	☐	☐		☐
• Create horizontal parting at nape, across both sections	☐	☐	☐		☐
• Use natural distribution	☐	☐	☐		☐
• Position fingers/shears parallel to parting	☐	☐	☐		☐
• Cut a horizontal stationary design line	☐	☐	☐		☐
• Work upward using horizontal partings, natural distribution and no projection	☐	☐	☐		☐
• Distribute hair naturally at crown area	☐	☐	☐		☐
• Complete back	☐	☐	☐		☐
• Create a horizontal parting at side and extend to back	☐	☐	☐		☐
• Distribute hair in natural fall	☐	☐	☐		☐
• Position fingers/shears parallel to part	☐	☐	☐		☐
• Cut horizontal line; continue upward; complete side	☐	☐	☐		☐
• Release and cut first parting on opposite side; check for balance	☐	☐	☐		☐
• Work upward using horizontal partings, natural distribution and no projection	☐	☐	☐		☐
• Complete side; crosscheck	☐	☐	☐		☐

Completion

	Level 1	Level 2	Level 3		Teacher Assessment
• Offer a prebook visit; recommend retail products; discard non-reusable materials, disinfect implements, arrange workstation in proper order and wash hands	☐	☐	☐		☐

TOTAL = ADDITION OF ALL TEACHER ASSESSMENT BOXES

TOTAL POINTS = ☐
54

PERCENTAGE = STUDENT SCORE / HIGHEST POSSIBLE SCORE

_____ %

204 UNIT 2 HAIR SERVICES

HAIRCUTTING

RUBRIC

This rubric is a self-assessment tool designed to compare your skill to industry standards. Indicate your present level of performance by checking the appropriate box. See overview for instructions.

Increase-Layered Form Haircut

Industry Standard – to meet entry-level proficiency, industry standards require that you:
- Consult with and provide a haircut in accordance with a client's needs or expectations.

Preparation

	Level 1	Level 2	Level 3	To Improve, I Need To:	Teacher Assessment
Disinfect workstation; assemble implements/supplies; wash hands; analyze hair/scalp; ask client to remove jewelry; drape/shampoo/condition client; replace towel with neck strip	☐	☐	☐		☐

Procedure

	Level 1	Level 2	Level 3		Teacher Assessment
Subdivide hair from hairline to nape	☐	☐	☐		☐
Position head upright	☐	☐	☐		☐
Take diagonal-forward partings on either side of center parting	☐	☐	☐		☐
Establish length guide at chin	☐	☐	☐		☐
Project length guide at 90°, cut parallel	☐	☐	☐		☐
Position fingers and shears parallel to floor	☐	☐	☐		☐
Take a diagonal-forward parting on one side	☐	☐	☐		☐
Use perpendicular distribution, direct the hair to stationary design line, projected at 90°; cut parallel to part	☐	☐	☐		☐
Cut one side, then other to maintain symmetry	☐	☐	☐		☐
Take subsequent diagonal-forward partings parallel to first on either side	☐	☐	☐		☐
Use perpendicular distribution, direct hair to stationary design line and cut parallel	☐	☐	☐		☐
Repeat same cutting procedures, working to nape; check symmetry	☐	☐	☐		☐
Crosscheck	☐	☐	☐		☐

Completion

	Level 1	Level 2	Level 3		Teacher Assessment
Offer a prebook visit; recommend retail products; discard non-reusable materials, disinfect implements, arrange workstation in proper order and wash hands	☐	☐	☐		☐

TOTAL = ADDITION OF ALL TEACHER ASSESSMENT BOXES   TOTAL POINTS = ☐
                                                                    45

PERCENTAGE = STUDENT SCORE / HIGHEST POSSIBLE SCORE   _____ %

SALON FUNDAMENTALS COSMETOLOGY   205

CHAPTER 9

RUBRIC

This rubric is a self-assessment tool designed to compare your skill to industry standards. Indicate your present level of performance by checking the appropriate box. See overview for instructions.

Graduated Form Haircut

Industry Standard — to meet entry-level proficiency, industry standards require that you:
- Consult with and provide a haircut in accordance with a client's needs or expectations.

	Level 1	Level 2	Level 3	To Improve, I Need To:	Teacher Assessment
Preparation					
Disinfect workstation; assemble implements/supplies; wash hands; analyze hair/scalp; ask client to remove jewelry; drape/shampoo/condition client; replace towel with neck strip	☐	☐	☐		☐
Procedure					
Section hair into four sections; position head upright	☐	☐	☐		☐
Take a diagonal-forward parting at either side of nape	☐	☐	☐		☐
Use perpendicular distribution and 0° projection	☐	☐	☐		☐
Position fingers/shears parallel to part	☐	☐	☐		☐
Cut one side, then other side establishing mobile design line	☐	☐	☐		☐
Continue to cut upward, using diagonal-forward partings and a mobile design line	☐	☐	☐		☐
Use perpendicular distribution and a medium-low (30°) projection angle	☐	☐	☐		☐
Extend diagonal-forward partings to front hairline in area above ear	☐	☐	☐		☐
Continue to alternate sides, avoiding tension over ears	☐	☐	☐		☐
Use a stationary design line once crest area is reached	☐	☐	☐		☐
Project at established 30° angle	☐	☐	☐		☐
Distribute naturally at the crown; cut parallel to parting	☐	☐	☐		☐
Continue to center top, alternating sides	☐	☐	☐		☐
Soften point at front using minimal projection; crosscheck	☐	☐	☐		☐
Completion					
Offer a prebook visit; recommend retail products; discard non-reusable materials, disinfect implements, arrange workstation in proper order and wash hands	☐	☐	☐		☐

TOTAL = ADDITION OF ALL TEACHER ASSESSMENT BOXES   TOTAL POINTS = ☐

48

PERCENTAGE = STUDENT SCORE / HIGHEST POSSIBLE SCORE   _____ %

UNIT 2 HAIR SERVICES

HAIRCUTTING

RUBRIC

This rubric is a self-assessment tool designed to compare your skill to industry standards. Indicate your present level of performance by checking the appropriate box. See overview for instructions.

Uniformly Layered Form Haircut

Industry Standard — to meet entry-level proficiency, industry standards require that you:
- Consult with and provide a haircut in accordance with a client's needs or expectations

	Level 1	Level 2	Level 3	To Improve, I Need To	Teacher Assessment
Preparation					
Disinfect workstation; assemble implements/supplies; wash hands; analyze hair/scalp; ask client to remove jewelry; drape/shampoo/condition client; replace towel with neck strip	☐	☐	☐		☐
Procedure					
Subdivide hair into five sections; position head upright	☐	☐	☐		☐
Establish length guide at center front hairline	☐	☐	☐		☐
Begin with center top section; take horizontal parting at front hairline	☐	☐	☐		☐
Use perpendicular distribution, 90° projection; position fingers parallel to head	☐	☐	☐		☐
Cut parallel to fingers to establish mobile design line	☐	☐	☐		☐
Take next parting, use perpendicular distribution, 90° projection	☐	☐	☐		☐
Position fingers parallel to head; cut parallel to fingers	☐	☐	☐		☐
Work toward back of top section; complete top section	☐	☐	☐		☐
Cut sides using top section as length guide	☐	☐	☐		☐
Use vertical partings, perpendicular distribution and 90° projection	☐	☐	☐		☐
Position fingers parallel to head, cut parallel to fingers	☐	☐	☐		☐
Use top and side section as length guide to cut back	☐	☐	☐		☐
Use pivotal partings, perpendicular distribution and 90° projection	☐	☐	☐		☐
Complete both sides and the back section using same cutting procedures; crosscheck	☐	☐	☐		☐
Completion					
Offer a prebook visit; recommend retail products; discard non-reusable materials, disinfect implements, arrange workstation in proper order and wash hands	☐	☐	☐		☐

TOTAL = ADDITION OF ALL TEACHER ASSESSMENT BOXES

TOTAL POINTS = ☐
48

PERCENTAGE = STUDENT SCORE / HIGHEST POSSIBLE SCORE _____ %

CHAPTER 9

RUBRIC

This rubric is a self-assessment tool designed to compare your skill to industry standards. Indicate your present level of performance by checking the appropriate box. See overview for instructions.

Combination Form Haircut

Industry Standard — to meet entry-level proficiency, industry standards require that you:
- Consult with and provide a haircut in accordance with a client's needs or expectations.

Preparation

	Level 1	Level 2	Level 3	To Improve, I Need To:	Teacher Assessment
Disinfect workstation; assemble implements/supplies; wash hands; analyze hair/scalp; ask client to remove jewelry; drape/shampoo/condition client; replace towel with neck strip	☐	☐	☐		☐

Procedure

Divide interior from exterior using horseshoe-shaped parting; subdivide exterior vertically at each ear	☐	☐	☐		☐
Begin center back; take vertical parting	☐	☐	☐		☐
Use high projection; position fingers along high line of inclination; cut parallel to fingers	☐	☐	☐		☐
Move to one side, take vertical parting at ear and cut using same technique; work to front; shift last two partings back; repeat same technique on opposite side	☐	☐	☐		☐
Use mobile design line, work from center to each ear	☐	☐	☐		☐
Project top exterior lengths straight out and notch; start at center back, work to front	☐	☐	☐		☐
Take partings parallel to sectioning line; distribute lengths to stationary design line and notch	☐	☐	☐		☐
Work up to center part using same technique to complete one side; repeat same techniques on opposite side	☐	☐	☐		☐
Release a thin center section from front hairline to weight area; use weight line from back section as a length guide	☐	☐	☐		☐
Project hair in center section at 90° and cut parallel to parting using razor-peeling technique to create uniformly layered length	☐	☐	☐		☐
Work toward one side using pivotal partings from crown, 90° projection and mobile design line; position your fingers parallel to part and cut using razor-peeling technique	☐	☐	☐		☐
Work to the front of section using horizontal partings and same cutting technique; distribute fringe toward face using low projection; personalize fringe using a razor etching technique	☐	☐	☐		☐
Use razor rotation in nape	☐	☐	☐		☐
Crosscheck	☐	☐	☐		☐

Completion

Offer a prebook visit; recommend retail products; discard non-reusable materials, disinfect implements, arrange workstation in proper order and wash hands	☐	☐	☐		☐

TOTAL = ADDITION OF ALL TEACHER ASSESSMENT BOXES   TOTAL POINTS = ☐

48

PERCENTAGE = STUDENT SCORE / HIGHEST POSSIBLE SCORE   _____ %

HAIRCUTTING

RUBRIC

This rubric is a self-assessment tool designed to compare your skill to industry standards. Indicate your present level of performance by checking the appropriate box. See overview for instructions.

Square Form/Uniform Haircut

Industry Standard — to meet entry-level proficiency, industry standards require that you:
- Consult with and provide a haircut in accordance with a client's needs or expectations.

	Level 1	Level 2	Level 3	To Improve, I Need To:	Teacher Assessment
Preparation					
Disinfect workstation; assemble implements/supplies; wash hands; analyze hair/scalp; ask client to remove jewelry; drape/shampoo/condition client; replace towel with neck strip	☐	☐	☐		☐
Procedure					
Begin with center top section; position head upright	☐	☐	☐		☐
Take a small section and front hairline and establish length guide	☐	☐	☐		☐
Take a parting through center top, project straight up, cut parallel to floor	☐	☐	☐		☐
Take horizontal partings at front hairline; establish mobile length guide	☐	☐	☐		☐
Take next parting; distribute hair straight up; position fingers horizontally; cut parallel to fingers	☐	☐	☐		☐
Work from front crown using directional distribution and mobile design line	☐	☐	☐		☐
Repeat with next section to the right; complete last top section	☐	☐	☐		☐
Distribute hair straight out at sides and back; use vertical partings; position fingers and shears perpendicular to floor; cut parallel to fingers up to second knuckle	☐	☐	☐		☐
Work from front hairline to center back, using top and previously cut section as length guide	☐	☐	☐		☐
Work from back to front hairline on other side	☐	☐	☐		☐
Work from one side to other side in the next lower section and repeat techniques	☐	☐	☐		☐
In nape, use vertical partings, perpendicular distribution and 90° projection, cut uniform layers; crosscheck	☐	☐	☐		☐
Personalize perimeter hairline; texturize ends with razor rotation and notching technique	☐	☐	☐		☐

TOTAL = ADDITION OF ALL TEACHER ASSESSMENT BOXES

TOTAL POINTS =

42

PERCENTAGE = STUDENT SCORE / HIGHEST POSSIBLE SCORE   _____ %

SALON FUNDAMENTALS COSMETOLOGY

CHAPTER 9

RUBRIC

This rubric is a self-assessment tool designed to compare your skill to industry standards. Indicate your present level of performance by checking the appropriate box. See overview for instructions.

Fade Haircut

Industry Standard – to meet entry-level proficiency, industry standards require that you:
- Consult with and provide a haircut in accordance with a client's needs or expectations.

	Level 1	Level 2	Level 3	To Improve, I Need To:	Teacher Assessment
Preparation					
Disinfect workstation; assemble implements/supplies; wash hands; analyze hair/scalp; ask client to remove jewelry; drape client for dry haircut service	☐	☐	☐		☐
Procedure					
Position head upright	☐	☐	☐		☐
Position clippers flat with adjustable and cutting blades even	☐	☐	☐		☐
Tilt head slightly forward; cut zone 1 against skin, up to established line	☐	☐	☐		☐
Start at center nape, work to either side; pull skin taut; work in multiple directions	☐	☐	☐		☐
Extend adjustable blade halfway to cut zone 2; start at the center back; move clippers outward at top of zone	☐	☐	☐		☐
Fully extend adjustable blade to cut zone 3; start at center back	☐	☐	☐		☐
Begin each stroke within zone 2, move the clipper outward at top of zone 3; work from center to either side	☐	☐	☐		☐
Add small guard to fully extended adjustable blade to cut zone 4; start at center back	☐	☐	☐		☐
Begin each stroke within zone 3 and move clippers out at top of zone 4; work to front hairline on either side	☐	☐	☐		☐
Position cutting and adjustable blades even with each other, switch to guard one size larger than previous guard; start at center front hairline, move the clippers toward crown	☐	☐	☐		☐
Cut uniform lengths throughout zone; move the clippers in multiple directions against growth patterns	☐	☐	☐		☐
Repeat the same procedure working toward the back of zone; blend between zones	☐	☐	☐		☐
Texturize ends to blend, cutting with tips of shears positioned vertically or diagonally; outline perimeter	☐	☐	☐		☐
Completion					
Offer a prebook visit; recommend retail products; discard non-reusable materials, disinfect implements, oil clippers, arrange workstation in proper order and wash hands	☐	☐	☐		☐

TOTAL = ADDITION OF ALL TEACHER ASSESSMENT BOXES

TOTAL POINTS = ☐

45

PERCENTANGE = STUDENT SCORE / HIGHEST POSSIBLE SCORE

_____ %

KNOWLEDGE GRID

Start at the top of the Knowledge Grid and work your way down, answering each question to check your understanding of *Chapter 9, Haircutting*. The questions found here will help you deepen your understanding, build self-confidence and increase your awareness of different ways of thinking about a subject.

KNOW	WHAT ARE THE BASIC FORMS USED IN HAIRCUTTING?	
COMPREHEND	EXPLAIN PROJECTION, ALSO KNOWN AS ELEVATION, IN YOUR OWN WORDS.	
APPLY	DEMONSTRATE THE CUTTING POSITIONS OF PALM DOWN, PALM UP AND PALM TO PALM.	
ANALYZE	ANALYZE THE FORM OF A HAIR SCULPTURE BY USING A PHOTO FROM A MAGAZINE. CONSIDER THE PROPERTIES OF NATURAL FALL AND NORMAL PROJECTION.	
SYNTHESIZE	DESIGN YOUR OWN POSTER USING DRAWINGS OR PHOTOS TO ILLUSTRATE THE FORMS USED IN HAIRCUTTING.	
EVALUATE	IN YOUR OPINION, WHICH GROWTH PATTERN WILL BE THE MOST DIFFICULT FOR YOU TO WORK WITH TO PRODUCE SATISFACTORY RESULTS?	

1 2 3 4 **5** 6 7

CHAPTER 9

BRAIN CONDITIONER
MULTIPLE CHOICE. CIRCLE THE CORRECT ANSWER.

1. The foundation of every haircut is:
   a. porosity   b. texture   c. color   d. form

2. Which of the following dimensions does a form have but a shape does not have?
   a. length   b. width   c. depth   d. texture

3. With unactivated texture, which part of the hair is not visible when viewed in natural fall?
   a. the root   b. the ends   c. the cortex   d. the medulla

4. The term used to describe the hair as the lengths lay naturally over the curve of the head is:
   a. normal projection   b. texture   c. natural fall   d. convex

5. What type of form would result from using a 180° angle cut?
   a. solid   b. graduated   c. increase-layered   d. uniformly layered

6. A uniformly layered form is also known as a:
   a. 0° angle cut   b. 45° angle cut   c. 90° angle cut   d. 180° angle cut

7. A solid form is also known as a one-length cut, bob, Dutch boy or blunt cut and is cut using a:
   a. 90° angle   b. 45° angle   c. 0° angle   d. 60° angle

8. All of the following descriptions are true about the uniformly layered form EXCEPT:
   a. circular shape   b. activated texture   c. same length throughout   d. oval shape

9. When cutting with a razor, all of the following results are achieved EXCEPT:
   a. ends are tapered   b. softer appearance to hair
   c. a diffused form line appears   d. regular alternation of short and long lengths

10. The term used for dividing the head into workable areas for the purpose of control is called:
    a. texturizing   b. positioning   c. designing   d. sectioning

11. The direction the hair assumes as it falls naturally from the head due to gravity is called:
    a. natural distribution   b. perpendicular distribution   c. shifted distribution   d. directional distribution

12. An angle of 45 degrees would be considered what type of projection?
    a. low   b. medium   c. high   d. very high

13. Holding the hair flat to the surface of the head while cutting is using what level of projection?
    a. low projection   b. medium projection   c. high projection   d. increased projection

14. An artistic guideline used while cutting is called a(n):
    a. projection line   b. elevation line   c. design line   d. crest line

15. When using this type of elevation, the hair is held straight out from the curve of the head while cutting:
    a. low   b. medium   c. high   d. very high

16. Texturizing is also known as:
    a. thinning   b. crosschecking   c. sectioning   d. parting

17. Texturizing involves cutting hair to:
    a. increase bulk   b. decrease fullness   c. decrease mobility   d. reduce bulk

HAIRCUTTING

18. Generally coarse hair should be texturized at least how far away from the scalp?
    a. ½" (1.25 cm)   b. 1" (2.54 cm)   c. 1½" (3.75 cm)   d. 2" (5 cm)

19. Which of the following statements is true when thinning the hair?
    a. avoid thinning the very ends of the hair
    b. always thin around the hairline last
    c. very curly hair should be thinned while it is wet
    d. coarse hair should be thinned ½" from the scalp

20. A prominent growth pattern that forms from a point at the front hairline and curves to one side is called a:
    a. widow's peak   b. cowlick   c. whorl   d. fringe

FINAL REVIEW

Check your answers as you did before. Place a check mark next to the page number for any incorrect answer. Review that material.

☐ 1. page 255	☐ 6. page 259	☐ 11. page 271	☐ 16. page 273
☐ 2. page 256	☐ 7. page 259	☐ 12. page 271	☐ 17. page 273
☐ 3. page 258	☐ 8. page 259	☐ 13. page 271	☐ 18. page 274
☐ 4. page 258	☐ 9. page 261	☐ 14. page 272	☐ 19. page 275
☐ 5. page 259	☐ 10. page 270	☐ 15. page 272	☐ 20. page 277

NOTES TO MYSELF

Experts tell us that it is important to summarize your feelings and reactions about what you are learning. Note especially things that surprised you, things you found difficult to learn, suggestions and ideas you received from friends that helped make learning this chapter easier and more enjoyable.

My reflections about Haircutting:

LESSONS LEARNED

- The two ways to analyze the structure of a haircut are natural fall and normal projection.
- The four basic forms are: solid form, graduated form, increase-layered form and uniformly layered form.
- Combination forms include two or more of the four basic forms.
- The five main sculpting tools are: shears, taper shears, razors, clippers and combs.
- The primary techniques performed in a haircut include sectioning, head position, parting, distribution, projection, finger and shear position, design line, cross-checking, texturizing, and/or outlining and special grooming.
- Other fundamental considerations when haircutting include fringe and nape variations, growth patterns and techniques used when children are clients.

CHAPTER 9

THINGS TO DO

THINGS TO DO

THINGS TO DO

CHAPTER 10
HAIRSTYLING

VALUE

Hairstyling is the heart of your craft. The reward any artist feels at the moment of accomplishment can be yours when your fingers finish an exciting and successful design for your client.

MAIN IDEA

Form + Texture + Direction + Movement = **A Hairstyle**

PLAN

10.1 HAIRSTYLING THEORY
Primary Hairstyling Considerations
Hairstyling Fundamentals
Hairstyling Essentials
Infection Control & Safety
Client Consultation

10.2 THERMAL STYLING
Thermal Styling Theory
Infection Control & Safety
Thermal Styling Procedure Overview
Air Forming Solid Form
Scrunching Layered Form
Air Forming Graduated Form: 9-Row Brush
Air Forming Layered Form: Round Brush
Air Forming Combination Form: 9-Row Brush
Air Forming Combination Form: Round Brush/Curling Iron
Pressing and Curling
Press and Curl Variation: Flat Iron

10.3 WET STYLING
Fingerwaves
Pincurls
Skip Waves
Rollers
Wet Styling Procedure Overview
Fingerwaves and Flat Pincurls
Straight Volume Rollers and Pincurls
Curvature Volume Rollers and Pincurls

10.4 LONG HAIR STYLING
Long Hair Fundamentals
Long Hair Styling Procedures
Three-Strand Overbraid
Three-Strand Underbraid
French Twist

CHAPTER 10

smartNOTES

10.1 HAIRSTYLING THEORY   pages 311-315

Hairstyling

Primary Hairstyling Considerations

Form   ROUND   TRIANGULAR   OVAL

Texture

Texture Character   WAVE   SPIRAL   CRIMPED

Draw the texture pattern

Texture Speed

Direction

Movement

Parallel

Radial

Formula for Success   Form + Texture + Direction + Movement = Beautiful Hairstyling

HAIRSTYLING

smartNOTES

10.1 HAIRSTYLING THEORY   pages 316-319

Hairstyling Fundamentals — Creating the desired direction and movement, combined with various degrees of volume and closeness.

Distribution and Molding

Radial Distribution

Curved, Parallel Distribution

Hair Wrapping

Sectioning

Straight Shapes

Draw the 7 straight shapes →

Curved Shapes

Draw the 4 curved shapes →

Partings

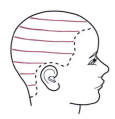

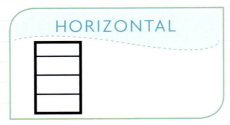

HORIZONTAL

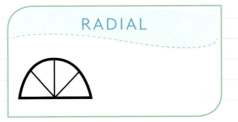

RADIAL

SALON FUNDAMENTALS COSMETOLOGY   217

CHAPTER 10

smartNOTES

10.1 HAIRSTYLING THEORY pages 319-322

Components of a Curl

Components of a Roller, Thermal-Iron or Round Brush Curl

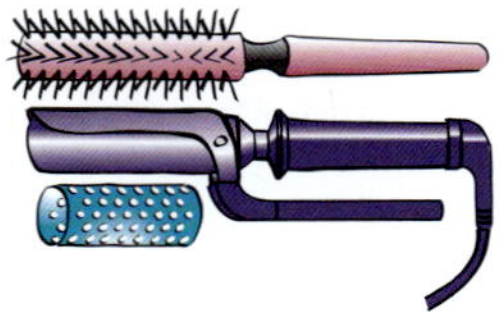

BASE	STEM (ARC)	CIRCLE

Base Controls for Hairstyling

Base Size

Tool Position

ON BASE (Full Base)

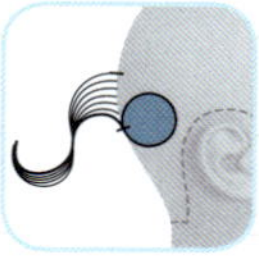

HALF-OFF BASE (Half base)

OFF BASE

UNDERDIRECTED

OVERDIRECTED (Volume Base)

HAIRSTYLING

smartNOTES

10.1 HAIRSTYLING THEORY   pages 323-325

HOW DID YOU DO THAT?
In the space provided below, describe the components used to create each hairstyle.

Base Control—
Indentation

Finishing the
Hairstyle

Comb-out   FIRST 1.

THEN 2.

NOW 3.

AFTER 4.

FINALLY 5.

1 2 3 4 5 6 7

SALON FUNDAMENTALS COSMETOLOGY   219

CHAPTER 10

smartNOTES

10.2 THERMAL STYLING   pages 330-333

Thermal Styling

Thermal Styling Theory

Air Forming

Air Forming Guidelines

-
-
-
-
-
-

| FINGER STYLING | ROUND BRUSH |

smartNOTES

10.2 THERMAL STYLING   page 333-338

Hair Pressing

FINE HAIR	MEDIUM HAIR	COARSE HAIR

Thermal Irons

Thermal Curling

MARCEL

ELECTRIC

Curling Iron Techniques

Base-to-Ends

Ends-to-Base

Ends

Marcel

Spiral

CHAPTER 10

RUBRIC

This rubric is a self-assessment tool designed to compare your skill to industry standards. Indicate your present level of performance by checking the appropriate box. See overview for instructions.

Air Forming Solid Form

Industry Standard – to meet entry-level proficiency, industry standards require that you:
- Provide styling and finishing techniques to complete a hairstyle to the satisfaction of the client.

Preparation
- Disinfect workstation; assemble implements/supplies; wash hands; analyze hair/scalp; ask client to remove jewelry; drape/shampoo/condition client

Procedure
- Remove excess moisture; detangle hair; apply appropriate styling product and distribute through hair
- Section head; take horizontal partings across nape; position medium-diameter round brush under hair
- Direct airflow downward; dry base, midstrand and then ends; work from center to either side
- Use same technique on subsequent horizontal partings, working up back of head from center to either side
- Use portion of previously air-formed section to blend bases
- Extend horizontal partings to front hairline
- Switch to larger-diameter round brush; use medium projection for off-base control
- Work to front hairline using same techniques; repeat same procedures working toward top of lighter side
- Use half-off base control at top of heavier side; work up to side part
- Use same technique throughout design
- Use finishing procedures to style hair as desired

Completion
- Offer a prebook visit; recommend retail products; disinfect implements, arrange workstation in proper order and wash hands

TOTAL = ADDITION OF ALL TEACHER ASSESSMENT BOXES   TOTAL POINTS =

39

PERCENTAGE = STUDENT SCORE / HIGHEST POSSIBLE SCORE   _____ %

222   UNIT 2 HAIR SERVICES

HAIRSTYLING

RUBRIC

This rubric is a self-assessment tool designed to compare your skill to industry standards. Indicate your present level of performance by checking the appropriate box. See overview for instructions.

Scrunching Layered Form

Industry Standard – to meet entry-level proficiency, industry standards require that you:

- Provide styling and finishing techniques to complete a hairstyle to the satisfaction of the client.

	Level 1	Level 2	Level 3	To Improve, Need To:	Teacher Assessment
Preparation					
• Disinfect workstation; assemble implements/supplies; wash hands; analyze hair/scalp; ask client to remove jewelry; drape/shampoo/condition client	☐	☐	☐		☐
Procedure					
• Distribute styling product through hair	☐	☐	☐		☐
• Attach diffuser	☐	☐	☐		☐
• Tilt head back	☐	☐	☐		☐
• Position diffuser beneath exterior strands	☐	☐	☐		☐
• Lift dryer up into lengths	☐	☐	☐		☐
• Lift hair at scalp with your fingers	☐	☐	☐		☐
• Dry ends, midstrand and then base	☐	☐	☐		☐
• Work toward interior and complete back using same techniques	☐	☐	☐		☐
• Tilt head to either side and use same techniques	☐	☐	☐		☐
• Work toward interior and complete using same techniques	☐	☐	☐		☐
Completion					
• Offer a prebook; recommend retail products; disinfect implements, arrange workstation in proper order and wash hands	☐	☐	☐		☐

TOTAL = ADDITION OF ALL TEACHER ASSESSMENT BOXES

TOTAL POINTS = ☐
36

PERCENTAGE = STUDENT SCORE / HIGHEST POSSIBLE SCORE

_____ %

CHAPTER 10

RUBRIC

This rubric is a self-assessment tool designed to compare your skill to industry standards. Indicate your present level of performance by checking the appropriate box. See overview for instructions.

Air Forming Graduated Form: 9-Row Brush

Industry Standard — to meet entry-level proficiency, industry standards require that you:
- Provide styling and finishing techniques to complete a hairstyle to the satisfaction of the client.

	Level 1	Level 2	Level 3	To Improve, I Need To:	Teacher Assessment
Preparation					
• Disinfect workstation; assemble implements/supplies; wash hands; analyze hair/scalp; ask client to remove jewelry; drape/shampoo/condition client	☐	☐	☐		☐
Procedure					
• Apply medium-hold styling product; use vent brush and air form hair to remove excess moisture; section hair for control	☐	☐	☐		☐
• Release diagonal-forward partings across nape	☐	☐	☐		☐
• Position brush at base using only first few rows of 9-row brush; air form base to ends in curved movement using low projection	☐	☐	☐		☐
• Continue taking diagonal-forward partings; work up back	☐	☐	☐		☐
• Extend slightly diagonal-forward partings to front hairline in area above ear; position brush parallel; continue using curved movement	☐	☐	☐		☐
• Work from center to either side using same techniques as you work from center to front hairline on either side	☐	☐	☐		☐
• Work toward top to complete air-forming techniques; direct lengths away from face at front hairline	☐	☐	☐		☐
• Style as desired	☐	☐	☐		☐
Completion					
• Offer a prebook visit; recommend retail products; disinfect implements, arrange workstation in proper order and wash hands	☐	☐	☐		☐

TOTAL = ADDITION OF ALL TEACHER ASSESSMENT BOXES   TOTAL POINTS = ☐
                                                                30

PERCENTAGE = STUDENT SCORE / HIGHEST POSSIBLE SCORE   _____ %

HAIRSTYLING

RUBRIC

This rubric is a self-assessment tool designed to compare your skill to industry standards. Indicate your present level of performance by checking the appropriate box. See overview for instructions.

Air Forming Layered Form: Round Brush

Industry Standard – to meet entry-level proficiency, industry standards require that you:
- Provide styling and finishing techniques to complete a hairstyle to the satisfaction of the client.

	Level 1	Level 2	Level 3	To Improve, I Need To:	Teacher Assessment
Preparation					
• Disinfect workstation; assemble implements/supplies; wash hands; analyze hair/scalp; ask client to remove jewelry; drape/shampoo/condition client	☐	☐	☐		☐
Procedure					
• Apply styling product	☐	☐	☐		☐
• Use vent brush and remove moisture from hair	☐	☐	☐		☐
• Section head for control	☐	☐	☐		☐
• Release horizontal parting across nape	☐	☐	☐		☐
• Position brush underneath hair and rotate brush upward	☐	☐	☐		☐
• Dry base, midstrand and ends	☐	☐	☐		☐
• Work from center to either side using volume base control	☐	☐	☐		☐
• Use diagonal-forward partings as you work up back of head	☐	☐	☐		☐
• Use portion of previously air-formed section and stagger bases	☐	☐	☐		☐
• Use vertical partings as you work toward crown	☐	☐	☐		☐
• Overdirect the fringe for exaggerated volume	☐	☐	☐		☐
• Use finishing procedures and style as desired	☐	☐	☐		☐
Completion					
• Offer a prebook visit; recommend retail products; disinfect implements, arrange workstation in proper order and wash hands	☐	☐	☐		☐

TOTAL = ADDITION OF ALL TEACHER ASSESSMENT BOXES   TOTAL POINTS = ____
42

PERCENTAGE = STUDENT SCORE / HIGHEST POSSIBLE SCORE   ____ %

CHAPTER 10

RUBRIC

This rubric is a self-assessment tool designed to compare your skill to industry standards. Indicate your present level of performance by checking the appropriate box. See overview for instructions.

Air Forming Combination Form: 9-Row Brush

Industry Standard – to meet entry-level proficiency, industry standards require that you:
- Provide styling and finishing techniques to complete a hairstyle to the satisfaction of the client.

	Level 1	Level 2	Level 3	To Improve, I Need To:	Teacher Assessment
Preparation					
Disinfect workstation; assemble implements/supplies; wash hands; analyze hair/scalp; ask client to remove jewelry; drape/shampoo/condition client	☐	☐	☐		☐
Procedure					
Find natural part; section back in half	☐	☐	☐		☐
Position 9-row brush on top of nape lengths and air form	☐	☐	☐		☐
Above nape, begin at center; position brush underneath hair	☐	☐	☐		☐
Take slight diagonal-forward partings and work from center to behind ear	☐	☐	☐		☐
Use portion of previous partings and continue to work toward crown	☐	☐	☐		☐
At sides, use same techniques from horizontal partings	☐	☐	☐		☐
At front hairline, position brush underneath hair and direct lengths toward face	☐	☐	☐		☐
Continue to work upward using same techniques	☐	☐	☐		☐
Lift hair along parting with first few rows of brush; repeat same procedures on opposite side	☐	☐	☐		☐
Use round brush throughout interior	☐	☐	☐		☐
Use finishing procedures to style hair as desired	☐	☐	☐		☐
Completion					
Offer a prebook visit; recommend retail products; disinfect implements, arrange workstation in proper order and wash hands	☐	☐	☐		☐

TOTAL = ADDITION OF ALL TEACHER ASSESSMENT BOXES   TOTAL POINTS = ☐
                                                                     39

PERCENTAGE = STUDENT SCORE / HIGHEST POSSIBLE SCORE   _____ %

HAIRSTYLING

RUBRIC

This rubric is a self-assessment tool designed to compare your skill to industry standards. Indicate your present level of performance by checking the appropriate box. See overview for instructions.

Air Forming Combination Form: Round Brush/Curling Iron

Industry Standard – To meet entry-level proficiency, industry standards require that you:
- Provide styling and finishing techniques to complete a hairstyle to the satisfaction of the client.

	Level 1	Level 2	Level 3	To Improve, I Need To:	Teacher Assessment
Preparation					
Disinfect workstation; assemble implements/supplies; wash hands; analyze hair/scalp; ask client to remove jewelry; drape/shampoo/condition client	☐	☐	☐		☐
Procedure					
Section hair; use 9-row brush to air form nape lengths; above nape, work from center to either side from horizontal partings	☐	☐	☐		☐
Lift hair at scalp to create volume, then position brush underneath the hair to create curved end texture	☐	☐	☐		☐
Work upward using same technique from diagonal-forward and vertical partings; direct hair away from face	☐	☐	☐		☐
Work toward front using same techniques from vertical partings	☐	☐	☐		☐
At front sides, create curvature movement away from face; complete front sides	☐	☐	☐		☐
Create volume curved end texture in back; work toward crown using progression of volume base controls	☐	☐	☐		☐
Create maximum volume at crown and top; overdirect hair at fringe area	☐	☐	☐		☐
Safely check temperature of curling iron; begin at back for curling-iron techniques on shorter lengths, create curved end texture	☐	☐	☐		☐
Create progression of volume curling-iron base controls as you work upward	☐	☐	☐		☐
Use portion of previous curl and progress to maximum-volume base control at crown; continue to use maximum-volume base control as you work from center top to sides	☐	☐	☐		☐
Use overdirected base control at fringe area	☐	☐	☐		☐
Use finishing procedures and style hair as desired	☐	☐	☐		☐
Completion					
Offer a prebook visit; recommend retail products; disinfect implements, arrange workstation in proper order and wash hands	☐	☐	☐		☐

TOTAL = ADDITION OF ALL TEACHER ASSESSMENT BOXES   TOTAL POINTS = 42

PERCENTAGE = STUDENT SCORE / HIGHEST POSSIBLE SCORE   _____ %

SALON FUNDAMENTALS COSMETOLOGY 227

CHAPTER 10

RUBRIC

This rubric is a self-assessment tool designed to compare your skill to industry standards. Indicate your present level of performance by checking the appropriate box. See overview for instructions.

Pressing and Curling

Industry Standard – to meet entry-level proficiency, industry standards require that you:
- Provide styling and finishing techniques to complete a hairstyle to the satisfaction of the client.

	Level 1	Level 2	Level 3	To Improve, I Need To:	Teacher Assessment
Preparation					
• Disinfect workstation; assemble implements/supplies; wash hands; analyze hair/scalp; ask client to remove jewelry; drape/shampoo/condition client	☐	☐	☐		☐
Procedure					
• Apply pressing cream or oil; section hair for air forming	☐	☐	☐		☐
• Air form to reduce natural curl pattern	☐	☐	☐		☐
• Section hair for thermal pressing; apply more pressing cream or oil if necessary	☐	☐	☐		☐
• Test temperature of pressing comb	☐	☐	☐		☐
• Insert teeth of pressing comb underneath parting	☐	☐	☐		☐
• Turn comb and press hair with spine as you work from base to ends	☐	☐	☐		☐
• Feed hair slowly through comb as you work down toward the ends	☐	☐	☐		☐
• Complete back using horizontal partings	☐	☐	☐		☐
• Press the front using diagonal partings	☐	☐	☐		☐
• Press hairline last	☐	☐	☐		☐
• Heat marcel irons	☐	☐	☐		☐
• Test the temperature of the irons	☐	☐	☐		☐
• Curl hair as desired	☐	☐	☐		☐
• Complete the comb-out style	☐	☐	☐		☐
Completion					
• Offer a prebook visit; recommend retail products; disinfect implements, arrange workstation in proper order and wash hands	☐	☐	☐		☐

TOTAL = ADDITION OF ALL TEACHER ASSESSMENT BOXES

TOTAL POINTS = ☐

48

PERCENTAGE = STUDENT SCORE / HIGHEST POSSIBLE SCORE

_____ %

smartNOTES

10.3 WET STYLING pages 365-369

Wet Styling

Fingerwaves

Pincurls

Components of a Pincurl

Types of Pincurls

| FLAT | VOLUME | INDENTATION |

Pincurl Base Shapes

-
-
-

Base Control – Pincurls
On Base (no stem)
Half-Off Base (half-stem)
Off Base (full-stem)
Underdirected
Overdirected

CHAPTER 10

smartNOTES

10.3 **WET STYLING** — pages 371-373

Skip Waves

Ridge Curl

Rollers

Roller Diameter

Roller Shapes

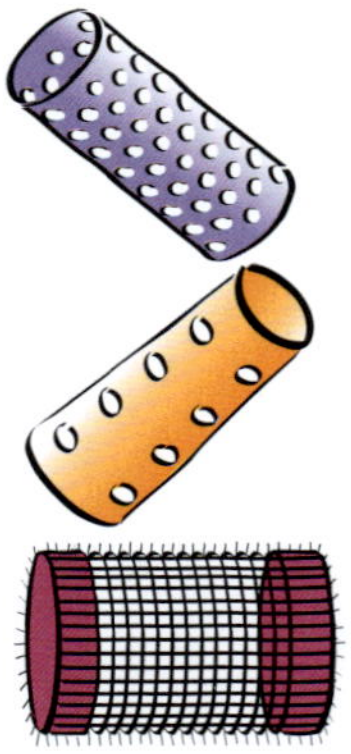

STRAIGHT	CURVATURE

1 2 3 4 5 6 7

230 UNIT 2 HAIR SERVICES

HAIRSTYLING

IT'S YOUR TURN!

Using the 7 facial shapes provided, sketch a design that best suits each shape. Colored pencils will allow you to add color to your creation.

REMEMBER YOUR FUNDAMENTALS OF HAIRSTYLING!

Form	Texture
Movement	Distribution
Molding	Sectioning
Air Forming	Roller Set
Wet Set	

1 2 3 4 **5** 6 7

SALON FUNDAMENTALS COSMETOLOGY   231

CHAPTER 10

RUBRIC

This rubric is a self-assessment tool designed to compare your skill to industry standards. Indicate your present level of performance by checking the appropriate box. See overview for instructions.

Fingerwaves and Flat Pincurls

Industry Standard — to meet entry-level proficiency, industry standards require that you:
- Provide styling and finishing techniques to complete a hairstyle to the satisfaction of the client.

	Level 1	Level 2	Level 3	To Improve, I Need To:	Teacher Assessment
Preparation					
• Disinfect workstation; assemble implements/supplies; wash hands; analyze hair/scalp; ask client to remove jewelry; drape/shampoo/condition client	☐	☐	☐		☐
Procedure					
• Apply styling product	☐	☐	☐		☐
• Create slightly curved diagonal side part	☐	☐	☐		☐
• Mold first direction (toward closed end) of oblong	☐	☐	☐		☐
• Position index finger in center of shape and mold second direction (toward open end)	☐	☐	☐		☐
• Create the ridge, starting at the concave end	☐	☐	☐		☐
• Complete ridge of first oblong	☐	☐	☐		☐
• Continue fingerwaving	☐	☐	☐		☐
• Complete fingerwaves	☐	☐	☐		☐
• Set flat pincurls beginning at concave end of last oblong	☐	☐	☐		☐
• Complete flat pincurls	☐	☐	☐		☐
• Use finishing procedures to style as desired	☐	☐	☐		☐
Completion					
• Offer a prebook visit; recommend retail products; discard non-reusable materials, disinfect implements, arrange workstation in proper order and wash hands	☐	☐	☐		☐

TOTAL = ADDITION OF ALL TEACHER ASSESSMENT BOXES

TOTAL POINTS = ☐
39

PERCENTAGE = STUDENT SCORE / HIGHEST POSSIBLE SCORE

_____ %

HAIRSTYLING

RUBRIC

This rubric is a self-assessment tool designed to compare your skill to industry standards. Indicate your present level of performance by checking the appropriate box. See overview for instructions.

Straight Volume Rollers and Pincurls

Industry Standard – to meet entry-level proficiency, industry standards require that you:
- Provide styling and finishing techniques to complete a hairstyle to the satisfaction of the client.

	Level 1	Level 2	Level 3	To Improve, I Need To:	Teacher Assessment
Preparation					
Disinfect workstation; assemble implements/supplies; wash hands; analyze hair/scalp; ask client to remove jewelry; drape/shampoo/condition client	☐	☐	☐		☐
Procedure					
Apply setting product	☐	☐	☐		☐
Begin at front hairline; mold hair away from face downward to nape, in curved movement around ears	☐	☐	☐		☐
Measure and part 1 diameter rectangular base; set roller on-base; secure	☐	☐	☐		☐
Begin next row; take center parting behind first roller; use diameter and length of roller to determine base size, continue using on-base roller control	☐	☐	☐		☐
Work from center to either side, setting rollers on base	☐	☐	☐		☐
Use pincurls to accommodate shorter lengths	☐	☐	☐		☐
Decrease projection angle to set rollers half-off base; use smaller diameter rollers for shorter lengths	☐	☐	☐		☐
Adjust angle of diagonal-forward partings to accommodate curves of head	☐	☐	☐		☐
Set last row in pincurls	☐	☐	☐		☐
Relax set with two cushion brushes; dry mold and backbrush in direction of design	☐	☐	☐		☐
Detail and finish using a wide-tooth tail comb	☐	☐	☐		☐
Completion					
Offer a prebook visit; recommend retail products; disinfect implements, arrange workstation in proper order and wash hands	☐	☐	☐		☐

TOTAL = ADDITION OF ALL TEACHER ASSESSMENT BOXES

TOTAL POINTS = ☐

39

PERCENTAGE = STUDENT SCORE / HIGHEST POSSIBLE SCORE _____ %

CHAPTER 10

RUBRIC

This rubric is a self-assessment tool designed to compare your skill to industry standards. Indicate your present level of performance by checking the appropriate box. See overview for instructions.

Curvature Volume Rollers and Pincurls

Industry Standard – to meet entry-level proficiency, industry standards require that you:
- Provide styling and finishing techniques to complete a hairstyle to the satisfaction of the client.

	Level 1	Level 2	Level 3	To Improve, I Need To:	Teacher Assessment
Preparation					
Disinfect workstation; assemble implements/supplies; wash hands; analyze hair/scalp; ask client to remove jewelry; drape/shampoo/condition client	☐	☐	☐		☐
Procedure					
Mold and scale half-circle at front hairline	☐	☐	☐		☐
Mold and scale expanded circle at sides	☐	☐	☐		☐
Mold and scale straight shape between circle shapes	☐	☐	☐		☐
Set half-circle using curvature volume base control	☐	☐	☐		☐
At sides, set expanded circle using curvature volume base control	☐	☐	☐		☐
In back, set straight shape using rollers and pincurls within straight volume base control within bricklay pattern	☐	☐	☐		☐
Position client underneath dryer	☐	☐	☐		☐
Remove rollers and use finishing procedures to style hair	☐	☐	☐		☐
Completion					
Offer a prebook visit; recommend retail products; disinfect implements, arrange workstation in proper order and wash hands	☐	☐	☐		☐

TOTAL = ADDITION OF ALL TEACHER ASSESSMENT BOXES   TOTAL POINTS = ☐
                                                                    30

PERCENTAGE = STUDENT SCORE / HIGHEST POSSIBLE SCORE   _____ %

HAIRSTYLING

smartNOTES

10.4 LONG HAIR STYLING   pages 384-392

Long Hair Fundamentals

Form

Three-Strand Overbraid

Three-Strand Underbraid

YOU BE THE JUDGE

Using your judgment skills, offer comments on the following statements. Share and discuss with a classmate the reasons that led to your choices.

1. What is the MOST POPULAR hairstyle worn today?

   Why is this style so popular?

2. What is the MOST DIFFICULT hairstyle for you to create?

   Why is this style difficult for you to create?

3. What is the EASIEST hairstyle for you to create?

4. Which hairstyle do you feel will be the most FINANCIALLY rewarding for you?

   Why do you feel this style will be the most financially rewarding?

SALON FUNDAMENTALS COSMETOLOGY   235

CHAPTER 10

RUBRIC

This rubric is a self-assessment tool designed to compare your skill to industry standards. Indicate your present level of performance by checking the appropriate box. See overview for instructions.

Three-Strand Overbraid

Industry Standard – to meet entry-level proficiency, industry standards require that you:
- Consult with and provide a long hair style in accordance with a client's needs or expectations.

	Level 1	Level 2	Level 3	To Improve, I Need To:	Teacher Assessment
Preparation					
• Disinfect workstation; assemble implements/supplies; wash hands; analyze hair/scalp; ask client to remove jewelry; drape/shampoo/condition client	☐	☐	☐		☐
Procedure					
• Distribute hair straight back	☐	☐	☐		☐
• Take crescent-shaped section at fringe area	☐	☐	☐		☐
• Subdivide hair into three equal strands	☐	☐	☐		☐
• Cross left strand over center strand, then cross right strand over center strand	☐	☐	☐		☐
• Cross left strand over center strand again	☐	☐	☐		☐
• Take diagonal parting on left side and join with center strand	☐	☐	☐		☐
• Switch hands and repeat same procedures on other side	☐	☐	☐		☐
• Pick up consistent-size partings and work side to side using same procedures	☐	☐	☐		☐
• Toward nape, conform hands to curve of head	☐	☐	☐		☐
• Continue three-strand overbraid technique toward ends	☐	☐	☐		☐
• Secure ends with coated elastic band	☐	☐	☐		☐
Completion					
• Offer a prebook visit; recommend retail products; disinfect implements, arrange workstation in proper order and wash hands	☐	☐	☐		☐

TOTAL = ADDITION OF ALL TEACHER ASSESSMENT BOXES

TOTAL POINTS = ☐
39

PERCENTAGE = STUDENT SCORE / HIGHEST POSSIBLE SCORE

_____ %

HAIRSTYLING

RUBRIC

This rubric is a self-assessment tool designed to compare your skill to industry standards. Indicate your present level of performance by checking the appropriate box. See overview for instructions.

Three-Strand Underbraid

Industry Standard — to meet entry-level proficiency, industry standards require that you:
- Consult with and provide a long hair style in accordance with a client's needs or expectations.

	Level 1	Level 2	Level 3	To Improve, I Need To:	Teacher Assessment
Preparation					
• Disinfect workstation; assemble implements/supplies; wash hands; analyze hair/scalp; ask client to remove jewelry; drape/shampoo/condition client; re-drape for dry service	☐	☐	☐		☐
Procedure					
• Distribute hair straight back	☐	☐	☐		☐
• Take crescent-shaped section at fringe area	☐	☐	☐		☐
• Subdivide hair into three equal strands	☐	☐	☐		☐
• Cross right strand under center strand, then cross left strand under center strand	☐	☐	☐		☐
• Cross right strand under center strand again	☐	☐	☐		☐
• Take diagonal parting on right side and join with center strand	☐	☐	☐		☐
• Switch hands and repeat same procedures on other side	☐	☐	☐		☐
• Pick up consistent-size partings and work side to side using same procedures	☐	☐	☐		☐
• Toward nape, conform hands to curve of head	☐	☐	☐		☐
• Continue three-strand underbraid technique toward ends	☐	☐	☐		☐
• Secure ends with coated elastic band	☐	☐	☐		☐
Completion					
• Offer a prebook visit; recommend retail products; disinfect implements, arrange workstation in proper order and wash hands	☐	☐	☐		☐

TOTAL = ADDITION OF ALL TEACHER ASSESSMENT BOXES

TOTAL POINTS = ☐
39

PERCENTAGE = STUDENT SCORE / HIGHEST POSSIBLE SCORE

_____ %

CHAPTER 10

RUBRIC

This rubric is a self-assessment tool designed to compare your skill to industry standards. Indicate your present level of performance by checking the appropriate box. See overview for instructions.

French Twist

Industry Standard – to meet entry-level proficiency, industry standards require that you:
- Consult with and provide a long hair style in accordance with a client's needs or expectations.

Preparation

	Level 1	Level 2	Level 3	To Improve, I Need To:	Teacher Assessment
Disinfect workstation; assemble implements/supplies; wash hands; analyze hair/scalp; ask client to remove jewelry; drape/shampoo/condition client; re-drape for dry service	☐	☐	☐		☐

Procedure

	Level 1	Level 2	Level 3		Teacher Assessment
Section fringe	☐	☐	☐		☐
Backcomb or backbrush right side diagonally toward center back	☐	☐	☐		☐
Smooth surface with brush	☐	☐	☐		☐
Secure with line of interlocked bobby pins slightly off center	☐	☐	☐		☐
Backcomb and smooth lengths on left side	☐	☐	☐		☐
Direct and twist lengths counterclockwise; create vertical roll	☐	☐	☐		☐
Secure roll using bobby pins and hairpins	☐	☐	☐		☐
Backcomb and arrange ends and fringe lengths	☐	☐	☐		☐
Finish hair as desired	☐	☐	☐		☐

Completion

	Level 1	Level 2	Level 3		Teacher Assessment
Offer a prebook visit; recommend retail products; disinfect implements, arrange workstation in proper order and wash hands	☐	☐	☐		☐

TOTAL = ADDITION OF ALL TEACHER ASSESSMENT BOXES   TOTAL POINTS = ☐
                                                                 33

PERCENTAGE = STUDENT SCORE / HIGHEST POSSIBLE SCORE   _____ %

238 UNIT 2 HAIR SERVICES

HAIRSTYLING

TALKING POINTS

Your next challenge is to be ready to talk about some of the important ideas in this chapter. Follow the directions listed next to each box. Then practice talking about your ideas with others.

Describe an invention that you have just created to use when styling hair

Create a promotional ad for wedding parties regarding hairstyling.

Create a promotional ad inviting prom attendees to visit the salon for prom styles.

THE CHALLENGE

Now it's time to see how well you know your new material. First answer these questions. Then use the Memory Box that follows to check yourself. Look up each answer on the corresponding page in the *Salon Fundamentals* textbook. Check "got it" for all correct answers and "not yet" for all incorrect responses. Using the "Know Chart," record all of your correct responses in the "I Know" column. After correcting incorrect answers, record all of your corrected responses in the "I Need to Study" column. That way you know exactly what to review before continuing in this study guide.

1. What are the four primary considerations a hairstylist must reflect upon before creating a style design?
   _____ _____ _____ _____

2. Define the following parts of a curl:
   Base _____
   Stem _____
   Circle _____

3. Base sizes are determined by the size of the tool being used. What are the most commonly used base sizes?
   _____ _____ _____

4. TRUE FALSE An on-base (full base) tool position will give more volume and will have a stronger base strength than a half-off base (half base) tool position.

5. _____ is the technique of drying and/or styling hair by using a hand-held dryer while simultaneously using your fingers, a variety of brushes, pressing comb and/or a thermal curling iron.

6. In a thermal styling procedure, it is the _____ bonds that are broken by both water and heat.

7. Thermal hairstyling is considered to have a _____ effect because additional heat or moisture will cause the hair to return to its original shape or configuration.

8. Describe how to tell if a stove-heated thermal iron is too hot. _____
   _____

9. TRUE FALSE The use of heat-protective styling products can help avoid damaging the hair during a thermal hair styling procedure.

10. _____ refers to the area of hairstyling in which the hair is manipulated into the desired shapes and movements while wet and then is allowed to dry.

1 2 3   6 7

SALON FUNDAMENTALS COSMETOLOGY 239

CHAPTER 10

MEMORY BOX

1. PAGE 312 — GOT IT / NOT YET
2. PAGE 319 — GOT IT / NOT YET
3. PAGE 320 — GOT IT / NOT YET
4. PAGE 321 — GOT IT / NOT YET
5. PAGE 330 — GOT IT / NOT YET
6. PAGE 330 — GOT IT / NOT YET
7. PAGE 330 — GOT IT / NOT YET
8. PAGE 331 — GOT IT / NOT YET
9. PAGE 332 — GOT IT / NOT YET
10. PAGE 365 — GOT IT / NOT YET

KNOW CHART

I KNOW:

I NEED TO STUDY:

SHOW YOU KNOW...

Sketch hairstyles from the following decades. A few have been done for you. Explain your sketch.

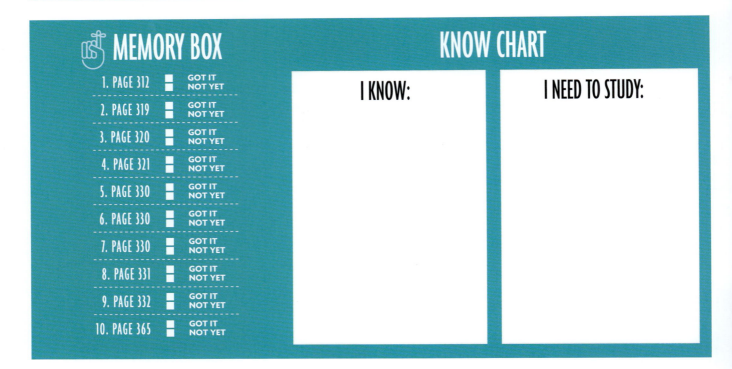

1900's   1920's   1930's   1940's   1950's

1960's   1970's   1980's   1990's   The Future!

240   UNIT 2 HAIR SERVICES   1 2 3 4 5 6 7

KNOWLEDGE GRID

Start at the top of the Knowledge Grid and work your way down, answering each question to check your understanding of *Chapter 10, Hairstyling*. The questions found here will help you deepen your understanding, build self-confidence and increase your awareness of different ways of thinking about a subject.

KNOW	WHAT ARE THE LINES CALLED THAT SUBDIVIDE SHAPES OR SECTIONS TO HELP DISTRIBUTE AND CONTROL THE HAIR?	
COMPREHEND	DESCRIBE WHAT DETERMINES THE AMOUNT OF MOVEMENT A PINCURL WILL HAVE.	
APPLY	DRAW AND LABEL THE STRAIGHT SHAPES USED IN HAIR DESIGN.	
ANALYZE	COMPARE THE EFFECT OF ON-BASE AND OFF-BASE TOOL POSITIONS FOR INDENTATION BASE CONTROL.	
SYNTHESIZE	CREATE A PROMOTIONAL AD FOR THE UPCOMING PROM SEASON THAT ADVERTISES YOUR SPECIALTY IN LONG HAIR STYLING.	
EVALUATE	IN YOUR OPINION, WHAT IS THE MOST POPULAR HAIRSTYLE TODAY?	

CHAPTER 10

A CLASS ACT

Now that you have completed your work in Hairstyling, it's time to demonstrate your creative talents in a class competition.

Each member of the class will create an entry for "Best Hair Design." Students will plan, sketch, demonstrate and explain their creations.

REMEMBER: Before starting you must sketch the design, list key features to be explained and name your creation!

SKETCH

KEY FEATURES

DESIGN NAME:

All designs will be judged for:

Design   1 2 3 4 5 6 7 8 9 10   points: _____

Technique   1 2 3 4 5 6 7 8 9 10   points: _____

Explanation   1 2 3 4 5 6 7 8 9 10   points: _____

TOTAL POINTS: _____

BRAIN CONDITIONER
MULTIPLE CHOICE. CIRCLE THE CORRECT ANSWER.

1. The term texture character refers to the:
   a. pattern of texture   b. thickness of texture   c. direction of texture   d. movement of texture

2. A long, slow wave would be an example of:
   a. crimped texture   b. a fast-speed texture pattern
   c. a slow-speed texture pattern   d. spiral curls

3. Which shape is generally recognized as the ideal face shape?
   a. oval   b. oblong   c. square   d. round

4. Center parts generally work well with what type of face shape?
   a. oval   b. oblong   c. square   d. long and thin

5. The process of combing wet hair into the desired position is referred to as molding or:
   a. parting   b. shaping   c. curving   d. distributing

6. An example of a straight shape used in sectioning the hair is a(n):
   a. triangle   b. oblong   c. oval   d. circle

7. Lines that subdivide shapes or sections to help distribute and control the hair are called:
   a. roller lengths   b. forms   c. partings   d. bases

8. What is the area between partings within a shape called?
   a. circle of a curl   b. curl base   c. form   d. stem

9. When working with rollers or thermal irons, partings will generally be:
   a. oval   b. curved   c. straight   d. round

10. The section of curl between the scalp and the first turn of the roller is called:
    a. form   b. base   c. circle   d. stem

11. What determines the size of the circle of a curl?
    a. diameter of the stem   b. diameter of the base   c. diameter of the tool   d. length of the tool

12. The combination of the size of the base and the position of the curl in relation to the base is called:
    a. diameter control   b. combination control   c. curl control   d. base control

13. Which diameter size means the area between partings is exactly the same as the diameter of the roller?
    a. ½   b. 1   c. 1½   d. 2

14. The length of a section to be placed on a roller should be:
    a. the same as the diameter of the roller   b. the same as the length of the roller
    c. 1½ times the length of the roller   d. 2 times the length of the roller

15. An on-base (full base) tool placement will result in the strongest base strength and:
    a. the most volume   b. the longest curl   c. the smallest diameter   d. the prettiest texture

16. Using a cushion brush to brush all the way to the scalp to integrate the bases is called:
    a. relaxing the set   b. indentation   c. sectioning   d. detailing

17. The technique of drying and/or styling hair by using a hand-held dryer while simultaneously using your fingers, a variety of brushes, pressing comb and/or a thermal curling iron is called:
    a. wet styling   b. directional styling   c. thermal styling   d. form styling

18. Before brushing or combing the hair after a thermal styling procedure, make sure the hair is:
    a. moist   b. warm   c. shampooed   d. completely cool

CHAPTER 10

19. Air forming is another term for:
    a. blow drying
    b. thermal ironing
    c. backcombing
    d. scrunching

20. Why does hair that is too wet not effectively transfer heat?
    a. water keeps disulfide bonds in a softened state
    b. water keeps hydrogen bonds in a softened state
    c. water keeps disulfide bonds in a strengthened state
    d. water keeps hydrogen bonds in a strengthened state

21. Another name for silking is:
    a. hair pressing
    b. scrunching
    c. fingerwaving
    d. wet styling

22. What type of hair can be resistant to hair pressing?
    a. fine
    b. medium
    c. coarse, tightly curled
    d. thin

23. Who was the first person to introduce thermal irons?
    a. Thomas Edison
    b. Benjamin Franklin
    c. Henry Ford
    d. Marcel Grateau

24. Manipulation of a thermal iron when styling involves all of the following techniques EXCEPT:
    a. rolling the iron
    b. quick clicking movement
    c. maintaining a closed clamp
    d. opening and closing the clamp

25. All of the following factors are true when using a thermal iron on tinted, white or very fine hair EXCEPT:
    a. lower iron temperature is used
    b. highest iron temperature is used
    c. hot iron is closed lightly on a damp towel before curling
    d. iron is tested on paper towel prior to service to prevent scorching

26. Which technique creates volume and support at the base and a consistent curl pattern throughout the strand?
    a. base-to-ends
    b. ends-to-base
    c. ends
    d. marcel technique

27. What type of thermal iron will produce an "S" pattern?
    a. straightening
    b. crimping
    c. undulating
    d. flat

28. Which of the following statements is true concerning safety while performing a thermal styling technique?
    a. use higher temperatures and longer contact time on hair that has been chemically altered
    b. allow the tool to come in contact with scalp
    c. if a burn should occur, flush with cold water and let the skin completely cool
    d. always perform procedure on wet hair

29. Which of the following steps would NOT be taken if a burn occurs on your client during a thermal styling procedure?
    a. flush with cold water
    b. flush with hot water
    c. blot dry
    d. apply first aid cream

30. When performing an air-forming procedure on a solid form, which of the following steps is taken first?
    a. detangle hair
    b. direct airflow on top of brush
    c. remove excess moisture
    d. section the head

31. Which of the following steps is NOT included in the completion phase of air forming?
    a. offer a chance to prebook visit to client
    b. use volume base control with a round brush
    c. disinfect implements and clear workstation
    d. wash your hands with liquid soap

32. All of the following statements are TRUE when working with double-processed hair EXCEPT:
    a. avoid high temperatures from the blow dryer
    b. avoid high temperatures from the thermal iron
    c. no additional care is needed
    d. use thermal-protectant products

33. What is created by two complete oblong shapings that are joined and connected by a ridge?
    a. a pincurl
    b. a flat pincurl
    c. a skip wave
    d. a fingerwave

34. Another name for a pincurl is:
    a. fingerwave
    b. skip wave
    c. sculpture curl
    d. volume wave

HAIRSTYLING

35. **Which types of pincurls are used for closeness?**
    a. flat pincurls
    b. volume pincurls
    c. indentation pincurls
    d. stand-up pincurls

36. **What section determines the amount of movement a pincurl will have?**
    a. base
    b. stem
    c. circle
    d. shape

37. **What determines the width and strength of a wave?**
    a. size of the base
    b. size of the arc
    c. size of the circle
    d. size of the stem

38. **What curls are large stand-up pincurls that achieve a similar effect to hair wound around a roller, but result in less volume?**
    a. barrel
    b. indentation
    c. flat
    d. fingerwave

39. **What type of curl is used to create hollow space and flair?**
    a. indentation pincurls
    b. flat pincurls
    c. volume pincurls
    d. skip waves

40. **A curl that is not quite a flat curl and not quite a stand-up curl and is used to create a blend from areas of volume to areas of closeness is called a:**
    a. transitional pincurl
    b. volume pincurl
    c. skip wave
    d. flat pincurl

41. **Alternating triangle base shapes helps avoid:**
    a. closeness
    b. splits
    c. volume
    d. texture

42. **What is used to keep the base flat while curving the stem with a comb when forming a pincurl?**
    a. spine of the comb
    b. tail of the comb
    c. little finger
    d. index finger

43. **A wave pattern that combines fingerwaves and flat pincurls is:**
    a. ridge curl
    b. connecting ridge
    c. skip wave
    d. volume wave

44. **Use of rollers instead of pincurls will:**
    a. increase the setting time
    b. double the setting time
    c. reduce the setting time
    d. produce a weaker set

45. **All of the following terms are used to describe backbrushing EXCEPT:**
    a. ratting
    b. matting
    c. relaxing
    d. French lacing

FINAL REVIEW

Check your answers as you did before. Place a check mark next to the page number for any incorrect answer. On the lines following the answers, jot down topics that you still need to review.

- [ ] 1. page 314
- [ ] 2. page 314
- [ ] 3. page 316
- [ ] 4. page 316
- [ ] 5. page 316
- [ ] 6. page 318
- [ ] 7. page 319
- [ ] 8. page 319
- [ ] 9. page 319
- [ ] 10. page 319
- [ ] 11. page 319
- [ ] 12. page 320
- [ ] 13. page 321
- [ ] 14. page 321
- [ ] 15. page 321
- [ ] 16. page 324
- [ ] 17. page 330
- [ ] 18. page 330

CHAPTER 10

FINAL REVIEW *continued*

☐ 19.	page 331	☐ 28.	page 339	☐ 37.	page 366
☐ 20.	page 332	☐ 29.	page 339	☐ 38.	page 367
☐ 21.	page 333	☐ 30.	page 343	☐ 39.	page 367
☐ 22.	page 334	☐ 31.	page 350	☐ 40.	page 367
☐ 23.	page 334	☐ 32.	page 358	☐ 41.	page 367
☐ 24.	page 336	☐ 33.	page 365	☐ 42.	page 370
☐ 25.	page 336	☐ 34.	page 366	☐ 43.	page 371
☐ 26.	page 337	☐ 35.	page 366	☐ 44.	page 372
☐ 27.	page 338	☐ 36.	page 366	☐ 45.	page 380

NOTES TO MYSELF

Experts tell us that it is important to summarize your feelings and reactions about what you are learning. Note especially things that surprised you, things you found difficult to learn, suggestions and ideas you received from friends that helped make learning this chapter easier and more enjoyable.

My reflections about Hairstyling:

LESSONS LEARNED

- *Hair design consists of working with form, texture, direction and movement to achieve the final design look.*
- *Wet design is achieved by manipulating the hair into set positions while wet and then maintaining it in these positions while drying.*
- *Thermal design uses heat energy to form the hair into new texture patterns.*
- *Long hair design combines long hair techniques and creativity to transform the hair into distinctive, dramatic or formal designs.*
- *Hair design, achieved by thermal design, wet design and long hair design, is considered temporary because the results can be undone by brushing, combing and shampooing.*

CHAPTER 11
WIGS AND HAIR ADDITIONS

VALUE
Meeting the needs of clients who desire a variety of styles or are in need of looking and feeling better due to hair loss will be rewarding and fulfilling to you as a stylist.

MAIN IDEA
Wigs and Hair Additions – Variety of Styles =
Looking and Feeling Better Following Hair Loss

PLAN

11.1 **WIGS AND HAIRPIECES**
History
Composition, Colors and Construction
Wig and Hairpiece Essentials
Infection Control and Safety
Client Consultation
Wig Services
Hairpieces

11.2 **HAIR ADDITIONS**
Hair Addition Methods

CHAPTER 11

smartNOTES

11.1 WIGS AND HAIRPIECES
pages 395-399

Wigs and Hairpieces

Composition, Colors and Construction

Wig Composition

STRUCTURE

COMPOSITION	COLORS	CONSTRUCTION

A human hair strand will burn slowly and produce an odor; a synthetic fiber will "ball up" on the end and extinguish itself or burn rapidly and produce no odor.

Modacrylic Fibers

Wig Construction

Cap Wigs

Capless Wigs

Wefts

Hair and/or synthetic fibers may attach to the wig cap or base in one of 3 methods: hand-tied, machine-made or semi-hand tied

WIGS AND HAIR ADDITIONS

smartNOTES

11.1 WIGS AND HAIRPIECES   pages 402-405

Wig Services

Client's comfort is as important as the way the wig looks

Wig Measurement and Fitting

Fitting Guidelines

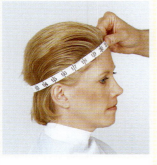

1. Circumference:

2. Forehead to Nape:

3. Ear to Ear:

4. Temple to Temple:

Putting on a Wig Guidelines

FIRST — 1.

THEN — 2.

NOW — 3.

FINALLY — 4.

Wig Blocking Guidelines

-
-
-

SALON FUNDAMENTALS COSMETOLOGY   249

CHAPTER 11

smartNOTES

11.1 WIGS AND HAIRPIECES pages 405-409

Customizing or Fitting a Wig

- DART
- TUCK

Stretching or Shrinking Cap Wigs

- STRETCHING
- SHRINKING

Human-hair wigs and synthetic wigs require slightly different methods of cleaning and conditioning

Cleaning and Conditioning

DIFFERENCES

HUMAN HAIR	SYNTHETIC HAIR

Coloring Services

Cutting and Shaping

250 UNIT 2 HAIR SERVICES

WIGS AND HAIR ADDITIONS

smartNOTES

11.1 WIGS AND HAIRPIECES   pages 410-414

Setting and Styling

 Don't put synthetic wigs and hairpieces under a dryer; excessive heat can melt fiber

Hairpieces Fill in the missing elements for the chart.

	WHAT IS IT?	HOW IS IT USED?
Wiglet		
Cascade		
Fall		
Switch		
Chignon		
Curl Segment		
Braid		
Integration Piece		

Toupees

Guidelines for Measuring
1.

2.

3.

CHAPTER 11

smartNOTES

11.2 HAIR ADDITIONS
pages 415–422

Remy Hair

Products, Implements and Equipment

Hair Addition Methods

Off-the-Scalp Braiding, Loose Hair/Fiber

On-the-Scalp Braiding Loose Hair/Fiber

Track and Sew

Tracking

Sewing Methods

Bonding

DIFFERENCES

HAIR ADDITIONS	WIGS

DIFFERENCES

WEFTS	STRAND-BY-STRAND

252 UNIT 2 HAIR SERVICES

WIGS AND HAIR ADDITIONS

WORD FIND

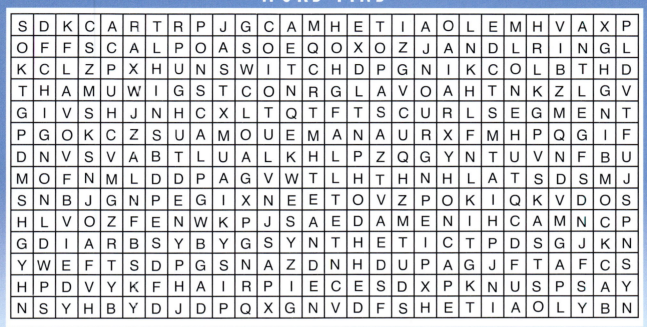

In the word find, circle the words listed below. Words are listed forward, backward and diagonally. Listings that have punctuation or two words are found without punctuation or spacing in the puzzle. How many of these words can you define?

WIGS	MSDS	J AND L RING	HAIRPIECES
MODACRYLICS	SYNTHETIC	SEW	CAP
CAPLESS	MACHINE MADE	BLOCKING	BACKCOMBING
WIGLET	TOUPEE	FALL	SWITCH
CASCADE	CHIGNON	WEFTS	CURL SEGMENT
BRAID	OFF SCALP	ON SCALP	TRACK

TALKING POINTS

Your next challenge is to be ready to talk about some of the important ideas in this chapter. Follow the directions listed next to each box. Then practice talking about your ideas with others.

	List three famous people from the past that you know wore wigs. Discuss the role wigs played in that society.
	List the feelings you imagine could be associated with hair loss. Circle the one that would be more difficult for you to empathize with as a stylist.
	Explain how you would add a hairpiece to this style to create a more dramatic effect.

1 2 **3** 4 **5** 6 7

SALON FUNDAMENTALS COSMETOLOGY 253

CHAPTER 11

THE CHALLENGE

Now it's time to see how well you know your new material. First answer these questions. Then use the Memory Box that follows to check yourself. Look up each answer on the corresponding page in the *Salon Fundamentals* textbook. Check "got it" for all correct answers and "not yet" for all incorrect responses. Using the "Know Chart," record all of your correct responses in the "I Know" column. After correcting incorrect answers, record all of your corrected responses in the "I Need to Study" column. That way you know exactly what to review before continuing in this study guide.

1. Wigs have been worn by men and women since the beginning of recorded history. Wigs are made of _____ , _____ , _____ or a blend of each.

2. Explain how to tell the difference between human hair and modacrylic (synthetic) wig fibers if you are uncertain of what the wig is made. _____

3. All the colors used for wigs are standardized according to the _____ colors on the _____ ring.

4. TRUE   FALSE   Wigs known as "machine made" consist of hair fiber sewn into long strips called wefts.

5. When performing wig services, it is important that the size of the wig is not compromised. Canvas-covered wig forms, called _____ , are available in many sizes for use during these services.

6. Ready-to-wear wigs may need to be altered to fit the client. An alteration made vertically to remove width in the nape area is a _____ , and an alteration made horizontally to shorten a wig from the front to the nape is a _____ .

7. TRUE   FALSE   A synthetic wig should not be put under a dryer because heat from the dryer can distort the curl patterns.

8. TRUE   FALSE   Human-hair wigs or hairpieces will need to be cleaned more often than those made with synthetic fibers.

9. Synthetic wigs are pre-designed with predetermined _____ patterns.

10. Hairpieces are worn for coverage in specific areas or simply to create particular effects. Name as many types of hairpieces you can think of. _____ _____ _____ _____

MEMORY BOX

1. PAGE 398   ☐ GOT IT ☐ NOT YET
2. PAGE 398   ☐ GOT IT ☐ NOT YET
3. PAGE 398   ☐ GOT IT ☐ NOT YET
4. PAGE 399   ☐ GOT IT ☐ NOT YET
5. PAGE 404   ☐ GOT IT ☐ NOT YET
6. PAGE 405   ☐ GOT IT ☐ NOT YET
7. PAGE 406   ☐ GOT IT ☐ NOT YET
8. PAGE 406   ☐ GOT IT ☐ NOT YET
9. PAGE 410   ☐ GOT IT ☐ NOT YET
10. PAGES 410-412   ☐ GOT IT ☐ NOT YET

KNOW CHART

I KNOW:

I NEED TO STUDY:

254   UNIT 2 HAIR SERVICES

1   2   3   **4**   **5**   6   7

KNOWLEDGE GRID

Start at the top of the Knowledge Grid and work your way down, answering each question to check your understanding of *Chapter 11, Wigs and Hair Additions*. The questions found here will help you deepen your understanding, build self-confidence and increase your awareness of different ways of thinking about a subject.

KNOW	LIST THE THREE METHODS IN WHICH HAIR AND/OR SYNTHETIC FIBERS MAY BE ATTACHED TO THE WIG CAP OR BASE.	
COMPREHEND	IDENTIFY THE GUIDELINES FOR PROPERLY FITTING A WIG TO A CLIENT'S PARTICULAR HEAD SIZE AND SHAPE.	
APPLY	OFFER AN EXAMPLE OF A HAIRPIECE THAT IS WORN PRIMARILY AS A BRAID OR PONYTAIL.	
ANALYZE	ANALYZE THE USE OF A TUCK AS COMPARED TO A DART IN CUSTOMIZING OR FITTING A WIG.	
SYNTHESIZE	IN YOUR OWN WORDS, DESCRIBE ONE OF THE "GIVEAWAYS" OF A POORLY FITTED TOUPEE.	
EVALUATE	STATE YOUR OPINION WHY IT IS NECESSARY TO PERFORM A PATCH TEST PRIOR TO THE APPLICATION OF BONDED HAIR ADDITIONS.	

CHAPTER 11

SHOW YOU KNOW...

The chapter you just reviewed, "Wigs and Hair Additions," offers information to assist you in reaching the level of performance indicated by these industry standards:

1. Consult with clients to determine their needs and preferences.
2. Provide non-surgical hair additions.
3. Market professional salon products.

Using the information you have gained from this chapter on wigs and hair additions, identify the famous silhouettes shown below:

BRAIN CONDITIONER
MULTIPLE CHOICE. CIRCLE THE CORRECT ANSWER.

1. Which of the following items are designed to cover the entire head?
   a. wigs	b. hairpieces	c. wiglets	d. cascades

2. Human-hair wigs are generally of what origin?
   a. African	b. South American	c. Canadian	d. Asian or European

3. How many different colors are there on the J and L color ring for wigs and hairpieces?
   a. 30	b. 50	c. 70	d. 90

4. Fantasy hairpieces, theatrical wigs or wigs meant to be worn by display mannequins are most often made of:
   a. human hair	b. synthetic fibers	c. animal hair	d. plastic

5. What type of wig or hairpiece is considered the most expensive?
   a. hand tied	b. machine tied	c. semi-hand tied	d. flammable

6. Capless wigs are cool, comfortable and:
   a. very heavy	b. available in several sizes	c. uncomfortable	d. weigh only a few ounces

7. To create a sturdy, natural-looking, reasonably priced product, the best toupees are:
   a. machine tied	b. hand tied	c. semi-hand tied	d. made of animal hair

8. Which of the following characteristics does NOT describe a cap wig?
   a. available in several sizes
   b. produced most often as handmade
   c. consists of an elasticized mesh-fiber base
   d. consists of rows of hair wefts sewn to elastic

9. How many different sizes of wig blocks are available?
   a. 2
   b. 4
   c. 6
   d. 8

10. A vertical alteration to remove width in the nape area is called a:
    a. dart
    b. tuck
    c. vertical tuck
    d. seam

11. A horizontal alteration made to remove width in the nape area of a wig is called a:
    a. dart
    b. tuck
    c. nip
    d. vertical tuck

12. What do you need to do before stretching a cap wig?
    a. put it in the dryer
    b. spray the inside of the cap with hot water
    c. put it in refrigerator
    d. color it to match your client's hair

13. Depending on the frequency worn, how often should a human-hair wig or hairpiece be cleaned?
    a. 1 to 2 weeks
    b. 2 to 4 weeks
    c. 4 to 6 weeks
    d. 6 to 8 weeks

14. Coloring procedures used on human-hair wigs or hairpieces can include all of the following procedures EXCEPT:
    a. temporary rinses
    b. semi-permanent colors
    c. high-level (lighter) oxidative colors
    d. fillers or low-level (darker) oxidative colors

15. The majority of thinning near the base of a wig is done to:
    a. provide volume
    b. decrease bulk
    c. form wispy ends
    d. prevent frizzing

16. Which hair addition is made up of hair fibers six inches or less in length attached to a round-shaped, flat base?
    a. wiglet
    b. chignon
    c. switch
    d. curl segment

17. A hairpiece consisting of long hair fiber attached to an oblong-shaped dome base is called a:
    a. wiglet
    b. fall
    c. cascade
    d. switch

18. A hairpiece worn primarily by a man to cover bald or thinning hair spots on top of the head is called a:
    a. braid
    b. toupee
    c. fall
    d. chignon

19. What type of hairpiece consists of individual pieces of curly hair worn to create a particular fashion look?
    a. braid
    b. curl segment
    c. chignon
    d. switch

20. A hairpiece with a base that covers the crown, occipital and nape areas is called a:
    a. switch
    b. chignon
    c. braid
    d. fall

21. A fairly long, bulky segment of looped hair usually sewn to a wire base or tied into a strong cord is called a:
    a. switch
    b. curl segment
    c. chignon
    d. toupee

22. Which hairpiece requires a plastic impression of the client's head?
    a. cascade
    b. toupee
    c. braid
    d. fall

23. Loose hair fiber intended for attachment to a client's own hair is called a:
    a. hair addition
    b. fall
    c. wiglet
    d. cascade

24. What is used as a support structure for hair wefts in a track-and-sew hair addition?
    a. a 2-strand twist
    b. a 3-strand off-the-scalp braid
    c. a 3-strand on-the-scalp braid
    d. any off-the-scalp braids

25. Which method of applying hair additions requires a patch test?
    a. sewing
    b. braiding
    c. bonding
    d. stitching

CHAPTER 11

FINAL REVIEW

Check your answers as you did before. Place a check mark next to the page number for any incorrect answer. On the lines following the answers, jot down topics that you still need to review.

☐ 1. page 395	☐ 8. page 399	☐ 15. page 409	☐ 22. page 413
☐ 2. page 398	☐ 9. page 404	☐ 16. page 410	☐ 23. page 415
☐ 3. page 398	☐ 10. page 405	☐ 17. page 410	☐ 24. page 418
☐ 4. page 398	☐ 11. page 405	☐ 18. page 411	☐ 25. page 420
☐ 5. page 399	☐ 12. page 406	☐ 19. page 411	
☐ 6. page 399	☐ 13. page 406	☐ 20. page 411	
☐ 7. page 399	☐ 14. page 408	☐ 21. page 411	

NOTES TO MYSELF

Experts tell us that it is important to summarize your feelings and reactions about what you are learning. Note especially things that surprised you, things you found difficult to learn, suggestions and ideas you received from friends that helped make learning this chapter easier and more enjoyable.

My reflections about Wigs and Hair Additions:

LESSONS LEARNED

- Wigs and hairpieces have been worn throughout history for both practical and aesthetic reasons.
- The fiber composition of a wig or hairpiece—human hair, animal hair, synthetic fibers or blends—affects the design services that can be performed and the products that can be used.
- A positive, supportive and respectful attitude helps build trust and rapport in clients who need wig services due to hair loss.
- The primary goals of most wig services are to achieve a look that resembles the client's own hair and to maintain the wig in good condition.
- Hairpieces are available in a variety of configurations, including: wiglets, cascades, falls, switches, chignons, curl segments, braids and toupees.
- Hair additions are loose fibers that are attached to the base of the client's own hair and are used to achieve added length, density, texture and color.

WIGS AND HAIR ADDITIONS

THINGS TO DO

THINGS TO DO

THINGS TO DO

CHAPTER 12
CHEMICAL TEXTURIZING

VALUE

Being able to chemically alter the texture of hair will greatly expand the services you offer your clients and the number of clients seeking your services.

MAIN IDEA

Perming + Chemically Relaxing + Curl Reforming =
The Three Major Options for Chemical Change

PLAN

12.1 PERMING
History of Perming
Perm Theory
Perming Essentials
Infection Control
  and Safety
Client Consultation
Perm Wrap Overview
Rectangle Perm Wrap
Bricklay Perm Wrap
Spiral Bricklay
  Perm Wrap
Bricklay With
  Directional Fringe
  Perm Wrap
Perm Problems
  and Solutions

12.2 CHEMICAL RELAXING
Chemical Relaxing Theory
Chemical Relaxing Essentials
Infection Control and Safety
Client Consultation
Product and Application Overview
Virgin Sodium Hydroxide Relaxer
Virgin Thio Relaxer
Relaxer Retouch

12.3 CURL REFORMING
Curl Reforming Theory
Curl Reforming Essentials
Infection Control and Safety
Client Consultation
Curl Reforming Service:
  Contour Wrap

CHEMICAL TEXTURIZING

smartNOTES

12.1 PERMING — pages 425-427

Chemical Texturizing

Three Classifications: PERMING RELAXING REFORMING

CHEMICAL TEXTURIZING TIMELINE

HISTORY OF PERMING	POPULAR TECHNIQUE	SPECIALIZED TREATMENT (pH)	CHANGE TO HAIR
Today			
1970			
1938			
1931			
1926			
1905			
Ancient Origin			

People to Know

Charles Nessler

Evans & Mcdonough

Arnold Willatt

CHAPTER 12

smartNOTES

12.1 PERMING
pages 426-428

Two Wrapping Methods

SPIRAL	CROQUIGNOLE

DIFFERENCES

COLD WAVE	HEAT WAVE

pH range of perms:

Acid and Endothermic

Exothermic

Perm Theory

Croquignole

Spiral

BASE-TO-ENDS	ENDS-TO-BASE

UNIT 2 HAIR SERVICES

CHEMICAL TEXTURIZING

smartNOTES

12.1 PERMING
pages 429-432

Perm Tools
-
-

STRAIGHT RODS

CONCAVE RODS

End Paper Techniques

BOOKEND   DOUBLE-PAPER   CUSHION

ALERT! When using multiple end papers, rinse and blot thoroughly

Base Size

Tool Position

ON BASE

HALF-OFF BASE

UNDERDIRECTED

OFF BASE

CHAPTER 12

smartNOTES

12.1 PERMING
pages 432–434

Wrapping Patterns

- RECTANGLE OR 9-BLOCK
- BRICKLAY
- SPIRAL
- DOUBLE-HALO
- OBLONG

Custom Wrapping Patterns
-
-
-

ALERT!

Always read and follow manufacturer's directions before you begin wrapping

Ergonomic Tips
1.

2.

3.

264   UNIT 2 HAIR SERVICES

CHEMICAL TEXTURIZING

smartNOTES

12.1 PERMING

pages 434-436

Chemical Phase

Basic Steps of Chemical Phase

1.
2.
3.
4.
5.
6.
7.

Perm Solution

In alkaline (cold) waves, the perm solution chemically breaks (or reduces) the strong _____ _____ while the hair is wrapped on the perm rods.

With acid (heat) waves, _____, _____ and _____ _____ break the disulfide bonds.

Test Curl

Rinsing

Blotting

Neutralizing or Rebonding (Oxidation)

Two Functions of Neutralizer

1.

2.

Rinsing

ALERT!

Always follow manufacturer's directions to achieve the best results from perm products

SALON FUNDAMENTALS COSMETOLOGY 265

CHAPTER 12

smartNOTES

12.1 PERMING
pages 436-443

Categories of Perm Solutions

DIFFERENCES

ALKALINE WAVES	ACID WAVES

Hair Analysis

POROSITY	ELASTICITY

TEXTURE	DENSITY

Test for Metallic Salt

ALERT! Do not perm until the metallic product has been cut from hair

Preliminary Test Curls

Scalp Analysis

CHEMICAL TEXTURIZING

RUBRIC

This rubric is a self-assessment tool designed to compare your skill to industry standards. Indicate your present level of performance by checking the appropriate box. See overview for instructions.

Rectangle Perm Wrap

Industry Standard – to meet entry-level proficiency, industry standards require that you:
- Perform wave formation techniques in accordance with manufacturer's directions.

	Level 1	Level 2	Level 3	To Improve, I Need To:	Teacher Assessment
Preparation					
Disinfect workstation; assemble implements/supplies; wash hands; analyze hair/scalp; ask client to remove jewelry; drape/shampoo client	☐	☐	☐		☐
Procedure					
Subdivide hair into five sections; begin at front hairline of center section; use diameter of rod to measure the base size	☐	☐	☐		☐
Take horizontal parting and project hair at 90° from center of base; apply end papers and use overlap technique	☐	☐	☐		☐
Position rod half-off base; secure each rod with picks; use same techniques to complete center section	☐	☐	☐		☐
Move to adjacent section, use same techniques to complete section	☐	☐	☐		☐
Adjust length of rod to size of section at back; complete back side section; complete front side section using same techniques	☐	☐	☐		☐
Repeat same procedures on opposite side	☐	☐	☐		☐
Apply barrier cream and cotton around entire hairline	☐	☐	☐		☐
Apply perm solution to each rod; follow manufacturer's directions regarding plastic cap, processing and timing	☐	☐	☐		☐
Take test curl; rinse hair thoroughly; towel blot each rod	☐	☐	☐		☐
Apply neutralizer to each rod; set timer according to manufacturer's directions; remove rods	☐	☐	☐		☐
Distribute remaining neutralizer through ends	☐	☐	☐		☐
Rinse thoroughly	☐	☐	☐		☐
Completion					
Offer a prebook visit; recommend retail products; discard non-reusable materials, disinfect implements, arrange workstation in proper order and wash hands	☐	☐	☐		☐

TOTAL = ADDITION OF ALL TEACHER ASSESSMENT BOXES

TOTAL POINTS = 42

PERCENTAGE = STUDENT SCORE / HIGHEST POSSIBLE SCORE _____ %

CHAPTER 12

RUBRIC

This rubric is a self-assessment tool designed to compare your skills to industry standards. Indicate your present level of performance by checking the appropriate box. See overview for instructions.

Bricklay Perm Wrap

Industry Standard — to meet entry-level proficiency, industry standards require that you:
- Perform wave formation techniques in accordance with manufacturer's directions.

	Level 1	Level 2	Level 3	To Improve, I Need To:	Teacher Assessment
Preparation					
Disinfect workstation; assemble implements/supplies; wash hands; analyze hair/scalp; ask client to remove jewelry; drape/shampoo client	☐	☐	☐		☐
Procedure					
Distribute hair straight back	☐	☐	☐		☐
Begin at center front hairline	☐	☐	☐		☐
Measure base size with diameter and length of rod	☐	☐	☐		☐
Wrap first rod away from face using overlap technique	☐	☐	☐		☐
Position rod half-off base	☐	☐	☐		☐
Part diagonally to include hairline in next row	☐	☐	☐		☐
Wrap two rods behind center of first rod using one-two bricklay method	☐	☐	☐		☐
Begin at the center of the next row	☐	☐	☐		☐
Secure rods with picks in direction hair was wrapped	☐	☐	☐		☐
Continue same procedures and one-two bricklay method as you work from the center to either side	☐	☐	☐		☐
Work toward lower crown and nape using one-two bricklay method along horizontal partings	☐	☐	☐		☐
Complete back	☐	☐	☐		☐
Follow manufacturer's directions for processing	☐	☐	☐		☐
Completion					
Offer a prebook visit; recommend retail products; discard non-reusable materials, disinfect implements, arrange workstation in proper order and wash hands	☐	☐	☐		☐

TOTAL = ADDITION OF ALL TEACHER ASSESSMENT BOXES

TOTAL POINTS = ☐
45

PERCENTAGE = STUDENT SCORE / HIGHEST POSSIBLE SCORE

_____ %

268 UNIT 2 HAIR SERVICES

CHEMICAL TEXTURIZING

RUBRIC

This rubric is a self-assessment tool designed to compare your skill to industry standards. Indicate your present level of performance by checking the appropriate box. See overview for instructions.

Spiral Bricklay Perm Wrap

Industry Standard – to meet entry-level proficiency, industry standards require that you:
- Perform wave formation techniques in accordance with manufacturer's directions.

	Level 1	Level 2	Level 3	To Improve, I Need To:	Teacher Assessment
Preparation					
• Disinfect workstation; assemble implements/supplies; wash hands; analyze hair/scalp; ask client to remove jewelry; drape/shampoo client	☐	☐	☐		☐
Procedure					
• Section front from back vertically from ear to ear; section nape horizontally from ear to ear	☐	☐	☐		☐
• In nape, use 1 diameter horizontal bases with overlap technique and staggered bases; secure with picks	☐	☐	☐		☐
• Wrap first horizontal row with larger diameter rods and spiral technique	☐	☐	☐		☐
• Work from one side of nape to other	☐	☐	☐		☐
• Wrap next row in opposite direction using smaller diameter rods	☐	☐	☐		☐
• Work to top of back alternating rod diameters and wrapping directions with each row	☐	☐	☐		☐
• Wrap sides using horizontal partings; alternate rod diameter and wrapping directions with each row; wrap larger diameter toward face; wrap smaller diameter away from face	☐	☐	☐		☐
• Work to top of one side alternating rod diameters and wrapping directions; secure top row with picks or stabilizers	☐	☐	☐		☐
• Repeat same wrapping procedures on other side to complete wrap	☐	☐	☐		☐
• Follow manufacturer's directions for processing	☐	☐	☐		☐
Completion					
• Offer a prebook visit; recommend retail products; discard non-reusable materials, disinfect implements, arrange workstation in proper order and wash hands	☐	☐	☐		☐

TOTAL = ADDITION OF ALL TEACHER ASSESSMENT BOXES

TOTAL POINTS = ☐
36

PERCENTAGE = STUDENT SCORE / HIGHEST POSSIBLE SCORE _____ %

SALON FUNDAMENTALS COSMETOLOGY

CHAPTER 12

RUBRIC

This rubric is a self-assessment tool designed to compare your skill to industry standards. Indicate your present level of performance by checking the appropriate box. See overview for instructions.

Bricklay With Directional Fringe Perm Wrap

Industry Standard – to meet entry-level proficiency, industry standards require that you:
- Perform wave formation techniques in accordance with manufacturer's directions.

	Level 1	Level 2	Level 3	To Improve, I Need To:	Teacher Assessment
Preparation					
Disinfect workstation; assemble implements/supplies; wash hands; analyze hair/scalp; ask client to remove jewelry; drape/shampoo client	☐	☐	☐		☐
Procedure					
Section fringe from diagonal side part using length of perm rod	☐	☐	☐		☐
On heavier side of part, direct fringe diagonally toward face; wrap using 1-diameter half-off base control with overlap technique; secure with picks or stabilizers	☐	☐	☐		☐
Begin wrapping bricklay pattern directly behind fringe; use one-two method with 1-diameter half-off base control	☐	☐	☐		☐
Extend first row behind fringe to incorporate lighter side of part; use end papers and wrap with same technique	☐	☐	☐		☐
Continue using 1-diameter half-off base control, extending partings to hairline on either side; secure with picks or stabilizers	☐	☐	☐		☐
Use one-two method and continue working toward back	☐	☐	☐		☐
Begin subsequent row with either one or two rods and continue working to hairline on either side	☐	☐	☐		☐
Repeat same technique throughout remainder of nape to complete nape and wrap	☐	☐	☐		☐
Apply barrier cream and cotton around hairline; follow manufacturer's directions for processing; finish as desired	☐	☐	☐		☐
Completion					
Offer a prebook visit; recommend retail products; discard non-reusable materials, disinfect implements, arrange workstation in proper order and wash hands	☐	☐	☐		☐

TOTAL = ADDITION OF ALL TEACHER ASSESSMENT BOXES

TOTAL POINTS = ☐
33

PERCENTAGE = STUDENT SCORE / HIGHEST POSSIBLE SCORE

____ %

270 UNIT 2 HAIR SERVICES

CHEMICAL TEXTURIZING

smartNOTES

12.2 CHEMICAL RELAXING   pages 461-464

Chemical Relaxing Theory

CHEMICAL PHASE

PHYSICAL PHASE

Types of Relaxers

SODIUM HYDROXIDE	AMMONIUM THIOGLYCOLATE	OTHER RELAXERS

Relaxer Strengths

Mild -

Regular -

Super -

ALERT! Do not apply hydroxide relaxer to hair that has been colored with permanent hair color or lightened hair; do not apply sodium hydroxide to hair that has been permed with ammonium thioglycolate or is going to be permed with thio

Hair Analysis

Identifying and Changing Existing Curl Patterns

SALON FUNDAMENTALS COSMETOLOGY   271

CHAPTER 12

smartNOTES

12.2 CHEMICAL RELAXING   pages 465-466

Stages of Reduction

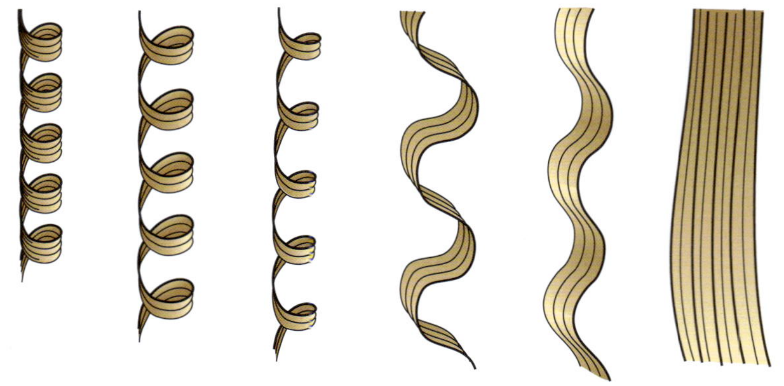

___ ___ ___ ___ ___ ___

Steps in Determining Curl Pattern

FIRST — 1.

THEN — 2.

NOW — 3.

FINALLY — 4.

Chemical Phase

Physical Phase

APPLYING AND SMOOTHING

RELAXATION TEST

CHEMICAL TEXTURIZING

smartNOTES

12.2 CHEMICAL RELAXING   pages 467-468; 473

Relaxation Application Methods

VIRGIN	RETOUCH
PARTIAL	CURL DIFFUSION

Timing Guide

THIO RELAXERS

STRENGTH	CONDITION OF HAIR	TIMING
Mild -		
Regular -		
Super -		

HYDROXIDE RELAXERS

STRENGTH	CONDITION OF HAIR	TIMING
Mild -		
Regular -		
Super -		

Product and Application Overview

 Never leave a client while the hair is processing

12

CHAPTER 12

RUBRIC

This rubric is a self-assessment tool designed to compare your skill to industry standards. Indicate your present level of performance by checking the appropriate box. See overview for instructions.

Virgin Thio Relaxer

Industry Standard — to meet entry-level proficiency, industry standards require that you:
- Perform hair relaxation techniques in accordance with manufacturer's directions.

	Level 1	Level 2	Level 3	To Improve, I Need To:	Teacher Assessment
Preparation					
Perform hair/scalp analysis; perform strand/elasticity test; disinfect workstation; assemble implements/supplies; wash hands; ask client to remove jewelry; drape/shampoo client	☐	☐	☐		☐
Procedure					
Section hair into five sections for control; apply base (protective cream) to entire hairline and ears	☐	☐	☐		☐
Begin at back top section or where hair is most resistant; use ¼" (.6 cm) horizontal partings	☐	☐	☐		☐
Apply relaxer ¼" (.6 cm) to ½" (1.25 cm) away from the scalp to both sides of the strand up to porous ends; work from top to bottom of each section; complete back sections	☐	☐	☐		☐
Move to side sections; complete one side section using diagonal-back partings; complete sides	☐	☐	☐		☐
Move to top and repeat same application techniques using horizontal partings; complete top	☐	☐	☐		☐
Apply relaxer to base in each section using same parting pattern	☐	☐	☐		☐
Comb, then smooth each section with back of comb using smooth, light, even strokes from scalp to ends; comb and smooth all sections	☐	☐	☐		☐
Perform comb test; if an indentation occurs, continue smoothing	☐	☐	☐		☐
Follow manufacturer's directions for processing	☐	☐	☐		☐
Once the hair has reached desired degree of relaxation, rinse relaxer from the hair until water runs clear	☐	☐	☐		☐
Follow manufacturer's directions for neutralizing	☐	☐	☐		☐
Completion					
Complete client record card; offer a prebook visit; recommend retail products; discard non-reusable materials, disinfect implements, arrange workstation in proper order and wash hands	☐	☐	☐		☐

TOTAL = ADDITION OF ALL TEACHER ASSESSMENT BOXES

TOTAL POINTS = ☐
39

PERCENTAGE = STUDENT SCORE / HIGHEST POSSIBLE SCORE

_____ %

CHEMICAL TEXTURIZING

RUBRIC

This rubric is a self-assessment tool designed to compare your skill to industry standards. Indicate your present level of performance by checking the appropriate box. See overview for instructions.

Sodium Hydroxide Relaxer Retouch

Industry Standard – to meet entry-level proficiency, industry standards require that you:
- Perform hair relaxation techniques in accordance with manufacturer's directions.

	Level 1	Level 2	Level 3	To Improve, I Need To:	Teacher Assessment
Preparation					
Perform hair/scalp analysis; perform strand/elasticity test; disinfect workstation; assemble implements/supplies; wash hands; ask client to remove jewelry; drape/shampoo client	☐	☐	☐		☐
Procedure					
Section hair into five sections for control	☐	☐	☐		☐
Apply base around entire hairline; apply base to scalp using a checkerboard pattern	☐	☐	☐		☐
Apply a protective cream or conditioning filler to previously relaxed hair using ½" (1.25 cm) partings	☐	☐	☐		☐
Begin at top back section or most resistant area; use ¼" (.6 cm) horizontal partings	☐	☐	☐		☐
Apply product slightly away from scalp up to previously relaxed hair to both sides of the parting; work from top to bottom of each section	☐	☐	☐		☐
Complete back sections	☐	☐	☐		☐
Apply to side sections using diagonal-back partings and same techniques	☐	☐	☐		☐
Move to top section; use same procedures from horizontal partings	☐	☐	☐		☐
Smooth each section with back of comb using same parting pattern	☐	☐	☐		☐
Follow manufacturer's directions for processing and perform comb test; smooth each section with back of comb	☐	☐	☐		☐
Rinse the hair until water runs clear after you have reached the desired degree of relaxation	☐	☐	☐		☐
Shampoo hair with a neutralizing shampoo, condition and finish as desired	☐	☐	☐		☐
Completion					
Complete client record card; offer a prebook visit; recommend retail products; discard non-reusable materials, disinfect implements, arrange workstation in proper order and wash hands	☐	☐	☐		☐

TOTAL = ADDITION OF ALL TEACHER ASSESSMENT BOXES

TOTAL POINTS = ☐
42

PERCENTAGE = STUDENT SCORE / HIGHEST POSSIBLE SCORE _____ %

SALON FUNDAMENTALS COSMETOLOGY

CHAPTER 12

smartNOTES

12.3 CURL REFORMING pages 481-486

Curl Reforming

Curl Reforming Theory

Three Steps to Curl Reformation

FIRST 1.

THEN 2.

NOW 3.

Infection Control and Safety

Special Safety Considerations

ALERT! Do not perform a curl reformation on hair that has been relaxed with a sodium hydroxide or no lye relaxer

276   UNIT 2 HAIR SERVICES

CHEMICAL TEXTURIZING

RUBRIC

This rubric is a self-assessment tool designed to compare your skill to industry standards. Indicate your present level of performance by checking the appropriate box. See overview for instructions.

Curl Reforming Service: Contour Wrap

Industry Standard – to meet entry-level proficiency, industry standards require that you:
- Perform hair relaxation techniques in accordance with manufacturer's directions.

Preparation
- Perform hair/scalp analysis; perform strand/elasticity test; disinfect workstation; assemble implements/supplies; wash hands; ask client to remove jewelry; drape/shampoo client

	Level 1	Level 2	Level 3	To Improve, I Need To:	Teacher Assessment

Procedure
- Apply protective base cream to hairline and ears
- Apply and smooth hair with curl rearranger, following the same procedures as for a virgin relaxer application
- Follow manufacturer's directions for processing
- Rinse and towel blot hair
- Wrap the center rectangle using ⅛" partings smaller than diameter of tool; use end papers to control hair; position tools half-off base; secure using picks or stabilizers to complete section
- Move to the adjacent section; wrap hair from front hairline to nape using diagonal and horizontal partings; wrap and complete last section using horizontal partings
- Wrap and complete remaining sections on opposite side using same procedures
- Place cotton around hairline; saturate hair with curl booster; follow manufacturer's directions regarding processing, plastic cap and test curl for "S" pattern
- Rinse using tepid water and tools in position
- Towel blot; apply neutralizer; follow manufacturer's directions for processing; rinse
- Rinse with low water pressure; Remove rods; apply moisturizer
- Style hair as desired

Completion
- Complete client record card; offer a prebook visit; recommend retail products; discard non-reusable materials, disinfect implements, arrange workstation in proper order and wash hands

TOTAL = ADDITION OF ALL TEACHER ASSESSMENT BOXES

TOTAL POINTS =

42

PERCENTAGE = STUDENT SCORE / HIGHEST POSSIBLE SCORE _____ %

SALON FUNDAMENTALS COSMETOLOGY   277

CHAPTER 12

TALKING POINTS

Your next challenge is to be ready to talk about some of the important ideas in this chapter. Follow the directions listed next to each box. Then practice talking about your ideas with others.

Locate three magazine photos, one with small, one medium and one large curl sizes. Compare with a partner the form, length, color and texture of the curls.

Compare directions from two different perm manufacturers and list similar and different instructions.

Create a promotion spotlighting perms as a service in the salon.

THE CHALLENGE

Now it's time to see how well you know your new material. First answer these questions. Then use the Memory Box that follows to check yourself. Look up each answer on the corresponding page in the *Salon Fundamentals* textbook. Check "got it" for all correct answers and "not yet" for all incorrect responses. Using the "Know Chart," record all of your correct responses in the "I Know" column. After correcting incorrect answers, record all of your corrected responses in the "I Need to Study" column. That way you know exactly what to review before continuing in this study guide.

1. Chemical texturizing is simply the process of using physical and chemical actions to permanently change the hair. What are the three major classifications of chemical texturizing? _____ _____ _____

2. _____ involves taking straight hair and making it curly or wavy.

3. Alkaline waves, also called _____ _____ are currently formulated with _____ or its derivatives and ammonia, which creates a compound called _____ _____.

4. Acid waves contain _____ _____ and have a pH of _____ to _____.

5. TRUE FALSE The chemical phase of perming involves applying the perm solution, rinsing it from the hair, then applying the neutralizer and rinsing it from the hair.

6. The most common ingredient found in products that completely relax the hair is _____ _____, and the most common ingredient found in products that reduce the curl pattern is _____ _____.

7. Once the hair has been relaxed and the relaxing solution has been completely rinsed from the hair, an _____ agent must be applied to reharden (lock) the hair into its new, straight shape.

8. TRUE FALSE Never apply a thio relaxer over hair that has been relaxed with a sodium hydroxide relaxer or vice versa, since these two chemicals are not compatible and severe damage or breakage can occur.

9. _____ _____ is a chemical service designed to change tightly curled hair to curly or wavy hair.

10. In a curl reforming procedure, the natural curl is reduced by applying a product known as a rearranger. _____ _____ is the main ingredient found in rearrangers.

278   UNIT 2 HAIR SERVICES

CHEMICAL TEXTURIZING

MEMORY BOX

1. PAGE 425 — GOT IT / NOT YET
2. PAGE 425 — GOT IT / NOT YET
3. PAGE 427 — GOT IT / NOT YET
4. PAGE 427 — GOT IT / NOT YET
5. PAGE 427 — GOT IT / NOT YET
6. PAGE 462 — GOT IT / NOT YET
7. PAGE 468 — GOT IT / NOT YET
8. PAGE 473 — GOT IT / NOT YET
9. PAGE 481 — GOT IT / NOT YET
10. PAGE 482 — GOT IT / NOT YET

KNOW CHART

I KNOW:

I NEED TO STUDY:

SHOW YOU KNOW...

Identify what type of tool and wrapping pattern was used for the following images.

SALON FUNDAMENTALS COSMETOLOGY 279

CHAPTER 12

A CLASS ACT

Now that you have completed your work in Chemical Texturizing, it's time to demonstrate your creative talents.

Each member of the class will plan, sketch, demonstrate and explain a wrap pattern. You may create a new directional pattern or use one from the chapter.

REMEMBER: Before starting the wrap on a mannequin you must sketch the wrapping pattern, list key features to be explained and name your creation!

SKETCH

KEY FEATURES

DESIGN NAME:

All designs will be judged for:

Plan/Sketch   1 2 3 4 5 6 7 8 9 10   points: _____

Demonstration 1 2 3 4 5 6 7 8 9 10   points: _____

Explanation   1 2 3 4 5 6 7 8 9 10   points: _____

TOTAL POINTS: _____

CHEMICAL TEXTURIZING

KNOWLEDGE GRID

Start at the top of the Knowledge Grid and work your way down, answering each question to check your understanding of *Chapter 12, Chemical Texturizing*. The questions found here will help you deepen your understanding, build self-confidence and increase your awareness of different ways of thinking about a subject.

KNOW	WHAT ARE THE TWO BASIC TECHNIQUES FOR WRAPPING HAIR AROUND A PERM TOOL?	
COMPREHEND	REPORT THE PURPOSE OF AN END PAPER IN THE PERMING PROCESS.	
APPLY	FILL IN THE BASIC STEPS INVOLVED IN THE CHEMICAL PROCESS OF PERMING.	The basic steps involved in the chemical phase of perming are: 1. Applying perm solution 4. 2. 5. Applying neutralizer 6. 3. 7. Rinsing
ANALYZE	COMPARE THE pH OF AN ALKALINE PERM TO THE pH OF AN ACID PERM.	
SYNTHESIZE	WRITE ABOUT THE IMPORTANCE OF ANALYZING THE POROSITY, ELASTICITY, TEXTURE AND DENSITY OF THE CLIENT'S HAIR PRIOR TO PERFORMING A PERM SERVICE.	
EVALUATE	JUSTIFY THE IMPORTANCE OF ANALYZING THE TEXTURE OF THE CLIENT'S HAIR IN SEVERAL AREAS OF THE HEAD PRIOR TO A CHEMICAL RELAXER SERVICE.	

1   2   3   4   **5**   6   7

SALON FUNDAMENTALS COSMETOLOGY

CHAPTER 12

BRAIN CONDITIONER
MULTIPLE CHOICE. CIRCLE THE CORRECT ANSWER.

1. The first machine capable of producing permanent curl was invented in:
   a. 1865   b. 1885   c. 1905   d. 1925

2. The inventor of the first permanent wave machine was:
   a. Eli Whitney   b. Thomas Edison   c. Charles Nessler   d. Benjamin Franklin

3. Heat waves that are self-timed and self-heated are called:
   a. acidic   b. endothermic   c. cold   d. exothermic

4. Acid waves that require the application of heat are:
   a. highly alkaline   b. endothermic   c. highly acidic   d. exothermic

5. What type of wave uses thioglycolic acid or its derivatives with ammonia and processes the hair without heat?
   a. endothermic   b. exothermic   c. acid   d. cold

6. The chemical phase of perms involves all of the following procedures EXCEPT:
   a. applying neutralizer   b. applying perm solution
   c. wrapping hair around the perm tool   d. rinsing the perm solution from the hair

7. The overlap method of wrapping hair around a perm tool is also called:
   a. base-to-ends spiral   b. ends-to-base spiral   c. croquignole   d. spring

8. To achieve the desired curl formation, hair should wrap around the rod at least how many times?
   a. once   b. 1 ½ times   c. 2 ½ times   d. 5 times

9. What type of rods produce a large curl pattern on either side and a smaller curl in the center?
   a. short   b. long   c. concave   d. small diameter

10. What type of rods produce small firm curls?
    a. small diameter rods   b. large diameter rods
    c. short rods with large diameters   d. long rods with large diameters

11. The most common end paper technique used to avoid bunching at the ends is the:
    a. bookend   b. double-paper (double-flat)   c. cushion   d. spiral

12. The base is defined as the area between two:
    a. sections   b. lengths   c. tools   d. partings

13. The most common base control for perming is a/an:
    a. half-off base   b. on-base   c. off base   d. underdirected

14. In perming a one-base size is:
    a. equal to the diameter of perm rod   b. 2 times the size of perm rod
    c. 3 times the size of perm rod   d. 4 times the size of perm rod

15. A larger base size will have which of the following effects on the curl?
    a. lengthen   b. tighten   c. reduce strength   d. increase strength

16. To achieve maximum volume, which tool position should be used?
    a. on-base   b. half-off base   c. off-base   d. underdirected

17. Which tool position is used in perimeter areas where closeness is desired?
    a. on-base   b. half-off base   c. off-base   d. underdirected

18. The tool position used when only a minimum degree of volume is desired is the:
    a. on-base b. half-off base c. off-base d. underdirected
19. What element do most acid waves use along with tension and waving lotion to process hair?
    a. heat b. cold c. alkalinity d. drying
20. What structure must be permanently broken to change the hair from a straight to a curly state?
    a. disulfide bonds b. carbon c. eumelanin d. melanocytes
21. What procedure removes the excess waving lotion?
    a. shampooing b. rinsing c. reducing d. processing
22. Alkaline waves carry a pH of:
    a. 4.5 to 5.5 b. 6.0 to 7.5 c. 8.0 to 9.5 d. 10 to 14
23. Neutralizing is also known as:
    a. rebonding
    c. relaxing
    b. processing
    d. breaking the disulfide bonds
24. What procedure reduces the swelling of the hair and hardens the bonds into the new size and shape during a perm process?
    a. rinsing with cold water
    c. applying a processing agent
    b. applying a neutralizer
    d. rinsing with hot water
25. Hydrogen peroxide, sodium perborate or sodium bromate are commonly used in:
    a. alkaline perm solutions
    c. conditioners
    b. acid perm solutions
    d. neutralizers
26. Which waving solution is not recommended for porous or damaged hair?
    a. acid b. heat c. endothermic d. alkaline
27. Which of the following chemicals is NOT one of the main ingredients found in most neutralizers?
    a. potassium b. sodium bromate c. sodium perborate d. hydrogen peroxide
28. Low pH alkaline waves have a pH of:
    a. 7 b. 8 c. 9.5 d. 9
29. Acid waves have a pH of:
    a. 4.9-5.2 b. 5.9-6.2 c. 6.9-7.2 d. 7.9-8.2
30. Hair must be wrapped without tension when using:
    a. endothermic acid waves
    c. acid waves without heat
    b. exothermic acid waves
    d. alkaline waves
31. Wrapping with firm, even tension when using an acid wave produces which of the following effects?
    a. boosts penetration of waving solution
    c. increases processing time
    b. decreases penetration of waving solution
    d. creates uneven wave pattern
32. It is essential to completely rinse the perm solution before applying the:
    a. conditioner b. shampoo c. neutralizer d. relaxer
33. Leaving the neutralizer on longer than recommended can:
    a. cause damage
    c. create an appearance with more luster
    b. create a firmer curl pattern
    d. add volume
34. Which of the following waving solutions has the shortest processing time?
    a. alkaline b. exothermic acid c. endothermic acid wave d. warm

35. Which of the following statements is true about acid perms?
    a. acid perms create soft, natural curls
    b. acid perms have a faster processing time
    c. acid waves are better for use on resistant hair
    d. acid waves do not require the addition of heat

36. Which term refers to the hair's ability to absorb moisture, liquids and chemicals?
    a. elasticity
    b. porosity
    c. texture
    d. density

37. The hair's ability to stretch and return to its original shape is called:
    a. elasticity
    b. porosity
    c. texture
    d. density

38. Thio-free perms use what as a reducing agent?
    a. thioglycolic acid
    b. glycerylmonothioglycolate
    c. cystemine hydrochloride
    d. peroxide

39. Which of the following items is NOT true about acid perms?
    a. better for fragile hair
    b. slower processing time
    c. create soft, natural curls
    d. better for use on resistant hair

40. Which of the following descriptions does NOT identify the meaning of porosity?
    a. the hair's ability to stretch
    b. the hair's ability to retain liquids
    c. the hair's ability to absorb liquids
    d. the hair's ability to absorb perming solution

41. Which of the following statements about permed hair is true?
    a. do not perm hair that has ever been colored
    b. do not perm hair that is limp
    c. do not perm hair if there are scalp abrasions present
    d. do not perm short hair near hairline

42. Which of the following statements about chemically treated hair is NOT true?
    a. hair that has been colored cannot be permed
    b. avoid perming damaged hair that shows breakage
    c. do not perm hair if there are scalp abrasions present
    d. never perm hair that has been treated with sodium hydroxide

43. Proper draping for chemical services accomplish all of the following EXCEPT:
    a. preventing burns
    b. preventing skin irritation
    c. protecting the client's clothing
    d. placing cape between client and chair back

44. What is the purpose of performing a 1:20 test?
    a. to indicate the processing time needed
    b. to determine if metallic salts are present
    c. to indicate allergies to the chemicals being used
    d. to determine the porosity of the hair

45. Which of the following statements is TRUE about a preliminary test curl?
    a. avoid shampooing prior to testing
    b. helps determine how a client's hair will react to a perm
    c. barrier cream is not necessary
    d. avoid testing hair that has been bleached

46. Which perm wrap is considered the most basic perm wrap pattern?
    a. rectangle
    b. bricklay
    c. spiral bricklay
    d. oblong bricklay

47. Rods too large for the desired curl can cause:
    a. frizziness
    b. breakage
    c. dryness
    d. a limp curl

48. Too much hair on a hair rod can cause:
    a. an uneven curl pattern
    b. dryness
    c. breakage
    d. frizziness

CHEMICAL TEXTURIZING

49. The most common ingredient found in products that completely straighten the hair is:
    a. sodium hydroxide   b. thioglycolate   c. potassium   d. bisulfate

50. Which relaxer is classified as a lye product?
    a. sodium hydroxide   b. calcium hydroxide   c. potassium hydroxide   d. lithium hydroxide

51. Sodium hydroxide relaxers have a pH of:
    a. 6.5 to 8   b. 8.5 to 10   c. 11.5 to 14   d. 5 to 6.5

52. What product should NOT be applied to hair that has been previously permed with ammonium thioglycolate?
    a. conditioner   b. neutralizer   c. sodium hydroxide   d. metallic salt

53. A pull test is performed to check for which of the following conditions?
    a. porosity   b. melanin   c. elasticity   d. brittleness

54. Sodium hydroxide relaxers are generally used on what type of hair?
    a. tightly curled   b. non-resistant   c. wavy   d. straight

55. A technique used to loosen or relax tightly curled hair patterns by approximately 50% of their natural shape is called:
    a. virgin relaxer   b. relaxer retouch
    c. partial relaxer   d. curl diffusion or chemical blow-out

56. What protects the scalp and hairline from caustic chemicals?
    a. protective base cream   b. sealer   c. conditioner   d. hand lotion

57. Which of the following steps is NOT performed when offering a virgin sodium hydroxide relaxer service?
    a. strand test   b. periodic comb tests
    c. pre-shampoo the client's hair   d. follow the service with a neutralizing shampoo

58. Virgin thio relaxers may be applied after all of the following procedures EXCEPT:
    a. a light shampoo   b. a vigorous shampoo
    c. an analysis of hair and scalp   d. a strand test and an elasticity test

59. What is the name of the chemical service designed to change tightly curled hair to curly or wavy hair?
    a. perming   b. relaxer retouch   c. curl reforming (soft curls)   d. stripping

60. Another term for a soft curl procedure is:
    a. alkaline wave perm   b. double-process perm   c. acid perm   d. thio-free perm

61. All of the following terms describe changing tightly curled hair to curly or wavy hair EXCEPT:
    a. curl reforming   b. relaxer retouch   c. reformation curls   d. double-process perm

62. Ammonium thioglycolate is the main ingredient in:
    a. curl rearranger   b. conditioners   c. shampoos   d. styling gels

63. When performing a curl reforming procedure, the rod diameter should be at least how many times larger than the diameter of the natural curl pattern?
    a. 2   b. 3   c. 4   d. 5

64. The main ingredient found in a booster is:
    a. sodium bromate   b. a mild form of potassium chloride
    c. a mild form of ammonium thioglycolate d. cystemine hydrochloride

65. Which of the following actions is NOT a step involved in curl reforming?
    a. reduction   b. restraightening   c. reforming   d. rebonding

CHAPTER 12

FINAL REVIEW

Check your answers as you did before. Place a check mark next to the page number for any incorrect answer. On the lines following the answers, jot down topics that you still need to review.

☐	1.	page 426	☐	23.	page 436	☐	45.	page 442
☐	2.	page 426	☐	24.	page 436	☐	46.	page 446
☐	3.	page 427	☐	25.	page 436	☐	47.	page 459
☐	4.	page 427	☐	26.	page 436	☐	48.	page 459
☐	5.	page 427	☐	27.	page 436	☐	49.	page 462
☐	6.	page 427	☐	28.	page 437	☐	50.	page 462
☐	7.	page 428	☐	29.	page 437	☐	51.	page 462
☐	8.	page 428	☐	30.	page 437	☐	52.	page 463
☐	9.	page 429	☐	31.	page 437	☐	53.	page 464
☐	10.	page 429	☐	32.	page 437	☐	54.	page 465
☐	11.	page 430	☐	33.	page 437	☐	55.	page 467
☐	12.	page 430	☐	34.	page 437	☐	56.	page 469
☐	13.	page 431	☐	35.	page 438	☐	57.	page 475
☐	14.	page 431	☐	36.	page 438	☐	58.	page 476
☐	15.	page 431	☐	37.	page 438	☐	59.	page 481
☐	16.	page 431	☐	38.	page 438	☐	60.	page 481
☐	17.	page 431	☐	39.	page 438	☐	61.	page 481
☐	18.	page 432	☐	40.	page 438	☐	62.	page 482
☐	19.	page 434	☐	41.	page 440	☐	63.	page 482
☐	20.	page 434	☐	42.	page 440	☐	64.	page 482
☐	21.	page 435	☐	43.	page 441	☐	65.	page 482
☐	22.	page 436	☐	44.	page 442			

FINAL REVIEW *continued*

On the lines below, jot down topics that you still need to review.

NOTES TO MYSELF

Experts tell us that it is important to summarize your feelings and reactions about what you are learning. Note especially things that surprised you, things you found difficult to learn, suggestions and ideas you received from friends that helped make learning this chapter easier and more enjoyable.

My reflections about Chemical Texturizing:

LESSONS LEARNED

- Chemical texturizing services offered in the salon include: perming, to transform hair from straight to curly; and relaxing, to transform hair from curly to straight.
- Perm results depend mainly on the distribution and sectioning, wrapping technique, base control, tool size and perm pattern used.
- Relaxer results depend mainly on the chemical relaxer product and smoothing technique used.
- A curl reformation service creates a new, looser curl pattern by first relaxing and then perming the hair.

CHAPTER 12

THINGS TO DO

THINGS TO DO

THINGS TO DO

HAIR COLORING

CHAPTER 13
HAIR COLORING

VALUE
Being able to change your client's existing hair color will allow you to maintain the best possible personal image for your client.

MAIN IDEA
Color + Identifying and Knowing How to Change the Client's Hair Color
= **Financial and Professional Reward**

PLAN

13.1 COLOR THEORY
What is Color?
The Law of Color

13.2 IDENTIFYING EXISTING HAIR COLOR
Melanin
Gray Hair
Identifying Natural Level and Tone
Identifying Artificial Level, Tone and Intensity
Additional Considerations

13.3 CHANGING EXISTING HAIR COLOR
Hair Color Chemistry
Hair Color Essentials
Hair Color Techniques
Infection Control and Safety
Client Consultation
Product and Application Overview
Temporary Color
Semi-Permanent Color
Oxidative Color: Darker Result
Oxidative Color: Lighter Result
Freehand Painting
Partial Highlights: Slicing
Full Highlights: Weaving
Cap Highlighting
Double-Process Blond
Tint Back
Hair Color Removal Techniques
Hair Color Problems and Solutions

SALON FUNDAMENTALS COSMETOLOGY 289

CHAPTER 13

smartNOTES

13.1 COLOR THEORY pages 494-496

The Law of Color

PRIMARY	SECONDARY	TERTIARY

Color Wheel

Hair & Skin Color

WARM	COOL

Complementary Colors

Neutralizing Effect

Color in these squares to achieve complementary colors neutralizing one another →

HAIR COLORING

smartNOTES

13.1 COLOR THEORY   pages 497-498

Levels of Hair Color

Degree of Lightness
or Darkness

Intensity of Hair
Color

LIGHT

DARK

13.2 IDENTIFYING EXISTING HAIR COLOR   pages 497-498

Melanin
Trichology
Quick Review

Melanocytes –

Melanosomes –

Melanin –

EUMELANIN

PHEOMELANIN

WHICH HAIR COLOR?

Dense amount of Eumelanin produces: _____

Small amount of Eumelanin produces: _____

Predominant amount of Pheomelanin produces: _____

Inactive Melanocytes produce: _____

1 2 3 4 5 6 7

SALON FUNDAMENTALS COSMETOLOGY   291

CHAPTER 13

smartNOTES

13.2 IDENTIFYING EXISTING HAIR COLOR pages 498–503

Gray Hair

25% – 30% Rule

| 25% | 50% | 75% |

Identifying Natural Level and Tone

Major Fields of Color

By level and name of color; levels of hair color identities on a scale of 1-10 fall into one of three major fields of hair color:

LIGHT		10 Lightest Blond
		9 Very Light Blond
		8 Light Blond
MEDIUM		7 Medium Blond
		6 Dark Blond
		5 Lightest Brown
		4 Light Brown
DARK		3 Medium Brown
		2 Dark Brown
		1 Black

Identifying Artificial Level, Tone and Intensity

TONES/BASE COLORS

Additional Considerations

INTENSITY

TEXTURE

POROSITY

292 UNIT 2 HAIR SERVICES

HAIR COLORING

smartNOTES

13.3 CHANGING EXISTING HAIR COLOR pages 504-507

Formula: Natural Melanin + Artificial Pigment = Final Color Result

Hair Color Chemistry

General Categories of Hair Color Products

NONOXIDATIVE COLORS

Function:

TEMPORARY	SEMI-PERMANENT
Use:	Use:

TYPES

Weekly Rinses: Color-Enhancing Shampoos/Conditioners:

Color Mousses/Gels:

                                  Glosses:

Color Crayons/Mascaras:

                                  Color Enhancers:

Pomades:

Spray-On Colors:

1 2 3 4 5 6 7

CHAPTER 13

smartNOTES

13.3 CHANGING EXISTING HAIR COLOR   pages 508-512

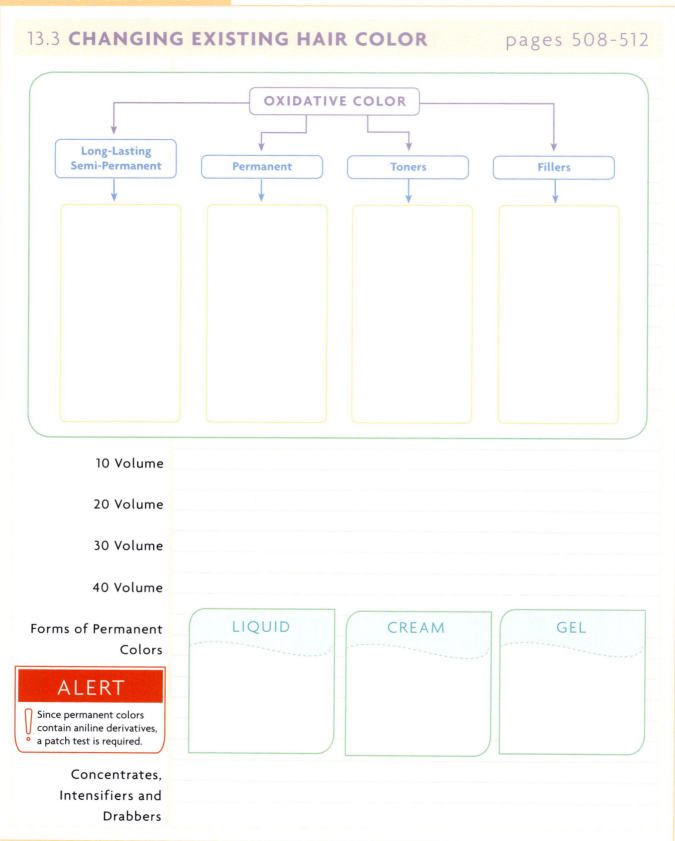

HAIR COLORING

smartNOTES

13.3 CHANGING EXISTING HAIR COLOR   pages 512-517

Lighteners

Degrees of Decolorization

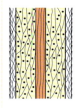 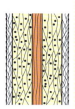

ON-THE-SCALP

OFF-THE-SCALP

Developers

Hydrogen Peroxide pH 2.5-4.5

Volume Formula

3% = _____   9% = _____

6% = _____   12% = _____

ALERT

! Increasing the strength of hydrogen peroxide in a formula beyond the manufacturer's recommendations may cause damage to the hair and chemical burns to the skin and scalp.

Vegetable, Metallic and Compound Dyes

Vegetable Dyes

Henna -

Chamomile -

Metallic

Compound

1 2 3 4 5 6 7

SALON FUNDAMENTALS COSMETOLOGY   295

CHAPTER 13

smartNOTES

13.3 CHANGING EXISTING HAIR COLOR pages 520-525

Hair Color Techniques

| BASE TO ENDS | MIDSTRAND TO ENDS THEN BASE (LIGHTER) | BASE (RETOUCH) |

Draw each technique in the boxes above.

Special Effects Coloring Techniques

	Method	Results
Freeform Painting	Brush used on the _____	Highlighted/lowlighted
Weaving and Slicing (Fine, Medium and Thick)	Tail comb weaves out _____ pattern or parts off section of hair	Adds depth and _____
Cap Method	Selected strands are pulled through holes in a perforated cap with crochet hook, then _____ or _____ is applied	Highlights

ALERT
Always follow manufacturer's directions and read material safety data sheets (MSDS).

Predisposition (Skin Patch) Test
Required when using _____ 24-48 hours prior to color service. Must use intended formula; test for _____ reaction; negative - formula may be used; positive - redness, blisters, have client seek _____ assistance.

Preliminary Strand Test
Color test, _____ hours before service - determine formula to be used; _____ time; reaction of hair

296 UNIT 2 HAIR SERVICES

1 2 3 4 5 6 7

HAIR COLORING

smartNOTES

13.3 CHANGING EXISTING HAIR COLOR — page 529

Product and Application Overview

CATEGORY	LASTING POWER	FUNCTION	APPLICATION METHOD
Nonoxidative (not mixed with developer)			
Temporary			
Semi-Permanent			
OXIDATIVE (mixed with developer)			
Demi-Permanent			
Permanent (also known as single process tints)			
LIGHTENERS (mixed with developer)			
On-the-Scalp			
Off-the-Scalp			

1 2 3 4 5 6 7

CHAPTER 13

THINKING MAP

Now that you have filled in your SmartNotes for "Hair Coloring," create a Thinking Map to help yourself make sense of how your SmartNotes fit together. Use some or all of the words in the Jump Start Box as well as your own words and pictures to make a visual that will help you connect the important ideas in this chapter to each other. Be creative!

HAIR COLORING

JUMP START BOX

LIGHTENERS	BASE TO ENDS	WEAVING	PREDISPOSITION TEST
INTENSITY	LEVEL	TEMPORARY	TONERS
CONCENTRATES	20 VOLUME	ON-THE-SCALP	HYDROGEN PEROXIDE
COMPOUND	MIDSTRAND	SLICING	DEVELOPER
MELANOCYTES	TONE	SEMI-PERMANENT	FILLERS
INTENSIFIERS	30 VOLUME	OFF-THE-SCALP	
METALLIC SALTS	RETOUCH	CAP	
EUMELANIN	NONOXIDATIVE	OXIDATIVE	
DRABBERS	40 VOLUME	DECOLORIZATION	

HAIR COLORING

TALKING POINTS

Your next challenge is to be ready to talk about some of the important ideas in this chapter. Follow the directions listed next to each box. Then practice talking about your ideas with others.

Good porosity Level 8 existing color	Role play a color consultation with a partner using the information to the left.
Good elasticity Active lifestyle	
Medium density Casual clothing preference	
Oval face shape Tall and lanky body shape	
Wants blond highlights	

Find photo examples of clothing from a magazine that show the use of complementary colors.

Create a salon promotion featuring hair color that could be offered during the month of May.

THE CHALLENGE

Now it's time to see how well you know your new material. First answer these questions. Then use the Memory Box that follows to check yourself. Look up each answer on the corresponding page in the *Salon Fundamentals* textbook. Check "got it" for all correct answers and "not yet" for all incorrect responses. Using the "Know Chart," record all of your correct responses in the "I Know" column. After correcting incorrect answers, record all of your corrected responses in the "I Need to Study" column. That way you know exactly what to review before continuing in this study guide.

1. Primary colors are colors that cannot be created by mixing together any other colors. The three primary colors are _____, _____ and _____.
2. A color wheel is a tool that has twelve colors positioned in a circle. Colors found opposite each other on the color wheel are called _____ colors and when mixed in equal proportions will produce a neutral color such as dark gray or brown.
3. TRUE   FALSE   When changing the color of hair, the colorist should keep in mind that the final hair color is the combination of the existing pigment and the artificial pigment applied to the hair.
4. _____ hair colors are mixed with hydrogen peroxide and are capable of both lifting natural pigment and depositing artificial pigment in one process.
5. As a general rule, a permanent color with a 20 volume level of hydrogen peroxide will lift the hair _____ color levels, and a 30 volume level of hydrogen peroxide will lift the hair _____ color levels.
6. Compound dyes are a mixture of _____ and _____ dyes.
7. TRUE   FALSE   The use of metallic and compound dyes is discouraged because they are unreliable and sometimes unsafe.
8. TRUE   FALSE   According to the U.S. Federal Food, Drug and Cosmetic Act, all permanent, aniline derivative tints require a skin patch test 24-48 hours prior to the hair color service.
9. How long are each of the following color services expected to last?
   temporary colors _____   semi-permanent colors _____
   demi-permanent colors _____   permanent colors _____   lighteners _____
10. The two-step coloring technique that involves lightening the hair first and then recoloring the hair to the desired tone is called _____.

1 2 3 **4** **5** 6 7

SALON FUNDAMENTALS COSMETOLOGY   299

13

CHAPTER 13

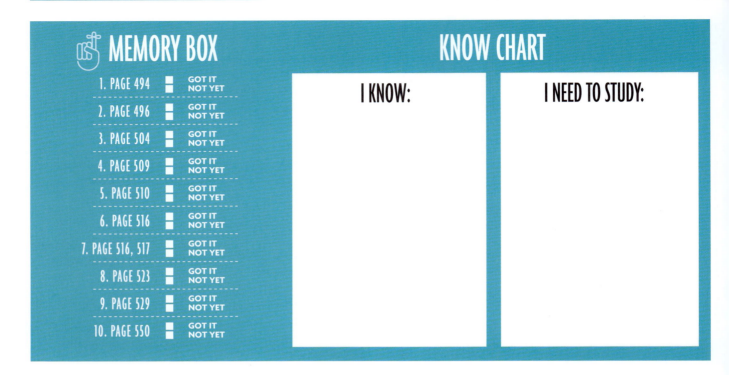

SHOW YOU KNOW...

Using the sketches shown below and colored pencils, indicate the color patterns you would use to best suit the length and style of the hair shown.

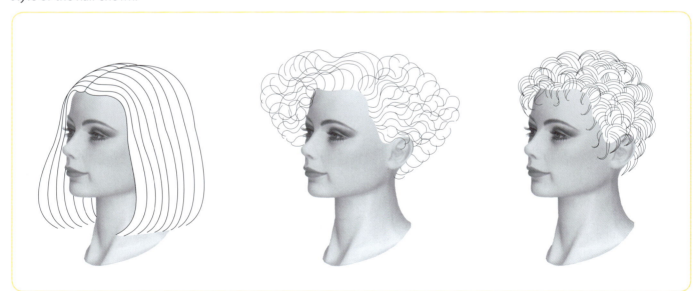

UNIT 2 HAIR SERVICES

HAIR COLORING

KNOWLEDGE GRID

Start at the top of the Knowledge Grid and work your way down, answering each question to check your understanding of *Chapter 13, Hair Coloring*. The questions found here will help you deepen your understanding, build self-confidence and increase your awareness of different ways of thinking about a subject.

KNOW	NAME THE THREE PRIMARY COLORS AND THE THREE SECONDARY COLORS.	
COMPREHEND	DESCRIBE HOW SECONDARY AND TERTIARY COLORS ARE PRODUCED.	
APPLY	CREATE A COLOR WHEEL.	
ANALYZE	COMPARE AN OXIDATIVE COLOR TO A NONOXIDATIVE COLOR.	
SYNTHESIZE	DESIGN A POSTER DISPLAYING THE DEGREES OF DECOLORIZATION.	
EVALUATE	SUPPORT THE IMPORTANCE OF PERFORMING A PREDISPOSITION (SKIN PATCH) TEST BEFORE USING ANY PERMANENT, ANILINE DERIVATIVE TINT.	

1　2　3　**5**　6　7

SALON FUNDAMENTALS COSMETOLOGY　301

13

CHAPTER 13

RUBRIC

This rubric is a self-assessment tool designed to compare your skill to industry standards. Indicate your present level of performance by checking the appropriate box. See overview for instructions.

Semi-Permanent Color

Industry Standard – to meet entry-level proficiency, industry standards require that you:
- Provide hair-related services in accordance with a client's needs or expectations in a safe environment.

	Level 1	Level 2	Level 3	To Improve, I Need To:	Teacher Assessment
Preparation					
• Perform predisposition test; disinfect color area; assemble implements/supplies; wash hands; drape client; analyze hair/scalp; wear protective gloves/color apron; perform preliminary strand test if needed; review client record card, if applicable	☐	☐	☐		☐
Procedure					
• Part hair into four sections; apply barrier cream; pour color into bottle	☐	☐	☐		☐
• Outline first back section; take 1" (2.5 cm) horizontal partings in back	☐	☐	☐		☐
• Apply color from base to midstrand, omitting porous ends	☐	☐	☐		☐
• Complete first back section; complete other back section	☐	☐	☐		☐
• Outline front sections, then apply color to these sections from diagonal partings	☐	☐	☐		☐
• Apply color to remaining midstrand and ends; work color through for even saturation	☐	☐	☐		☐
• Apply cotton around hairline; place plastic cap over hair	☐	☐	☐		☐
• Position client under pre-heated dryer if applicable; set timer	☐	☐	☐		☐
• Perform strand test if desired	☐	☐	☐		☐
• Rinse, shampoo and remove any color stains	☐	☐	☐		☐
• Condition and finish hair as desired	☐	☐	☐		☐
Completion					
• Complete record card; offer a prebook visit; recommend retail products; discard non-reusable materials, disinfect implements, arrange workstation in proper order and wash hands	☐	☐	☐		☐

TOTAL = ADDITION OF ALL TEACHER ASSESSMENT BOXES   TOTAL POINTS = ☐
                                                                                                    39

PERCENTAGE = STUDENT SCORE / HIGHEST POSSIBLE SCORE   _____ %

HAIR COLORING

RUBRIC

This rubric is a self-assessment tool designed to compare your skill to industry standards. Indicate your present level of performance by checking the appropriate box. See overview for instructions.

Oxidative Color: Darker Result

Industry Standard – to meet entry-level proficiency, industry standards require that you:
- Consult with and provide color services in accordance with a client's needs or expectations in a safe environment.

	Level 1	Level 2	Level 3	To Improve, I Need To:	Teacher Assessment
Preparation					
Perform predisposition test; disinfect color area; assemble implements/supplies; wash hands; drape client; analyze hair/scalp; wear protective gloves/color apron; perform preliminary strand test if needed; review client record card, if applicable	☐	☐	☐		☐
Procedure					
Subdivide hair into four sections; apply barrier cream	☐	☐	☐		☐
Measure and mix color formula	☐	☐	☐		☐
Begin at nape; apply color from base to ends using ¼" (.6 cm) horizontal partings	☐	☐	☐		☐
Work from bottom to top of section; complete back sections; work product through hair and ensure coverage	☐	☐	☐		☐
Move to one side of front and repeat same procedures using diagonal-back partings; start at top of sections and direct hair back away from face	☐	☐	☐		☐
Use same procedures on opposite side	☐	☐	☐		☐
Outline hairline	☐	☐	☐		☐
Cross-check and comb color through	☐	☐	☐		☐
Set timer; perform strand test	☐	☐	☐		☐
Rinse, shampoo and remove any color stains	☐	☐	☐		☐
Condition and finish hair as desired	☐	☐	☐		☐
Completion					
Complete client record card; offer a prebook visit; recommend retail products; discard non-reusable materials, disinfect implements, arrange workstation in proper order and wash hands	☐	☐	☐		☐

TOTAL = ADDITION OF ALL TEACHER ASSESSMENT BOXES

TOTAL POINTS = ☐
39

PERCENTAGE = STUDENT SCORE / HIGHEST POSSIBLE SCORE

_____ %

CHAPTER 13

RUBRIC

This rubric is a self-assessment tool designed to compare your skill to industry standards. Indicate your present level of performance by checking the appropriate box. See overview for instructions.

Freehand Painting

Industry Standard – to meet entry-level proficiency, industry standards require that you:
- Consult with and provide color services in accordance with a client's needs or expectations in a safe environment.

	Level 1	Level 2	Level 3	To Improve, I Need To:	Teacher Assessment
Preparation					
Perform predisposition test; disinfect color area; assemble implements/supplies; wash hands; drape client; analyze hair/scalp; wear protective gloves/color apron; perform preliminary strand test if needed; review client record card, if applicable	☐	☐	☐		☐
Procedure					
Establish an off-center part; section vertically from ear to ear	☐	☐	☐		☐
On heavier side, take a horizontal parting approximately 2" (5 cm) to 2 ½" (6.25 cm) thick	☐	☐	☐		☐
Position brush vertically and apply product away from base, starting at various points of strand; follow through to ends	☐	☐	☐		☐
Work toward top using same technique	☐	☐	☐		☐
Subdivide wider partings for control	☐	☐	☐		☐
Leave hair near side part natural	☐	☐	☐		☐
Repeat same color techniques on lighter side	☐	☐	☐		☐
Move to nape and take a horizontal parting, same thickness used in the front	☐	☐	☐		☐
Subdivide section for control	☐	☐	☐		☐
Apply product to one side then other	☐	☐	☐		☐
Work towards top using same technique, leaving surface natural	☐	☐	☐		☐
Follow processing directions	☐	☐	☐		☐
Rinse, shampoo, condition and finish hair as desired	☐	☐	☐		☐
Completion					
Complete client record card; offer a prebook visit; recommend retail products; discard non-reusable materials, disinfect implements, arrange workstation in proper order and wash hands	☐	☐	☐		☐

TOTAL = ADDITION OF ALL TEACHER ASSESSMENT BOXES   TOTAL POINTS = ☐
                                                                          45

PERCENTAGE = STUDENT SCORE / HIGHEST POSSIBLE SCORE   _____ %

HAIR COLORING

RUBRIC
This rubric is a self-assessment tool designed to compare your skill to industry standards. Indicate your present level of performance by checking the appropriate box. See overview for instructions.

Partial Highlights: Slicing

Industry Standard — to meet entry-level proficiency, industry standards require that you:
- Consult with and provide color services in accordance with a client's needs or expectations in a safe environment.

	Level 1	Level 2	Level 3	To Improve, I Need To:	Teacher Assessment
Preparation					
Perform predisposition test; disinfect color area; assemble implements/supplies; wash hands; drape client; analyze hair/scalp; wear protective gloves/color apron; perform preliminary strand test if needed; review client record card, if applicable	☐	☐	☐		☐
Procedure					
Create a triangle section at fringe area; mix formula	☐	☐	☐		☐
Begin at large end of triangle; make a horizontal parting and part off a fine slice from top of parting; position foil underneath slice	☐	☐	☐		☐
Apply lightener in a zigzag pattern away from scalp to ends; fold foil in half	☐	☐	☐		☐
Release a section to remain natural	☐	☐	☐		☐
Continue to alternate between highlighted and natural sections	☐	☐	☐		☐
Work toward narrow end of triangle	☐	☐	☐		☐
Clip highlighted section upward	☐	☐	☐		☐
Set timer and follow processing directions	☐	☐	☐		☐
Perform strand test	☐	☐	☐		☐
Remove foils	☐	☐	☐		☐
Rinse, shampoo, condition and finish hair as desired	☐	☐	☐		☐
Completion					
Complete client record card; offer a prebook visit; recommend retail products; discard non-reusable materials, disinfect implements, arrange workstation in proper order and wash hands	☐	☐	☐		☐

TOTAL = ADDITION OF ALL TEACHER ASSESSMENT BOXES

TOTAL POINTS = ☐
39

PERCENTAGE = STUDENT SCORE / HIGHEST POSSIBLE SCORE

_____ %

CHAPTER 13

RUBRIC

This rubric is a self-assessment tool designed to compare your skill to industry standards. Indicate your present level of performance by checking the appropriate box. See overview for instructions.

Full Highlights: Weaving

Industry Standard – to meet entry-level proficiency, industry standards require that you:
- Consult with and provide color services in accordance with a client's needs or expectations in a safe environment.

	Level 1	Level 2	Level 3	To Improve, I Need To:	Teacher Assessment

Preparation
- Perform predisposition test; disinfect color area; assemble implements/supplies; wash hands; drape client; analyze hair/scalp; wear protective gloves/color apron; perform preliminary strand test if needed; review client record card, if applicable ☐ ☐ ☐ ☐

Procedure
- Section hair into four basic sections; mix formula ☐ ☐ ☐ ☐
- Begin at nape; take a horizontal parting and weave out selected strands ☐ ☐ ☐ ☐
- Position prefolded edge of foil underneath woven strands; apply lightener from edge of foil to ends ☐ ☐ ☐ ☐
- Fold foil upward twice; fold sides of foil inward ☐ ☐ ☐ ☐
- Create a bricklay pattern; alternate between natural and highlighted sections; complete back section ☐ ☐ ☐ ☐
- Continue weaving from diagonal-back partings, using a bricklay pattern at front side ☐ ☐ ☐ ☐
- Complete other side; set timer; perform strand test ☐ ☐ ☐ ☐
- Remove foils; rinse, shampoo and dry hair ☐ ☐ ☐ ☐
- Mix toner; apply toner using a base-to-ends technique from diagonal-back and horizontal partings ☐ ☐ ☐ ☐
- Set timer; perform strand test ☐ ☐ ☐ ☐
- Rinse, shampoo and finish hair as desired ☐ ☐ ☐ ☐

Completion
- Complete client record card; offer a prebook visit; recommend retail products; discard non-reusable materials, disinfect implements, arrange workstation in proper order and wash hands ☐ ☐ ☐ ☐

TOTAL = ADDITION OF ALL TEACHER ASSESSMENT BOXES   TOTAL POINTS = ☐
                                                                    39

PERCENTAGE = STUDENT SCORE / HIGHEST POSSIBLE SCORE   _____ %

HAIR COLORING

RUBRIC

This rubric is a self-assessment tool designed to compare your skills to industry standards. Indicate your present level of performance by checking the appropriate box. See overview for instructions.

Double-Process Blond

Industry Standard — to meet entry-level proficiency, industry standards require that you:
- Provide hair-related services in accordance with a client's needs or expectations in a safe environment.

Preparation

Task	Level 1	Level 2	Level 3	To Improve, I Need To:	Teacher Assessment
Perform predisposition test; disinfect color area; assemble implements/supplies; wash hands; drape client; analyze hair/scalp; wear protective gloves/color apron; perform preliminary strand test if needed; review client record card, if applicable	☐	☐	☐		☐

Procedure

Task	Level 1	Level 2	Level 3	To Improve, I Need To:	Teacher Assessment
Section hair into four sections; apply barrier cream; measure and mix formula	☐	☐	☐		☐
Release ⅛" (.3cm) horizontal partings at nape, place cotton under strand	☐	☐	☐		☐
Apply lightener ½" (1.25 cm) away from scalp through to ends; apply to both sides of strand if necessary	☐	☐	☐		☐
Place cotton at base	☐	☐	☐		☐
Work upward to complete back; lift and bring each parting down	☐	☐	☐		☐
Complete other side of back	☐	☐	☐		☐
Move to sides and use same procedures	☐	☐	☐		☐
Set timer according to manufacturer's directions	☐	☐	☐		☐
Perform strand test	☐	☐	☐		☐
Remove cotton and apply newly mixed lightener to base only, beginning at top of back; outline each section; bring down each section	☐	☐	☐		☐
Perform strand test periodically	☐	☐	☐		☐
Rinse with cool water, shampoo and towel dry	☐	☐	☐		☐
Re-examine scalp for abrasions and any irritations	☐	☐	☐		☐
Mix and apply toner; apply toner from ¼" (.6cm) diagonal back partings at sides and horizontal partings at back	☐	☐	☐		☐
Set timer	☐	☐	☐		☐
Perform strand test	☐	☐	☐		☐
Rinse, shampoo and condition hair	☐	☐	☐		☐
Finish hair as desired	☐	☐	☐		☐

Completion

Task	Level 1	Level 2	Level 3	To Improve, I Need To:	Teacher Assessment
Complete client record card; offer a prebook visit; recommend retail products; discard non-reusable materials, disinfect implements, arrange workstation in proper order and wash hands	☐	☐	☐		☐

TOTAL = ADDITION OF ALL TEACHER ASSESSMENT BOXES

TOTAL POINTS = _____ / 60

PERCENTAGE = STUDENT SCORE / HIGHEST POSSIBLE SCORE _____ %

CHAPTER 13

BRAIN CONDITIONER
MULTIPLE CHOICE. CIRCLE THE CORRECT ANSWER.

1. All of the following statements are true about color, EXCEPT:
   a. it is a phenomenon of light
   b. it is a group of electromagnetic waves
   c. it can be seen if wavelengths are reflected off an object
   d. it does not depend on presence of light

2. What are the three primary colors?
   a. red, blue and yellow   b. green, black and purple   c. green, orange and purple   d. red, white and blue

3. What colors are produced by mixing two primary colors in varying proportions?
   a. secondary   b. tertiary   c. infrared   d. ultraviolet

4. A varying mixture of red and yellow creates what color?
   a. blue   b. green   c. violet   d. orange

5. Varying proportions of blue and yellow create:
   a. black   b. green   c. violet   d. orange

6. An example of a tertiary color would be:
   a. yellow-orange   b. blue-yellow   c. violet   d. blue

7. Mixing varying proportions of a primary color with its neighboring secondary color will produce:
   a. white   b. black   c. gray   d. a tertiary color

8. Which of the following combinations is NOT a tertiary color?
   a. red-violet   b. blue-green   c. red-orange   d. blue-yellow

9. Mixing colors found opposite one another on the color wheel produces which color?
   a. green   b. white   c. brown or dark gray   d. blue

10. Which of the following descriptions identifies warm colors?
    a. colors that contain blue hues
    b. colors that contain green hues
    c. colors that fall into the orange and red half of the color wheel
    d. colors that are opposite each other on the color wheel

11. Cool colors include?
    a. blues   b. yellows   c. reds   d. oranges

12. Colors found opposite each other on the color wheel are called:
    a. complementary colors   b. primary colors   c. secondary colors   d. tertiary colors

13. An application of what colors would help rid a client of unwanted orange tones?
    a. green-based   b. brown-based   c. blue-based   d. black-based

14. The brightness or vividness of a hair color is referred to as:
    a. level   b. texture   c. intensity   d. porosity

15. A small population of eumelanin will produce:
    a. black hair   b. red hair   c. light blond hair   d. dark brown hair

16. A predominant amount of pheomelanin will produce:
    a. black hair   b. brown hair   c. red hair   d. blond hair

17. A level 10 color is:
    a. the darkest level   b. the lightest level   c. a medium level   d. a neutral level

HAIR COLORING

18. Which hair texture may tend to process slightly lighter than the intended level?
    a. coarse
    b. medium
    c. fine
    d. thinning

19. Which colors coat the cuticle but do not enter the cortex?
    a. semi-permanent
    b. long-lasting semi-permanent
    c. permanent
    d. temporary

20. Temporary colors are available in all of the following forms EXCEPT:
    a. weekly rinses
    b. color mousses
    c. mascaras
    d. developers

21. Which of the following products requires the use of a skin patch test?
    a. temporary color
    b. color mousses
    c. permanent color
    d. weekly rinses

22. A nonoxidative process that uses large and small color molecules and allows small color molecules to penetrate the cuticle and enter the cortex is called:
    a. temporary coloring
    b. semi-permanent coloring
    c. demi-permanent coloring
    d. permanent coloring

23. Which of the following characteristics does NOT describe semi-permanent colors?
    a. only deposits color
    b. retouches are not required
    c. leaves a line of demarcation
    d. does not use chemicals to alter the hair

24. Hair color products that are mixed with a developer are called:
    a. oxidative colors
    b. nonoxidative colors
    c. temporary colors
    d. semi-permanent colors

25. A type of coloring using a low-volume peroxide that can only deposit color or add tone to the hair would be:
    a. temporary coloring
    b. permanent coloring
    c. semi-permanent coloring
    d. long-lasting semi-permanent coloring

26. Long-lasting semi-permanent colors will generally last:
    a. 1 to 2 weeks
    b. 2 to 3 weeks
    c. 4 to 6 weeks
    d. at least 3 months

27. Demi-permanent colors are NOT designed to:
    a. add tone
    b. deposit color
    c. last 4 to 6 weeks
    d. lift or lighten existing color

28. Permanent hair colors are sometimes called:
    a. oxidative tints with ammonia
    b. color pomades
    c. color crayons
    d. weekly rinses

29. Paraphenylenediamine or paratoluenediamine would be found in which of the following:
    a. temporary colors
    b. semi-permanent colors
    c. vegetable dyes
    d. permanent hair colors

30. A 20 volume peroxide solution will generally lift the hair:
    a. two levels
    b. three levels
    c. four levels
    d. five levels

31. A 30 volume hydrogen peroxide solution will lift the hair how many more levels than a 20 volume solution?
    a. 1 level
    b. 2 levels
    c. 3 levels
    d. 4 levels

32. What may be required if the desired amount of lift is not achieved using a single-process color?
    a. prelightening
    b. addition of a temporary color
    c. addition of a filler
    d. addition of a demi-permanent color

33. What product is used before a color service to provide an even base?
    a. toner
    b. intensifier
    c. filler
    d. drabber

34. Which of the following statements is true of lighteners?
    a. used to add melanin to the hair
    b. generally applied to wet hair
    c. used to add polymers and melanin
    d. used to diffuse or remove melanin

CHAPTER 13

35. On-the-scalp lighteners have a pH of:
    a. 2.5 to 3.5
    b. 4.0 to 5.5
    c. 6.5 to 7.5
    d. about 9.0

36. Off-the scalp lighteners are generally used for:
    a. virgin coloring
    b. retouch coloring
    c. special effects such as painting
    d. soap capping

37. What item is the most commonly used developer or oxidizing agent?
    a. aniline
    b. nitrogen
    c. oxygen
    d. hydrogen peroxide

38. A 10 volume developer in the United States would be equivalent to what level of developer in Europe?
    a. 3%
    b. 6%
    c. 20 volume
    d. 30 volume

39. What instrument is used to measure the strength of hydrogen peroxide?
    a. pH meter
    b. ammeter
    c. hydrometer
    d. patch test

40. An organic product that produces reddish highlights is commonly known as:
    a. henna
    b. metallic color
    c. filler
    d. chamomile

41. Chemical services should not be performed on hair that has been colored with any of the following products EXCEPT:
    a. henna
    b. metallic dyes
    c. compound dyes
    d. weekly rinses

42. Chamomile would be an example of a:
    a. vegetable dye
    b. metallic dye
    c. compound dye
    d. permanent dye

43. What technique is used to add tone or darken the existing color?
    a. midstrand to ends
    b. ends to base
    c. base to ends
    d. ends to midstrand

44. A highlighting technique in which a crochet hook is used to pull hair strands through a perforated cap is called:
    a. reverse highlighting
    b. cap method
    c. double-process blond
    d. weaving

45. A skin patch test will help determine:
    a. the processing time for a lightener
    b. the processing time for the color procedure
    c. the correct formula for the color procedure
    d. if the client has a sensitivity or an allergic reaction to the chemicals being used

46. If redness and swelling are found around the test area when performing a predisposition test, which of the following steps should NOT be taken?
    a. stop the service
    b. proceed with the service
    c. ask the client how they are feeling
    d. have the client seek medical assistance

47. Which of the following statements is true of products that contain aniline derivatives?
    a. they are always temporary
    b. they may be applied to the eyebrows
    c. a skin patch test is not required
    d. a skin patch test is required

48. A skin patch test must be done at least how many hours before the actual procedure that requires the predisposition test?
    a. 2
    b. 6
    c. 12
    d. 24

49. What test can detect the presence of previous applications that may not be compatible with the planned application?
    a. skin patch
    b. preliminary strand
    c. porosity
    d. pH

50. What factor would be a consideration regarding a preliminary strand test?
    a. it is not necessary to drape the client for this test
    b. position the test strand so the client can't see the results
    c. position the test strand so the client can see the results
    d. if the hair is going to be cut, cancel the preliminary strand test

HAIR COLORING

51. Which light gives a true color reflection?
    a. incandescent light   b. fluorescent light   c. sunlight   d. ultraviolet light

52. Which light generally makes the hair appear warmer than it actually is?
    a. incandescent light   b. fluorescent light   c. sunlight   d. ultraviolet light

53. Which light generally makes the hair appear cooler?
    a. incandescent light   b. fluorescent light   c. sunlight   d. ultraviolet light

54. Applying a nonoxidative color product or an oxidative color without ammonia over previously colored hair to refresh the color is referred to as:
    a. virgin darker   b. virgin lighter   c. double-process blond   d. color glazing

55. When lightening hair for the first time, what technique should be used?
    a. base to ends
    b. midstrand to ends, then base
    c. ends to base
    d. base, then midstrand to ends

56. Darker result retouch procedures will generally need to be performed every:
    a. 1 to 2 weeks   b. 2 to 4 weeks   c. 6 to 8 weeks   d. 12 to 16 weeks

57. Upon completion of an oxidative color procedure, be sure to do all of the following procedures EXCEPT:
    a. complete a client record card
    b. perform a strand test
    c. wash your hands with a liquid antibacterial soap
    d. offer a rebook visit

58. Lighter result retouch applications should not exceed:
    a. 2 minutes   b. 10 minutes   c. 30 minutes   d. 60 minutes

59. Which technique is performed on the surface of hair to create a highlighted or lowlighted color effect?
    a. surface painting   b. lighter result touchup   c. virgin lightener   d. color glazing

60. Coloring hair back to its natural color is called:
    a. stripping   b. tinting back   c. repositioning   d. lightening

FINAL REVIEW

Check your answers as you did before. Place a check mark next to the page number for any incorrect answer. Review that material.

☐	1. page 494	☐	7. page 495	☐	13. page 496	☐	19. page 505
☐	2. page 494	☐	8. page 495	☐	14. page 497	☐	20. page 506
☐	3. page 494	☐	9. page 496	☐	15. page 498	☐	21. page 506
☐	4. page 494	☐	10. page 496	☐	16. page 498	☐	22. page 507
☐	5. page 494	☐	11. page 496	☐	17. page 499	☐	23. page 507
☐	6. page 495	☐	12. page 496	☐	18. page 502	☐	24. page 508

CHAPTER 13

FINAL REVIEW *continued*

☐ 25.	page 508	☐ 34.	page 512	☐ 43.	page 520	☐ 52.	page 526
☐ 26.	page 508	☐ 35.	page 513	☐ 44.	page 522	☐ 53.	page 526
☐ 27.	page 508	☐ 36.	page 513	☐ 45.	page 523	☐ 54.	page 537
☐ 28.	page 509	☐ 37.	page 514	☐ 46.	page 523	☐ 55.	page 537
☐ 29.	page 509	☐ 38.	page 514	☐ 47.	page 523	☐ 56.	page 537
☐ 30.	page 510	☐ 39.	page 515	☐ 48.	page 524	☐ 57.	page 537
☐ 31.	page 510	☐ 40.	page 516	☐ 49.	page 525	☐ 58.	page 538
☐ 32.	page 510	☐ 41.	page 516	☐ 50.	page 525	☐ 59.	page 539
☐ 33.	page 511	☐ 42.	page 516	☐ 51.	page 526	☐ 60.	page 555

NOTES TO MYSELF

Experts tell us that it is important to summarize your feelings and reactions about what you are learning. Note especially things that surprised you, things you found difficult to learn, suggestions and ideas you received from friends that helped make learning this chapter easier and more enjoyable.

My reflections about Hair Coloring:

LESSONS LEARNED

- Color is the visual perception of the reflection of light, and its main characteristics are tone, level and intensity.
- The color wheel is a tool used to describe any mixed color in relation to the primary colors. Colors opposite one another on the color wheel are complementary colors and are used in hair coloring to neutralize unwanted tones.
- Natural and artificial hair colors are identified by their level, which specifies the lightness or darkness of the color from blond to black, and their tone, which specifies whether the color is warm, cool or neutral.
- The client's final hair color is the result of its contributing pigment and the formula of artificial pigments, developers and/or lighteners applied to the hair.
- Nonoxidative colors produce temporary or semi-permanent results and oxidative colors produce long-lasting or permanent results. Lighteners are used to decolorize pigment and to achieve lighter color results.
- Color designs are achieved using base-to-ends, midstrand-to-ends and base application techniques and freeform painting, weaving and slicing and the cap method coloring techniques.

THINGS TO DO

THINGS TO DO

CHAPTER 14

THE STUDY OF NAILS

VALUE

Providing specialized nail services for your clients will help improve their total image and in turn assist you in retaining more loyal clients.

MAIN IDEA

Knowing the Theory Behind Nails + Performing Natural and Artificial Nail Care Procedures = **Meeting Client's Total Image Needs**

PLAN

14.1 NAIL THEORY
Nail Structure
Nail Growth
Nail Diseases, Disorders and Conditions

14.2 NATURAL NAIL CARE
Nail Shapes
Nail Essentials
Infection Control and Safety
Client Consultation
Basic Manicure
Male Manicure
Pedicure Essentials
Basic Pedicure
Special Nail Services

14.3 ARTIFICIAL NAIL CARE
Artificial Nail Essentials
Infection Control and Safety
Nail Tips
Tips With Acrylic Overlay
Pink and White Sculptured Nails
Additional Artificial Nail Services

smartNOTES

14.1 NAIL THEORY   pages 563-564

Onychology — The study of _____

Nail Structure

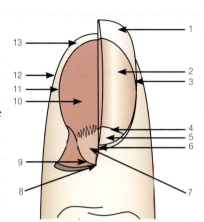

1. Free Edge — Extends beyond the end of the finger or toe
2. Nail Body — Visible nail area
3. Nail Wall — Folds of skin on either _____ of nail groove
4. Lunula — Whitened half-moon shape at _____ of nail
5. Eponychium — Cuticle that overlaps lunula at nail base
6. Cuticle — Loose, overlapping _____ around the nail
7. Nail Matrix — Generates cells that make the nail
8. Nail Root — Attached to matrix
9. Mantle — Holds _____ and matrix
10. Nail Bed — Area of nail on which nail body rests
11. Nail Grooves — Tracks that nail _____ on as it grows
12. Perionychium — Skin that _____, overlaps and surrounds nail
13. Hyponychium — Skin underneath the free _____

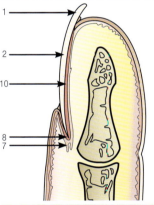

Nail Growth

Keratin — Protein that hardens to make the _____

Rate — Under normal circumstances it takes 4 to 6 _____ to grow a new nail; ⅛" (.3 cm) per month in adults; faster in summer; toenails grow slower

Injuries — Can result in shape distortions or nail discoloration
- A nail is lost due to _____ and, without the protection of the nail plate, the nail bed or matrix is injured
- A nail is lost through _____ or infection. The regrown nail, in these circumstances, is often distorted in shape

CHAPTER 14

smartNOTES

14.1 NAIL THEORY pages 564-565

Nail Diseases, Disorders and Conditions

Onychosis

Etiology

Hand and Nail Examination

Six Signs of Infection

SYMPTOM OBSERVED:	MAY INDICATE:
Coldness	_____
Heat	_____
Dry Texture	_____
Redness	_____
Color of Nail Bed	_____
Condition of Free Edge	_____
Tenderness/Stiffness	_____
Nail Plate Shape/Thickness	_____

THE STUDY OF NAILS

DISEASE	DESCRIPTION	ETIOLOGY (CAUSE)	SYMPTOMS/PROGNOSIS	SERVICE
Onychomycosis Tinea Unguium	Ringworm of the Nail	Fungus		No service may be performed
Tinea Manus	Hand Ringworm	Fungus		No service may be performed
Tinea Pedis	Athlete's Foot/Foot Ringworm	Fungus		No service may be performed
Paronychia/Felon	Inflammation	Bacterial Infection		No service may be performed
Onychoptosis	Shedding of Nails	Disease/Injury		No service may be performed
Onychia	Inflammation of Matrix	Bacterial Infection		No service may be performed
Onychatrophia	Wasting Away of Nail	Injury/Systemic		No service may be performed
Onycholysis	Loosening of Nail	Internal Disorder/Systemic		No service may be performed

DISORDER	DESCRIPTION	ETIOLOGY (CAUSE)	SYMPTOMS/PROGNOSIS	SERVICE
Blue Nails	Bluish in Color	Systemic/Injury		Manicure with caution
Eggshell Nails	Thin, Soft Nails	Hereditary/Nervous Condition		Polish to protect
Corrugations	Ridges Across Nail	Injury/Systemic		Lightly buff; apply base coat

CHAPTER 14

DISORDER	DESCRIPTION	ETIOLOGY (CAUSE)	SYMPTOMS/PROGNOSIS	TREATMENT
Koilonychia	Spoon Nails	Systemic/Illness		File carefully; polish to protect
Furrows	Vertical Lines	Injury/Nutritional Deficiencies		Lightly buff; apply base coat
Onychogryposis	Claw Nails	Systemic		Clean under free edge; file
Onychocryptosis	Ingrown Nails	Environmental/ Poor Trimming		Soften skin; trim nail
Melanonychia	Brown or black darkening of nail	Trauma/Systemic/ Medications		Make client aware of problem/causes; suggest seeing a physician
Onychauxis Hypertrophy	Thickening of Nail Plate	Injury/Systemic		Lightly buff

CONDITIONS	DESCRIPTION	ETIOLOGY (CAUSE)	SYMPTOMS/PROGNOSIS	TREATMENT
Agnails	Hangnails	Split Cuticle		Trim hangnail; moisturize
Bruised Nails (Splinter Hemorraghes)	Purple Nails	Trauma/Environmental/ Trapped Blood		No pressure on nail plate
Leuconychia	White Spots	Injury/Heredity/ Systemic		Perform nail service as usual
Pterygium	Living, Excess Skin Attached to Nail Plate	Severe Injury; Other Disease		No service can be performed on affected nails
Beau's Lines	Indentations that run across the nail	Major Injury/ Severe Illness		Make client aware of possible cause; perform nail service as usual
Onychophagy	Bitten Nails	Habit		Perform nail service weekly
Onychorrhexis	Split or Brittle Nails	Injury/Improper Filing/ Chemicals		Soften nails before trimming; hot oil manicure

THE STUDY OF NAILS

smartNOTES

14.1 NAIL THEORY   page 570

Pigmentation
Problems

Discoloration

Bacterial Infection

Health of Body

14.2 NATURAL NAIL CARE   pages 570-574

Purpose of Nail
Service

Nail Shapes

**Infection Control
and Safety**

Blood Spill Procedure

1.
2.
3.
4.
5.
6.
7.

SALON FUNDAMENTALS COSMETOLOGY   319

CHAPTER 14

RUBRIC

This rubric is a self-assessment tool designed to compare your skill to industry standards. Indicate your present level of performance by checking the appropriate box. See overview for instructions.

Basic Manicure

Industry Standard – to meet entry-level proficiency, industry standards require that you:
- Provide and conduct basic manicure and pedicure services in a safe environment, free from disease.

	Level 1	Level 2	Level 3	To Improve, I Need To:	Teacher Assessment
Preparation					
Clean nail table; place fresh soaking lotion and disinfected nail implements on nail table; review and arrange products in order of use	☐	☐	☐		☐
Procedure					
Wash and sanitize hands; perform visual examination of hands and nails; remove polish	☐	☐	☐		☐
Analyze skin and nails thoroughly; consult with client	☐	☐	☐		☐
File and shape nails; place hand in finger bowl	☐	☐	☐		☐
Repeat filing, shaping and cuticle care on opposite hand	☐	☐	☐		☐
Pat first hand dry; apply cuticle remover; push back cuticles; scrub hand and nails	☐	☐	☐		☐
Clean under free edge; pat hand dry	☐	☐	☐		☐
Repeat cuticle care and cleaning on opposite hand	☐	☐	☐		☐
Apply massage lotion or cream; perform massage techniques	☐	☐	☐		☐
Remove all traces of massage lotion or cream from nails	☐	☐	☐		☐
Apply base coat; apply two coats of polish; apply top coat	☐	☐	☐		☐
Remove excess polish from skin	☐	☐	☐		☐
Apply quick-dry product or small amount of cuticle oil	☐	☐	☐		☐
Completion					
Offer a prebook visit; recommend retail products; discard non-reusable materials, replace used towels with fresh towels, arrange all products and implements in proper order; disinfect nail service implements and top of the nail service table; wash your hands with liquid soap.	☐	☐	☐		☐

Total = addition of all Teacher Assessment boxes

TOTAL POINTS = ☐

42

Percentage = student score / highest possible score

_____ %

THE STUDY OF NAILS

RUBRIC

This rubric is a self-assessment tool designed to compare your skill to industry standards. Indicate your present level of performance by checking the appropriate box. See overview for instructions.

Basic Pedicure

Industry Standard – to meet entry-level proficiency, industry standards require that you:
- Provide and conduct basic manicure and pedicure services in a safe environment, free from disease.

	Level 1	Level 2	Level 3	To Improve, I Need To:	Teacher Assessment
Preparation					
Clean and disinfect implements; set up equipment and lay out tools on sanitized table; review and arrange products in order of use; prepare foot bath; wash hands	☐	☐	☐		☐
Procedure					
Wash and sanitize hands; sanitize client's feet; perform a visual examination; soak and dry feet	☐	☐	☐		☐
Remove nail polish; examine nails; trim and file nails; repeat on other foot	☐	☐	☐		☐
Apply cuticle remover cream; push back cuticles; repeat on opposite foot	☐	☐	☐		☐
Apply sloughing lotion or foot scrub, and massage to remove dead skin cells	☐	☐	☐		☐
Dry thoroughly; massage with lotion	☐	☐	☐		☐
Remove excess lotion from nail surface; apply position toe separators	☐	☐	☐		☐
Apply base coat; apply two coats of polish; apply top coat, clean excess polish followed by quick-drying product or cuticle oil	☐	☐	☐		☐
Allow drying time	☐	☐	☐		☐
Remove toe separators when dry	☐	☐	☐		☐
Completion					
Offer a prebook visit; recommend retail products; discard non-reusable materials, replace used towels with fresh towels, arrange all products and implements in proper order; disinfect pedicure service implements and equipment; wash your hands with liquid soap.	☐	☐	☐		☐

Total = addition of all Teacher Assessment boxes

Percentage = student score / highest possible score

TOTAL POINTS = ☐
33

_____ %

SALON FUNDAMENTALS COSMETOLOGY 321

CHAPTER 14

smartNOTES

14.2 NATURAL NAIL CARE   pages 584-585

Special Nail Services

French Manicure

White polish on free edge; pink or peach polish applied to entire nail

Nail Repair (Mending with Silk)

1. Smooth over broken or split area with black side of 3-way buffer
2. Apply _____ to nail
3. Cut fiber, slightly larger than split or break
4. Apply _____ to split or broken area
5. Place _____ over split or break with tweezers; cut away uneven edges
6. Smooth and apply second layer of _____
7. Dry and _____ smooth
8. Soak and scrub nail repair area

Hot Oil or Cream Manicure

Hand is placed in warm oil or cream; great for moisturizing

Electric Nail Services

Special tools that file, buff, smooth and push _____

Nail Art

14.3 ARTIFICIAL NAIL CARE   pages 586-588

Three General Product Systems

1. Acrylic nails (_____ or liquid)
2. Nail wraps (fiberglass, silk, linen and nylon)
3. _____ nails (light-cured)

MMA (Methyl Methacrylate)

Liquid methyl methacrylate is a poisonous _____; should not be used in acrylic monomers

MMA is safe to use in acrylic polymers

THE STUDY OF NAILS

RUBRIC

This rubric is a self-assessment tool designed to compare your skill to industry standards. Indicate your present level of performance by checking the appropriate box. See overview for instructions.

Nail Tips

Industry Standard – to meet entry-level proficiency, industry standards require that you:
- Provide and conduct basic manicure and pedicure services in a safe environment, free from disease.

	Level 1	Level 2	Level 3	To Improve, I Need To:	Teacher Assessment
Preparation					
Clean nail table; place fresh soaking lotion and disinfected nail implements on nail table; review and arrange products in order of use	☐	☐	☐		☐
Procedure					
Wash and sanitize hands; perform visual analysis	☐	☐	☐		☐
Remove nail polish; perform thorough hand and nail examination and consultation	☐	☐	☐		☐
Select correct size of nail tips; file and shape natural free edge	☐	☐	☐		☐
Buff nail surface gently; remove oil and debris from nail plate	☐	☐	☐		☐
Apply thin line of adhesive to free edge of natural nail and to well of plastic tip; rock tip onto natural nail slowly; hold nail for a few seconds	☐	☐	☐		☐
Apply second drop of adhesive on top of seam; spray with adhesive accelerator	☐	☐	☐		☐
Trim free edge of nail tip; measure length of all nails	☐	☐	☐		☐
File and buff top of seam; then free edge; buff to shine or polish	☐	☐	☐		☐
Blend and smooth imperfections	☐	☐	☐		☐
Completion					
Offer a prebook visit; recommend retail products; discard non-reusable materials, replace used towels with fresh towels, arrange all products and implements in proper order; disinfect nail tips service implements and equipment; wash your hands with liquid soap.	☐	☐	☐		☐

Total = addition of all Teacher Assessment boxes

Percentage = student score / highest possible score

TOTAL POINTS = ☐
33

_____ %

CHAPTER 14

RUBRIC

This rubric is a self-assessment tool designed to compare your skill to industry standards. Indicate your present level of performance by checking the appropriate box. See overview for instructions.

Tips With Acrylic Overlay

Industry Standard – to meet entry-level proficiency, industry standards require that you:
- Provide and conduct basic manicure and pedicure services in a safe environment, free from disease.

	Level 1	Level 2	Level 3	To Improve, I Need To:	Teacher Assessment
Preparation					
• Clean nail table; place fresh soaking lotion and disinfected nail implements on nail table; review and arrange products in order of use	☐	☐	☐		☐
Procedure					
• Wash and sanitize hands; perform visual analysis	☐	☐	☐		☐
• Remove nail polish; perform thorough hand and nail examination and consultation	☐	☐	☐		☐
• Prepare natural nail – buff, and apply appropriate nail preparation solution	☐	☐	☐		☐
• Apply tips; buff nails and tips	☐	☐	☐		☐
• Form bead on side or tip of acrylic brush	☐	☐	☐		☐
• Apply acrylic at free edge (zone 1)	☐	☐	☐		☐
• Pat and press with belly of brush to blend	☐	☐	☐		☐
• Blend acrylic toward middle of nail plate (zone 2)	☐	☐	☐		☐
• Place second acrylic bead in middle of nail plate (zone 2)	☐	☐	☐		☐
• Pat and press toward free edge	☐	☐	☐		☐
• Place third acrylic bead at cuticle area (zone 3)	☐	☐	☐		☐
• Pat and press toward middle of nail plate (zone 2)	☐	☐	☐		☐
• File and shape nail; buff to smooth finish; apply cuticle oil	☐	☐	☐		☐
Completion					
• Offer a prebook visit; recommend retail products; discard non-reusable materials, replace used towels with fresh towels, arrange all products and implements in proper order; disinfect acrylic overlay service implements and equipment; wash your hands with liquid soap.	☐	☐	☐		☐

Total = addition of all Teacher Assessment boxes

TOTAL POINTS = ☐
45

Percentage = student score / highest possible score

_____ %

324   UNIT 3 NAIL AND SKIN SERVICES

THE STUDY OF NAILS

RUBRIC

This rubric is a self-assessment tool designed to compare your skill to industry standards. Indicate your present level of performance by checking the appropriate box. See overview for instructions.

Pink and White Sculptured Nails

Industry Standard – to meet entry-level proficiency, industry standards require that you:
- Provide and conduct basic manicure and pedicure services in a safe environment, free from disease.

	Level 1	Level 2	Level 3	To Improve, I Need To:	Teacher Assessment
Preparation					
Clean nail table; place fresh soaking lotion and disinfected nail implements on nail table; review and arrange products in order of use	☐	☐	☐		☐
Procedure					
Wash and sanitize hands; perform visual analysis; remove nail polish	☐	☐	☐		☐
Perform thorough hand and nail examination and consultation	☐	☐	☐		☐
File free edge; buff surface of nail lightly; remove filing residue	☐	☐	☐		☐
Apply dehydrant; apply nail form; apply primer if directed	☐	☐	☐		☐
Measure out required amount of pink and white acrylic powder; form bead of white acrylic on side of brush	☐	☐	☐		☐
Apply acrylic bead to form to create free edge (zone 1); rotate brush; pat and press toward edges of nail form	☐	☐	☐		☐
Define shape and length of free edge	☐	☐	☐		☐
Create second acrylic pink bead; place second bead in middle section (zone 2); pat, press and stroke acrylic into place	☐	☐	☐		☐
Place smallest pink acrylic bead just below cuticle (zone 3); pat, press and stroke acrylic down to base of nail	☐	☐	☐		☐
Apply fourth bead across stress area (optional); repeat on remaining nails	☐	☐	☐		☐
Remove form; file and buff; remove nail dust; buff	☐	☐	☐		☐
Completion					
Offer a prebook visit; recommend retail products; discard non-reusable materials, replace used towels with fresh towels, arrange all products and implements in proper order; disinfect acrylic overlay service implements and equipment; wash your hands with liquid soap.	☐	☐	☐		☐

Total = addition of all Teacher Assessment boxes

TOTAL POINTS = ☐
39

Percentage = student score / highest possible score ____ %

CHAPTER 14

smartNOTES

14.3 ARTIFICIAL NAILS pages 597-598

Fill-Ins and Re-Balancing Acrylic Nails

Removing Nail Tips, Tips with Overlays and Sculptured Nails

Additional Artificial Nail Services

Nail Wraps

TYPES

FIBERGLASS	SILK
• Synthetic fiber • Almost invisible when applied	• Natural fiber • Creates a smooth overlay

LINEN	NYLON
• Thicker fabric • Remains visible	• Used for repair • Not as strong as other wraps

Liquid nail wrap – acts as a nail strengthener; basically a polish containing fibers

Light-Cured Gel Nails

THE STUDY OF NAILS

TALKING POINTS

Your next challenge is to be ready to talk about some of the important ideas in this chapter. Follow the directions listed next to each box. Then practice talking about your ideas with others.

	Select the three nail diseases that you feel would be the most difficult to recognize and then discuss with a partner.
	Identify the step in applying artificial nails that gives you the most difficulty and discuss with a partner.
	List three occupations where having long fingernails might be a nuisance, distraction or detrimental.

THE CHALLENGE

Now it's time to see how well you know your new material. First answer these questions. Then use the Memory Box that follows to check yourself. Look up each answer on the corresponding page in the textbook. Check "got it" for all correct answers and "not yet" for all incorrect responses. Using the "Know Chart," record all of your correct responses in the "I Know" column. After correcting incorrect answers, record all of your corrected responses in the "I Need to Study" column. That way you know exactly what to review before continuing in this study guide.

1. The study of the structure and growth of nails is known as_____.
2. The nail is made of a hardened protein called _____,
3. TRUE FALSE Nail growth is very similar to the growth of hair.
4. Onychosis is defined as any disease, disorder or _____ of the nail.
5. Can you name the six signs of infection in the nail and hands?
   _____   _____
   _____   _____
   _____   _____
6. TRUE FALSE A healthy nail is flexible, translucent and pinkish in color.
7. The cosmetic care of the hands and fingernails is defined as_____.
8. Explain the first step in a basic manicure procedure. _____
   _____
9. There are three general product systems by which artificial nails can be created. Can you name them?
   _____   _____
   _____
10. Fill-in services are required approximately two weeks following coating the entire nail with an acrylic. Explain why this is a very important procedure.
    _____

14

1   2   3   4   5   6   7

SALON FUNDAMENTALS COSMETOLOGY   327

CHAPTER 14

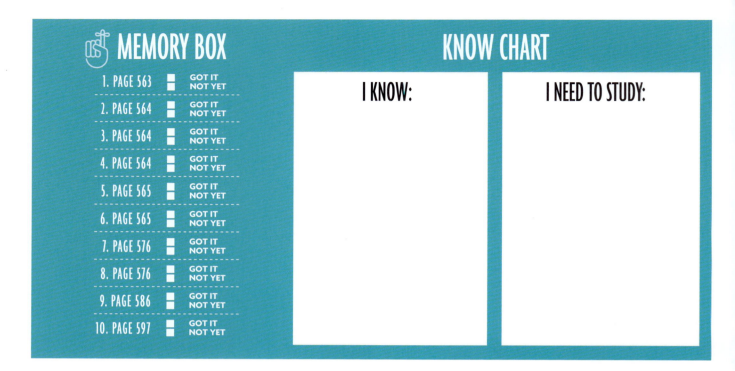

SHOW YOU KNOW...

The manager of the salon has just announced at the staff meeting that a prize will be awarded to the stylist or group of stylists that creates the best nail promotion. The nail promotion will be held during the month of May. The manager has requested that the following items be included in the promotion: 1) theme 2) special pricing 3) ad for the newspaper 4) flyer for clients visiting the salon.

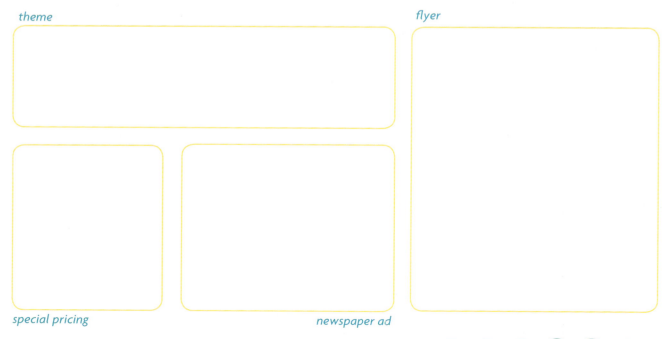

THE STUDY OF NAILS

KNOWLEDGE GRID

Start at the top of the Knowledge Grid and work your way down, answering each question to check your understanding of *Chapter 14, The Study of Nails*. The questions found here will help you deepen your understanding, build self-confidence and increase your awareness of different ways of thinking about a subject.

KNOW	WHAT IS THE FUNCTION OF THE NAIL MATRIX?	
COMPREHEND	IDENTIFY THE GUIDELINES FOR WHETHER A NAIL SERVICE MAY BE PERFORMED IF A NAIL DISEASE, DISORDER OR CONDITION IS PRESENT.	
APPLY	OFFER AN EXAMPLE OF WHAT YOU MIGHT OBSERVE IN A HAND AND NAIL EXAMINATION THAT MIGHT INDICATE THAT THE CLIENT HAS POOR CIRCULATION.	
ANALYZE	CLASSIFY THE FOLLOWING DISEASES, DISORDERS AND CONDITIONS INTO THE PROPER CATEGORY.	
SYNTHESIZE	IN YOUR OWN WORDS, DESCRIBE THE PURPOSE OF THE CONSULT STEP OF THE CLIENT CONSULTATION.	
EVALUATE	DEFEND THE IMPORTANCE OF FOLLOWING INFECTION CONTROL GUIDELINES WHEN PERFORMING AN ARTIFICIAL NAIL SERVICE.	

CHAPTER 14

A CLASS ACT

Now that you have completed your work in *The Study of Nails*, it's time to demonstrate your creative talents.

Each member of the class will plan, sketch, demonstrate (either on a nail tip or a fellow student) and explain a flat nail art design.

REMEMBER: Before starting the design you must sketch it, list key features to be explained and name your creation.

SKETCH

KEY FEATURES

DESIGN NAME:

All designs will be judged for:

	1 2 3 4 5 6 7 8 9 10	
Plan/Sketch	☐ ☐ ☐ ☐ ☐ ☐ ☐ ☐ ☐ ☐	points: _____
Demonstration	☐ ☐ ☐ ☐ ☐ ☐ ☐ ☐ ☐ ☐	points: _____
Explanation	☐ ☐ ☐ ☐ ☐ ☐ ☐ ☐ ☐ ☐	points: _____

TOTAL POINTS: _____

THE STUDY OF NAILS

BRAIN CONDITIONER
MULTIPLE CHOICE. CIRCLE THE CORRECT ANSWER.

1. What term describes the technical name for the nail?
   a. onyx
   b. cuticle
   c. mantle
   d. lunula

2. What term describes the deep pocket-like area that holds the root and matrix of the nail?
   a. nail groove
   b. mantle
   c. lunula
   d. onyx

3. The active tissue that generates cells that harden as they move outward from the root to the nail is called the:
   a. eponychium
   b. nail matrix
   c. mantle
   d. nail plate

4. What term describes the whitened, half-moon shaped area at the base of the nail?
   a. matrix
   b. eponychium
   c. lunula
   d. nail root

5. The loose and pliable overlapping skin around the nail is the:
   a. hyponychium
   b. leuconychia
   c. cuticle
   d. nail wall

6. The area on which the nail plate rests is the:
   a. hyponychium
   b. mantle
   c. nail bed
   d. nail root

7. The skin under the free edge of the nail is the:
   a. lunula
   b. eponychium
   c. hyponychium
   d. nail root

8. The folds of skin on either side of the nail groove are called the:
   a. nail plate
   b. nail bed
   c. nail wall
   d. perionychium

9. The visible area from the nail root to the free edge is called the:
   a. nail matrix
   b. nail body
   c. mantle
   d. perionychium

10. The study of the structure and growth of nails is called:
    a. etiology
    b. neurology
    c. onychology
    d. onychosis

11. The part of the nail that extends beyond the end of the finger is called the:
    a. free edge
    b. cuticle
    c. lunula
    d. nail wall

12. The nail is made from a hardened protein called:
    a. keratin
    b. onyx
    c. lunula
    d. glucose

13. Damage to which portion of the nail could cause permanent distortions?
    a. perionychium
    b. matrix or nail bed
    c. free edge
    d. hyponychium

14. Under normal conditions, growth of a new nail plate takes approximately:
    a. 2 weeks
    b. 4 to 6 months
    c. 1 year
    d. 2 years

15. Any disease, disorder or condition of the nail is called an:
    a. onychomycosis
    b. onychology
    c. etiology
    d. onychosis

16. Medical attention is required for a nail:
    a. disorder
    b. condition
    c. disease
    d. cuticle

17. What item contains lymph, blood vessels and nerves that create cells?
    a. matrix
    b. nail plate
    c. lunula
    d. free edge

18. In what season of the year do nails tend to grow fastest?
    a. autumn
    b. winter
    c. spring
    d. summer

CHAPTER 14

19. **Which fingernail grows the slowest?**
    a. ring fingernail   b. middle fingernail   c. little fingernail   d. thumb nail

20. **Which of the following statements is true about toenails?**
    a. they grow faster than fingernails   b. they grow slower than fingernails
    c. they are softer than fingernails   d. they are thinner than fingernails

21. **Which of the following conditions does NOT indicate a decreasing rate of nail growth?**
    a. aging   b. winter   c. summer   d. poor nutrition

22. **Nail services may be performed with care and the client may want to consult a physician, if the client has a nail:**
    a. condition   b. disorder   c. disease   d. plate

23. **A healthy nail is smooth, curved, translucent, pinkish in color and:**
    a. is without hollows or wavy ridges   b. has wavy hollows and ridges
    c. is slightly rough   d. is filed deep into the corners

24. **The cause of a disease, disorder or condition is called:**
    a. prognosis   b. etiology   c. symptom   d. identification

25. **What disease is commonly called athlete's foot?**
    a. tinea manus   b. onychomycosis   c. paronychia   d. tinea pedis

26. **What condition appears as rings containing tiny blisters, dark pink to reddish in color, and can be confused with eczema or contact dermatitis?**
    a. paronychia   b. tinea manus   c. onychia   d. onychoptosis

27. **What condition could result when hangnails become infected?**
    a. paronychia   b. tinea manus   c. tinea pedis   d. onychia

28. **All of the following descriptions identify possible causes of paronychia EXCEPT:**
    a. systemic disease   b. infected hangnail
    c. bacterial infection   d. prolonged exposure to water

29. **The technical name for the disease referred to as ringworm of the nail is:**
    a. tinea manus   b. tinea pedis   c. onychomycosis   d. paronychia

30. **Poor circulation can cause a disorder called:**
    a. onychia   b. corrugations   c. blue nails   d. furrows

31. **Which term refers to a loosening or separation of the nail?**
    a. onycholysis   b. corrugations   c. onychogryposis   d. tinea pedis

32. **The shedding or falling out of nails is called:**
    a. onychia   b. tinea pedis   c. onychoptosis   d. felon

33. **Atrophy or wasting away of the nail is called:**
    a. onychatrophia   b. paronychia   c. onychomycosis   d. onychia

34. **Which of the following nail diseases is NOT caused by fungus?**
    a. tinea pedis   b. onychomycosis   c. tinea manus   d. onychatrophia

35. **The disorder in which the nail grows into the edge of the nail groove causing ingrown nails is called:**
    a. onychocryptosis   b. onchopgryposis   c. onychauxis   d. leuconychia

THE STUDY OF NAILS

36. Spoon nails is another term for:
    a. koilonychia   b. corrugations   c. furrows   d. claw nails

37. Living skin that becomes attached to the nail plate is referred to as:
    a. onychophagy   b. agnails   c. leuconychia   d. pterygium

38. Small white spots in the nail in which a small separation between the nail and nail bed has occurred due to injury are called:
    a. leuconychia   b. blue nails   c. bruised nails   d. agnails

39. Agnails is another name for:
    a. bruised nails   b. hangnails   c. claw nails   d. thin nails

40. What term refers to the thickening of the nail plate or an abnormal outgrowth of the nail?
    a. tinea manus   b. onychia   c. onychauxis   d. pterygium

41. What sign can indicate serious problems in the nail bed or nail plate?
    a. hangnails   b. leuconychia   c. discoloration   d. onychophagy

42. Improper filing, injuries or harsh chemicals can be causes of which of the following?
    a. hangnail   b. split nails   c. fungus   d. bruised nails

43. When performing a manicure, what product may be used to loosen dead skin?
    a. antiseptic   b. cuticle remover cream   c. first aid cream   d. acetone

44. How many basic shape classifications for nails are there?
    a. 2   b. 4   c. 5   d. 6

45. Nail service implements must be disinfected or discarded:
    a. once every hour   b. after every service   c. at closing time   d. on a weekly basis

46. A colorless polish that evens out the nail plate and prevents pigments from penetrating the nail plate is called a:
    a. base coat   b. sealer   c. nail enamel   d. nail strengthener

47. A colorless polish that keeps colored polish from chipping is called a:
    a. base coat   b. sealer   c. nail enamel   d. nail strengthener

48. Proper infection control, safety and blood spill procedures are practiced:
    a. only with sick clients   b. during warm season
    c. when someone is watching you   d. at all times

49. When not in use, nail service implements should be stored:
    a. in a covered container   b. in an open container   c. in soapy water   d. in distilled water

50. The manicurist and client are required to wash their hands with what product prior to performing a manicure service?
    a. liquid soap   b. moisturizing lotion   c. soaking solution   d. hydrogen peroxide

51. What procedure should be followed for any cut that may occur during a manicure?
    a. sanitizing   b. cleaning   c. blood spill   d. antiseptic

52. In which direction should a nail be shaped to avoid splitting?
    a. from top to bottom   b. from the bottom to the top
    c. from the outer edge toward the center   d. from the center toward the outer edge

CHAPTER 14

53. How should nail polish be applied?
    a. from the free edge toward the base
    b. on the sides first
    c. using light, sweeping strokes
    d. in one stroke per nail

54. What term is used to describe the cosmetic care of the feet and toenails?
    a. pedicuring
    b. manicuring
    c. etiology
    d. onychology

55. What item can be used to smooth calluses on the feet?
    a. foot brush
    b. foot powder
    c. foot file
    d. toenail clipper

56. A hot oil or cream manicure is helpful for all of the following conditions EXCEPT:
    a. dry, aging hands
    b. ingrown toenails
    c. brittle nails
    d. ridged nails

57. All of the following product systems can be used to create artificial nails EXCEPT:
    a. oil and rubber
    b. wraps
    c. light-cured gels
    d. powder and liquid acrylic

58. Bacteria under the artificial nail is reported most often by clients who wear which type of nail?
    a. acrylic
    b. press-on
    c. gel
    d. sculptured

59. How often is a fill-in service for artificial nails required?
    a. every 2 weeks
    b. every 2 months
    c. every 6 months
    d. once a year

60. Which nails use a special light to create a chemical reaction to harden the product?
    a. gel
    b. acrylic
    c. wrapped
    d. fiberglass

FINAL REVIEW

Check your answers as you did before. Place a check mark next to the page number for any incorrect answer. On the lines following the answers, jot down topics that you still need to review.

☐	1.	page 563	☐	8.	page 563	☐	15.	page 564
☐	2.	page 563	☐	9.	page 563	☐	16.	page 564
☐	3.	page 563	☐	10.	page 563	☐	17.	page 564
☐	4.	page 563	☐	11.	page 563	☐	18.	page 564
☐	5.	page 563	☐	12.	page 564	☐	19.	page 564
☐	6.	page 563	☐	13.	page 564	☐	20.	page 564
☐	7.	page 563	☐	14.	page 564	☐	21.	page 564

FINAL REVIEW *continued*

☐ 22.	page 564	☐ 35.	page 568	☐ 48.	page 574
☐ 23.	page 565	☐ 36.	page 568	☐ 49.	page 574
☐ 24.	page 565	☐ 37.	page 569	☐ 50.	page 574
☐ 25.	page 566	☐ 38.	page 569	☐ 51.	page 574
☐ 26.	page 566	☐ 39.	page 569	☐ 52.	page 577
☐ 27.	page 566	☐ 40.	page 569	☐ 53.	page 579
☐ 28.	page 566	☐ 41.	page 570	☐ 54.	page 581
☐ 29.	page 566	☐ 42.	page 570	☐ 55.	page 581
☐ 30.	page 567	☐ 43.	page 571	☐ 56.	page 585
☐ 31.	page 567	☐ 44.	page 571	☐ 57.	page 586
☐ 32.	page 567	☐ 45.	page 571	☐ 58.	page 593
☐ 33.	page 567	☐ 46.	page 572	☐ 59.	page 593
☐ 34.	page 567	☐ 47.	page 572	☐ 60.	page 598

NOTES TO MYSELF

Experts tell us that it is important to summarize your feelings and reactions about what you are learning. Note especially things that surprised you, things you found difficult to learn, suggestions and ideas you received from friends that helped make learning this chapter easier and more enjoyable.

My reflections about The Study of Nails:

LESSONS LEARNED

- Understanding the structure and growth of nails and the diseases, disorders and conditions of the nail are essential in order to provide nail services that protect clients' health and safety.
- Well-groomed and cared-for natural nails improve clients' overall appearance.
- Artificial nail services enhance your clients' appearance and in turn assist you in retaining more loyal clients.

CHAPTER 15

CHAPTER 15
THE STUDY OF SKIN

VALUE

Your understanding of how to maintain and enhance the skin will allow you to provide services to help your clients look better and feel good.

MAIN IDEA

Ongoing Skin Maintenance + Creatively Applied Makeup = **Healthy, Glowing Skin**

PLAN

15.1 SKIN THEORY
Functions of the Skin
Composition of the Skin
Types of Skin
Skin Diseases and Disorders

15.2 SKIN CARE
Massage
Facial Masks
Skin Care Essentials
Infection Control and Safety
Client Consultation
Basic Facial

15.3 HAIR REMOVAL
Hair Removal Essentials
Infection Control and Safety
Client Consultation
Temporary Hair Removal
Basic Waxing
Permanent Hair Removal

15.4 MAKEUP
Facial Shapes
Color Theory
Makeup Essentials
Infection Control and Safety
Client Consultation
Makeup Techniques and Products
Basic Makeup Application

THE STUDY OF SKIN

smartNOTES

15.1 SKIN THEORY
pages 601-605

Dermatology

Functions of the Skin

1.
2.
3.
4.
5.
6.

Composition of the Skin

Three Main Layers

EPIDERMIS	DERMIS	SUBCUTANEOUS
		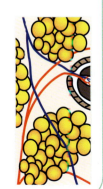

5 LAYERS OF THE EPIDERMIS

UPPERMOST STRATUM

PROTECTIVE
Stratum _____
Common Name _____
Special Cells _____
Function _____

CLEAR
Stratum _____
Common Name _____
Special Cells _____
Function _____

GRANULAR
Stratum _____
Common Name _____
Special Cells _____
Function _____

SPINY
Stratum _____
Common Name _____
Special Cells _____
Function _____

BEGINNING
Stratum _____
Common Name _____
Special Cells _____
Function _____

LOWEST STRATUM

THE STUDY OF SKIN

smartNOTES

15.1 SKIN THEORY
pages 603-606

Dermis (True Skin)

Sudoriferous Glands

THREE FUNCTIONS
1.
2.
3.

Sebaceous Glands

Sebum

Acid Mantle

Subcutaneous Tissue/Adipose (Fatty Layer)

Label the Parts of Skin

1.
2.
3.
4.
5.
6.
7.

Skin Pigmentation

CHAPTER 15

smartNOTES

15.1 SKIN THEORY   pages 606-614

Types of Skin

WEB

Topic: TYPES OF SKIN
- Dry
- Oily
- Combination
- Normal

Skin Diseases and Disorders

Objective Symptoms

Subjective Symptoms

Signs of Infection

DANGER INFECTION
CAUTION INFECTION

1.
2.
3.
4.
5.
6.

340 UNIT 3 NAIL AND SKIN SERVICES

SKIN LESIONS

After completing the charts on pages 341-342, with a partner use the charts to quiz each other in creative and thorough ways.

NAME	CHARACTERISTICS	EXAMPLE	SERVICE?
PRIMARY			
Macules			Yes - Service
Papules			Yes - Service
Vesicles			No service on affected areas
Bulla			
Pustules			
Wheals			
Tumors			
SECONDARY			
Scales			
Crusts			
Excoriations			
Fissures			
Scars			
Ulcers			
HYPERTROPHIES			
Callus			
Verruca			
Skin Tags			

CHAPTER 15

PIGMENTATION ABNORMALITIES

NAME	CHARACTERISTICS	EXAMPLE	SERVICE?
MELANODERMA			
Chloasma			
Moles			
Nevus			
LEUKODERMA			
Albinism			
Vitiligo			

DISORDERS

NAME	CHARACTERISTICS	SERVICE?
SEBACEOUS GLANDS		
Comedones		
Milia		
Acne		
Rosacea		
Asteatosis		
Seborrhea		
Steatoma		
Furuncles		
Carbuncles		
SUDORIFEROUS GLANDS		
Bromidrosis		
Anhidrosis		
Hyperhidrosis		
Milia Rubra		
OTHER INFLAMMATORY DISORDERS		
Dermatitis		
Eczema		
Impetigo		
Folliculitis		
Pseudofolliculitis barbae		
Conjunctivitis		

THE STUDY OF SKIN

smartNOTES

15.2 SKIN CARE   pages 614-620

Skin Care

4 Steps to Skin Care
1.
2.
3.
4.

Massage

MOVEMENT	EFFECT

Effleurage

Petrissage

Tapotement

Friction

Vibration

Facial Masks
Types of Facial Masks
Benefits of Facial Masks

Contraindications   Conditions or factors that serve as reasons to withhold certain treatments
Examples:

SALON FUNDAMENTALS COSMETOLOGY   343

CHAPTER 15

RUBRIC

This rubric is a self-assessment tool designed to compare your skill to industry standards. Indicate your present level of performance by checking the appropriate box. See overview for instructions.

Basic Facial

Industry Standard — to meet entry-level proficiency, industry standards require that you:
- Provide basic skin care services, perform hair removal services and apply appropriate cosmetics to enhance a client's appearance.

	Level 1	Level 2	Level 3	To Improve, I Need To:	Teacher Assessment
Preparation					
Disinfect facial area; assemble products and supplies; check equipment	☐	☐	☐		☐
Procedure					
Wash and sanitize hands; drape client (cocoon wrap)	☐	☐	☐		☐
Cleanse face; obtain cleansing cream with spatula; apply cleansing cream; remove without dragging or pulling skin	☐	☐	☐		☐
Apply toner with piece of cotton to skin surface	☐	☐	☐		☐
Place eyepads over client's eyes	☐	☐	☐		☐
Analyze client's skin	☐	☐	☐		☐
Apply exfoliant; remove exfoliant with hot towel or cotton pad	☐	☐	☐		☐
Apply toner with piece of cotton to skin surface	☐	☐	☐		☐
Obtain massage cream; apply massage cream; perform massage movements; remove without dragging or pulling skin	☐	☐	☐		☐
Apply toner with piece of cotton to skin surface	☐	☐	☐		☐
Apply facial mask; allow mask to set; remove mask	☐	☐	☐		☐
Apply toner with piece of cotton to skin surface	☐	☐	☐		☐
Apply moisturizing cream over the entire face and neck using effleurage movements	☐	☐	☐		☐
Completion					
Offer a prebook visit; recommend retail products; discard non-reusable materials, replace used towels with fresh towels, arrange all products and implements in proper order; disinfect facial service implements and equipment; wash your hands with liquid soap.	☐	☐	☐		☐

Total = addition of all Teacher Assessment boxes   TOTAL POINTS = ☐
                                                                    42

Percentage = student score / highest possible score   ____ %

THE STUDY OF SKIN

smartNOTES

15.3 HAIR REMOVAL
pages 628-637

Hypertrichosis

Two Types of Hair Removal

TEMPORARY | **PERMANENT**

Temporary Hair Removal

Shaving

Chemical Depilatories

Tweezing

Waxing

Threading

Sugaring

Draw in the guidelines for eyebrow shaping

Permanent Hair Removal

| GALVANIC | THERMOLYSIS | BLEND | LASER | PHOTO EPILATION OR PULSED LIGHT |

1 2 3 4 5 6 7

SALON FUNDAMENTALS COSMETOLOGY 345

CHAPTER 15

RUBRIC

This rubric is a self-assessment tool designed to compare your skill to industry standards. Indicate your present level of performance by checking the appropriate box. See overview for instructions.

Basic Waxing

Industry Standard – to meet entry-level proficiency, industry standards require that you:
- Provide basic skin care services, perform hair removal services and apply appropriate cosmetics to enhance a client's appearance.

	Level 1	Level 2	Level 3	To Improve, I Need To:	Teacher Assessment

Preparation
- Disinfect/assemble the essential products, implements/supplies and equipment for the procedure; cut strips; warm wax

Procedure
- Wash and sanitize hands; drape client
- Examine area to be waxed; cleanse area to be waxed
- Apply powder on area to be waxed
- Test temperature of wax; obtain wax with clean spatula
- Apply wax at a 45° angle in direction of hair growth
- Apply removal strip; press down; pull skin taut; remove strip quickly in opposite direction; apply pressure immediately
- Apply antiseptic
- Repeat procedure
- Apply and remove wax cleanser; apply soothing lotion
- Tweeze stray hairs if neccessary
- Show client results

Completion
- Offer a prebook visit; recommend retail products; discard non-reusable materials, replace used towels with fresh towels, arrange all products and implements in proper order; disinfect waxing service implements, work area and facial bed; wash your hands with liquid soap.

Total = addition of all Teacher Assessment boxes   TOTAL POINTS = ☐
                                                                          39

Percentage = student score / highest possible score   _____ %

346   UNIT 3 NAIL AND SKIN SERVICES

THE STUDY OF SKIN

smartNOTES

15.4 MAKEUP   pages 638-640

Chiaroscuro

Facial Shapes

Color Theory

Hue

Tint

Shade

Value

Intensity

Tone

CHAPTER 15

smartNOTES

15.4 MAKEUP
pages 641; 644-651

Color Schemes

Monochromatic:
Analogous:
Triadic:
Complementary:
Warm and Cool:
Remember: Dark diminishes; light advances

Makeup Techniques and Products

Base

Makeup Corrections/Concealer:

Foundation:

Contouring and Highlighting:

Eyes

Eyebrows:

Eyeliner:

Eyeshadow:

Mascara:

Artificial Lashes:

348 UNIT 3 NAIL AND SKIN SERVICES   1 2 3 4 5 6 7

THE STUDY OF SKIN

smartNOTES

15.4 MAKEUP

pages 652-655

Powder and Blush

Facial Powder:

Cheek Blush:

Lips

Lip Liner:

Lip Color:

Basic Guidelines for Lip Makeup

ANALYZE	APPLY	LINE	SHAPE	COMPLETE

Lip Shapes

CHAPTER 15

smartNOTES

15.4 MAKEUP   pages 655-658

Corrections for Facial Features

Using a pencil, sketch in the proper technique to correct the corresponding facial feature.

WIDE NOSE   LONG NOSE/   UNDEFINED
                    PROMINENT CHIN   CHEEKBONES

RECEDING CHIN   POINTED CHIN   "DOUBLE" CHIN   BROAD OR SQUARE JAW/ HIGH OR BROAD FOREHEAD

Brow Design and Placement of Lights and Darks

350 UNIT 3 NAIL AND SKIN SERVICES

THE STUDY OF SKIN

RUBRIC

This rubric is a self-assessment tool designed to compare your skill to industry standards. Indicate your present level of performance by checking the appropriate box. See overview for instructions.

Basic Makeup Application

Industry Standard – to meet entry-level proficiency, industry standards require that you:
- Provide basic skin care services, perform hair removal services and apply appropriate cosmetics to enhance a client's appearance.

	Level 1	Level 2	Level 3	To Improve, I Need To:	Teacher Assessment
Preparation					
• Disinfect/assemble the essential products, implements/supplies and equipment for the procedure	☐	☐	☐		☐
Procedure					
• Wash and sanitize hands	☐	☐	☐		☐
• Prepare client (drape, including headband, and position chair); consult with client	☐	☐	☐		☐
• Cleanse, tone, moisturize and protect skin	☐	☐	☐		☐
• Analyze skin, face, brows, eyes and lips	☐	☐	☐		☐
• Groom brows if needed (brush and tweeze)	☐	☐	☐		☐
• Select appropriate foundation color; apply concealer as needed; apply foundation	☐	☐	☐		☐
• Shade brows (brush and fill in as needed); check brows for symmetry	☐	☐	☐		☐
• Apply eyeshadow(s); apply eyeliner	☐	☐	☐		☐
• Apply blush, if cream, liquid or gel; apply tinted or translucent powder	☐	☐	☐		☐
• Apply blush if powder	☐	☐	☐		☐
• Apply mascara	☐	☐	☐		☐
• Apply lip liner; apply lip color	☐	☐	☐		☐
• Check coverage, balance accuracy; remove draping	☐	☐	☐		☐
Completion					
• Offer a prebook visit; recommend retail products; discard non-reusable materials, replace used towels with fresh towels, arrange all products and implements in proper order; disinfect makeup service implements, work area and makeup chair; wash your hands with liquid soap.	☐	☐	☐		☐

Total = addition of all Teacher Assessment boxes

TOTAL POINTS = ☐
45

Percentage = student score / highest possible score

_____ %

CHAPTER 15

THE CHALLENGE

Now it's time to see how well you know your new material. First answer these questions. Then use the Memory Box that follows to check yourself. Look up each answer on the corresponding page in the *Salon Fundamentals* textbook. Check "got it" for all correct answers and "not yet" for all incorrect responses. Using the "Know Chart," record all of your correct responses in the "I Know" column. After correcting incorrect answers, record all of your corrected responses in the "I Need to Study" column. That way you know exactly what to review before continuing in this study guide.

1. The skin is the largest organ of the body. It and its layers make up the _____ system of the body.

2. Name the six basic functions of the skin. _____ _____ _____ _____ _____ _____

3. The three main layers of the skin are the _____, _____ and the _____.

4. The layer of skin found only on the palms of the hands and the soles of the feet is known as the stratum _____.

5. TRUE FALSE Deterioration of collagen and elastin fibers in the skin's aging takes place in the dermis.

6. From a cosmetologist's point of view, the surface of the skin falls into four basic types. They are _____, _____, _____ and _____.

7. Disorders and diseases of the skin are often accompanied by lesions, which are any abnormal changes in the structure of an organ or tissue. There are three main categories of lesions, two of which the cosmetologist needs to be able to recognize. These two categories are _____ and _____ lesions.

8. Can you name the six signs of infection that may be associated with a disorder or disease? _____ _____ _____ _____ _____ _____

9. TRUE FALSE Only a dermatologist or a medical doctor should diagnose and treat skin disorders and diseases.

10. Keeping the skin in good condition requires a minimum of four steps. These steps are _____, _____, _____ and _____.

11. Massages and facial masks are additional treatments that can help keep your client's skin in optimum condition. List six benefits derived from a facial massage. _____ _____ _____ _____ _____ _____

12. List three benefits that may be derived from a facial mask. _____ _____ _____

13. The two types of hair removal procedures are _____ and _____.

14. Most regulating agencies will not license a cosmetologist to perform _____ hair removal procedures without additional specialized training.

15. TRUE FALSE The effects of temporary hair removal can last anywhere from a few hours to several weeks, depending on the system used.

16. Most corrective makeup and contouring are done to achieve the illusion of the oval face. Can you name six other facial shapes? _____ _____ _____ _____ _____ _____

17. Darker tones are used to shadow or contour areas and features you wish to diminish or _____.

18. What is considered to be the most important makeup product because it creates the canvas on which other cosmetics appear? _____

352 UNIT 3 NAIL AND SKIN SERVICES

THE STUDY OF SKIN

MEMORY BOX

1. PAGE 601 — GOT IT / NOT YET
2. PAGE 601 — GOT IT / NOT YET
3. PAGE 602 — GOT IT / NOT YET
4. PAGE 603 — GOT IT / NOT YET
5. PAGE 603 — GOT IT / NOT YET
6. PAGE 607 — GOT IT / NOT YET
7. PAGE 609 — GOT IT / NOT YET
8. PAGE 609 — GOT IT / NOT YET
9. PAGE 608 — GOT IT / NOT YET
10. PAGE 614 — GOT IT / NOT YET
11. PAGE 615 — GOT IT / NOT YET
12. PAGE 617 — GOT IT / NOT YET
13. PAGE 628 — GOT IT / NOT YET
14. PAGE 628 — GOT IT / NOT YET
15. PAGE 630 — GOT IT / NOT YET
16. PAGE 639, 640 — GOT IT / NOT YET
17. PAGE 641 — GOT IT / NOT YET
18. PAGE 647 — GOT IT / NOT YET

KNOW CHART

I KNOW:

I NEED TO STUDY:

TALKING POINTS

Your next challenge is to be ready to talk about some of the important ideas in this chapter. Follow the directions listed next to each box. Then practice talking about your ideas with others.

| | Discuss with a partner the most difficult skin disease for each of you to recognize and list your findings in the box to the left. |
| | With a partner discuss your daily skin care and makeup routines. List similarities and differences in the box to the left. |

1 2 3 **4** **5** 6 7

SALON FUNDAMENTALS COSMETOLOGY 353

CHAPTER 15

SHOW YOU KNOW...

Finally, it is time to show off your new invention at the annual convention. It is the first time you will have the opportunity to demonstrate the benefits of the ergonomic features and innovative design your new product for the skin has to offer. The coordinator of the convention has asked you to complete the informational card below to offer a profile of your product.

Product Profile

Product Name Product Use

Features: Benefits:

Profile of Consumer Most Likely to Purchase this Product:

Suggested Retail Price of this Product:

KNOWLEDGE GRID

Start at the top of the Knowledge Grid and work your way down, answering each question to check your understanding of *Chapter 15, The Study of Skin*. The questions found here will help you deepen your understanding, build self-confidence and increase your awareness of different ways of thinking about a subject.

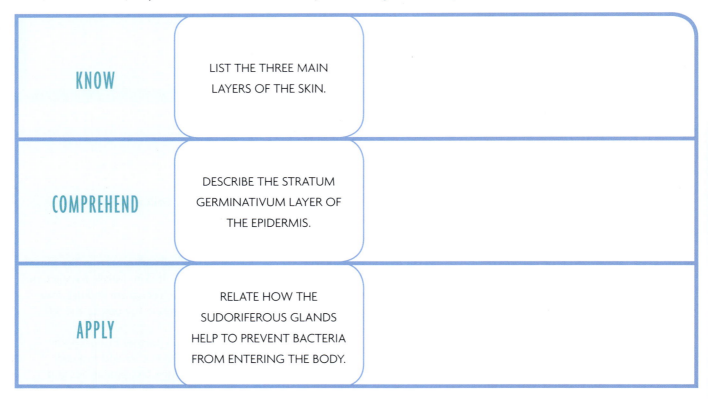

KNOW	LIST THE THREE MAIN LAYERS OF THE SKIN.	
COMPREHEND	DESCRIBE THE STRATUM GERMINATIVUM LAYER OF THE EPIDERMIS.	
APPLY	RELATE HOW THE SUDORIFEROUS GLANDS HELP TO PREVENT BACTERIA FROM ENTERING THE BODY.	

KNOWLEDGE GRID *continued*

ANALYZE	COMPARE THE DIFFERENCE BETWEEN A SUBJECTIVE AND OBJECTIVE SYMPTOM.	
SYNTHESIZE	DISCUSS THE BENEFITS A CLIENT CAN RECEIVE FROM A PROFESSIONAL FACIAL SERVICE.	
EVALUATE	EVALUATE HOW BROW DESIGN AND PLACEMENT OF LIGHTS AND DARKS CAN VISUALLY ALTER THE POSITION OF THE EYES ON THE FACE.	

BRAIN CONDITIONER
MULTIPLE CHOICE. CIRCLE THE CORRECT ANSWER.

1. Which of the following organs is considered to be the largest of the human body?
   a. liver   b. brain   c. stomach   d. skin
2. The skin has how many basic functions?
   a. 3   b. 5   c. 6   d. 9
3. Which of the following terms is NOT a function of the skin?
   a. sensation   b. secretion   c. absorption   d. lymph production
4. Functions of the skin include regulation of body temperature, respiration and:
   a. reproduction   b. protection   c. digestion   d. circulation
5. Which body system is made up of the skin and its layers?
   a. excretory   b. respiratory   c. sensation   d. integumentary
6. What is the technical name for the study of skin, including its structure, functions, diseases and treatment?
   a. pathology   b. etiology   c. anatomy   d. dermatology
7. The dermis is also referred to as which of the following?
   a. cuticle   b. epidermis   c. true skin   d. scarf skin
8. Which of the following terms is the outermost layer of the skin?
   a. dermis   b. epidermis   c. stratum granulosum   d. stratum corneum

CHAPTER 15

9. In which layer of the epidermis does mitosis (cell division) or replacement of the skin take place?
   a. stratum lucidum   b. stratum granulosum   c. stratum corneum   d. stratum germinativum
10. The conversion of living cells into dead protein cells is called:
    a. mitosis   b. cell division   c. keratinization   d. lucidum
11. Melanocytes start out in which of the following layers of the epidermis?
    a. stratum granulosum   b. stratum germinativum   c. stratum corneum   d. subcutaneous layer
12. Which layer of the skin is known as the epidermis?
    a. innermost   b. third   c. second   d. outer
13. Which of the following skin layers does NOT contain blood vessels?
    a. cutis   b. dermis   c. corium   d. epidermis
14. Which of the following layers of cells is NOT part of the epidermis?
    a. stratum corneum   b. stratum lucidum   c. subcutaneous layer   d. stratum germinativum
15. Which of the following skin layers is the toughest and is composed of keratin cells?
    a. stratum lucidum   b. stratum germinativum   c. stratum granulosum   d. stratum corneum
16. In which layer do the cells become more regularly shaped and look like tiny granules?
    a. stratum lucidum   b. stratum granulosum   c. stratum germinativum   d. stratum corneum
17. The soles of the feet and the palms of the hand are the only places where which layer of the skin is found?
    a. stratum spinosum   b. stratum germinativum   c. stratum lucidum   d. stratum corneum
18. What type of tissue makes up the dermis?
    a. muscular   b. epithelial   c. connective   d. nerve
19. The effects of the skin's aging process can be seen in the:
    a. epidermis   b. dermis   c. cuticle   d. scarf skin
20. What part of the skin is often referred to as "true skin?"
    a. stratum lucidum   b. epidermis   c. dermis   d. stratum germinativum
21. Which layer of the skin contains collagen protein and elastin fibers that help give the skin its elasticity and pliability?
    a. dermis   b. epidermis   c. stratum lucidum   d. stratum granulosum
22. All of the following statements describe the cells in the stratum granulosum, EXCEPT:
    a. they become more regularly shaped   b. they look like tiny granules
    c. they eventually replace cells that are shed   d. they are called squamous cells
23. Sudoriferous glands produce which of the following?
    a. lymph   b. oil   c. sweat   d. collagen
24. What is a major function of the sudoriferous gland?
    a. give skin texture   b. give skin a healthy color
    c. help to regulate body temperature   d. protect the skin's elasticity
25. Which of the following glands regulate body temperature?
    a. eccrine   b. sebaceous   c. oil   d. ductless
26. The small openings of the sweat glands in the skin are called:
    a. follicles   b. pores   c. glands   d. ducts
27. The sudoriferous glands function to do all of the following EXCEPT:
    a. produce oil   b. help regulate body temperature
    c. excrete waste   d. help to maintain the proper pH of the skin
28. All of the following are examples of duct glands EXCEPT:
    a. eccrine   b. endocrine   c. sebaceous   d. sudoriforous

THE STUDY OF SKIN

29. The papillary canal takes oil (sebum) to the:
    a. blood vessels   b. surface of the skin   c. nerves   d. keratin

30. The acid mantle is a mixture of all of the following EXCEPT:
    a. sebum   b. oil   c. toner   d. sweat

31. Which of the following is NOT true about the acid mantle?
    a. helps prevent chapping   b. helps prevent entry of dirt particles
    c. provides a protective cushion for the skin   d. keeps skin smooth

32. Most skin problems are caused by the:
    a. sudoriferous glands   b. eccrine glands   c. sebaceous glands   d. arrector pili muscles

33. What part of the skin is composed of fatty and loose connective tissue?
    a. subcutaneous layer   b. dermis   c. acid mantle   d. epidermis

34. Which of the following structures is a protective cushion for the skin?
    a. subcutaneous tissue   b. epidermis   c. cuticle   d. dermis

35. The pH of the acid mantle for most people is:
    a. 2.5 to 3.5   b. 4.5 to 5.5   c. 7   d. 7.5 to 8.5

36. The subcutaneous layer contains all of the following EXCEPT:
    a. stratum corneum
    b. the glandular parts of some sudoriferous glands
    c. large blood vessels that transport nourishment to the skin and nerves
    d. some sense organs for touch, pressure and temperature

37. The subcutaneous tissue includes all of the following functions EXCEPT:
    a. body insulation   b. support of delicate structures, such as blood vessels
    c. protein digestion   d. protective cushioning for the skin

38. Which of the following statements is NOT true about dark skin?
    a. contains more melanocytes   b. contains more melanin
    c. better barrier to damaging rays   d. can be damaged by overexposure to UV rays

39. Which of the following statements is true of melanin?
    a. contains sebum   b. tans the skin   c. may harm the skin   d. produces perspiration

40. Which type of skin is NOT prone to acne?
    a. dry   b. oily   c. normal   d. combination

41. The least common skin type is:
    a. oily   b. dry   c. normal   d. combination

42. The most common skin type is:
    a. dry   b. oily   c. normal   d. combination

43. A disease that spreads by personal contact is known as:
    a. systemic   b. congenital   c. contagious   d. occupational

44. The term used to identify conditions that are brief and severe is known as:
    a. acute   b. chronic   c. objective   d. subjective

45. Chronic is the term used to identify conditions that are:
    a. brief and severe   b. frequent and habitual   c. influenced by weather   d. visible

46. What is the technical term for the study of the cause of disease?
    a. etiology   b. pathology   c. anatomy   d. dermatology

47. Anticipating the most probable course a disease may follow is known as:
    a. diagnosis   b. prognosis   c. recognition   d. analysis

CHAPTER 15

48. Abnormal changes in the structure of organs or tissues are called primary, secondary and tertiary:
    a. fissures   b. infections   c. lesions   d. papules

49. Which of the following terms is used for symptoms that are visible?
    a. seasonal   b. subjective   c. objective   d. visible

50. Which of the following symptoms is NOT considered subjective?
    a. itching   b. inflammation   c. burning   d. pain

51. A freckle is a type of:
    a. chloasma   b. macule   c. leukoderma   d. vitiligo

52. Herpes simplex is the technical name for which of the following conditions?
    a. fever blister b. eczema   c. psoriasis   d. acne

53. Which of the following lesions is characterized by a solid formation above the skin, often caused by an insect bite or allergic reaction?
    a. pustules   b. macules   c. papules   d. wheals

54. Treatment for secondary skin lesions needs to be performed by a medical doctor or which of the following?
    a. dermatologist b. cosmetologist   c. radiologist   d. esthetician

55. A cyst is defined by which of the following descriptions?
    a. oozing sore   b. wheal lesions   c. crack in the skin   d. abnormal membranous sac

56. Which of the following secondary lesions are shedding dead cells of the uppermost layer of the epidermis?
    a. scales   b. crusts   c. excoriations   d. fissures

57. A secondary lesion appearing as round, dry patches of skin covered with rough, silvery scales is called:
    a. eczema   b. psoriasis   c. herpes simplex d. acne

58. Which of the following secondary lesions are cracks in the skin?
    a. wheals   b. fissures   c. tumors   d. crusts

59. The dried remains of an oozing sore are known as:
    a. scales   b. crusts   c. scars   d. excoriations

60. The lesion found following the healing of an injury is called a:
    a. mole   b. scale   c. scar   d. fissure

61. All of the following secondary skin lesions are considered hypertrophies (new growth) EXCEPTa:
    a. callus   b. verruca   c. nevus   d. skin tag

62. Which of the following describes a thickening of the epidermis from pressure and friction applied to the skin?
    a. ulcer   b. callus   c. verruca   d. skin tag

63. A congenital failure of the skin to form melanin pigment is known as:
    a. lentigines   b. chloasma   c. vitiligo   d. albinism

64. What is another name for a stain in the skin caused by the dilation of the small blood vessels which is also known as a birthmark?
    a. scar   b. callus   c. verruca   d. nevus

65. Which term is used to describe any hyperpigmentation caused by overactivity of the melanocytes in the epidermis?
    a. albinism   b. leukoderma   c. vitiligo   d. melanoderma

66. Masses of sebum trapped in the hair follicle are known as comedones or which of the following?
    a. blackheads   b. acne   c. rosacea   d. steatoma

67. Accumulations of hardened sebum beneath the skin are called whiteheads or:
    a. milia   b. comedones   c. acne   d. rosacea

68. **A condition characterized by dry, scaly skin caused by a decreased production of sebum is called:**
    a. seborrhea　　　b. steatoma　　　c. asteatosis　　　d. rosacea
69. **Which disorder is caused by excessive secretion of the sebaceous glands?**
    a. seborrhea　　　b. bromidrosis　　　c. asteatosis　　　d. milia
70. **Which of the following is the term used for foul-smelling perspiration?**
    a. anhidrosis　　　b. bromidrosis　　　c. hyperhidrosis　　　d. psoriasis
71. **The lack of perspiration caused by fever or disease is known as:**
    a. osmidrosis　　　b. bromidrosis　　　c. anhidrosis　　　d. hyperhidrosis
72. **What sebaceous gland disorder appears in the dermis and epidermis and is caused by an acute bacterial infection?**
    a. boils　　　b. moles　　　c. skin tags　　　d. scars
73. **Which of the following terms is NOT a disorder of the sudoriferous glands?**
    a. seborrhea　　　b. anhidrosis　　　c. hyperhidrosis　　　d. miliaria rubra
74. **Which of the following massage movements involves a light, gentle stroking or circular motion?**
    a. petrissage　　　b. effleurage　　　c. tapotement　　　d. vibration
75. **All of the following results are benefits of massage EXCEPT:**
    a. increasing circulation of blood supply to skin　　　b. stimulating glandular activity of skin
    c. improving texture of skin　　　d. weakening muscle tissue
76. **Which of the following areas is a cosmetologist NOT licensed to massage?**
    a. feet　　　b. face　　　c. hands　　　d. lower back
77. **Which of the following is NOT one of the five basic movements of massage?**
    a. effleurage　　　b. petrissage　　　c. tapotement　　　d. cleansing
78. **A light or heavy kneading and rolling of the muscles is known as which of the following massage movements?**
    a. effleurage　　　b. tapotement　　　c. petrissage　　　d. vibration
79. **Which of the following massage movements is a light tapping or slapping movement applied with the fingertips?**
    a. effleurage　　　b. tapotement　　　c. petrissage　　　d. vibration
80. **Which of the following massage manipulations is a circular or wringing movement usually carried out with the fingertips or palms of the hands?**
    a. friction　　　b. vibration　　　c. petrissage　　　d. tapotement
81. **Massage should NOT be performed when:**
    a. vitiligo is present　　　b. abrasions are present　　　c. fillings are present　　　d. tension is present
82. **Which of the following massage movements should NOT be used if the client needs soothing?**
    a. gliding　　　b. stroking　　　c. effleurage　　　d. tapotement
83. **Which of the following is NOT a type of facial mask?**
    a. cream　　　b. clay　　　c. paraffin　　　d. astringent
84. **All of the following statements are true about paraffin masks EXCEPT:**
    a. heated then applied　　　b. applied over a layer of gauze
    c. made from clay, sand, zinc oxide or mud　　　d. act to draw oil and perspiration to the top layer of skin
85. **Electricity is required for which of the following procedures?**
    a. permanent hair removal　　　b. removing dirt and oil
    c. temporary hair removal　　　d. preventing growth of bacteria
86. **Which of the following permanent hair removal methods uses wavelengths of light to penetrate and diminish or destroy hair bulbs?:**
    a. laser　　　b. galvanic electrolysis　　　c. waxing　　　d. chemical depilatory

CHAPTER 15

87. Most corrective makeup and contouring techniques are done to help the face to appear as what shape?
    a. round b. square c. diamond d. oval

88. What face shape is characterized by a narrow forehead and jaw area with predominant width in the cheekbone area?
    a. square b. round c. oval d. diamond

89. Hue is another term for which of the following terms?
    a. shade b. tint c. color d. tone

90. Which of the following products is used to complete the balance of color in makeup application?
    a. foundation b. blush c. lipstick d. eyeliner

FINAL REVIEW

Check your answers as you did before. Place a check mark next to the page number for any incorrect answer. On the lines following the answers, jot down topics that you still need to review.

☐	1.	page 601	☐	23.	page 604	☐	45.	page 608
☐	2.	page 601	☐	24.	page 604	☐	46.	page 608
☐	3.	page 601	☐	25.	page 604	☐	47.	page 608
☐	4.	page 601	☐	26.	page 604	☐	48.	page 609
☐	5.	page 601	☐	27.	page 604	☐	49.	page 609
☐	6.	page 601	☐	28.	page 604	☐	50.	page 609
☐	7.	page 602	☐	29.	page 605	☐	51.	page 609
☐	8.	page 602	☐	30.	page 604	☐	52.	page 609
☐	9.	page 602	☐	31.	pages 604, 605	☐	53.	page 610
☐	10.	page 602	☐	32.	page 605	☐	54.	page 610
☐	11.	page 602	☐	33.	page 605	☐	55.	page 610
☐	12.	page 602	☐	34.	page 605	☐	56.	page 610
☐	13.	page 602	☐	35.	page 605	☐	57.	page 610
☐	14.	page 602	☐	36.	page 605	☐	58.	page 611
☐	15.	page 603	☐	37.	page 605	☐	59.	page 611
☐	16.	page 603	☐	38.	page 606	☐	60.	page 611
☐	17.	page 603	☐	39.	page 606	☐	61.	page 611
☐	18.	page 603	☐	40.	page 607	☐	62.	page 611
☐	19.	page 603	☐	41.	page 607	☐	63.	page 612
☐	20.	page 603	☐	42.	page 607	☐	64.	page 612
☐	21.	page 603	☐	43.	page 608	☐	65.	page 612
☐	22.	page 603	☐	44.	page 608	☐	66.	page 613

FINAL REVIEW *continued*

☐	67.	page 613	☐	75.	page 615	☐	83.	page 617
☐	68.	page 613	☐	76.	page 615	☐	84.	page 617
☐	69.	page 613	☐	77.	pages 615, 616	☐	85.	page 636
☐	70.	page 613	☐	78.	page 616	☐	86.	page 637
☐	71.	page 613	☐	79.	page 616	☐	87.	page 638
☐	72.	page 613	☐	80.	page 616	☐	88.	page 640
☐	73.	pages 613, 614	☐	81.	page 616	☐	89.	page 640
☐	74.	page 615	☐	82.	page 616	☐	90.	page 653

NOTES TO MYSELF

Experts tell us that it is important to summarize your feelings and reactions about what you are learning. Note especially things that surprised you, things you found difficult to learn, suggestions and ideas you received from friends that helped make learning this chapter easier and more enjoyable.

My reflections about The Study of Skin:

LESSONS LEARNED

- The skin is the largest organ of the body and performs six specific functions.
- Cleansing, toning, moisturizing and protecting are the four basic steps of proper skin care.
- Salon hair removal services include temporary methods — shaving, depilatories, tweezing and waxing — and permanent methods known as electrolysis, which use an electric current to inhibit hair growth.
- Makeup design and application combine principles of art and science to enhance desirable features, balance uneven proportions and diminish facial flaws.

CHAPTER 15

THINGS TO DO

THINGS TO DO

THINGS TO DO

GLOSSARY

A

Abductor (ab-DUK-tor) – Muscles that separate the fingers

Abductor Digiti Minimi (ab-DUK-tohr dij-it-ty MIN-eh-mee) – Muscle that moves the smallest toe away from the other toes

Abductor Hallucis (ab-DUK-tohr ha-LU-sis) – Muscle that moves the big toe away from the other toes

Abraded hair – The technical term for broken hair or excessive stretching or traction of the hair

Absorption – The skin's ability to permit substances like water and oxygen to pass through its tissues

AC current – Alternating current; electrons flow first in one direction and then in the other

Accountant – A financial advisor

Acid – Water-based solution measuring more positive hydrogen ions than negative hydroxide ions; measures less than 7 on the pH scale

Acid-balanced rinse – Used to close the cuticle after a color service to prevent the color from fading

Acid-balanced shampoo – Non-stripping; used to cleanse hair types, especially lightened, color-treated or dry, brittle hair

Acid mantle – A layer of oil and sweat found in the sebaceous glands; keeps the skin smooth, prevents dirt and grime from entering the outer layer of the epidermis and also prevents the skin from drying or chapping; protects the cuticle or outer covering of the hair fiber and maintains the acid balance of hair and skin

Acid rinse – Used to remove soap scum

Acid waves – A method of perming using a thioglycolic derivative called glycerol monothioglycolate without ammonia; a more gentle perming method because the chemicals penetrate the hair slowly; to speed the process heat is added by placing a plastic cap on the client's head and placing her under a pre-heated dryer; pH range of 6.9 to 7.2

Acne (AK-nee) – A chronic inflammatory disorder of the sebaceous glands; occurs most often on the face, back and chest

Acrylic brush – Builds the acrylic nail; may be flat, oval or rounded in shape and is made from natural hair

Activator – Booster used to increase the speed of the oxidation process

Active immunity – Results when exposure to a disease organism triggers the immune system to produce antibodies to that disease

Active stage – The stage at which bacteria (germs) grow and reproduce rapidly

Acute – A term used to identify conditions that are brief and severe

ADA – Americans with Disabilities Act

Adductor (Ah-DUK-tor) – Muscles that draw the fingers together

Adhesive – A tacky (sticky) substance that bonds a plastic tip to a natural nail; specially formulated for the nail industry

Advertising – A means of telling the public about your salon, the services you perform, the quality of work you produce and any other reasons that clients should patronize your salon

Agnails (hangnails) – Split cuticles; loose skin partially separated from the cuticle

Afferent nerves – Also called sensory nerves; carry messages to the brain and spinal cord

AIDS – Acquired Immunodeficiency Syndrome – A disease caused by HIV (Human Immunodeficiency Virus); HIV interferes with the body's natural immune system and causes the immune system to break down

Airbrushing – The use of an airbrush gun and airbrush paints to decorate the nails

Air forming – Refers to the process of drying the hair and styling it simultaneously to create a new form. Also called blow drying

Air-forming brush (7 or 9-row) – A brush that smooths wavy or curly textures; adds directional emphasis when air forming

Albinism (AL-bin-izm) – A congenital failure of the skin to produce melanin pigment

Albino – A person lacking pigmentation in the hair and skin

Alkaline – Water-based solution measuring more negative hydroxide ions than positive hydrogen ions; measures higher than 7 on the pH scale

Alkaline perm – Perm wave processed with heat and thioglycolate

Alkaline waves – Today's highly improved cold waves; formulated with thioglycolic acid and its derivatives and ammonia, which creates a compound called ammonium thioglycolate; pH of approximately 8.0 to 9.5

Allergy – A sensitivity that may develop from contact with normally harmless substances; symptoms of an allergy may include itching, redness, swelling and/or blisters

All-purpose comb – Detangles and combs the hair after the shampoo service

All-purpose shampoo – Used to cleanse the hair without correcting any special condition

Alopecia – Excessive hair loss

Alopecia areata – Sudden loss of hair in round or irregular patches without display of an inflamed scalp

Alopecia Areata Totalis – Total loss of hair on the scalp

Alopecia Areata Universalis – Loss of hair over the entire scalp and body

Alopecia Prematura – Baldness that occurs early in life, beginning as early as late adolescence

Alternation – Design principle; a pattern in which an element changes from one to another repeatedly

Amines – Ingredient found in conditioners; makes hair easier to comb and control static

Amino acid – Compounds consisting of carbon, oxygen, hydrogen and nitrogen

Ammonium hydroxide – An ingredient found in alkaline waves to shorten the processing time

Ammonium thioglycolate – A chemical reducing agent that causes the hair to soften and swell; also called thio relaxers

Amp – A unit of electric strength

Anabolism (ah-NAB-oh-lizm) – The process of building up larger molecules from smaller ones during metabolism

GLOSSARY

Anagen – The active or growing stage of hair, during which time each hair bulb has an attached root sheath

Analogous color – Color scheme using three colors that are adjacent to each other on the color wheel

Anaphoresis – Negative pole of Galvanic Current that produces an alkaline effect

Anatomy – The study of the organs and systems of the body

Androgenetic alopecia – Hair loss caused by a combination of heredity, hormones and age that causes progressive shrinking or miniaturization of certain scalp follicles

Angles – Formed at the point where two lines meet; used in haircutting to create the shape and form of the haircut

Angular artery – Artery that supplies blood to the sides of the nose

Anhidrosis (an-heye-**DROH**-sis) – A lack of perspiration caused by fever or disease; requires medical attention

Anode – A positively charged electrode; usually red in color or displays a large "P" or a positive sign (+)

Anterior (an-**TER**-e-er) – In front of

Anterior auricular – Artery that supplies blood to the anterior part of the ear

Anterior dilator naris – One of the four muscles of the nose; controls contraction and expansion of the nostrils

Anterior Tibial (an-**TEER**-ee-ur **TIB**-ee-al) **Artery** – Supplies blood just below the knee; passes down between the tibia and fibula; branches off into smaller arteries in the lower leg

Anti-dandruff shampoo – Used to control dandruff and other scalp conditions

Antiseptic – Product that can be applied to the skin to reduce microbes

Apex – Top or highest point of the head

Aponeurosis (ap-o-noo-**ROH**-sis) – A tendon that connects the frontalis and the occipitalis muscles in the epicranium

Application – A form used to submit information to an employer

Apprentice – A salon stylist in training; also called an assistant

Aromatherapy – The combination of our sense of smell and the use of plant extracts and their healing abilities

Arrector pili muscle – Comes from cells in the dermis that attach to the follicle just below the sebaceous gland. This is the muscle that causes the hair to stand on end when a person is scared or cold

Arteries – Tubular, elastic, thick-walled branching vessels that carry pure blood from the heart through the body

Artificial lashes – Eyelashes made from human hair or synthetic material applied to one's own lashes or in place of them for enhancement

Artificial nail care – The use of various man-made materials and techniques to enhance the appearance of natural nails

Assets – All properties owned

Asteatosis (as-tee-ah-**TOH**-sis) – Condition of dry, scaly skin with reduced sebum production

Asymmetrical balance – Created when weight is positioned unequally from a center axis

Asymptomatic – Condition that allows a person to carry disease-producing bacteria without symptoms

Atom – The smallest complete unit of an element

Atomic number – The number of protons in the nucleus of an atom

Attitude – The specific and identifiable emotion and/or reaction one experiences and projects in dealing with the demands of life

Auricle – Also called atrium; upper right and left chambers of the heart

Auricularis (aw-rik-ya-**LA**-ris) **anterior** – Muscle located in front of the ear

Auricularis (aw-rik-ya-**LA**-ris) **posterior** – Muscle located behind the ear

Auricularis (ae-rik-ya-**LA**-ris) **superior** – Muscle located above the ear

Auriculo temporal (aw-**RIK**-u-lo **TEM**-po-ral) – Nerve that extends to the ear and to the area from the top of the head to the temple

Autonomic (aw-to-**NOM**-ik) **nervous system** – Responsible for all involuntary body functions

Axons (**AK**-sonz) – Long threadlike fibers that extend from nerve cells

B

Bacilli (ba-**SIL**-i) – The most common form of bacterial cells; bar or rod-shaped cells that can produce a variety of diseases including tetanus, bacterial influenza, typhoid fever, tuberculosis and diphtheria

Backbrushing – A technique used to add volume to a hairstyle with a brush by systematically pushing the shorter lengths of the hair toward the base to create a cushion effect

Backcombing – The use of a comb to add volume to a hairstyle and further connect the shapes within a set, while adding longevity to the style

Back-wash systems – A free-standing sink for shampooing hair

Bacteria – One-celled microorganisms; sometimes called germs or microbes

Bactericidal – Disinfectant designed to kill bacteria

Bacteriology – The study of bacteria

Balance – The state of equilibrium existing between contrasting, opposite or interacting elements

Bargain buyer – Someone interested in saving money at all costs and not as interested in quality of products as price

Base (retouch) – Color application used for a retouch; color or lightener is applied to the new growth only to match the existing color

Base coat – Colorless polish that evens out nail plate; holds nail color to nail; prevents pigments from penetrating nail plate

Base color – In artificial hair coloring, the tone or base color identifies the warmth or coolness of a color

Base size – The area between two partings for an individual perm rod

Base texturizing – Performed between the scalp up to 1" (2.5 cm) away from the scalp; creates expansion and fullness

Base-to-ends technique – Hair color application technique used when you want to add tone to or darken the existing color; also known as a virgin darker technique

Battery – A source of electrical current with a positive and negative terminal; produces direct current only

Beau's Lines – Indentations that run across the nail; growth at the area under the cuticle is interrupted by major injury or severe illness

Belly – The term applied to the midsection of the muscle, between the two attached sections

Bicep (BI-cep) – The primary muscle in the front of the upper arm; this muscle raises the forearm, bends the elbow and turns the palm of the hand down

Block buffer – Implement used to smooth surface of the nail

Blood – The sticky, salty fluid that circulates through the body bringing nourishment and oxygen to all body parts and carrying toxins and waste products to the liver and kidneys to be eliminated

Bloodborne pathogens – Disease-causing bacteria or viruses that are carried through the blood or body fluids

Bloodborne Pathogen Standards – Regulations requiring the use of an EPA-registered disinfectant with an efficacy against HIV and HBV or tuberculocidal. This requirement applies to implements that accidentally come into contact with blood or body fluids

Blood vessels – Any vessels through which blood circulates through the body

Blotting – Removes excess water before the neutralizing solution is applied in order to prevent a weak curl that relaxes prematurely

Blow dryer – An implement used to air form wet hair while using brushes, combs and your fingers to create temporary direction and texture changes

Blue nails – Blue color in skin under nails; caused by systemic problems of the heart, poor circulation or injury

Blush – Makeup that adds color or contour to the cheeks

Bobby pins – Implements used to secure hair in place for finished style, especially in long hair designs

Body-building conditioner – Used to displace excess moisture, providing more body to the hair; made from protein

Body language – Nonverbal communication in which messages are exchanged without speaking

Body shapes – The height and bone structure of the body often referred to as tall and lanky, average and short and sturdy

Bonding – The attachment of additional hair fiber to a client's own hair with a special adhesive

Bone – Composed of 2/3 mineral matter and 1/3 organic matter and produces red and white blood cells and stores calcium

Bookend technique – An end paper wrapping technique that uses one end paper folded in half; used to control sections of hair when a shorter rod length is selected or to wrap sections of very short hair

Boric Acid – An ingredient used in eye washes, mouthwashes and powders because of its bactericidal and fungicidal properties

Braid – A switch that has three swatches of hair braided together, often with a thin wire running through it

Brain – Organ that controls all three subsystems of the nervous system; referred to as the command center; weighs between 44 and 48 ounces

Bricklay perm pattern – Positions tools in a staggered configuration; compared to the way a bricklayer arranges the bricks in a building

Broad spectrum – Group of disinfectants that kill bacteria, viruses, fungi, pseudomonas

Bromidrosis (broh-mih-DROH-sis) – A foul-smelling perspiration; also called osmidrosis

Brow pencil/powder – Makeup used to fill in or correct the shape of eyebrows

Bruised nails – Dark purplish discoloration under the nail caused by trauma to nail, environmental problem, blood trapped under nails or hemorrhage of small capillaries

Brush cleaner – A solution that removes any residual nail enhancement product from the bristles of a sable brush

Buccal nerve – Nerve that extends to the muscles of the mouth

Buccinator (BUK-si-na-ter) – Muscle located between the jaws and cheek; responsible for compressing the cheek to release air outwardly, as in blowing

Bulla – Lesions, like vesicles, but larger; found above and below the skin, they contain a clear watery fluid

Bursitis – An inflammation of the fluid-filled sac (bursa) that lies between a tendon and skin or a tendon and bone

Business card – A card listing vital information about salon and employees used to promote both

C

Calibrated – Standardized and measured adjustments used to regulate sterilization equipment

Callus – Sometimes called hyperkeratosis or keratoma; thickening of the epidermis, which occurs from pressure and friction applied to the skin

Calories – Unit measuring energy found in food

Caninus (kay-NEYE-nus) – (also known as the levator angulioris) Muscle located above the corners of the mouth; raises the angle of the mouth, as in snarling

Canities (ka-NEESH-eez) – Refers to the grayness or whiteness of the hair

Canvas block – Canvas-covered head form that holds wig while services are being performed

Capillaries – Small vessels that take nutrients and oxygen

Capilli – The technical term for the hair on the head

Cap method – A hair coloring technique in which selected hair strands are pulled through perforated holes in a rubber coloring cap with a crochet hook

Cap wig – Consists of an elasticized mesh-fiber base to which the hair fiber is attached

Capless wig – Consists of rows of hair wefts sewn to strips of elastic

Carbohydrates – Energy nutrient found in food; carbohydrates make up 60% of RDA guidelines

Carbon – Element found in everything that is living or was once living

GLOSSARY

Carbuncles (KAR-bun-kels) – Clusters of furuncles caused by an acute bacterial infection of several adjoining hair follicles

Cardiac muscle – The muscle of the heart itself; the only muscle of its type in the human body

Cardiovascular or blood-vascular system – Responsible for the circulation of blood, includes the heart, arteries, veins and capillaries

Carpal tunnel – A tunnel in the wrist, surrounded by bone and tissue

Carpal tunnel syndrome – A condition caused by tendonitis in which the tendons swell and the nerve in the tunnel gets pinched, making the hand numb and weak

Carpals – Eight small bones held together by ligaments to form the wrist or carpus

Carrier – A person or thing that carries or transmits a disease

Cascade – A hairpiece worn to create bulk or special effects; consists of long hair fiber attached to an oblong-shaped dome base

Cash value – Total value of assets owned

Cash value items – Best assets such as IRA, certificates of deposit, savings bonds

Casual style – Clients who like comfortable, practical clothes and styles

Catabolism (kah-TAB-oh-lizm) – The process of breaking down larger molecules or substances into smaller ones during metabolism

Cataphoresis – Positive pole of electric current that produces an acidic current

Catagen – A brief transitional stage of hair growth, when all cell division stops

Cathode – A negatively charged electrode; usually black in color or displays a large "N" or a negative sign (-)

Cell membrane – The outer surface of the cell

Cells – The basic units of living matter (life)

Central nervous system – Also called the cerebrospinal nervous system; composed of the brain and spinal cord; responsible for all voluntary body action

Centrosome – The part of the cell that affects cell reproduction

Cerebellum (ser-e-BEL-um) – Area of the brain responsible for the control and coordination of muscle movement, located in the occipital area directly below the cerebrum

Cerebrospinal nervous system – Also called the central nervous system; composed of the brain and spinal cord; the central nervous system is responsible for all voluntary body action

Cerebrum (se-RE-bum) – Area of the brain responsible for mental activity, located in the upper, front portion of the cranium

Cervical (SUR-vi-kal) **cutaneous** (ku-TA-ne-us) **nerve** – Extends into the side and front of the neck to the breastbone

Cervical nerve – Extends to the muscles on the side of the neck

Cervical vertebrae (SUR-vi-kel VURT-e-bray) – The seven bones that form the top part of the spinal column

Chemical bond – Bond involving the sharing of electrons of two or more atoms

Chemical change – A change in a substance that creates a new substance with chemical characteristics different from those of the original substance

Chemical depilatory – A method of hair removal in the form of a cream, paste or powder; the main ingredient is a thioglycolic acid derivative, with an alkaline pH, that chemically softens and degrades the protein structure of the hair

Chemical relaxing – Involves two major phases: the chemical phase, which is application of the straightening product, and the physical phase, which is smoothing the hair, rinsing the product from the hair and applying neutralizer or neutralizing shampoo (also known as fixative or stabilizer)

Chemical texturizing – The process of using physical and chemical actions to permanently change the texture of hair

Chemistry – The scientific study of matter and the physical and chemical changes of matter

Chiaroscuro – An arrangement of light and dark; lighter colors stand out and darker colors recede

Chignon – A fairly long, bulky segment of looped hair, usually sewn to a wire base or tied into a strong cord

Chin strap – Holds wig in place on client's head during services

Chloasma (kloh-AZ-mah) – A group of brownish macules (non-elevated spots) occurring in one place; commonly called liver spots; often occurs on the hands and face

Chronic – A term used to identify conditions that are frequent and habitual

Cilia (SIL-ee-a) – Also called flagella (flah-JEL-ah); hair-like projections that propel bacterial movement

Circulatory or vascular system – Controls the circulation of blood and lymph through the body

Circuit – Flow of electrons along a path called a conductor

Circuit breaker – Reusable device that breaks the flow of current when an overload occurs

Clarifying shampoo – Used to remove residue such as product build-up

Classic style – Clients who are very coordinated in their wardrobe; they wear classic colors, such as navy, black, white, cream, beige, brown and gray

Clavicle (KLAV-i-kel) – The bone that forms the area from the throat to the shoulder

Cleanser – Skin care product used to remove dirt, makeup and impurities

Clientele – Client base developed and maintained by a cosmetologist

Clippers – Implement used to create precise lines or soft, broom-like effect; various blade attachments (guards) allow the hair to be cut at various distances from the scalp

Clipper-over-comb – A cutting technique in which the hair is directed up and held in position with the comb; clipper is positioned on top of the comb, which can be positioned horizontally, vertically or diagonally

Closed circuit – A path on which electrons leave a source and operate an appliance

Cloth cape – Used for dry styling or dry haircutting services

Cocci (KOK-si) – Spherical cells that appear singularly or in groups

Code of Professional Ethics – A system of codes designed to protect the public and guarantee that they are treated honestly and fairly

Cold waves – Machineless method of perming hair; the hair is wrapped on rods while a waving lotion (thioglycolic acid or its derivatives) processes the hair without heat

Color – The visual perception of the reflection of light; if white light (sunlight or light from a light bulb) passes through a prism, the wavelengths are separated and become visible to the eye as color

Color crayons and mascaras – Come in a variety of colors and are used for a number of effects ranging from blending in the regrowth to creating fun, colorful designs

Color mousses/gels – Come in a variety of colors and are used to brighten the existing color, tone gray hair and create dramatic effects

Color psychology – The emotional effects of color; many designers consider color to be the most powerful design element, since it has both an esthetic and emotional value

Color removers – Products used to remove artificial pigment from the hair

Color rinse – Used to add temporary color to the hair, which lasts from shampoo to shampoo

Color shampoo – Used to enhance color-treated hair and tone non-color-treated hair temporarily; available in a variety of colors

Color wheel – A tool in which the twelve colors (three primary, three secondary and six tertiary) are positioned in a circle, allowing any mixed color to be described in relation to the primary colors

Comb control – The use of various comb sizes and shapes to control the hair while cutting

Combination equipment – Generates heat and produces a flow of air (for example, hooded dryers, blow dryers and blow combs)

Combination form – Two or more haircut forms in any combination

Combination skin – Recognized by the shiny "T" zone (forehead, nose and chin), and the presence at the same time of a noticeable dryness in the cheek, jawline and hairline areas; blackheads and enlarged pores are often evident on the nose and chin

Comedones (KOM-e-donz) – Also called black heads; masses of sebum (oil) trapped in the hair follicles

Commission – A percentage of the dollar income the individual stylist creates by performing cosmetology services

Common carotid (kah-ROT-id) **arteries** – Located on either side of the neck; split into the internal carotid artery (ICA) and external carotid artery (ECA)

Common Peroneal Nerve (KAHM-un per-oh-NEE al NURV) – Runs alongside the sciatic nerve from the femur to the buttocks, then down along the knee and behind the fibula

Communicable disease – Contagious infection that can be transmitted from one person to another, usually through touch or through the air

Communication – An exchange of thoughts and information by conversation or writing

Complementary colors – Colors found opposite one another on the color wheel; in hair color they neutralize or cancel out one another when they are mixed together; used to neutralize unwanted tones

Compound – Molecule formed when two or more different atoms combine chemically

Compound dyes – Combination of metallic and vegetable dyes; metallic salts are added to vegetable dyes to create a wider range of colors and a longer lasting color than achieved with vegetable dyes alone

Compress – Squeeze together; make smaller by pressure

Concave lines – Lines that curve inward, like the inside of a sphere

Concave profile – A concave profile has an inward curve, which is most often the result of a dominant, protruding forehead and chin or a small nose

Concave rods – Produce a smaller, tighter curl in the center

Concealer – Makeup used to eliminate discolorations on the skin and reduce the appearance of blemishes

Concentrated solution – Solution that contains a large quantity of the solute in comparison to the quantity of solvent

Conditioner – Used to fortify damaged hair and help prevent further damage

Conditioning shampoo – Used to improve the tensile strength and porosity of the hair

Conductor – A material that allows electricity to flow through it easily

Conical rollers – Cone-shaped tool used to create progression of curl diameter from narrow end of base toward wide end; used in curvature-shape roller setting

Congenital – Occurring at or before birth

Conjunctivitis (kuhn-juhngk-tuh-VAHY-tis) – Referred to as pink eye; inflammation of the transparent membrane that lines the eyelid and eyeball; characterized by itching and redness; spreads easily

Connective tissue – Supports, protects and holds the body together

Consultation – A complete profile of the client resulting in a discussion between stylist and client with the goal of creating the best hairstyle for the client

Contagious disease – Communicable by contact; also known as an infectious or communicable disease

Contaminated – Not free from dirt, oil or microbes

Contraindications – Conditions or factors that serve as reasons to withhold certain treatments; high blood pressure, heart problems, diabetes, pregnancy, pacemaker or metal implants and/or medications are examples

Contour tips – Applying darker contour can narrow a wide jaw; applying lighter cosmetic shades along the hairline can broaden narrow foreheads

Contouring – Outlining of a figure

Contrast – A pattern in which an element has a relationship of opposites that create interest, variety and excitement

Converter – Machine that changes direct current to alternating current

Convex lines – Lines that curve outward, like the outside of a sphere

Convex profile – A convex profile has a strong outward curvature resulting from either a protruding nose or a sloping forehead or chin

GLOSSARY

Cool colors – Violet, blue and green ranges; these colors produce a calming effect by lowering the blood pressure and pulse rate and, in a sense, provide a "cooling off" effect

Corporation – A legal entity, separate from its shareholders, that is formed under legal guidelines

Corrugations (kor-u-**GA**-shuns) – Horizontal ridges across the nail; caused by injury, systemic conditions

Corrugator (**KOR**-e-gat-er) – Muscle located between the eyebrows; controls the eyebrows, drawing them in and downward

Cortex – The inside of the second layer of the hair fiber (gives hair most of its pigment and strength [elasticity])

Cosmetology – The art and science of beauty care

Cover letter – Introduces you to the salon by providing a brief description of your qualities and why you would like to work at the salon

Cowlick – Usually found in straight or wavy hair at the front hairline or crown; represented by strong growth pattern that moves to the right or left

Cranium – Consists of eight bones that form the top, sides and back of the head; encloses and protects the brain and primary sensory organs

Cream hair colors – Applied with a bowl and brush technique; generally mixed with a cream developer; have conditioners and thickening agents

Cream rinse – Used to soften, add shine and smoothness to the hair while making the hair tangle-free for ease in combing

Crimping irons – Consist of two irons that have an angular or serrated pattern

Croquignole wrap – A method of wrapping hair around a perm tool in which the hair is wrapped from the ends up to the scalp

Crosschecking – A technique used to check a haircut for balance and accuracy

Crown – The area of the head above the occipital bone

Crusts – Dried masses that are the remains of an oozing sore; the scab on a sore is an example of a crust

Curl activator – Product that helps new curl configurations retain their shape and provides moisture; applied frequently after every shampoo

Curl base – The area between partings within a shape or the section of hair on which the roller, thermal iron or round brush is placed

Curl booster – Product that helps hair assume new shape of rod when wrapping hair in perm rods; milder form of thio

Curl circle – The hair that is positioned around the roller, thermal iron or round brush

Curl diffusion – A technique used to loosen or relax tightly curled hair patterns by approximately 50% of their natural shape

Curl rearranger – Reduces peptide bonds so hair can relax and become straight; thio-based product

Curl reforming – Also known as soft curls, reformation curls or, in technical terms, a double-process perm service; a chemical service designed to change tightly curled hair to curly or wavy hair; the hair is first relaxed to reduce the curl pattern and then permed to create a new curl pattern

Curl segment – Consists of individual pieces of curly hair that vary in bulk depending on the desired effect

Curl stem – The hair between the scalp and the first turn of the hair around the roller, thermal iron and round brush; the stem determines the amount of movement of the section of hair

Cushion brush – A brush used to relax sets, also for backbrushing, dry molds, styles or the refinement of the form

Cushion-end-paper technique – Incorporates several end papers; known as cushion wrapping because it provides an extra layer of protection between the revolutions of hair wrapped around the rod

Customized shampoo – Used to moisturize and build body

Cuticle – The outer covering of the hair shaft; the loose and pliable skin around the nail

Cuticle cream or oil – Moisturizer used to soften cuticle skin, moisturizes brittle nails

Cuticle nipper – Cutting implement used to trim hangnails

Cuticle pusher – Implement used to push cuticles

Cuticle remover cream – Low percent hydrogen peroxide, sodium or potassium hydroxide used to loosen dead skin

Cuticle scale – The outer covering of the hair fiber

Cutting comb – Parts and distributes the hair; primary comb for cutting and overcomb techniques

Cutting lotion – A product used to control hair while cutting

Cylindrical rollers – A tool to create uniform curl formation/diameter across width of base; used in straight-shape roller setting

Cytoplasm (**SI**-to-plazm) – The production department of the cell, where most of the cell's activities take place

D

Dandruff – Pityriasis; overabundance of epithelial cells that have accumulated on the scalp or fallen to the shoulders

Dappen dish – Holds monomer and polymer separately

Darts – Alterations made vertically to remove width in the nape area (from ear to ear) of a wig

DC current – Direct current; electrons move at an even rate and flow in one direction

Deep Peroneal Nerve – One of two nerves of the lower leg and foot that splits inside the neck of the fibula; also known as the anterior tibial nerve

Degrees of decolorization – The stages or degrees the hair goes through as the melanin changes; dark hair goes through 10 levels, from black to palest yellow

Dehydrant – A solution that allows better adhesion of nail enhancements; reduces the amount of moisture in the nail when brushed over the nail plate

Deltoid (**DEL**-toid) – Muscle that covers the shoulder; triangular-shaped muscle that lifts the arm or turns it

Demi-permanent colors – Contain very little or no ammonia and are designed to deposit color or add tone to the hair; use a low-volume peroxide to develop the color molecules and aid in the color processing; not designed to lift or lighten the existing hair color and generally last 4-6 weeks

Dendrites (**DEN**-dritz) – Short nerve fibers responsible for sending messages in the form of nerve impulses

Density – The number of active hair follicles per square inch on the scalp

Depilatories – Chemical substances that dissolve the hair at skin level; cream, paste or powder form

Depressor (de-**PRES**-er) – Draws down or depresses

Depressor septi – One of the four muscles located inside the nose, controls contraction and expansion of the nostrils

Dermatitis (dur-mah-**TYE**-tis) – An inflammatory disorder of the skin

Dermatitis venenata (**VEN**-eh-nay-tah) – An allergic reaction to certain cosmetics or chemicals; sometimes referred to as contact dermatitis

Dermatology – Study of the skin, its structure, functions, diseases and treatment

Dermis – The underlying, or inner layer of the skin; also called derma, corium, cutis or true skin; made up of connective tissues; the sweat (sudoriferous) glands, oil (sebaceous) glands, sensory nerve endings and receptors, blood vessels, arrector pili muscles and a major portion of each hair follicle are found in the dermis

Design line – The artistic guideline used while cutting; the two types of design lines are stationary (a stable guide to which all lengths are directed) and mobile (a movable guide that consists of a small amount of previously cut hair, which is used as a length guide to cut subsequent partings)

Design principles – The artistic arrangement patterns for the design elements of form, texture and color to follow

Detailing – Smaller, more refined touches, such as pleated textures or creative "piecing" of the hair, for a more personalized hairstyle

Developers – Referred to as a catalyst or conductor; oxidating agents used with demi-permanent and permanent color, lighteners and toners; hydrogen peroxide is the most common developer

Diagonal lines – Lines that fall between horizontal and vertical, slanting right or left, or toward or away from the face; these lines create the illusion of movement and excitement

Diamond facial shape – The diamond face is elongated and angular; its widest area is at the cheekbones, while the forehead and chin are narrow

Diaphragm – Muscular organ that separates the chest cavity from the abdomen

Diffuser – A blow dryer attachment used to spread a gentle air flow over a larger area; generally used for freeform drying techniques such as scrunching

Digestive system – Breaks food down into simpler chemical compounds that can be easily absorbed by cells or, if not absorbed, eliminated from the body in waste products

Digital nerve – Mixed nerve of the arm and hand; extends into the fingers of the hand

Digits – Phalanges or fingers; fourteen bones that form the fingers; each finger has three phalanges; thumb has two

Dilator (**DI**-la-ter) – Opens, enlarges or expands

Dilute solution – Solution that contains a small quantity of the solute in comparison to the quantity of solvent

Dimethicone – Ingredient found in conditioners; gives softness to the feel of hair without weighing it down

Diplococci (dip-lo-**KOK**-si) – Bacterial cells that grow in pairs and are the cause of certain infections, including pneumonia

Directional distribution – Hair is distributed vertically, or straight up from the head, and horizontally, or straight out from the head

Direct mail advertising – Involves sending postcards or flyers to prospective clients encouraging them to try your salon

Disease – Sickness; illness; unhealthy condition

Disease-related cause – The invasion of the skin or nail tissues by an agent like bacteria or fungi

Disinfectants – Chemical products used to destroy or kill bacteria and some viruses (except bacterial spores)

Disinfection – The act of destroying or killing a broad spectrum of microbes on a nonporous surface. Disinfection is the second level of infection control

Disulfide bond – Important side bond containing sulfur; directly affected by perming and relaxing

Dorsal Nerve (**DOOR**-sal **NURV**) – Nerve of the lower leg and foot that is connected to the superficial peroneal nerve

Dorsalis Pedis (**DOR**-sul-is **PEED**-is) **Artery** – Carries blood to the upper surface of the foot

Double-flat-end-paper technique – Incorporates two end papers, one on the top and one on the bottom; the most common end paper technique because it allows maximum control of tapered ends and avoids bunching the ends

Double-halo perm pattern – Features a center part with two rows of perm rods that follow the curves of the head

Double-process blond – A two-step hair coloring process that involves lightening (decolorizing) the hair first and then recoloring the hair to the desired tone

Double-prong clips – Implements used to secure molded shapes/sectioning; also secure rollers if picks are not used

Drabbers – Also called concentrates, intensifiers and pigments; refers to products designed to increase the vibrancy of a color formula or to neutralize tones

Dramatic style – Clients who like anything out of the ordinary; they want to draw attention and make heads turn

Draping – Performed prior to hair care services, such as shampooing and scalp massage, to protect the client's skin and clothing

Drawing Board – Flat mat used to hold hair extension fibers during a hair addition service

Dry skin – Characterized by signs such as peeling and flaking; chaps easily and has a general all-over taut feeling; has fewer blemishes and is not prone to acne

Duct glands – Canal-like structures that deposit their contents on the surface of the skin; part of the endocrine system

Ductless glands – Canal-like structures that secrete hormones into the blood stream; part of the endocrine system

Dye solvent – Products known as color removers; dye solvents are designed to remove artificial pigment

GLOSSARY

E

Ecology – The science of living beings in relationship to their environment

Eczema (EK-sah-mah) – Characterized by dry or moist lesions with inflammation of the skin; requires medical attention

Efferent nerves – Also called motor nerves; carry messages from the brain to the muscles; cause a muscle to contract or expand

Efficacy label – Informs product user regarding what the product is effective in fighting

Effleurage (EF-loo-rahzh) – Light, gliding massage strokes or circular motions made with the palms of the hands or pads of the fingertips; often used to begin and/or end a treatment; used on the face, neck and arms

Eggshell nails – Very thin, soft nails

Elasticity – The ability of hair to stretch and return to its original shape without breaking

Electric curling irons – A styling tool containing a heating element controlled by a thermostat that maintains a constant temperature during use; parts of the iron include: rod handle, shell handle, barrel or rod (the round heating element) and groove or shell (the clamp that holds the hair against the barrel)

Electric current – The movement of electricity along a path called a conductor

Electric heater – Heats cream for specialized nail services

Electricity – A form of energy that produces light, heat, magnetic and chemical changes

Electric nail services – Special electrically powered tools are used to perform many of the same procedures as the implements in a basic nail service

Electrochemical effect – Electric current traveling through a water-based solution to produce relaxing or stimulating effects

Electrode – Safe contact point through which current can pass

Electrolysis – A permanent method of hair removal that uses electric current to damage the cells of the papilla and disrupt hair growth; usually performed by a licensed professional called an electrologist

Electrons – Negatively charged particles that orbit around the nucleus of an atom

Electrotherapy – The application of electrical currents during treatments to the skin

Elements of matter – Basic substances that cannot be broken down into simpler substances

Elevation – Also known as projection; angle at which the hair is held in relation to the curve of the head prior to cutting

Eleventh cranial nerve – The nerve that affects the muscles of the neck and back; also known as the accessory nerve

Embedded – Lodged in a surrounding mass

Emery board – Shortens and shapes natural nails and smooths rough edges by using sandpaper-like fine and coarse sides

Emotional buyer – The impulsive, spontaneous person that reacts to the color of packaging or aroma of product

Emulsion – Two or more nonmixable substances united with help of a binder

End bond – Linked together end to end (peptide bond)

Endocrine system – Carefully balanced mechanism that directly affects hair growth, skin conditions and energy levels

End papers – Papers that are used to control the hair ends and keep hair smoothly wrapped around the perm tool

End texturizing – Performed on the ends of the hair, reduces bulk and weight to allow for mobility

Environmental cause – Diseases, disorders or conditions of the nail caused by nail services or products (chemicals) that have adversely altered the skin or nail

Enzymes (EN-zimz) – Secretions from the salivary glands that assist in breaking down food during digestion

EPA (Environmental Protection Agency) – Approves the efficacy of products used for infection control

Epicranium (ep-i-KRA-ne-um) – Consists of all of the structures above the cranium, including muscle, skin and aponeuroses

Epicranius (ep-i-KRA-ne-us) or **occipitofrontalis** (ok SIP-ih-to-fron-TA-les) – Broad muscle covering the scalp or epicranium

Epidermis – The outermost layer of the skin; also referred to as cuticle or scarf skin

Epithelial (ep-i-THE-le-el) **tissue** – Covers and protects body surfaces and internal organs

Eponychium (ep-o-NIK-ee-um) – The cuticle that overlaps the lunula at the base of the nail

Ergonomics – The science that looks at how body movements and positions and environment work in conjunction with tools and equipment and the effect they have on health and comfort

Erythrocytes (RBC) – Red blood cells or corpuscles; carry oxygen and contain a protein called hemoglobin

Esophagus (e-SOF-ah-gus) – Tube that goes from the pharynx to the stomach

Essential oils – Provides invigorating, stimulating or soothing scents; allows fluid movement on the scalp

Ethics – Moral principles and values

Ethmoid (ETH-moid) – The spongy bone between the eyes that forms part of the nasal cavity

Etiology (e-te-OL-o-je) – Cause of a disease, disorder or condition

Eumelanin – The type of melanin that produces brown/black hair color

Excoriations – Mechanical abrasions to the epidermis (or injuries to the epidermis); scratches to the surface of the skin are considered excoriations

Excretion – The skin's ability to eliminate sweat, salt and wastes from the body, therefore helping to remove toxins from the internal systems

Excretory system – Eliminates solid, liquid and gaseous waste products from the body

Exercise – Helps to stimulate the blood; helps you feel better and work better

Exhaust – The escape of used steam, vapors or dust

Exothermic perms – Self-timing and self-heating; use an additive that creates heat through a chemical reaction mixed with perm solution; range from acid to alkaline

Extensor (eks-TEN-sor) – Muscle located mid-forearm, on the inside of the arm; straightens the fingers and wrist

Extensor Digitorum Longus (eck-STEN-sur dij-it-TOHR-um) – Muscle located on the outside of the lower leg; bends the foot up and extends the toes

Extensor Hallucis Longus (eck-STEN-sur ha-LU-sis LONG-us) – Muscle located between the tibialis interior and extensor digitorum longus; extends the big toe and flexes the foot

External carotid artery (ECA) – Supplies blood to the skin and muscles

External jugular (EJV) – Vein that collects blood from the head, face and neck

External maxillary (EKS-tur-nal MAK-si-ler-e) – Facial artery; supplies the lower portion of the face with blood, including the mouth and nose

External parasites (PAR-ah-sights) – Plants or animals that live on or obtain their nutrients from another organism

Eyedropper – Removes acrylic liquid from container to dappen dish

Eye liner – Makeup used to accentuate and define the shape of eye

Eye shadow – Makeup used to accentuate the shape and color of eye; also contours

Eye tabbing – The process of applying individual synthetic lashes to the client's own lashes

F

Facial – The analysis, cleansing, exfoliation, massage and treatment of the face

Facial artery – External maxillary nerve; supplies the lower portion of the face, including the mouth and nose

Facial masks – Solutions applied to the skin to hydrate, tighten pores or reduce excess oil; include clay packs, cream masks and paraffin (warm wax)

Facial nerve – Emerges from the brain at the lower part of the ear and is the primary motor nerve of the face; also known as the seventh cranial nerve

Facial powder – A makeup product primarily designed to "set" other makeup products so that they last longer without fading, streaking or rubbing off

Facial skeleton – Fourteen bones that compose the front of the skull

Facial steamer – A machine that sprays warm, humid mist on skin to open follicles for cleansing

Fade haircut – Incorporates gradation and consists of extremely short lengths in the exterior progressing to longer interior lengths

Fall – A hairpiece with a base that covers the crown, occipital and nape areas

Fantasy pins – Implements used to define textural detail and movement

Faradic Current – Alternating current with a mechanical effect that stimulates the nerve and muscle tissue

Fat – Energy nutrient found in food and stored by the body for later use; fat makes up 10% of the RDA guidelines

Fatty alcohol – Ingredient found in conditioners; gives hair a smooth feel when dry and makes it easier to comb; creamy in texture and helps retain moisture

Femoral (FEM-or-ahl) **Vein** – Transports blood to the heart and lungs for oxygenation

Femur (FEE-mur) – Leg bone also know as the thigh bone

FEI – Federal Employer Identification; identifies an employer to the government

Fibula (FIB-u-lah) – Outer and narrower of the two lower leg bones extending from the knee to the ankle

Fifth cranial nerve – The largest of the cranial nerves; also known as the trifacial or trigeminal nerve

Fillers – Provide an even base color by filling in porous, damaged or abused areas with materials such as protein or polymers; they equalize the porosity of the hair and deposit a base color in one application

Finger bowl – A bowl that allows comfortable soaking of nails for a manicure service

Finger/shear position – Refers to the position of the fingers and shears relative to the parting; the two basic types of finger/shear positions are parallel (fingers are positioned at an equal distance away from the parting) and nonparallel (fingers are positioned unequally away from the parting)

Finger styling – A technique in which the fingers are used to manipulate and style the hair

Fingerwaves – Created by two complete oblong shapings that are joined and connected by a ridge

Fingerwaving – The art of shaping and defining the hair in graceful waves

First Aid – Techniques used to assist individuals in emergency situations.

Fissures – Cracks in the skin; chapped lips are one example of a fissure

Fixed rent – A set dollar amount paid each month to the lessor that allows you to predict monthly expenses

Flagella (flah-JEL-ah) – Also called cilia (SIL-ee-a); hair-like projections that propel bacterial movement

Flat bones – Plate-shaped and located in the skull

Flexor (FLEX-er) – Muscle located mid-forearm, on the inside of the arm; this muscle bends the wrist and closes the fingers

Flexor Digiti Minimi Brevis (FLEK-sur dij-it-ty MIN-eh-mee BREV-us) – Muscle of the foot that flexes the joint of the small toe

Flexor Digitorum Brevis (FLEK-sur dij-ut-TOHR-um BREV-us) – Muscle that lies in the middle of the sole of the foot; flexes toe digits 2 through 4

Floor plan – A drawing or blueprint depicting the various areas, fixtures and operations of the salon

Fluorescent light – An economical and long-lasting light source

Follicle – A cluster of cells in the upper layer of the skin; the cell cluster pulls the upper layer down with it, creating a tube-like pocket called the root sheath, out of which the hair will grow

Folliculitis (FO-lik-u-li-tis) – Infection in the hair follicles caused by bacteria, shaving or clothing irritation; usually looks like red pimples with a hair in the center of each one

Foot brush – A stiff brush that cleans nails and removes debris

Foot file – A paddle with a gritty surface that softens and removes calluses

Foreign conductor – An outside element that interrupts the flow of electric current

GLOSSARY

Form – A hair design element describing the outline or silhouette of an object; three-dimensional representation of shape

Forms of matter – Exists in solid, liquid and gas form

Foundation – Makeup used to create an even skin tone and uniform surface

Fragilitis crinium (frah-**JIL**-I-tas **KRI**-nee-um) – The technical term for split ends, small cracks in the cuticle that deepen into the cortex

Franchise – An operating agreement in which a fee is paid to a parent corporation in exchange for fixtures, promotion, advertising, education and management techniques

Free edge – The part of the nail that extends beyond the end of the finger

Freckles – Commonly found on the face, neck and chest and are considered macules

Freeform painting – A technique in which a brush is used to strategically position color or lightener on the surface of the hair

French manicure – A nail polishing technique/design with white polish applied to the free edge of the nail and pink or peach polish applied to the nail bed

French twist – A style in which hair can be incorporated into a roll for an elongated smooth finish, or the roll can be positioned up to the crown area and finished with curls for a combination of textures; also known as the vertical roll

Frequency – The number of times per second of alternating current from positive to negative

Friction (**FRICK**-shun) – Circular or wringing movement with no gliding used on the scalp or with a facial when less pressure is desired; applied with the fingertips or palms; a way in which the hair cuticle can be damaged by combing and brushing

Fringe – The hair that partially or completely covers the forehead in a hairstyle

Frontal – Bone that extends from the top of the eyes to the top of the head and forms the forehead

Frontal artery – Artery that supplies the forehead with blood

Frontalis (frun-**TA**-les) – Muscle that extends from the forehead to the top of the skull; it raises eyebrows or draws the scalp forward

Full stem – Off base; stem and circle of curl positioned below the base and pick-up line; used when closeness and direction are required

Fungicidal – Disinfectant designed to kill fungus

Furrows – Indented vertical lines down the nail plate

Furuncles (fu-**RUN**-kels) – Boils; appear in the dermis and the epidermis and are caused by an acute bacterial infection

Fuse – A device that contains a fine metal wire that allows current to flow

G

Galvanic Current – A direct current (DC) of low voltage and high amperage; has an electrochemical effect and is the oldest form of electrotherapy in the salon

Galvanic electrolysis – Multiple needle method of permanent hair removal

Gamine style – Clients who are very fashion-oriented and enjoy wearing the latest looks; playful and very feminine

Gas – Form of matter having definite weight but indefinite volume and shape

Gastrocnemius (gas-truc-**NEEM**-e-us) – Muscle at the back of the leg attached to the lower rear surface of the heel; pulls the foot down

Gel – Creates wet-look finishes in haircutting; creates maximum control and support in wet styling

Gel masks – Designed for a wide variety of purposes; may contain botanicals and ingredients that are designed to calm and soothe sensitive skin

General infection – Also called systemic infection; occurs when the circulatory system carries bacteria and their toxins to all parts of the body

General shock – Passes through the nervous system

Generator – Power source most often used in a salon; produces alternating current; uses mechanical energy to produce a flow of electrons

Germinal matrix – The area of the hair bulb where cell division (mitosis) takes place

Germinal matrix cells – Produce the cells that ultimately keratinize (harden) and form the three major layers of the hair

Glands – Organs in the body by which certain substances are separated from the blood and changed into some secretion for use in the body, such as oil (sebaceous gland)

Glyceryl monothioglycolate – Thioglycolic derivative; found in acid waves

Good Samaritan Laws – Give legal protection to people who provide emergency care to ill or injured persons

Graduated form – A combination of activated and unactivated cut texture achieved by projecting (lifting) the hair and using mobile and stationary design lines; also known as a wedge or 45° angle cut

Gradation – Very short exterior progressing to longer interior; similar to graduated form but shorter

Grammar – The standard use of language

Gray hair – Sometimes referred to as mottled hair, indicating white spots scattered about the hair shaft, caused by reduced color pigment in the cortex layer of the hair

Greater auricular nerve – Extends into the side of the neck and external ear

Greater occipital nerve – Extends up the back of the scalp to the top of the head

Gross anatomy – The study of the structures of the body that can be seen with the naked eye

Grounding wire – A safety device designed to protect you when operating certain kinds of appliances

Growth pattern – The natural growth pattern determines the angle and direction at which the hair grows out of the scalp

H

Habit – An action performed repeatedly

Hackle – Metal plate with rows of pointed needles used to blend or straighten hair during a hair addition service

Half stem – Half of circle of curl is positioned below the base and pick-up line; half-off base; used when equal degree of predetermined direction and volume is required

Hair – A form of protein called keratin

Hair additions – Loose hair fiber intended for attachment to a client's own hair

Haircutting – The artistic carving or removing of hair lengths with shears, taper shears, razors and/or clippers to create various forms and shapes

Haircutting station – Place for stylist's tools to be displayed and organized; workstation

Hair density – Measure of the amount of hair per square inch on the scalp; usually referred to as light, medium or heavy (or thin, medium or thick)

Hair fiber – Sometimes referred to as the hair shaft or strand; the portion of the hair that extends above the skin's surface

Hair lightener – The oldest form of hair color service; bleaches or decolorizes hair

Hairpieces – Designed to cover specific areas of the head and for definite purposes; made of human hair, animal hair, synthetic fibers or a blend of each

Hairpins – Implements used to secure the hair in place for a finished style, especially in long hair designs

Hair pressing – Also called silking; a form of temporarily straightening tightly curled hair by applying a protective oil and then using a hot pressing comb or silking iron on small sections of the hair to straighten the curl

Hair root – The portion of hair that is inside the hair follicle under the skin's surface

Hairstyling – The art of dressing and arranging hair to create temporary changes in the form and texture of the finished hairstyle

Hair texture – Refers to the surface appearance or feel of the hair as well as the diameter of the hair strand itself; unactivated texture – having a smooth and unbroken surface, activated – having a rough surface

Half-off base – The tool or curl sits directly on the bottom parting of the base, with half the curl on the base and half the curl off the base

Half-off-base tool position – With a one-diameter base size, the tool is positioned half on its base and half off its base, directly on the bottom parting

Halitosis (hal-eh-TOH-sis) – A term referring to bad breath

Hand lotion – Lubricant used to soften skin; aids when providing massage manipulations

Hand-tied wig – Produced by actually hand tying strands of hair into a fine meshwork foundation

Hard press – Pressing action that is repeated twice with more pressure and heat

Hard water – Contains salts of calcium, magnesium and other metals; does not allow shampoo to lather freely

Head Lice – Parasitic insects transmitted directly from one person to another, or by contact with articles that have come in contact with an infested person (such as combs and brushes, etc.)

Head position – The position of the client's head during the haircut; the most common head positions are upright, forward or tilted to either side

Heart – A cone-shaped, muscular organ located in the chest cavity, normally about the size of a closed fist

Heart facial shape – The heart-shaped (triangle) face is long; the heart face shape is angular and the chin area is sometimes elongated and pointed, while the forehead is wide

Heart rate – A normal heart beats 60-80 times per minute

Hemoglobin (HE-mo-glo-bin) – A protein in the red blood cells that attracts oxygen molecules through the process know as oxygenation

Henna – Vegetable dye that produces reddish highlights in the hair

Heredity – The genes that people inherit from their parents

Herpes Simplex – Also known as fever blister; a contagious, chronic condition characterized by a single vesicle or group of vesicles on a red, swollen base; usually appears on the lips, nostrils or other parts of the face

Hertz – A rating providing the number of cycles per second that a generator alternates the current from the source

High frequency machine – A machine that creates current that is thermal, or heat producing, and germicidal for treatment of the skin

Hirsuties – Hypertrichosis; superfluous hair; abnormal coverage of hair on areas of the body where normally only lanugo hair appears

Histology – The study of the structures of the body too small to be seen except through a microscope; also called microscopic anatomy

Horizontal lines – Lines that are parallel to the horizon and are considered stable or restful; these lines create a feeling of maximum weight or stability

Hot oil or cream manicure – The client's hand is placed in oil or cream instead of warm water soaking solution

Hue – Name of a color, also referred to as tone; is identified by its position on the color wheel

Human Hepatitis B (HBV) – A highly infectious disease that infects the liver

Human relations – The psychology of getting along with others

Humectant – A moisturizing ingredient

Humerus (HU-mur-us) – The largest bone of the upper arm, extends from the elbow to the shoulder

Hydration – The ability to keep the skin soft, supple and maintain moisture through water

Hydraulic chair – Provides proper back support for client during the haircutting service; adjustable

Hydrochloric (hi-dro-KLO-rik) acids – Break down food in the stomach

Hydrogen – Element with the simplest atomic structure

Hydrogen bond – Side bond that works on the principle that unlike charges attract

Hydrogen peroxide – The most often used oxidizing or developing agent

Hydrometer – Implement used to measure the strength (volume) of hydrogen peroxide

Hydrophilic – Refers to the water-loving part of a molecule

Hygiene – The science that deals with healthful living

Hyoid (HI-oid) – The u-shaped bone at the base of the tongue that supports the muscles of the tongue

GLOSSARY

Hyperhidrosis (hyper-hy-**DROH**-sis) – An overproduction of perspiration caused by excessive heat or general body weakness; requires medical attention

Hypertrichosis (hi-per-tri-**KOH**-sis) – Referred to as hirsuties (hur-sue-**SHEEZ**) or superfluous hair; the abnormal coverage of hair on areas of the body where normally only lanugo hair appears

Hypertrophies – new growths; overgrowths; excesses of skin

Hyponychium (heye-poh-**NIK**-ee-um) – The skin underneath the free edge of the nail

I

Image – A person's total look based on the care of hair, skin, hands, feet and clothing

Immunity – The ability of the body to destroy infectious agents that enter the body

Impetigo (im-peh-**TIE**-go) – A highly contagious bacterial infection that produces a honey-yellow, crusted lesion, usually on the face

Inactive stage – Stage during which bacteria become dormant

Incandescent – Lighting used in the salon to balance tones

Increase-layered form – A form with an activated cut texture that can be achieved using a stationary design line and the conversion layering technique; also known as a shag or 180° angle cut

Indentation – The amount of hollow space or flatness (closeness) achieved through the position of the tool and the size of the base

Infection – Occurs when disease-causing (pathogenic) bacteria or viruses enter the body and multiply to the point of interfering with the body's normal state

Infection control – The efforts taken to prevent the spread of disease and kill certain or all microbes

Inferior labial – Artery that supplies blood to the lower lip

Inferioris (in-**FIR**-e-or-es) – Located below or is smaller

Inflammation – An objective symptom characterized by redness, pain, swelling and/or increased temperature

Infraorbital nerve – Extends to the lower eyelid, side of the nose, upper lip and mouth

Infrared lamp – A lamp that provides a soothing heat that penetrates into the tissues of the body; softens the skin to allow penetration of product and increased blood flow

Infrared light therapy – The use of infrared light in the treatment of skin

Infratrochlear Nerve – Emerges on the skin of the upper eyelid and side of the nose

Ingrown nails – Onychocryptosis; nails that grow into the edge of the nail groove

Inorganic chemistry – Studies all matter that is not alive, has never been alive and does not contain carbon, such as rocks, water and minerals

Insertion – The portion of the muscle joined to movable attachments: bones, movable muscles or skin

Instant conditioner – Used to coat the hair shaft and restore moisture to the hair

Insulator – Material that does not allow the flow of electric current

Insurance agent – Person who gives advice on insurance needs to safely open and operate a business

Integumentary system – The skin and its layers

Intensity of hair color – Refers to the brightness or vividness of a color or the strength of the tone

Internal carotid artery (ICA) – Supplies blood to the brain, eyes and forehead

Internal jugular (IJV) – Vein that collects blood from the head, face and neck

Inventory control – Applies to procedures used in the salon that will ensure that products are accounted for from the time they are brought into the salon until they are sold or used

Invisible light therapy – The use of light or visible rays in the treatment of skin

Involuntary or non-striated (**STRI**-at-ed) – Muscles that respond automatically to control various body functions including the functions of internal organs

Iontophoresis (eye-on-to-fo-**REE**-sis) – The use of a Galvanic Current machine to introduce water-soluble treatment products into the skin

Irregular bones – Found in the wrist, ankle or spinal column (the back)

IRS – Internal Revenue Service; the governing body that controls taxes paid on income

J

JL color ring – A ring containing numbered samples of hair colors from black to palest blond

Job benefits – Key factors offered to an employee by an employer, which include salary, insurance, paid holidays, vacation time and sick days, among other things

Jugular veins – Internal and external veins; all blood from head, face and neck returns to heart by jugular veins

K

Keratin – A protein that accounts for 97% of the makeup of hair

Keratinization – The process whereby cells change their shape, dry out and form keratin protein; once keratinized, the cells that form the hair fiber or strand are no longer alive

Kidneys – Organs that receive urea from the liver and then pass the urea through small tubelike structures known as nephrons

Kilowatt – Equals 1,000 watts

Koilonychia (koi-loh-**NIK**-ee-uh) – Nails with a concave shape; caused by systemic or long-term illness or nerve disturbance; also called spoon nails

L

Lacrimal (**LAK**-ri-mal) – The smallest two bones of the facial skeleton that form the front part of the inner, bottom wall of the eye socket

Language – Human speech, spoken or written; wording

Lanthionization – Process that occurs when chemically relaxing hair with sodium hydroxide; the disulfide bonds are broken at point X between the first sulphur atom and the adjacent carbon atom, resulting in one sulphur atom being lost; results in a lanthionine bond (contains only one sulphur atom)

Lanugo – The term for baby fine, silky hair, which covers most of the body and is shed shortly after birth and replaced with vellus hair

Large intestine – Includes the colon; stores undigested food for eventual elimination through the anal canal

Large-tooth comb – Comb that controls and distributes larger amounts of hair; also used for over-comb techniques

Latissimus dorsi – Flat, triangular muscle that covers the lumbar (lower back) region and lower half of the thoracic region. This muscle aids in swinging of the arms.

Law of color – Out of all the colors in the universe, only three – yellow, red and blue, called primary colors – are pure

Lawyer – Someone who gives advice on the legal obligations of business ownership, borrowing money, signing rental agreements and assuming tax responsibilities

Lease – A rental agreement

LED – Acronym for Light Emitting Diode

Left atrium or auricle – Upper chamber of the heart

Left ventricle – Lower chamber of the heart

Lentigines (len-tih-JEE-nees) – Appears larger and darker than a freckle; an example of a macule

Lesser occipital nerve – Extends into the muscles at the back of the skull

Leuconychia (loo-ko-NIK-e-a) – White spots appearing in the nail caused by injury to the nail, heredity, signs of systemic disorders or nutritional deficiency

Leukocytes (WBC) – White blood cells or corpuscles; fight bacteria and other foreign substances and increase in number when infection invades the body

Leukoderma (Loo-ko-DUR-mah) – Describes hypopigmentation (lack of pigmentation) of the skin caused by a decrease in activity of melanocytes

Levator palpebrae (POL-pe-bra) superioris – Muscle located above the eyelids, functions to raise the eyelid

Level of hair color – The degree of lightness or darkness of hair color; identified on a scale of 1 to 10 with 1 being the darkest and 10 the lightest

Liabilities – Debts owed to others

Lifestyle – Factors in a person's life such as job/career, hobbies (such as sports), family, time willing to spend on hair, skill or ability to care for hair and the money the client is willing to invest in hair maintenance

Lifter – A comb used for detailing, lifting and backcombing

Light-cured or gel nails – An acrylic gel applied to the nail plate and then cured or hardened to reinforce weak nails or add sheen and strength over nail tips

Lighteners – Also called bleaches; used to remove or diffuse melanin; utilize ingredients, such as ammonia and peroxide, to facilitate the oxidation process; generally applied to dry hair; come in oil or cream form (on-the-scalp lighteners) or powder form (off-the-scalp lighteners)

Light therapy – The production of beneficial effects on the body through treatments using light rays or waves

Lighting – The way in which lights are arranged

Line – Consists of a series of points that are connected with each other in a variety of directions

Line of demarcation – Area along the hairstrand where two colors meet; the area where the new growth meets the previously colored hair

Lip glosses – Makeup used to add color to lips; impart a shiny appearance to the lips; generally have less concentration of color than lipsticks; have moisturizing properties

Lip liner – Makeup used to define natural shape of the lips or correct the shape

Lipophilic – Refers to the oil-loving part of a molecule

Lipstick – Makeup used to add color and texture to the lips

Liquid – Form of matter having definite weight and volume, but no definite shape

Liquid-dry shampoo – Used to cleanse the scalp and hair for clients who are unable to receive a normal shampoo; effective in cleaning wigs and hairpieces

Liquid hair colors – Applied with a bottle; contain fewer conditioning agents and a greater ammonia content; have a good penetration ability

Liquid polish – Colored polish, enamel, which creates a colored effect on the nail

Liquid tissue – Carries food, waste products and hormones

Liver – Organ that converts and neutralizes ammonia from the circulatory system to urea

Load – The technical name for any electrically powered appliance

Local infection – Located in a small, confined area; often indicated by a pus-filled boil, pimple or inflamed area

Local shock – Passes through a small part of the body causing burns and muscle contractions

Logarithmic – Each step or number increases by multiples of 10

Logical buyer – The careful person who wants the facts about a product and thinks about buying without much regard for who else likes or uses the product

Long bones – Found in the arms and legs

Loss – Occurs when the expenses of a salon are greater than the income produced

Lungs – Spongy organs composed of cells into which air enters during inhalation

Lunula – The whitened area, half-moon shape at the base of the nail

Lymph – Colorless liquid produced as a byproduct in the process through which plasma passes nourishment to capillaries and cells

Lymphatic system – A vascular system that interacts with the blood system by collecting excess tissue fluid and filtering toxins; helps increase the body's resistance to disease

Lymph nodes – Glands that filter out toxic substances, like bacteria

GLOSSARY

Lymph vascular system – Responsible for the circulation of lymph through lymph glands, nodes and vessels

M

Machine-made wig – Wig consisting of hair fiber sewn into long strips called wefts, which are then sewn to the cap of the wig in a circular or crisscross pattern

Macules – Discoloration appearing on the skin's surface; a freckle is an example of a macule

Magnetic effect – A push-pull effect causing motors to turn

Magnifying lamp – A lamp that provides thorough examination of skin's surface using magnification and glare-free light

Makeup – The application of products that add color, highlights, contour and other enhancements to the face

Malpractice insurance – A policy that protects the salon owner from financial loss that can result from a stylist-employee's negligence while performing hair, nail and skin care services on salon clients

Mandible (MAN-di-bl) – The lower jaw and the largest bone of the facial skeleton

Mandibular nerve branch – Main nerve branch to the lower 1/3 of the face

Marginal mandibular (mahr-JUH-nl man-DIB-u-lur) **nerve** – Extends to the muscles of the chin and lower lip

Manicure – The cosmetic care of the hands and finger nails; the Latin word "manus" means hand and "cura" means care

Mantle – The pocket-like structure that holds the root and matrix

Marcel curling irons – A styling tool, heated in a stove, used to create curls or waves for a finished hairstyle

Marcel waving – The process of curling hair with thermal irons

Mascara – Makeup used to define, lengthen and thicken the eyelashes

Massage – A scientific method of manipulating the body by rubbing, pinching, tapping, kneading or stroking with the hands, fingers or an instrument

Masseter (MAS-se-ter) – Muscle covers the hinge of the jaw and aids in closing the jaw, as in chewing (mastication)

Master Sketcher comb – A comb used to remove tangles from the hair and to backcomb the hair

Matter – Refers to anything that occupies space

Maxillae (mak-SIL-e) – The two bones of the upper jaw

Maxillary (MAK-si-ler-e) **nerve branch** – Main nerve branch to the middle 1/3 of the face

Measuring tape – Measures client's head to determine correct wig size

Mechanical equipment – Any equipment with a motor (for example, clippers and massagers)

Median nerve – Extends down the mid-forearm into the hand

Medicated rinse – Used to control minor dandruff and scalp conditions

Medicated shampoo – Prescribed by the client's doctor to treat scalp and hair problems and disorders such as minor dandruff conditions; may affect color-treated hair

Medulla – The central core of the hair shaft, also called the pith (often absent in fine or very fine hair)

Medulla oblongata (me-DOOL-ah ob-long-GA-ta) – Connects parts of the brain to the spinal column; located just below the pons

Melanin – A pigment that gives skin and hair their color

Melanocytes – Cells that exist among the dividing cells within the hair bulb

Melanoderma – The term used to describe any hyperpigmentation caused by overactivity of the melanocytes in the epidermis

Melanonychia (mel-uh-nuh-NIK-ee-uh) – Brown or black darkening of the nail caused by increased production of melanin by melanocytes in the nail matrix; due to trauma, systemic disease or medications

Melanosomes – Bundles of a pigment protein complex that rest near the hair bulb's nourishment center, the dermal papilla

Mental nerve – Extends to the lower lip and chin

Mentalis (men-TAL-us) – Muscle located at the tip of the chin, pushes the lower lip up and/or wrinkles the chin, as in expressing doubt

Metabolism (me-TAB-e-lism) – The chemical process in which cells receive nutrients (food) for cell growth and reproduction

Metacarpals (met-ah-KAR-pels) – The five long, thin bones that form the palm of the hand

Metallic dyes – Hair dyes containing metals; also known as progressive dyes because the hair turns darker with each application

Metatarsals (met-ah-TAHR-sul) – Five long, slender bones (one for each digit) that connect the phalanges to the tarsals

Microbe – Another word for bacteria or germ; small living organism

Microbiology – The study of small living organisms called microbes, such as bacteria

Microscopic – Too small to be seen except through a microscope

Middle temporal – Artery that supplies blood to the temples

Midstrand texturizing – Performed between the end of the base area up to 1" (2.5 cm) before the ends to reduce bulk and weight

Midstrand to ends – Hair color technique to lighten the existing color; the color or lightener is first applied to the midstrand, generally ½" (1.25 cm) away from the scalp, then up to but not including any porous ends later, since they will lighten faster

Milia (MIL-ee-uh) – Also called whiteheads; caused by the accumulation of hardened sebum beneath the skin

Miliaria rubra (mil-ee-AY-re-ah ROOB-rah) – Prickly heat; an acute eruption of small red vesicles with burning and itching of the skin caused by excessive heat

Mixed nerves – Large nerves that perform both sensory and motor functions

Mixture – Two or more substances that combine physically

Modeling masks – Masks that are mixed with water and applied in a thick consistency to the face; these masks dry and harden to a rubber-like consistency, then can be pulled from the face in one piece; these masks seal the skin, locking in moisture and creating a firm, taut feeling

Moisturizer – Skin care product used to replenish moisture/oil and protect skin

Moisturizing agent – Replenishes or restores moisture to dry scalp; formulated as creams, oils or lotions

Moisturizing conditioner – Used to add moisture to dry, brittle hair

Molding – The process of combing or shaping wet hair into the desired position

Molecule – Two or more atoms joined together by a chemical bond

Moles – Small brown pigmented spots that may be raised; hair often grows through moles, but should not be removed, unless advised by a physician

Monilethrix (mo-NIL-e-thriks) – Beads or nodes formed on the hair shaft

Monochromatic color – Color scheme using the same color (with variations in value and intensity)

Monomer – Mixes with the powder to form an acrylic nail; liquid in form

Motor nerves – Also called efferent nerves; carry messages from the brain to the muscles

Mottled hair – Hair with white spots scattered about in the hair shafts

Mousse – A product used to define texture; creates light-to-firm hold on wet or dry hair

MSDS (Material Safety Data Sheets) – An information sheet designed to provide the key data on a specific product regarding ingredients, associated hazards, combustion levels, and storage requirements

Muscles – Fibrous tissues that contract, when stimulated by messages carried by the nervous system, to produce movement

Muscular system – Supports the skeleton, produces body movements, contours the body, involved in the functions of other body systems

Muscular tissue – Contracts, when stimulated, to produce motion

Myology (mi-OL-o-je) – The study of the structure, function and diseases of the muscles

N

Naevus or nevus (NEE-vus) – A birthmark or a congenital mole; reddish purple flat mark; caused by dilation of the small blood vessels in the skin

Nail and cuticle scissors – Implement used to cut nails or trim mending fiber

Nail art – The use of nail paints, striping tape, beads, jewelry and other accessories arranged creatively on the nail

Nail bed – The area of the nail bed on which the nail body rests; nerves and blood vessels found here supply nourishment

Nail bleach – Lightener or high percent hydrogen peroxide used to remove stains and whiten nails

Nail body – Nail plate; visible nail area from the nail root to free edge; made of layers; no nerves or blood vessels can be found here

Nail brush – Small brush used to clean nails and remove debris before polishing

Nail cuticle – The loose and pliable overlapping skin around the nail

Nail file – Shortens, files and shapes artificial nails; coarse grit

Nail forms – Plastic, paper or metal templates that form an acrylic extension to the natural nail

Nail groove – The tracks on either side of the nail that the nail moves on as it grows

Nail matrix – The active tissue that generates cells that harden as they move outward from the root to the nail

Nail mend fiber – Mending material; silk, paper, fiberglass used to repair splits or cracks on the nail

Nail root – Attached to the matrix at the base of the nail, under the skin and inside the mantle

Nail service table – A table that provides a place for all tools to be laid out; is the proper height for comfort; may have an attached light

Nail strengthener – Usually a clear polish; may contain strengthening fibers used to prevent nails from splitting and peeling

Nail technician – Specializes in nail care services

Nail tips – Plastic extensions that adhere to natural nail; they have a hollowed area on one end called the nail well, which is attached to the natural nail

Nail wall – The folds of skin on either side of the nail groove

Nail wraps – Woven materials that are applied to the natural nails or nails with tips to add strength

Nape – The area of the head below the occipital bone

Nasal (NA-zel) – The two bones that join to form the bridge of the nose

Nasal bones - Two bones that join to form the bridge of the nose

Nasalis – One of the four muscles located inside the nose, controls contraction and expansion of the nostrils

Nasal nerve – Extends to the tip and lower side of the nose

Natural-bristle hair brush – A brush that increases blood circulation to the scalp, removes dirt, debris and product build-up from the hair prior to the shampoo service

Natural distribution – The direction the hair assumes as it falls naturally from the head due to gravity

Natural fall – Describes the hair as the lengths lay or fall naturally over the curve of the head

Natural style – Clients who like to wear colors that are found in nature and made from natural materials

Neck strip – Protects client's skin from contact with the cape; replaces towel during the haircutting services

Needle and thread – Used to create darts and tucks in wigs; secure wefts in track-and-sew technique; used to sew wefts for fantasy hairpieces

Nerve cell – Neuron; cells with long and short threadlike fibers called axons; responsible for sending messages in the form of nerve impulses

Nerve terminal (synapse) – Appears at the end of axon; connects the neuron to muscles, organs or other nerve cells

Nerve tissue – Carries messages to and from the brain and coordinates body functions

GLOSSARY

Nervous system – Coordinates and controls the overall operation of the human body

Networking – Building professional relationships through meeting and greeting people

Net worth – Assets minus liabilities

Neurology – The study of the nervous system

Neutral or base – Indicates equal number of positive hydrogen ions and negative hydroxide ions

Neutralizer – Product that reforms disulfide bonds in a perm procedure

Neutralizing – Rebonding or oxidation; final step in the perm process; restores the disulfide bonds; reduces the swelling caused by the alkalinity of the perm solution and hardens the bonds in the new shape

Neutron – Particle with no electric charge found in the nucleus of an atom

Nitrazine paper – Used to indicate if solution is acidic, neutral or alkaline

Nodes – Glands

No-lye relaxers – Contain a derivative of sodium hydroxide; contain calcium, potassium, guanidine, lithium hydroxide, or bisulfate as the active ingredient; usually recommended for less resistant hair and require frequent conditioning follow-up treatments

Non-corrosive – Prevents eating away of implements when placed in a disinfectant

Nonoxidative – Hair colors that contain no developers

Nonpathogenic bacteria – Non-disease-producing bacteria; they are harmless and can be beneficial

Non-striated muscle – Involuntary muscle; responds automatically to control various body functions including functions of internal organs

Normalizing conditioner – Used to close the cuticle after alkaline chemical services

Normal projection – The hair is viewed abstractly as if it were sticking straight out from the various curves of the head; this view allows the stylist to analyze the structure or length arrangement of the hair

Normal skin – Characterized by a fresh and healthy color, a firm, moist and smooth texture, freedom from blackheads and blemishes, and does not appear oily

No-stem – Curl placed directly on base

Nucleus (NU-kle-us) – The control center of cell activities; the dense core of an atom that contains protons and sometimes neutrons

Nutrition – The intake of appropriate dietary requirements

O

Objective symptoms – Signs of a disorder or disease that are visible; for example, pimples or inflammation

Oblong facial shape – The oblong (rectangle) face is long, narrow and angular. The jawline is wide and almost horizontal; the hairline on the oblong face is only slightly curved

Oblong perm pattern – Positions rods within oblongs using diagonal partings; creates strong wave patterns

Occipital (ak-SIP-e-tal) – The bone that forms the back of the skull, indenting above the nape area

Occipital artery – Supplies blood to the back of the head, up to the crown

Occipitalis (ok-sip-i-TAL-is) – Muscle located at the nape of the neck; draws the scalp back

Occupation disorders – Occur in certain types of work situations due to reactions to certain chemicals used or as a result of repeated actions

Off base – The tool or curl sits below the bottom parting of the base, creating minimum base strength and the least volume or lift

Off-base tool position – The hair is held at 45° below the center of the base while wrapping so that the tool sets completely off its base; used for a minimal degree of volume and a curl pattern concentrated on the midstrand and ends

Off-the-scalp lightener – Strong lightener that lightens the hair quickly and is not intended to touch the scalp

Ohm – A unit of electric resistance

Ohm's rating – Measure of the resistance to the motion of the electrons through a conductor

Oily skin – An all-over shiny look and/or rough texture with blackheads and enlarged pores

Ointment – Mixtures of organic substances and a medicinal agent, usually found in a semi-solid form

On base – The tool or curl is centered between the top and bottom partings of the base

On top of the fingers – Haircutting position used when lifting lengths on top of the head by cutting the hair along the top of your fingers

On-base tool position – A one-diameter base is directed 45° above the center of the base and wrapped so the tool sits between two partings; used to create more volume

On-the-scalp lightener – Lightener that when applied to the hair can touch the scalp without harm

Onychatrophia (o-ni-ka-TRO-fe-a) – Atrophy of the nail or wasting away of nail

Onychauxis (o-ni-KOK-sis) – Hypertrophy; thickening of the nail plate or an abnormal outgrowth of the nail

Onychia (o-NIK-e-a) – Inflammation of the nail matrix

Onychocryptosis (o-ni-ko-KRIP-to-sis) – Ingrown nails; causes include environmental or poor nail trimming practices; can become infected

Onychogryposis (o-ni-ko-GRI-po-sis) – Represents an increased curvature of the nails; also called "claw nails"

Onychology (on-ih-KOL-o-gee) – The study of the structure and growth on the nails

Onycholysis (o-ni-KOL-I-sis) – Refers to a loosening or separation of the nail

Onychomycosis (o-ni-ko-mi-KO-sis) – Fungus of the nail

Onychophagy (o-ni-KOF-a-je) – Refers to bitten nails

Onychophosis – Overgrowth of the nail bed

Onychophyma – Swelling of the nail; also known as onychauxis

Onychoptosis (o-ni-kop-TO-sis) – Refers to shedding or falling off of nails

Onychorrhexis (o-ni-ko-REK-sis) – Split or brittle nails

Onychosis – Any disease, disorder or condition of the nail

Onyx (ON-iks) – The technical name for the nail

Open circuit – A broken path of electron flow

Open-minded buyer – A ready buyer; the person who will take a chance on new products without hesitation

Ophthalmic (of-THAL-mik) **nerve branch** – Main nerve branch to the top 1/3 of the face

Opponens – Muscles located in the palm (palmor view) of the hand and cause the thumb to move toward the fingers, giving the ability to grasp or make a fist

Oral hygiene – The act of maintaining healthy teeth and keeping the breath fresh

Orangewood stick – Implement made of orangewood used to loosen debris and apply creams and clean under the free edge of the nail

Orbicularis oculi (or-bik-ye-LAR-e AK-yu-le) – Muscle that circles the eye socket and functions to close the eyelid

Organic chemistry – Deals with all matter that is now living or was alive at one time, with carbon present, such as plants and animals

Organs – Separate body structures that perform specific functions; composed of two or more different tissues

Orientation – A salon program developed to familiarize the new employee with work habits and standards of the salon

Origin – Nonmoving (fixed) portion of the muscle attached to bones or other fixed muscles

Orbicularis Oris (Or-bik-ye-LAR-es (O-ris) – Muscle that circles the mouth and is responsible for contracting, puckering and wrinkling the lips, as in kissing or whistling

OSHA (The Occupational Safety and Health Administration) – The regulating agency under the Department of Labor that enforces safety and health standards in the workplace

Osteology (as-te-AL-e-je) – The study of bones

Outlining – A cutting technique used to define the perimeter hairline

Oval facial shape – The oval face is rounded, long and narrow rather than wide and short

Overdirected – The tool or curl sits in the upper portion of the base, but not on or above the parting

Overlap – Application of chemical products like hair color or relaxer on top of previously treated hair; to be avoided

Overload – The passage of more current than the line can carry

Oxidation – The process of combining oxygen with other chemical ingredients

Oxidative – Hair color containing developers (oxidant)

Oxygen – One of five elements that make up hair

P

Palatine (PAL-ah-tin) – The two bones that form the roof of the mouth and the floor of the eye sockets

Palm down – Haircutting position with the palm of your cutting hand downward; commonly used for cutting solid form lengths

Palm to palm – Haircutting position used when cutting graduated lengths by holding the hair away from the head

Palm up – Haircutting position with the palm of your cutting hand upward; commonly used when cutting along diagonal lines

Papilla – Filled with capillaries (small blood vessels) that supply nourishment to the cells around it, called germinal matrix cells

Papillary (PAP-e-lairy) **canal** – Oil (sebum) is secreted onto the surface of the skin by way of the papillary canal

Papules – Hardened red elevations of the skin in which no fluid is present; a pimple is an example of a papule

Parallel wiring – Wiring system with the ability to power several loads all at once or at different times

Parietal (pah-RI-e-tal) – The two bones that form the crown and upper sides of the head

Parietal artery – Artery that supplies blood to the crown and sides of head

Paronychia (par-o-NIK-e-a) – Inflammation of the skin around nail; also called Felon

Partial relaxer – A virgin relaxer applied only to selected areas of the head; used mainly when the nape area and sides are closely tapered or when the perimeter hairline is frizzy

Parting – Lines that subdivide sections of hair in order to separate, distribute and control the hair

Partnership – Salon business owned by two or more persons

Passive immunity – Provided when a person is given antibodies to fight a disease rather than producing them through his or her own immune system

Patella (pah-TEL-lah) – Kneecap, sits over the front of the knee joint

Patch test – A test used to see if a client has a negative or positive allergic reaction to a chemical product; required 24 hours prior to aniline derivative tints

Pathogenic bacteria – Disease-producing bacteria; they are harmful because they cause infection and disease; some produce toxins

Pathogenic bacterial cells – Bacterial cells that cause disease, infection and may produce toxins

Pathology – The study of a disease

Pear facial shape – The pear-shaped (trapezoid) face is most often elongated, with a forehead that is narrow and a jaw that is the widest area of the face

Pectoralis (pek-to-RAL-us) **major and pectoralis minor** – Muscles that extend across the front of the chest; these muscles assist in swinging the arms

Pediculosis capitis (pe-dik-u-LOH-sis) – Medical term for head lice; infestation of head lice on the scalp causing itching and eventual infection

Pedicure – Cosmetic care of the feet and toenails; the Latin word "ped" means foot and "cura" means care

Pelvic tilt – A motion that keeps one from arching backward by bending the knees slightly and pulling in the abdominal muscles when reaching up

GLOSSARY

Peptide bond – End bond of amino acids where amino end attaches to acid end

Pericardium (per-i-KAR-de-um) – A membrane that encases the heart and contracts and relaxes to force blood to move through the circulatory system

Perimeter – The area all around the hairline

Perimeter perm – Eliminates texture in the top and crown and focuses on the perimeter and ends of the hair; also called drop crown wrap

Perionychium (PER-I-o-nik-ee-um) – The skin that touches, overlaps and surrounds the nail

Peripheral (pe-RIF-ur-al) **nervous system** – Composed of sensory and motor nerves that extend from the brain and spinal cord to other parts of the body

Peristalsis (per-I-STAL-sis) – The twisting and turning motion of the esophagus

Perm – A chemical procedure to add curl or wave to hair

Permanent colors – Colors mixed with hydrogen peroxide capable of both lifting natural pigment and depositing artificial pigment in one process; add tone or darken existing hair or lighten and deposit color in a single process

Perm rods – Tools on which hair is wrapped; come in various lengths, diameters, shapes and colors; determine the size and shape of a new curl configuration (small diameter rods produce small, firm curls and large diameter rods produce large curls)

Perm solution – Reduces disulfide bonds so hair can assume new shape of rod

Peroneus Brevis (per-oh-NEE-us BREV-us) – Muscle that originates in the lower third of the fibula; bends the foot down and out

Peroneus Longus (per-oh-NEE-us LONG-us) – Muscle that originates in the upper two-thirds of the outer fibula; causes the foot to invert and turn outward

Perpendicular distribution – The hair is combed at a 90°angle from its parting

Personal ethics – The proper conduct one displays in life through positive values and beliefs, such as honesty and fairness

Personal goals – A personal motivation statement that describes or defines the path life and career may take

Personal hygiene – The individual system for maintaining cleanliness and health

Personality – The outward reflection of inner thoughts, feelings, attitude and values

Personal loan rate – Individual loan rate based on your net worth

Personal Service Workers (**PSWs**) – Those workers and professionals, such as nurses, doctors, teachers and cosmetologists, who work with the public and are often asked to take precautions against HBV

Petrissage (PAY-tre-sahzh) – Light or heavy kneading and rolling of the muscles; performed by kneading muscles between the thumb and fingers or by pressing the palm of the hand firmly over the muscles, then grasping and squeezing with the heel of the hand and fingers; generally performed from the front of the head to the back; used on the face, arms, shoulders and upper back

Pharynx (FAR-ingks) – Passageway at the back of the mouth; part of the digestive tract

Pheomelanin – The type of melanin that produces red hair color

pH meter – Determines the pH value of a solution

Phalanges (fuh-LAN-jeez) – Fourteen bones that form the digits of fingers and toes; three phalanges in each finger and toe with the exception of two in the big toe

Phoresis – The process that allows bleaching of the skin

Physical change – A change in the physical characteristics of a substance without creating a new substance

Physiology – The study of the functions bodily organs and systems perform

Picks – Implements used to secure rollers in place while hair dries; also secure perm rods

Piggyback perm – Perm that positions two rods along a single strand; designed for longer lengths to ensure complete saturation of chemicals

Pilica polonica – Refers to excessive matting of hair, characterized by a mass of hair strands tangled together in a mat that cannot be separated

Pincurl base – The area of the strand at the scalp between partings within a shape

Pincurl circle – The end of the strand that forms the curl

Pincurls – A means of temporarily changing the direction and texture of hair by creating smoothly wound curls without the use of rollers

Pincurls, full-stem – Off-base control; stem and circle are positioned below the base and pick-up line in a pincurl

Pincurls, half-stem – Half-off base control; half of the circle is positioned below the base and pick-up line in a pincurl

Pincurls, no-stem – On-base; entire circle of curl is positioned on the base; produces lift or strong curl effect or strong wave

Pincurls, semi-stand up – Transitional pincurls; used to create blend from areas of volume to areas of closeness; not quite a stand-up curl and not quite a flat curl

Pincurls, stand up – Volume pincurl or cascade pincurl; used to create fullness and height; placed directly on base with the circle at a 90° angle to the head

Pincurl stem (arc) – The beginning portion of the strand that demonstrates the direction of the curl (between base and first turn)

Pityriasis (pit-i-REYE-ah-sis) – The medical term for dandruff; overabundance of epithelial cells (small, white scales) that have accumulated on the scalp or fallen to the shoulders

Pityriasis capitis simplex (kah-PEYE-tis SIM-pleks) – The medical term for dry dandruff; dry epithelial cells attached to the scalp or on the hair; itchy; caused by poor circulation, poor diet, uncleanliness or emotional disturbance

Pityriasis steatoides (ste-a-TOY-dez) – Medical term for greasy or waxy dandruff; epithelial cells combine with sebum (oil) and stick to the scalp in clusters; itchy

Plain shampoo – Used to cleanse normal hair but not recommended for chemically treated or damaged hair

Plasma – The fluid part of the blood in which red and white blood cells and blood platelets are suspended, to be carried throughout the body by this liquid's flow; plasma is about 90% water

Plastic cap – Covers hair to allow deeper penetration of conditioning treatment

Plastic cape – A waterproof cape used for shampooing, wet haircutting, wet styling and chemical services

Platelets – Thrombocytes; responsible for clotting of blood

Platysma (plah-TIZ-mah) – Muscle that extends from the tip of the chin to the shoulders and chest and depresses the lower jaw and lip, as in expressing sadness

Podiatrist – A foot doctor

Polish remover – Acetone or non-acetone solution used to dissolve polish

Pollutant – Product that causes odors or harmful effects to the air

Polymer – Mixes with the monomer to form an acrylic nail; powder in form

Polypeptide bond – Several peptide bonds connecting amino acids to form chains

Pomade – A product used to add gloss and sheen to dry hair; creates texture separation; also referred to as polisher, glosser, lusterizer and brilliantine

Pons – Connects other parts of the brain to the spinal column and is located below the cerebrum and directly in front of the cerebellum

Popliteal (pop-lih-TEE-ul) Artery – Supplies blood to the knee joint and muscles in the thigh and calf

Porosity – Refers to the ability of the hair to absorb moisture, liquids or chemicals

Positive attitude – Identifiable emotions and/or reactions expressed favorably

Posterior (pos-TER-e-er) – Behind or in back of

Posterior auricular (pos-TER-e-or aw-RIK-u-lar) **artery** – Supplies blood to the scalp above and behind the ears

Posterior auricular nerve – Extends to the muscles behind and below the ear

Posterior dilator naris – One of the four muscles located inside the nose, controls contraction and expansion of the nostrils

Posterior Tibial (poh-STEER-ee-ur TIB-ee-al) Artery – Supplies blood beneath the calf muscle to the skin, muscles and other tissues of the lower leg

Postpartum alopecia – The temporary hair loss at the conclusion of pregnancy

Posture – The position of the body while standing, sitting and moving

Potential hydrogen (pH) – Unit of measurement that determines if a substance is acidic, neutral or alkaline

Powder-dry shampoo – Used to cleanse the hair of clients whose health prohibits them from receiving a wet shampoo service

Powders – Equal mixtures of inorganic and organic substances that do not dissolve in water and that have been sifted and mixed until free of coarse, gritty particles

Prebooking – The act of making a future appointment for a client after their present service is complete

Premise insurance – A policy that covers the actual salon equipment and physical location in case of natural disasters, fire, theft or burglary, or accidents occurring at the business

Pressing and curling – A natural way to straighten tightly curled hair by pressing the hair straight with a pressing comb and curling with marcel irons

Pressing oil – Prepares and protects hair during pressing service; helps prevent scorching and breakage; conditions and adds shine; helps hair stay pressed longer

Primary colors – Yellow, red and blue; cannot be created by mixing together any other colors

Primary health hazards – The improper public hygiene practices that endanger the public such as: impure air from poor ventilation, inadequate lighting, improper disinfection practices, and improper storage or use of food

Primer – A solution that ensures adhesion of acrylic product to nail

Prism – A three-sided glass object that produces individual wavelengths when white light passes through it

Procerus (pro-SER-us) – Muscle located between the eyebrows across the bridge of the nose; draws brows down and wrinkles the area across the bridge of the nose

Product liability insurance – Protection for the salon owner regarding the sale and use of professional products from the client

Professional development – A commitment to constantly improving oneself

Professional ethics – The proper conduct one displays in relationships with employer, co-workers and clients

Profit – Occurs when the salon income is more than the cost of doing business

Progression – A pattern in which an element changes gradually in an ascending or descending scale

Projection – Also known as elevation; the angle at which the hair is held in relation to the curve of the head prior to cutting

Promotional literature – Flyers, newsletters or postcards with information about a salon operation

Pronator – Muscle that turns the palm inward and down; located in forearm

Properties of matter – Characteristics such as color, weight, odor, hardness or softness

Proportion – All parts and components coming together into a total image

Protection – The skin's ability to shield the body from the direct impact of heat, cold, bacteria and other aspects of the environment that could be detrimental to one's health

Protein – Formed by amino acids; hair is a form of protein called keratin; hair is made up of 97% keratin protein and 3% trace minerals; energy nutrient in food, protein makes up 10% of the RDA guidelines

Proton – Positively charged particle in the nucleus of an atom

Protoplasm (PRO-to-plazm) – Gel-like substance found in cells containing water, salt and nutrients obtained from food

Pseudofolliculitis Barbae (SOO-doh-fo-lik-u-li-tis bar-be) – Medical term for razor bumps or irritation following shaving

Pseudomonacidal – Disinfectant designed to kill pseudomonas

Psoriasis (soh-REYE-ah-sis) – Round, dry patches of skin, covered with rough, silvery scales; condition is chronic and not contagious

GLOSSARY

Pterygium (te-RIJ-e-ge-uhm) – Refers to the living skin that becomes attached to the nail plate either at the eponychium (dorsal pterygium) or the hyponychium (inverse pterygium)

Public hygiene – The codes of safety that protect the well-being of the public; example code areas include ventilation, lighting and disinfection

Pulmonary circulation – The system that allows blood to travel through the pulmonary artery to the lungs where it is oxygenated (combined with oxygen)

Pustules – Small elevations of skin similar to vesicles in size and shape, but containing pus; a pimple with pus is an example of a pustule

Q

Quadratus labii (kwod-RA-tus LA-be) **inferioris** – (also known as the Depressor Labii Inferioris) Muscle located below the lower lip; pulls the lower lip down or to the side, as in expressing sarcasm

Quadratus labii (kwod-RA-tus LA-be) **superioris** – (also known as the Levatator Labii Superioris) Muscle located above the upper lip; raises both the nostrils and the upper lip, as in expressing distaste

R

Radial (RAY-dee-ul) **Artery** – Supplies blood to the thumb side of the arm and hand

Radial nerve – Extends down the thumb side of the arm into the back of the hand

Radius (RAD-e-us) – The small bone on the thumb side of the lower arm or forearm

Rake comb – A comb used to remove tangles from hair; also used to style curly hair and define texture

Razor – Implement used to create a tapered effect on the edge of each strand, which produces a softer, somewhat diffused line; the razor consists of a blade and usually a guard, which is used to protect you from coming in direct contact with the edge of the blade; the shank is used to hold the razor, while the handle, which is sometimes foldable, is used to rest your fingers; the tang is used to rest the little finger

Razor etching – A technique in which the ends of the hair are carved into with a razor using a back-and-forth motion

Razor rotation – Performed by rotating the razor and comb along the hair strand to remove weight

RDA (Recommended Dietary Allowances) – The appropriate nutrient intake for people in the United States established by the U.S. government

Ready buyer – An open-minded buyer who will take a chance on new products without hesitation

Receptors – Nerve cells located in the papillary layer of the dermis

Rectangle perm pattern – 9-block; consists primarily of rectangular shapes throughout the pattern; most basic perm pattern

Rectifier – Changes alternating current to direct current

Red corpuscles – Erythrocytes or red blood cells; contain hemoglobin and carry oxygen

Reduction (Redox) – Process that occurs in color/perming/relaxing services where a substance gains an electron and oxygen is released; overprocessed hair can also be a result

Referrals – Clients sent to the cosmetologist by clients telling their friends about the cosmetologist's reputation

Reflex – Action caused by interaction of sensory and motor nerves

Regulation – The skin's ability to help maintain the body's temperature

Relaxation test – Also known as the comb test, allows you to determine if additional smoothing is required; performed with the spine or back of the comb

Relaxer – A chemical used to soften the disulfide bond in a hair straightening procedure

Relaxer retouch – Uses the same procedure as a virgin application, except that the product is applied only to the new growth area at the scalp

Remy Hair – Hair with the cuticle intact and facing the same direction

Repetition – Design principle; a pattern in which an element is identical

Reproductive system – Responsible for the process by which a living organism procreates others of its kind.

Resistance – The measure of how difficult it is to push electrons through a conductor; also called impedance

Respect – Honor; esteem

Respiratory system – Responsible for the intake of oxygen and the exhalation of carbon dioxide

Resumé – A document describing one's attributes in a brief, concise manner, including personal data, educational background, employment and skills

Ribs – Twelve bones of the chest

Ridge curls – Pincurls placed behind a fingerwave ridge; two sets of ridge curls create a skip wave

Right atrium or auricle – Upper chamber of the heart

Right ventricle – Lower chamber of the heart

Ringed hair – Alternating bands of gray and dark hair

Rinse – Helps close the cuticle of hair and makes hair feel soft and manageable

Rinsing – Removes excess waving (or reforming) solution from the hair before neutralizing or rebonding

Risorius (re-SOR-e-us) – Muscle located at the corner of the mouth; draws the mouth up and out, as in grinning

Roller – A cylindrical hairstyling tool of various diameters and lengths on which hair is wound to create various hairstyles

Romantic style – Clients who like silk, flower prints, lace, beads and pastel shades of color

Rosacea (ro-ZA-sha) – A chronic inflammatory congestion of the cheeks and nose, observed as redness, with papules and sometimes pustules present; also called acne rosacea

Round brushes – Brushes that impart varying degrees of curved or curled texture and volume; comes in various diameters

Round facial shape – The round face has a low, round hairline and a short chin with a very rounded jawline; it appears to be rather short and wide rather than long and narrow

S

Salary – Compensation system that guarantees a set income on a weekly or monthly basis

Salary plus commission – Guarantees a certain amount of money on a regular basis and allows for additional payment based on the number of clients brought in

Salivary (SAL-i-ver-e) gland – A gland in the mouth that produces saliva

Salon design – The layout of a salon, including the amount of space needed for each stylist, reception area, dispensary, restroom, service areas and efficient traffic patterns

Salon ecology – The study of the ways to keep the larger, expanded environment of the salon in balance to guarantee the well-being and safety of all involved

Salon research factors – Important factors in the success of a salon are location, market and cost of improvements

Salt bond – Side bond that helps organize protein chains

Sanitation – The process of removing dirt to aid in reducing the growth of microbes; it is the first level of infection control; sanitation methods clean and reduce microbes on the surface but do not kill germs

Saphenous Nerve – Nerve of the lower leg and foot that begins in the thigh

Saphenous (SA-FEEN-us) Vein – Transports blood from veins in the foot to the femoral vein

Saprophytes – Nonpathogenic bacteria that live on dead matter and do not produce disease

Saturated solution – Solution that cannot take or dissolve any more solute than it already holds

Scabies – Medical term for itch mite; red and watery vesicles or pus-filled areas caused by an animal parasite

Scales – Shedding, dead cells of the uppermost layer of the epidermis

Scalp toner – Adds a refreshing, stimulating feeling to the scalp; may have mild antiseptic properties and cleansing ability

Scapula (SKAP-yu-lah) – The large, flat bone extending from the middle of the back upward to the joint where it attaches to the clavicle

Scars – Formations resulting from a lesion, which extend into the dermis or deeper, as part of the normal healing process; keloids are thick scars

Sciatic Nerve (sy-AT-ik NURV) – Begins in the lower back and runs through the buttock and down the lower limb

Sculptured nails – A nail extension produced with a nail form rather than a tip; can be applied faster and used as an alternative to tips and overlays; sculptured nails are created by combining two ingredients, which are the polymer and the monomer

Seasonal disease – Disease influenced by the weather

Sebaceous (sih-BAY-shus) glands – Oil glands; partially controlled by the nervous system; sac-like glands that are attached to hair follicles; result in oily skin when an over-abundance of sebum is produced by the glands

Seborrhea (seb-oh-REE-ah) – A condition caused by excessive secretion of the sebaceous glands

Secondary colors – Orange, green and violet; when primary colors are mixed in varying proportions; orange contains varying amounts of red and yellow; green contains varying proportions of blue and yellow, and violet contains varying proportions of red and blue

Sectioning – The division of the hair into workable areas for the purpose of control

Semi-hand-tied wig – Combination of hand-tied and machine-made wig and hairpiece

Semi-permanent colors – Direct-dye colors that need no mixing; the color you see in the bottle is the color that is deposited on the hair; alkaline and generally last through several shampoos, depending on the porosity of the hair; deposit color and cannot lighten the hair

Sensation – Feelings generated by the nerve ending just under the outer layer of the skin that makes you aware of heat, cold, touch, pain and pressure; the reaction to a sensation is called a reflex

Sensory nerves – Also called afferent nerves; carry messages to the brain and spinal cord; determine the sense of touch, sight, smell, hearing and taste

Series wiring – Travels from one load to the next forcing the user to have all loads running at the same time

Serratus anterior (ser-RA-tus an-TER-e-er) – Muscle located under the arm; this muscle helps in lifting the arm and in breathing

Seventh cranial nerve – The main motor nerve of the face; also known as the facial nerve

Shampoo – Used to clean hair and scalp and remove foreign matter

Shampoo bowl – Supports client's neck and holds water and shampoo products during a shampoo service

Shampoo chair – Allows client to sit or lay down during the shampoo service

Shampoo dispensary – Displays shampoos and conditioners

Shape – Two-dimensional figure consisting of points, lines and angles

Shaving – A hair removal method using an electric shaver, clipper or razor

Shears – A haircutting implement used to create a clean, blunt edge or line; a pair of shears consists of a still or stationary blade, which is controlled by a finger grip, and a movable or action blade, which is controlled by the thumb grip

Shear-over-comb – A cutting technique using straight shears or taper shears in which both the shears and comb move upward in unison

Shell orbit – The part of an atom where electrons spin around the nucleus

Shifted distribution – When the hair is combed out of natural distribution in any direction except perpendicular to its parting

Short circuit – Occurs anytime a foreign conductor comes in contact with a wire carrying current to the load

Side bond – Bond formed when amino acids are lined up side by side

Single process – Method used to add tone or darken the existing hair or lighten and deposit color in a single process

Single-prong clips – Implements used to secure pincurls

Sinusodial Current – An alternating current with a mechanical effect

GLOSSARY

Skeletal system – The physical foundation of the body, composed of 206 bones of different shapes and sizes, each attached to others at movable or immovable joints

Skin – The largest organ of the body, covers nearly 20 square feet of the body surface and protects it from invasion from outside particles

Skin patch test – A test to determine how a permanent, aniline derivative tint will react on the client; the intended formula is applied inside the elbow or behind the ear and evaluated in 24 hours for negative (no signs) results or positive (signs of redness, swelling, blisters, itching or burning of the skin and /or respiratory distress) reactions

Skin tags – Small elevated growths of skin

Skip waves – A wave pattern that combines fingerwaves and flat pincurls

Skull – The skeleton of the head that encloses and protects the brain and primary sensory organs

Sleep recommendation – Six to eight hours per night are recommended to maintain a healthy lifestyle

Slicing – A hair coloring technique in which a section of hair is positioned over a piece of paper or thermal strip and color is applied

Slithering – A haircutting technique in which the shears are opened and closed rhythmically while moving upward from the ends; also referred to as effilating

Sloughing lotion – A lotion that removes dead skin cells

Small intestine – Part of the intestine between the stomach and large intestine, where assimilation of nutrients begins

Soaking solution – Liquid soap used with warm water in finger bowl to soften skin, loosen dirt and aid in pushing back cuticle

Soap – Mixtures of fats and oils converted to fatty acids by heat and then purified

Soapless shampoo – Used to cleanse hair with either soft or hard water

Social security tax – A planned savings/retirement fund for every worker in the United States

Sodium hydroxide – Relaxer chemical with a high oil content (the base) and conditioning agents that help protect the hair and scalp from irritation; also known as lye relaxer; pH of 11.5-14

Soft press – Pressing action that uses less heat and pressure

Soft water – Rain water or water with very small amounts of minerals

Soleus (SO-lee-us) – Muscle that originates in the upper portion of the fibula from just below the knee to the heel; bends the foot down

Sole proprietorship – A business owned by one person who is in complete control of the business

Solid – Form of matter having definite weight, volume and shape

Solid form – Haircuts that have a totally smooth cut texture, which is achieved by cutting the hair in natural fall with 0° projection. Also known as a one-length cut, bob, Dutch boy, blunt cut or 0° angle cut

Solute – Any substance that dissolves into a liquid to form a solution

Solution – Mixtures of two or more kinds of molecules, evenly dispersed

Solvent – Any substance that is able to dissolve another substance

Source – Provides the force to move electrons in conducting material in an electric current

Spatula - Implement used to remove product from container

Speed dry – Drying agent; spray or polish that aids in fast drying of polish

SPF – Sun protection factor; rating system for sunscreen to determine how long one can stay out in the sun without burning

Sphenoid (SPE-noid) – Bone located behind the eyes and nose; connects all the bones of the cranium

Spinal cord – Composed of long nerve fibers; originates in the base of the brain and extends to the base of the spine; holds 31 pairs of spinal nerves that branch out to muscles, internal organs and skin

Spiral bricklay perm pattern – Horizontal rows that are subdivided in a staggered bricklay pattern; tools are positioned vertically within square bases

Spiral wrap – A method of wrapping hair around a perm tool base-to-ends and ends-to-base

Spirilla (speye-RIL-a) – Spiraled, coiled, corkscrew-shaped bacterial cells that cause highly contagious diseases such as syphilis and cholera

Spray gel – A product used to support volume and movement; firmer hold than lotion; liquid consistency

Spray-on colors – Come in an aerosol can in a multitude of colors and are a quick and easy way to add color to the hair for special effects

Squamous (SQUAW-mus) cells – Cells with a flat, scale-like appearance; found in the palms of the hands and the soles of the feet (stratum lucidum)

Square combination form – Also known as a box cut; uniform at center top to increase layered at front and crown; graduated and uniform sides and back

Square facial shape – The square face is short and wide; it looks very angular with a lot of straight lines; the front hairline and jawline is almost horizontal while the cheekbones protrude very little on the sides

Staphylococci (staf-i-lo-KOK-si) – Pus-forming bacterial cells that form grape-like bunches or clusters and are present in abscesses, pustules and boils

Steatoma (stee-ah-TOH-mah) – A sebaceous cyst or wen; a subcutaneous tumor of the sebaceous gland, filled with sebum

Stem – The part of a curl between the scalp and the first turn of the curl

Sterilization – The most effective level of infection control; sterilization procedures kill or destroy all microbes

Sternocleido mastoideus (stur-no-KLI-do mas-TOID-e-us) – Muscle that extends along the side of the neck from the ear to the collarbone and causes the head to move from side to side and up and down, as in nodding "yes" or "no"

Sternum – Two of the bones of the chest

Stomach – Organ that digests food

Straight back bend – A bend at the hips instead of the waist

Straightening or flat irons – Consist of two flat, heated plates

Straight profile – A straight profile has a very slight outward curvature from the front hairline to the tip of the nose and from the tip of the nose to the chin

Straight rods – Produce curls or waves that are uniform throughout the hair strands

Strand test – A preliminary color test performed 24-48 hours before the actual hair color service; the intended color formula is mixed and applied to a section of hair to predict the final results

Stratum corneum – The uppermost layer of the epidermis; the toughest layer, composed of keratin protein cells that are continually shed and continually replaced by new cells from below

Stratum germinativum – The lowest level of the epidermis where mitosis or cell division takes place; begins with the stratum basale, or basal cell layer, which is a single layer thick

Stratum granulosum – The layer of the epidermis below the stratum lucidum and above the stratum spinosum; in this layer the cells become more regularly shaped and look like many tiny granules

Stratum lucidum – The layer of the epidermis just below the stratum corneum; it is the palms of the hands and the soles of the feet, where there are no hair follicles

Stratum spinosum – The layer of the epidermis just above the stratum germinativum; sometimes considered part of the stratum germinativum; includes cells that have absorbed melanin to distribute pigmentation to other cells

Streptococci (strep-to-KOK-si) – Pus-forming bacterial cells that form in long chains and can cause septisemia (sometimes called poisoning), strep throat, rheumatic fever and other serious infections

Striated muscle – Voluntary muscle; responds to commands regulated by will

Structure – In haircutting, structure refers to the arrangement of lengths across the various curves of the head, such as shorter on top to longer at the bottom or nape

Stubborn buyer – A skeptical buyer who puts up a struggle and has a strong desire to debate with the seller

Styling lotion – A product used to support volume and movement; liquid consistency

Styptic product – Liquid or spray product used to stop bleeding

Styrofoam heads – A head form used to store and display wigs

Subcutaneous layer (tissue) – Fatty layer below the dermis of the skin; protective cushion for the skin; acts as a shock absorber to protect the bones and to help support the delicate structures such as blood vessels and nerve endings

Subjective symptoms – Signs of a disorder or disease that are felt but not necessarily visible; for example, itching, burning

Submental artery – Artery that supplies blood to the chin and lower lip

Sudoriferous (soo-dohr-IF-er-us) **glands** – Controlled by the nervous system of the body; each gland consists of a coiled base and tube-like duct opening on the surface of the skin to form sweat pores; control and regulate body temperatures; excrete waste products; help to maintain the acidic pH factor of the skin

Sugaring – A hair removal technique that utilizes a paste made primarily of sugar that is applied to the skin in a rolling motion

Sulfur – One of five elements that make up hair

Supercilia – Technical name for the hair of the eyebrows

Superficial Peroneal Nerve – Nerve of the lower leg and foot that sits closer to the skin than the deep nerve; becomes the dorsal nerve

Superficial temporal (su-pur-FI-shul TEM-po-ral) – Artery that supplies the sides and top of the head with blood and branches farther into five smaller arteries that supply more precise locations

Superior labial – Artery that supplies blood to the upper lip and septum

Superioris (super-e-OR-es) – Located above or is larger

Supinator (SU-pi-nat-or) – Muscle that runs parallel to the ulna; this muscle turns the palm of the hand up

Supraorbital artery – Supplies blood to parts of the forehead and eyes

Supraorbital nerve – Extends to the skin of the upper eyelid, eyebrow, forehead and scalp

Supratrochlear nerve – Extends to the skin of the upper side of the nose and between the eyes

Sural Nerve (SUR-ul NURV) – Runs down the back of the leg to the outside of the foot and little toe

Surfactant – Used to remove oil from hair; also called surface active agent

Suspension – Mixtures of two or more kinds of molecules that will separate if left standing

Switch – A long weft of one to three swatches of hair, mounted on a loop base, worn primarily as a braid or ponytail

Symmetrical balance – Created when weight is positioned equally on both sides of a center axis, creating a mirror image

Systemic cause – Meaning throughout the system; causes are internal; related to illness, nutrition or heredity

Systemic circulation – The process of blood traveling from the heart throughout the body and back to the heart

Systems – Group of body structures and/or organs that together perform one or more vital functions for the body

T

Tact – The act of saying the proper thing to a person without giving offense

Tail comb – A comb used to section, part and distribute the hair during styling

Talus (TA-lus) – Sits above the heel bone and forms the lower part of the ankle joint; also called anklebone

Taper shears – A haircutting implement used to create a distinct and regular alternation of shorter and longer lengths for mobility; one blade of the taper shear is straight and the other is notched (serrated); also called thinning shears; taper shears come in various sizes, such as with teeth 1/8" apart, 1/16" apart, 1/32" apart and with wider notches called channeling shears that produce dramatic chunky effects

Tapotement (tah-POHT-mant) – Also called percussion or hacking; light tapping or slapping movement applied with the fingers or partly flexed fingers; used on the arms, back and shoulders

Tarsal (TAHR-sul) – One of seven bones that makeup the mid foot and rear foot

Teamwork – The act of considering and cooperating with others

Telogen – The resting stage of hair growth when each bulb has no attached root sheath, at which time hair falls out; eventually, cell division is again stimulated, producing new hair, and the growth cycle starts again

GLOSSARY

Telogen effluvium – Premature shedding of hair in the resting phase (telogen) resulting from various causes such as childbirth, shock, drug intake, fever, etc.

Temporal (TEM-poh-ral) – The two bones located on either side of the head, directly above the ears and below the parietal bones

Temporalis (tem-po-RA-lis) – Muscle located above and in front of the ear; performs both opening and closing the jaw, as in chewing (mastication)

Temporal nerve – Extends to the muscles of the temple, the side of the forehead, the eyebrows, eyelid and upper cheek

Temporary colors – Used to create temporary changes that last from shampoo to shampoo; nonreactive, direct dyes, which means no chemicals are needed to develop them

Tendonitis – A condition that occurs when tendons in the hand and fingers get inflamed

Tertiary colors – Created by mixing primary colors with their neighboring secondary color in varying proportions; there are six tertiary colors: yellow-orange, yellow-green, blue-green, blue-violet, red-violet and red-orange

Tesla Current – High frequency current known as the violet ray

Test curl – A test to determine complete processing of a perm; positive test shows an "S" shape or pattern

Texture – The degree of coarseness or fineness in the hair fiber; as a design element, texture identifies the surface appearance of the hair, whether it is curly or straight, smooth or layered; in haircutting texture refers to the hair's surface appearance as unactivated (smooth) or activated (rough)

Texturizing – Sometimes referred to as thinning, involves cutting shorter lengths within the form to reduce bulk and create support, closeness, fullness, mobility and visual texture in the haircut

Thermal equipment – Used to generate heat (for example, curling irons, heat lamps, color machines, manicure heaters, facial steamers, and scalp steamers)

Thermal irons – Tools used to temporarily add texture to hair or straighten hair

Thermal styling – The technique of drying and/or styling hair by using a hand-held dryer while simultaneously using your fingers, a variety of brushes, pressing comb and/or a thermal curling iron

Thermolysis – High frequency/short wave method of permanent hair removal

Thinning hair shampoo – Used to cleanse the hair without weighing it down

Thioglycolate – The main ingredient found in alkaline perms

Thoracic (tho-RAS-ik) **vertebrae** (VURT-e-bray) – One of the bones of the bony cage that encloses and protects the heart, lungs and other internal organs

Thorax (THO-raks) – The bony cage composed of the spine, vertebrae, sternum and the ribs; also known as the chest

Threading – An ancient method of hair removal that utilizes 100% cotton thread that is twisted and rolled along the surface of the skin

Three-sectioning – An effective way of measuring the proportions of the face; section one – the front hairline to the middle of the eyebrows; section two – the middle of the eyebrows to the tip of the nose and section three – the tip of the nose to the tip of the chin

Three-strand overbraid – Braiding technique that produces a braid that is raised by crossing the outside strands under the center strands; also known as the French or invisible braid

Three-strand underbraid – Braiding technique that produces a braid that is raised by crossing the outside strands under the center strand; also known as cornrow braiding

Three-wire system – A three-prong plug serving as a safety device; added to appliances to act as grounding wire

Thrombocytes (Clot) – Blood platelets; responsible for the clotting of blood, starting the process of coagulation (clotting) when they are exposed to air or rough surfaces (bruised skin)

Tibia (TIB-ee-ah) – Inner and larger of the two lower leg bones extending from the knee to the ankle; also known as shinbone

Tibial Nerve (TIB-ee-al NURV) – Passes behind the knee and the common peroneal nerve

Tibialis Anterior (tib-ee-AHL-is an-TEHR-ee-ohr) – Muscle that covers the front of the shin; bends the foot upward and inward

Tinea (TIN-ee-ah) – Medical term for ringworm; red, circular patch of small blisters; caused by a vegetable parasite

Tinea capitis – Medical term for ringworm of the scalp; enlarged open hair follicles that are surrounded by clusters of red spots (papules); hair is likely to break in area infected

Tinea favosa (fa-VO-sah) or **Favus** (FAY-vus) – Medical term for honeycomb ringworm; dry, yellow, encrusted areas on the scalp called scutula (SKUT-u-la); may have a peculiar odor; shiny pink or white scars may result

Tinea manus – Ringworm of the hand

Tinea pedis (PED-is) – Athlete's foot or ringworm of the feet

Tinea unguim (UN-gwee-um) – Ringworm of the nail; also called unguis (UN-gwees)

Tint back – Coloring the hair back to its natural color

Tissues – Groups of cells of the same kind performing a specific function in the body

Toenail clipper – Clippers used to shorten toenails

Toe separators – Separates toes during polish technique; made of foam, rubber or cotton

Tone – Identifies the warmth or coolness of a color

Toner – Skin care product used to purify the skin and restore pH

Toners – Light pastel colors used to tone prelightened hair; used to deposit color and neutralize unwanted pigment after prelightening, such as brassy golds or yellows

Top coat or sealer – Colorless hard polish that protects colored polish from chipping, fading and peeling

Total assets – All property owned by an individual

Toupee – A hairpiece worn by men to cover bald or thinning hair spots, particularly on top of the head

Tourniquet – Device for stopping bleeding by compressing a blood vessel

Towels – Absorbant material used to protect the client's skin and clothing; also used to dry the hair

Track and sew – A hair addition technique in which a three-strand, on-the-scalp braid is used as a support structure to which a hair weft (a strip of human or artificial hair) is then sewn

Traction or traumatic alopecia – Hair loss due to repetitive traction on the hair by pulling or twisting

Transverse artery – Artery that supplies blood to the masseter

Trapezius (trah-PE-ze-us) Flat, triangular muscle covering the upper and back part of the neck and shoulders. It aids in drawing the head back and elevating the shoulder blades

Triadic color – Color schemes using three colors located in a triangular position on the color wheel

Triangularis (tri-an-gu-LAR-us) – (also known as the Levator Anguli Oris) Muscle located below the corners of the mouth; draws the corners of the mouth down, as in expressing depression

Tricep (TRI-cep) – Muscle that extends the length of the upper arm to the forearm; this muscle controls forward movement of the forearm

Trichology – The technical term for the study of hair

Trichoptilosis (tri-kop-ti-LOH-sis) – Fragilitis crinium or brittle hair; technical name for split ends

Trichorrhexis nodosa (TRIK-o-rek-sis no-DO-sa) – Knotted hair, characterized by the presence of lumps or swelling along the hair shaft

Trifacial (trigeminal) nerve – The largest of the cranial nerves, responsible for transmitting facial sensation to the brain and for controlling the muscle movements of chewing (mastication)

Trimmer – Implement used to outline the hairline, beard and sideburns

Tubercle – A large papule; hardened red elevation of the skin with no fluid present

Tuberculocidal – Disinfectant designed to kill tuberculosis microbes

Tucks – Alterations made horizontally to shorten a wig from the front to the nape

Tumors – Solid masses in the skin; may be soft or hard, depending upon their makeup, and may be fixed or freely movable; generally have a rounded shape; a nodule is a small tumor

Turbinal (TUR-bi-nal) – Two spongy bones that form the sides of the nasal cavity

Tweezers – Small metal implements used to remove hair; implement used to manage detail work such as nail art

Tweezing – A hair removal method that uses tweezers; commonly used to remove unwanted hair from smaller areas, such as eyebrows, chin or around the mouth

Two-way communication – The act of listening and asking questions to gather information

T-zone – Oily residue of the skin on the chin, nose, nasal labial groove and forehead

U

Ulcers – Open lesions visible on the skin surface that may result in the loss of portions of the dermis and may be accompanied by pus

Ulna (UL-nah) – The bone located in the little finger side of the lower arm

Ulnar artery – An artery that supplies blood to the arm and small finger side of the hand

Ulnar nerve – Extends down the little finger side of the arm into the palm of the hand

UL rating – Underwriters Laboratory designation; means the appliance has been certified to operate safely under the conditions the instructions specify

Ultrasonic cleaners – Use high-frequency sound waves to create a cleansing action that cleans areas on implements or tools that are difficult to reach with a brush

Ultraviolet light therapy – The use of ultraviolet light rays to produce both positive and negative effects on the skin; depending on the exposure time can tan the skin and produce vitamin D

Ultraviolet rays – A shorter wavelength and can be more damaging than infrared rays; also know as actinic rays

Underbevel – Cutting technique that turns the ends of the hair under; hair in the nape is shorter than the surface lengths

Underdirected – The tool or curl sits in the lower portion of the base, but not on or below the parting

Underdirected tool position – Base size is at least 1.5 diameters; tool is positioned in the lower half of the base to achieve moderate lift

Undulating irons – Consist of two undulating or curved irons that create an "S" pattern

Uniformly layered form – A form with a totally activated texture; also known as a layered cut or 90° angle cut

Universal precautions – The practice of using infection control procedures for all clients, regardless of their health history

Universal solvent – Capable of dissolving more substances than any other; water is considered a universal solvent

Unstable atom – Results when electrons are missing from the outer shell of an atom

V

Vacuum – Creates mild suction; increases circulation to the surface

Vagus – tenth cranial nerve; helps regulate heartbeat

Van der Waals forces – Side bond based on the theory that atomic groups prefer an environment with other groups that have structures similar to theirs; this type of bonding is of no importance to the cosmetologist

Variable rent – Monthly rent that varies with the amount of income generated by the salon; normally found in malls and larger shopping centers

Varicose veins – Bulges that form if veins stretch and lose their elasticity

Vascular system – Circulatory system; responsible for circulation of the blood; includes heart, arteries, veins and capillaries

Vegetable dyes – Natural products to color the hair; henna is an example of a vegetable dye that produces reddish highlights in the hair; considered a less professional category of hair color

Veins – Tubular, elastic, thin-walled branching vessels that carry the blood from the capillaries to the heart

Vellus – Hair that covers most of the body, including the head; often not visible to the naked eye

Vent brush – A brush used to achieve lift or volume when air forming smoother textures or creating directional emphasis

GLOSSARY

Ventilation – The opening for the escape and exchange of air so that the air does not have a stale, musty odor or contain the odor of sprays, bleaches and various chemical solutions

Verbal communication – Refers to how one speaks by emphasizing the meaning of what one says through the tone or inflection of voice, level and rate of speech

Verbal energy – The ability to speak up clearly with a good rate, inflection and tone

Verruca – A name give to a variety of warts

Vertical lines – Lines that go straight up and down. These lines create a feeling of weightlessness or equilibrium, as with a standing human body

Vesicles – Fluid-filled elevations in the skin caused by localized accumulation of fluids or blood just below the epidermis

Vibration (vi-**BRAY**-shun) – Shaking movement; your arms shake as you touch the client with your fingertips or palms

Villi (**VIL**-i) – Finger-like projections of the intestine walls

Vinegar and lemon rinse – Used to keep the cuticle compact, remove soap scum, return the hair to its pH balance and counteract the alkalinity present after a chemical service

Virgin darker technique – A base-to-ends application used to add tone to or darken the existing color

Virgin lighter technique – Midstrand-to-ends-then-base application used to lighten existing hair color

Virgin relaxer – A chemical relaxer applied to untreated or "virgin" hair to the most resistant area and 1/4" (.6 cm) to 1/2" (1.25 cm) away from the scalp and up to the porous ends; then product is applied to scalp area

Virucidal – Disinfectant designed to kill viruses

Virus – Sub-microscopic particles that cause familiar diseases like the common cold and other respiratory and gastrointestinal infections, chicken pox, mumps, measles, small pox, yellow fever, rabies, HIV (AIDS), hepatitis and polio

Viscosity – A descriptive term identifying the thickness of a solution

Visible light – The portion of the electromagnetic spectrum humans can see

Visible light therapy – The use of visible or white light in therapy procedures to allow absorption or reflection by the skin or body

Vitiligo (vit-i-**LYE**-goh) – Characterized by oval or irregular patches of white skin that do not have normal pigment

Volt – A unit of electric pressure

Voluntary or striated (**STRI**-at-ed) **muscles** – Muscles that respond to commands regulated by will

Vomer (**VO**-mer) – The bone in the center of the nose that divides the nasal cavity; also called the Nasal System

W

Wall plate – A portable appliance that reduces power to an appliance.

Warm colors – Orange, red and yellow range of the color wheel; warm tones

Warts – A skin growth caused by a virus; can be contagious and can spread all over the body

Watt – A measure of how much electrical energy is being used

Wave or styling clamp – Implements used to keep finger waves in place

Waxing – A temporary hair removal method of applying hot or cold wax to skin, allowing the wax to adhere to the skin and finally pulling off the wax/hair

Weaving – The use of a tail comb to weave out selected strands of hair in an alternating pattern for the application of hair color

Wet disinfectant container – A container with disinfectant solution into which tools and implements are completely immersed

Wet styling – Refers to the area of hairstyling in which the hair is manipulated into the desired shapes and movements while wet then allowed to dry

Wheals – A solid formation above the skin, often caused by an insect bite or allergic reaction; hives, also called Urticaria (ur-ti-**KAR**-e-uh), are an example of wheal lesions

White corpuscles – Leukocytes or white blood cells; fight bacteria and other foreign substances

Whorl – Strong circular directional growth of hair on either side of the nape or crown

Widow's peak – Prominent hair growth pattern that forms from a point at the front hairline and curves to one side

Wig – A head covering designed to cover the entire head and worn for specific purposes; made of human hair, animal hair, synthetic fibers or a blend of each

Wig block – Canvas-covered head form used during wig blocking (sizing) services

Wig cap – Holds client's hair in place and helps wigs to stay in place

Wiglet – A hairpiece usually worn to create fullness or height at the top or crown area of the head; consists of hair fiber usually six inches or less in length attached to a round-shaped, flat base

Wig pins – Used to hold wigs and hairpieces in place on canvas block during setting, cleaning and maintenance services

Wood's lamp – A lamp with ultraviolet light used for analysis of skin surface and deeper layers to aid in determining skin treatment

Word-of-mouth advertising – An effective way of building clientele when satisfied customers recommend your services to others

Workers' compensation insurance – A state-controlled insurance required by law to protect employees if injured in the salon

Wrapped or fiberglass nails – A piece of fiberglass applied over the natural nail or tips reinforced with a resin (thick adhesive) and then hardened with a catalyst and finally filed and buffed smooth to produce a natural-locking nail

Z

Zygomatic (zi-go-**MAT**-ik) or **malar** (**MA**-ler) – The two bones that form the upper cheeks and the bottom of the eyesockets

Zygomatic nerve – Extends to the side of the forehead, temple and upper part of the cheek

Zygomaticus (zi-go-**MAT**–ik-us) – Muscle located outside the corners of the mouth; draws the mouth up and back, as in laughing